A COVENANT OF CREATURES

Cultural Memory
in
the
Present

Mieke Bal and Hent de Vries, Editors

A COVENANT OF CREATURES

Levinas's Philosophy of Judaism

Michael Fagenblat

STANFORD UNIVERSITY PRESS

STANFORD, CALIFORNIA

Stanford University Press
Stanford, California

Material in Chapters 3 and 4 was originally published as "Levinas and Maimonides:
From Metaphysics to Ethical Negative Theology" in *The Journal of Jewish Thought
and Philosophy*, 16: 1 (2008), Koninklijke Brill N.V. Reprinted with permission.

Printed in the United States of America on acid-free, archival-quality paper
Library of Congress Cataloging-in-Publication Data
Fagenblat, Michael.
  A covenant of creatures : Levinas's philosophy of Judaism / Michael Fagenblat.
    p. cm. — (Cultural memory in the present)
  Includes bibliographical references and index.
  ISBN 978-0-8047-6869-6 (cloth : alk. paper) — ISBN 978-0-8047-6870-2 (pbk. :
alk. paper)
  1. Lévinas, Emmanuel—Ethics. 2. Ethics, Modern. 3. Judaism—Philosophy.
4. Philosophy, French—20th century. I. Title. II. Series: Cultural memory in the
present.
  B2430.L484F34 2010
  194—dc22

                          2010000664

Typeset by Bruce Lundquist in 11/13.5 Adobe Garamond

To Melanie Landau

אוֹר זָרֻעַ לַצַּדִּיק וּלְיִשְׁרֵי לֵב שִׂמְחָה

Psalms 97:11

"They encamped in the wilderness" (Exodus 19:2)

The Torah was given [*démos, parrésia*] in an ownerless place. For had the Torah been given in the land of Israel, the Israelites could have said to the nations of the world, "You have no share in it." But now that it was given in the wilderness publicly and openly, in an ownerless place, everyone who desires to receive it can come and receive it.
　　　　　—*Mekhilta de R. Yishmael, Bahodesh* 1

Contents

Preface: Judaism as a Philosophical Way of Life

> I am not a particularly Jewish thinker. I am just a thinker.
> —Emmanuel Levinas

Another book on Emmanuel Levinas? In the context of the incomplete and still unpredictable "return of religion" to academic and public discourse, the work of Levinas becomes more pertinent, even as criticism of it becomes more caustic. As the interaction but also the tension between the religious and the secular increases, Levinas stands out among modern thinkers for the original way he weaves together the religious and the secular without opposition. In 1922, Carl Schmitt formulated his now well known dictum that "all the significant concepts of the theory of the modern state are secularized theological concepts."[1] According to this view, the contemporary deployment of concepts such as sovereignty, fraternity, legality, right, and enemy in the context of modern secular political life is best understood in light of the distinctly religious intellectual heritage that gave rise to them. Indeed, the unavoidable use we make of such concepts involves a repetition of that religious heritage in a secular key. Secularization would mark less a break with our religious heritage than its extension to a new historical situation. The assumption of this book is that a similar phenomenon applies to fundamental secular moral concepts and, therefore, that the best way to understand such concepts is by exploring the religious intellectual heritage that they secularize. Immanuel Kant's moral philosophy is often taken as a paradigmatic example of the secularization of an essentially Christian conception of morality (more precisely, a Protestant Prussian conception). This book advances a similar claim about Levinas's work, with two crucial differences. First, Levinas's account of ethics is phenomenological, and so to understand the religious heritage at work in what he calls ethics we need to understand not simply the religious concepts it secularizes but the way it transforms fundamental religious experiences into ethical intuitions. Second, the secularization at work in Levinas's account of ethics is best understood in relation to the particular religious heritage in which he thought, a heritage that is first and foremost Judaic but also, more generally, Judeo-Christian. Not that the religious dimension of Levinas's thought ever went unnoticed. On the contrary, it was from the outset the subject of complex and spirited debate, beginning with Jacques Derrida's seminal 1967 essay, "Violence and Metaphysics." In more recent years, several interesting studies have commented on, and sometimes vigorously critiqued, the religious aspect of Levinas's thought. And yet most of the debate has circled around the vague notion of religion without due consideration of the concrete and particular religious character of his thought. But Levinas, who was born in 1906 into the Russian-Jewish *haskalah* (enlightenment) milieu of Kaunas, Lithuania, was a committed Jew for the duration of his adult life, and his philosophical account of "religion" is distinctively Judaic.

The aim of this book is to provide an interpretation of Levinas's philosophy from the Judaic heritage he was secularizing. Such an interpretation is crucial for a proper understanding of Levinas's work, but its significance extends beyond these exegetical concerns. By proposing an interpretation of Levinas's philosophy from the sources of Judaism, I raise in this study broader questions concerning the nature and scope of both philosophy and Judaism. By relying on a philosophical interpretation of Judaism, Levinas expands the significance of this particular tradition beyond the conventional social, historical, and legal limits of being Jewish. In so doing, he provides an interpretation of Judaism addressed to the Gentiles, or to Jews and Gentiles alike. In this sense Levinas's enterprise recalls that of Paul, the first apostle to the Gentiles, who likewise interpreted the sources of Judaism for the nations at large.

I will argue that Levinas's philosophical claims are saturated by interpretations of Judaism. But if Levinas's philosophy depends on Jewish texts and traditions, does this not compromise its claims? What sort of philosophical status does this work have if it is generated out of a particular—indeed, a particularistic—tradition, such as Judaism? It was, of course, Martin Heidegger, Levinas's most important philosophical influence and an unrepentant member of the Nazi party, who placed hermeneutics at the center of modern philosophy. Levinas learned many things from Heidegger, but for our purposes two of them should be emphasized. First, Levinas accepted Heidegger's fundamental claim that thinking itself is an interpretative engagement with the intellectual heritage that constitutes the historical situation of the philosopher. With Heidegger, philosophy becomes hermeneutics, a thoughtful disclosure of the "meaning of being" that severely modifies the old philosophical questions (those concerned with relations among truth, knowledge, reality, values, mind, nature, time, and space) by approaching them as the nexus of a historical situation. There is no avoiding the fact that Levinas's philosophical approach to Judaism—his understanding, interpretation, and application of the Judaic tradition—is primarily indebted to the Heideggerian breakthrough, chiefly for the way it foregrounds the interpretative character of thought itself. Second, as Heidegger himself understood, the argument of *Being and Time* leads to a "post-metaphysical" way of doing philosophy guided by the conviction that "Being" (whatever that is) cannot be approached in terms of its correspondence to a concept or a representation and cannot be analyzed as an object-like phenomenon or set of phenomena, but instead gives itself to us without becoming a ground or principle from which a stable, metaphysical picture of the world could be derived. If "Being" in the preceding sentence reminded some thinkers of an old god called YHWH, that is either a coincidence (as Heidegger thought) or a call "to hear a God not contaminated by Being" (as Levinas thought).[2] Consequently, the assumption of this book, that Levinas's philosophical work is based on an interpretation of Judaism, leads to a dialogue, a confrontation, and an implication between a certain Judaism, a certain Paul, and a certain Heidegger, and thereby raises complex and at times painful questions.

Levinas's biography is inextricably bound to the turbulence of the European twentieth century. The Russian Revolution, the aftermath of the Dreyfus affair, the 1930s, and the Holocaust touched Levinas personally, vocationally, and intellectually. His philosophical output commenced in 1929 with pioneering studies of Husserlian phenomenology, and his first publications on issues relating to Judaism began with "Some Reflections on the Philosophy of Hitlerism" in 1934. By the time of his death in 1995 Levinas had produced a corpus of major philosophical writings, most of it concerned with "ethics," as well as six collections of philosophical commentary on Jewish texts such as the Hebrew Bible, the Talmud,

and works by medieval and modern Jewish thinkers. While clearly working on two fronts throughout his life, Levinas sought to distinguish his
"confessional" writings from his strictly philosophical work by publishing each with separate presses and denying, in several published interviews
and discussions, that his philosophy was in any way based on faith. Such
safeguards are commonly deployed among French philosophers of various
religious persuasions. The French tradition of *laïcité* separates not only the
state but also its philosophers from religion; it is in fact forbidden to teach
theology at almost all universities of the French Republic. Like many of
Levinas's colleagues, such as Paul Ricoeur or, more recently, Jean-Luc Marion, Levinas accepted the rules of the game of French philosophy and went
to lengths to downplay or even deny the religious element of his thinking.
If that is a common stance of Christian philosophers whose religion tacitly
pervades the French intellectual milieu, for Levinas it was indispensable.
Denying the Jewish element of his thought was quite simply the price of
its admission into the arena of French philosophy. Yet several points mili-
tate against separating the philosophy from the Judaism.

   The most obvious is that Levinas himself articulated the same philosophical views, or what amounts to the same views, in both his confessional and his philosophical works. If scholars of the Talmud have been
surprised that Levinas finds hidden poststructuralist intentions in the debates of Abbaye and Rabba, contemporary philosophers have been concerned by his occasional citation from and copious allusions to Jewish
texts and ideas in his philosophical corpus. Maintaining his stance as a
philosopher, Levinas nevertheless acknowledged an "infiltration" from Judaism to his philosophy.[3] Moreover, unlike so many of his Nietzschean
colleagues on the Continent, Levinas never thought that either God or religion is dead. That conviction was reinforced by a desire to affirm a certain Judaism after the Holocaust, which claimed his parents, brothers, and
most other Jews of Kaunas. The visceral effect of the destruction of European Jewry on Levinas's thinking is impossible to deny, even if its explicit
presence in his work is more difficult to determine.[4] But even before and
independently of the Destruction, Levinas's existential commitment to Judaism was palpable.

   After all, his early years were spent shuttling between the elite intellectual culture of interwar Paris—at the soirees of Gabriel Marcel and

the colloquia of Jean Wahl, in company with the likes of Alexandre Ko-jève, Jean-Paul Sartre, Maurice Merleau-Ponty, and Maurice Blanchot—and his day job as an administrator of the Alliance Israélite Universelle, a Jewish teachers' college charged with educating Jews from the French Mediterranean colonies. Although his pioneering study as a brilliant twenty-four-year-old master's student was published in 1930 to prize-winning acclaim[5]—the book introduced the immensely influential Ger-man phenomenological movement to young French philosophers such as Sartre, Ricoeur, and, later, Derrida—Levinas was, for thirty years to come, a lay philosopher employed in a largely administrative role in the field of Jewish education. While fascism spread through Europe during the 1930s, he read Moses Maimonides' *Guide for the Perplexed* and Franz Rosenzweig's *The Star of Redemption* and published several articles in the all-too-rare genre of Jewish philosophical journalism, including the essay on the philosophy of Hitlerism and a related discussion on "The Con-temporary Relevance of Maimonides."[6] For almost five years, from June 1940 until the end of World War II, Levinas was incarcerated as a French POW in Stalag IX-B in the region of Hannover, along with other Jew-ish soldiers protected by the Geneva Conventions. By day he labored as a woodcutter and by night he read—G. W. F. Hegel, Marcel Proust, and Jean-Jacques Rousseau, among others—and composed an important philosophical fragment on "the horror of existence" that was evidently as much shaped by his view of the war as by his analysis of Hegel and Hei-degger, against whom he argues.[7] Upon returning to Paris after the war at the age of forty, Levinas characteristically expressed his dual loyalty to philosophy and Judaism. Among the first things he did was to extend the philosophical fragment he had composed during captivity into a su-perb phenomenological essay, *From Existence to the Existent* (1947), and to deliver a series of lectures, later published as *Time and the Other*, at the College Philosophique established by Wahl. Another was to assume the position of director of a prestigious Jewish high school, the École Nor-mal Israélite Orientale. Many years later Levinas confessed that working as an administrator at a Jewish educational institution instead of forg-ing an academic career was a vocational decision: "After Auschwitz . . . I was responding to a historical calling. It was my little secret."[8] Like Levi-nas's commitment to Jewish education, the role of Judaism in his general philosophy is also a little secret, even if the philosopher was not much good at keeping secrets.

It was during these years, from 1946 to 1961, that Levinas composed his first major philosophical account of ethics—in lectures, articles, and essays that culminated in his first magnum opus, *Totality and Infinity* (1961), the work that also earned him his *doctorat d'État*, a prerequisite for teaching philosophy at a French university. During this same period of productive philosophizing, Levinas began studying the Talmud with a brilliant and enigmatic teacher, Monsieur Chouchani; delivered weekly Shabbat lessons on Rashi's classical commentary on the Torah (from the eleventh century, but largely based on important rabbinic commentaries from Talmudic times); and involved himself in the rituals of Shabbat, including the synagogue liturgy. By 1960 he was sufficiently emboldened to present his first "Talmudic Reading," which he would do again for most of the next thirty years at the annual Colloquium of French Jewish Intellectuals that he helped found; apparently he would often consult Maimonides' legal code, the *Mishneh Torah*, in order to select a Talmudic passage to suit the conference theme.[9] Such incidental biographical details must be recalled because the sources of Levinas's Judaism determine the shape it assumes in his philosophical work. It is particularly important to bear in mind the significance of the close, prolonged exposure Levinas received to canonical Jewish texts, in Hebrew, through the liturgy of Judaism,[10] as well as the education in rabbinic lore he received from Rashi, Maimonides, Hayim Volozhin, Chouchani, and contemporary scholars such as Gershom Scholem. Although Levinas surely never received a formal advanced Jewish education, neither of the academic nor of the yeshiva variety, he embraced the intellectual heritage of Judaism: the Hebrew Bible, rabbinic commentaries, medieval masters (those just mentioned, but also Judah Halevi and Solomon Ibn Gabirol), and modern Jewish philosophers from Moses Mendelssohn to Hermann Cohen, Martin Buber, and Rosenzweig. Even those who accept Levinas's claim that his philosophy stands independently of his Judaism do not for a moment separate the philosopher from the Jew. It was only at the age of fifty-seven, in 1963, that Levinas assumed his first appointment as a philosopher.[11] Perhaps he thought of professional philosophy as a form of early retirement. In any case, the argument of this book is that one cannot separate Levinas's work from its Jewish provenance, even though the philosopher enjoined his readers to do so. Levinas was a remarkably creative and original thinker as well as a broad and penetrating reader, and it must be borne in mind that during this intensely fertile period from after World War II to his first appointment as a professional philosopher, he was all the while thinking of Judaism philosophically and philosophy Judaically. Accordingly, despite his attempt to regulate our reading of his work by partitioning the Judaic from the philosophical, what is required, rather, is to determine the contours of the profound unity of Judaism and philosophy to which his thought attests.

*

Since I hope some readers of this book will come from Jewish studies and religious studies generally and therefore may not have read much of Levinas's major philosophical works, I will briefly elucidate his core philosophical idea, although I make no claim whatsoever to offer an "introduction to Levinas," of which by now there are numerous.[12] Levinas's project is best understood, at least provisionally, as an attempt to formulate a post-Heideggerian account of ethics that draws its inspiration from Kantian morality while avoiding the critique of Kant waged by Heidegger. For Levinas, following Kant, ethics involves a sense of categorical obligation, obligations that rely on no particular moral feeling or empathy and no personal interest or gain. Levinas's constant use of heady terms like "transcendence" and "infinity" or "otherwise" and "beyond" was driven by a desire to articulate the view that moral obligation is an "end in itself," as Kant called it, an ultimate term of reference that cannot be reduced to more basic conceptual language such as "biology" or "ontology" or "instrumental reason." Levinas was largely right in his perception that Heidegger had sought to destroy the very ground of this Kantian view of morality, even if Levinas's interpretation of *Being and Time* was also influenced by its author's accommodation to Nazism. The young Jewish philosopher was among the first to promote Heidegger's groundbreaking work, published in 1927. By 1934, however, his enthusiasm for *Being and Time* had already been tempered by the realization that Heidegger's political commitments were not accidentally related to his philosophical views. For reasons that are not pondered often enough, Levinas's critique of Heidegger focused almost entirely on the moral rather than the political flaws of *Being and*

Time. At the end of this book I suggest that this exclusive attention to Heidegger's critique of morality did not prevent Levinas from repeating some of the fundamental problems of political ontology. At that point I confront the question of the politics of Levinasian ethics, a question made more acute by interpreting Levinas Judaically. For now, though, let me clarify the quasi-Kantian critique of Heidegger that led Levinas to develop his distinct sense of "ethics."

According to Levinas, Heidegger had subordinated and devalued ethics within his philosophical project by historicizing and instrumental-izing it. After World War II this became not merely a theoretical argu-ment but one that Levinas waged against the culture of modern Western morality in which ethics was commonly dismissed by intellectuals as merely relative, ideological, or emotive. In place of such prevalent ideas Levinas sought to revive the Kantian view that morality was categorically binding and that to fail to heed a moral imperative is to miss something crucial about the ultimate structure of reality. And yet for Kant, the cat-egorical nature of morality was derived from a view of the fundamentally rational nature of human beings. It is only because human beings have the capacity to conform their will to Reason that morality, according to Kant, is possible. Heidegger argued against just this notion of human na-ture. In his view, Kant's notion of the transcendence of Reason is itself based on prior "ontological" conditions that are neither purely rational nor particularly moral, conditions that constitute our being-in-the-world temporally (such as sociality, historicality, language, and much else). He showed that morality could not be explained by appeal to the rational na-ture of humanity and that the idea of the human as a fundamentally ra-tional being, and thus the idea of rational morality, was but a contingent, historical, and even "inauthentic" interpretation of the experience of con-science (*Gewissen*). According to *Being and Time*, the truth of conscience lies not in conforming one's will to the universal law of Reason but in the disclosure of the finitude of one's concrete situation. In Heidegger's view, the very idea of absolute moral imperatives is merely an inauthentic in-terpretation of a much more fundamental experience of the finitude of being, which is itself ethically neutral. This ontological reduction of Rea-son to the fundamental horizon of being-in-the-world historicizes and relativizes morality. It exorcises the very idea of immutable moral values based on the free and rational inner nature of the human will. Worse, Heidegger argued that the notion of a "public conscience" belonged to the realm of "inauthentic" existence.[13] Experiences of guilt or conscience that are interpreted according to universal "values" or derived from formal reasoning are "ontologically inadequate."[14] For Heidegger, morality is but a set of platitudes reified by a particular community at a particular historical moment and misconstrued by inauthentic individuals as the authoritative grounds for action or a guilty conscience. We might say that for Heidegger, Kantian morality is but common cant. From these ruins of Kant's categorical morality Levinas sought to restore a new sense of an unconditional ethical imperative that could not be dismissed as merely abstract, formal, ahistorical, inauthentic, and ontologically inadequate. He did this by developing a phenomenology of the moral imperative that was derived not from the fact of Reason but from the face of the Other. This account of a pre-rational but still categorical imperative constitutes his signature contribution to contemporary phenomenology and moral philosophy.

It should be noted how Levinas's attempt to describe a post-Heideggerian account of ethics that preserves the categorical nature of moral imperatives involves a fundamental acceptance of Heidegger's critique of Kantian anthropology and epistemology. Kant constructs morality on the basis of a metaphysical view of the primacy of Reason and of the freedom of the human will to conform to it, but for Levinas ethics is generated out of the immediate, concrete expression of the mortality, vulnerability, and singularity of the other person, metaphorically encapsulated in "the face." This account of "ethics" therefore looks quite different from much contemporary moral philosophy and from its Kantian progenitor.[15] In place of arguments that appeal solely to reason, Levinas provides descriptions that seek to "awaken" our pre-rational moral sensitivity to others. For Levinas, it is not the universal form of reason but the singular manifestation of the other that has moral authority in the modern world. Many of his descriptions of ethics, what can loosely be called his "phenomenological" method, aim to show how the relationship between self and other is the very condition, or the foundation, for there being an intelligible world at all. These descriptions are meant to explain why it is that "ethics" is our ultimate transcendental condition (in the Kantian sense), which is to say that ethics is the condition for the possibility of meaningful experience as such. But contrary to Kant, Levinas maintains that it is not the formal concept of morality that generates its exalted significance but its material presentation in the encounter with the other as a singular figure, a face, or a proper name.

We can point to three features of Levinas's account of ethics that distinguish it from most moral philosophy. First, in his view, ethics makes demands calling for an *individuated responsiveness* that he calls "responsibility." The ethical response must be radically individuated because it relates directly to the concrete person whom one encounters rather than some preconceived idea of human nature. The uniqueness of the other calls for a singular ethical response on the part of oneself; indeed, it calls one to become oneself by implicating one's own "identity" in the relationship to the other, a relationship that Levinas insists is ethical. Why does the relationship to the other have a specifically ethical sense? Why is this relationship characterized as fundamentally ethical rather than as biological, ontological, or instrumental? Levinas's answer, which we will modify in the course of this book, is that the uniqueness of the other presented in his or her "face" cannot be approached without ethics. The face is never equivalent to a phenomenon seeking to be seen or described, or to a set of concepts or narratives that are to be explained or understood. The face cannot be captured by description, explanation, or narration; it can only be respected or desired, loved or hated. To exclude the ethical significance of the face is to miss what makes it unique. The face thus presents a distinctly ethical excess that neither perception nor cognition, neither epistemology nor semantics, neither biography nor psychology can contain. Ethics involves the "mutation" of ordinary experience and "the opening of a new dimension" in which the face exposes an ethical obligation that cannot be articulated in terms of reasons, causes, or rules (TI, 197/TeI, 172).[16] Levinas's customary way of indicating the distinctly ethical sense of the face is to argue that language "reduces"—in the technical phenomenological sense of *leading back* to a primordial manifestation—to the vocative case, to the occasion of direct address in which the "expression" of the face says more than what is conveyed by its semantic values, a distinction he regularly marks by the excess of "the saying" over "the said." It is here, in the ethical presentation of the face, beyond semantics, epistemology, and even manifestation, that "the person presents himself as unique" (TI, 66/ TeI, 37). Accordingly, although Levinas argues that "the face speaks," the point is that it speaks only ethically; its saying does not appear in the ordinary sense of a meaning made manifest to consciousness but only as a moral command—"Do not kill!" or "Love me!" "Give me!" or "Help me!"—addressed to me in a manner than cannot be readily generalized.

A second distinctive feature of Levinas's view thus follows from the account of ethics as individuated responsiveness. Since ethics arises from the singular way in which one responds to the uniqueness of the other, it cannot be abstracted into a set of rules, values, or principles. It is therefore not a *theory* of ethics, as Derrida astutely observed, but an "Ethics of Ethics" that "does not seek to propose laws or moral rules, does not seek to determine *a* morality, but rather the essence of the ethical relation in general."[17] In Levinas's words, "The presentation of being in the face does not have the status of a value" (TI, 202/TeI, 177). Or as he rehearsed the idea in his second magnum opus, "Responsibility is what first enables one to catch sight of and conceive of value" (OB, 123/AE, 159).[18] Levinas insists that ethics is as fluid, open, and even indeterminate as a human relationship itself. The language of ethics therefore involves "respect," "responsibility," and "obligation" rather than "rules," "principles," and "rights" because his principal point is not to argue for particular norms but to cultivate a sense of responsibility and indebtedness to the other that constitutes the very idea of oneself. That rights, procedures, and institutions will enshrine the ethicality of the other is a second-order moral and political requirement derived from the basic ethical experience of the other.

A third feature of Levinas's account is that ethics is not derivative of any more basic condition but is the very origin and opening of intelligibility. This is what he means by the bold assertion that "ethics is first philosophy" (TI, 304/TeI, 340). In his view ethics constitutes the basis of meaning in general, which is to say that all of our philosophical and nonphilosophical concerns—for knowledge and truth, for politics and economics, for science and art, for oneself and one's family, for eros and thanatos—are indebted and obliged to ethical relationships from the ground up. For Levinas, then, *ethics is the individuated responsiveness to the singularity of the other that gives rise to meaning in general and to which one is indebted for one's "own" ultimate purpose and identity.* Responsibility, or "response-ability," is not merely what one does but who one "is."

*

It will have been noticed that none of what I said in this brief explication of what Levinas calls "ethics" made any reference to Judaism, either to the biblical revelation of the Jews or to their commentaries, traditions, and history. Levinas wrote as a philosopher. The ethics he describes appeals to dimensions of human experience that presuppose none of Judaism's doctrinal beliefs and no commitments to its history, tradition, or destiny. Yet the claim of this book is that the descriptions Levinas makes of ethics draw from the Judaic tradition in a decisive way. The precise nature of the Judaism smoldering within Levinas's philosophy is admittedly not obvious, even if his thought binds Judaism and philosophy together at all its crucial sutures. The attempt to analyze these junctures thus requires a type of "reverse engineering" of Levinas's philosophical project that unbuilds its midrashic structure or unravels its numerous but unstated exegetical threads. As I turn the fabric of Levinas's philosophical works inside out we will discover the Judaic threads they have woven. If I am right, we will see that what is sometimes understood as an exercise in pure phenomenology is at the same time a coherent philosophy of Judaism.[19]

The task of interpreting Levinas's philosophy out of the sources of Judaism is inseparable from an analysis of the barely tested possibility that there may be such a thing as a philosophy of Judaism that is both philosophically and Jewishly rigorous. To be sure, Judaism and philosophy have long kept company; we find them intermingling in rapturous accord, briefly in Philo but pervasively in medieval and modern Jewish thought. Yet for most of its history Judaism has turned to philosophy only to shine the light of wisdom back onto itself. Maimonides' *Guide of the Perplexed*, like Joseph B. Soloveitchik's *Halakhic Man*, is infused with philosophy, but as with almost all examples of what is tellingly called "Machshevet Yisrael"—which refers to "the thought of the Jewish people" rather than Jewish philosophy—it is addressed solely to Jews.[20] One of the great novelties of *Totality and Infinity* and *Otherwise than Being or Beyond Essence* is the possibility they herald of a philosophy of Judaism whose claims are not restricted or even addressed primarily to Jews. In this respect, Levinas's understanding of Judaism goes beyond the traditional practice of pouring philosophy into kosher vessels, with the standard boiling and souring of the vine. His is a much bolder venture that has been dared only on the rarest occasions—for example, in the epistles of St. Paul or the *Fons Vitae* of Ibn Gabirol, which likewise provide interpretations of Judaism for the nations of the world.[21] In both these cases the new branch was lopped off; indeed, in both cases, all proportions aside, it was transplanted into Christianity. Throughout his life Levinas's work seemed destined for the same fate. For a long time his philosophical works were better known to Christian thinkers and postmodern philosophers than to those interested in "the thought of the Jewish people"; the latter often read only Levinas's Talmudic readings and essays on Judaism, if they read him at all. Contrary to this reception history, the wager of this book is that Levinas's *philosophical works* are midrashically determined from beginning to end. If I am right, then far from playing into the identity politics of "being Jewish," as Levinas has been accused of doing, his work confounds conventional identity politics and theoretical frameworks that continue to distinguish between Jew and Gentile, Israel and the nations, Jerusalem and Athens, and so on. I argue that although *Totality and Infinity* and *Otherwise than Being* are explicitly addressed to non-Jewish European philosophers, or Westerners generally, they nevertheless encode interpretations of Judaism in their core arguments. Indeed, despite the well-trodden path leading from a philosophical interpretation of Judaism to some determined account of a proper "Jewish identity," Levinas's calculated indifference to a philosophical account of Jewish identity is precisely what is needed today. Only a Judaism that goes beyond the identity politics of being Jewish is able to make a Judaic contribution to thinking about ethics and politics in our world today. This book, then, is a sometimes timorous, sometimes brazen act of *giluy 'arayot*, in both senses: an act of *illicit union* that desires to give birth to Judaism as a philosophical way of life and an *exposure* of the philosophical nakedness of Judaic spirituality.

*

In his outstanding historical study of Levinas's philosophy, Samuel Moyn has argued that its genesis should be understood within the context of a burgeoning interest in Protestant existential theology among the Parisian intelligentsia of the interwar period. Moyn entirely discounts the influence of the Judaic on Levinas's thinking and goes so far as to call Levinas's description of Judaism an "invention."[22] Moyn's account thus seems to belie the basic assumptions and methods of this book. In Chapter 1, I argue that Moyn brilliantly elucidates an understandable but unduly partial and ultimately mistaken perspective that does not account for the genuinely Judaic character of Levinas's philosophy. This exercise required me to analyze the meaning and possibility of a philosophy of Judaism, a possibility that is available precisely in the context of the post-Heideggerian hermeneutical philosophy in which Levinas operated.

In Chapter 2, I begin a sustained reading of Levinas's philosophy as a covert interpretation of certain aspects of classical Jewish thought. I argue that Levinas's phenomenological description of the emergence of subjectivity recapitulates the great myth in Genesis 1, according to which creation takes place on the basis of the "unformed and void." Like the Priestly author in the Bible, Levinas argues that creation does not happen ex nihilo but is wrought from the chaos of the anonymous darkness of existence. Creation makes order out of chaos, but the chaos threatens to return, like a deluge or a holocaust, if the moral covenant is broken. Chapter 3 delves into Levinas's phenomenology of creation from an altogether different angle. Whereas Chapter 2 argued that Levinas provides a covert and secularized account of the fragility of creation that is sustained by covenantal fidelity (among people, of course), Chapter 3 explores the more classical notion of *creatio ex nihilo* as it appears in Levinas's work. I argue that Levinas's use of the term in its classical sense borrows from Maimonides and implies a thoroughly metaphysical conception of creation. Maimonides' argument is directed against Aristotle, but Levinas wages his argument against Heidegger. In both cases, however, it is a matter of the Jewish thinker arguing for the transcendence of freedom and responsibility for particularity. Levinas's critique of Heidegger is thereby read as a repetition of Maimonides' critique of Aristotle, a parallel buttressed by the well-known thesis that *Being and Time* is an ontological "translation" of Aristotle's *Ethics*.

After Chapter 3, I shift gears, for although *Totality and Infinity* can be read as a sustained midrash on creation, it remains, like the notion of creation itself, invested in a metaphysical account of agency and transcendence. Creation is a quintessentially metaphysical concept that implies a being at a distance from the world by virtue of its freedom. The Interlude shows how Levinas came to reject the notion of creation by opening a new direction for his later work to be read as a post-metaphysical secularized philosophy. Where formerly there was creation, Levinas's later, post-meta-physical work is a midrash on creatureliness. I argue that there is a seismic shift between the two great works, *Totality and Infinity* and *Otherwise than Being*, that leads Levinas from a metaphysical to a post-metaphysical account of ethics, correlative to similar distinctions invoked nowadays in philosophy and theology. The quite radical nature of this turn, which warrants speaking of Levinas 1 and Levinas 2, has not been sufficiently appreciated in the literature, although awareness of it is indispensable for answering most of Levinas's critics, almost all of whom attack his metaphysical views.

A traditional way of surpassing metaphysics is to turn from positive to negative theology. Chapter 4 argues that *Otherwise than Being*, in which Levinas develops his post-metaphysical position, is best understood as a work of negative theology, in particular of Judaic ethical negative theology. I therefore turn again to Maimonides in this chapter, since his metaphysics harbors a radical and quite disturbing form of negative theology. By separating the metaphysical Maimonides from the Maimonides of negative theology I show how Jewish negative theology culminates with an acknowledgment of the unique referential function of the proper name, a train of thought that takes a remarkably ethical turn with Levinas. Chapter 5 continues to explore Levinas's later philosophy by making explicit another major claim of this book, that what the philosopher calls "ethics" is best understood as a secularized and generalized account of the Jewish covenant of faith. I argue that Jewish faith ought to be understood phenomenologically rather than cognitively, and that theological beliefs, like moral and epistemic beliefs, are derived from the noncognitive experience of covenantal faith. Having outlined an account of ethics in terms of covenantal faithfulness, I turn, in Chapter 6, to the problem of political identity as it relates to Levinas's philosophy of Judaism.

Levinas's work is striking for the way it weaves together the secular and the religious, the Jewish and the Christian, the particular and the universal, the phenomenological and the hermeneutical. This is not a wild patchwork of postmodern syncretism but a testament to the implicatedness of thinking historically about our ethical and political condition together. This implicatedness is not simply a banal historical fact but an ethical and political axiom with repercussions for how we think through and live our historical coexistence. Modern ethics does not stand on a neutral ahistorical platform, and it does not take place within natural borders or determinate historical and political identities. Today it is clear that our futures are inseparable, perilous, and absolutely unassured, and at the same time that we are moored to our origins far more than most modern thinkers imagined. Levinas's constant recourse to Judaism as a philosophical way of life springs from this very sentiment, which remains our predicament. Ethics happens as an exposure to singular demands in light of a heritage. But heritage is as unstable as it is unavoidable and as fiercely possessed as it is factually shared. Ethics thus inevitably involves a contestation over the goods we desire. The heterodoxy of Levinas's philosophy of Judaism, which eschews every strict division between the religious and the secular, Judaism and Christianity, Jew and Gentile, is both the source of its vitality and of its significance for the unforeseeable that faces us.

Acknowledgments

Many people and institutions have enabled me to write this book. My studies led me from the Philosophy Department to the Centre for Comparative Literature and Cultural Studies, both at Monash University, and then to Jerusalem for several years where I studied at the Hebrew University of Jerusalem, the Shalom Hartman Institute, and as a Jerusalem Fellow at the Mandel Leadership Institute. I will single out only Kevin Hart, my PhD supervisor at Monash, who is now at the University of Virginia, and Moshe Halbertal, my mentor as a Golda Meir Postdoctoral Fellow at the Hebrew University of Jerusalem, although my gratitude extends to many scholars and administrators of those institutions. I am particularly aware that from my teachers in Jerusalem I have taken only what a paintbrush can take from the sea. Since returning to Monash University I have been involved in the establishment of the Australian Centre for Jewish Civilisation within the School of Historical Studies and have greatly benefited from the generous and supportive encouragement of my colleagues at Monash. I thank the administrative staff of the School of Historical Studies and the librarians at the Matheson Library who have greatly assisted me over the years. I thank also Mark Crees and James Cannon for providing me with valuable research assistance, and Andrew Markus and Mark Baker, the directors of the Australian Centre for Jewish Civilisation, for their support and trust.

Chapters 3 and 4 are modified versions of an article published in the *Journal of Jewish Thought and Philosophy* 16:1 (2008). My thanks to Koninklijke Brill N.V. for allowing me to reprint the article. The arrival of Andrew Benjamin at Monash has been of great benefit and pleasure to me and I thank him for the attention and encouragement he has given my work. My thanks also go to members of the Phenomenology and Theology Research Group who read and commented on a couple of chapters. Emily-Jane Cohen at Stanford University Press provided much valuable assistance, as did Sarah Crane Newman, Carolyn Brown, and Alison Rainey.

It is a pleasure to acknowledge the unwavering support of my parents, Mark and Hannah Fagenblat. I am especially grateful to Naor Bar-Zeev and Nathan Wolski for innumerable conversations, references, criticisms, readings of my work, and, above all, friendship. To Melanie Landau I am grateful for the same, and a lot more. Our children, Ktoret and Ariel, provide a constant source of learning and delight.

A COVENANT OF CREATURES

1

Levinas's New Creation

A PHILOSOPHY OF JUDAISM, WITHOUT *AND* OR *BETWEEN*

> The Jew is split, and split first of all between the two dimensions of the letter: allegory and literality.
>   —Jacques Derrida

A Philosophy of Judaism?

When asked, as he frequently was and, indeed, from the earliest occasions, Emmanuel Levinas rejected the notion that he was "a Jewish philosopher." His arguments and conclusions made claims independent of his particular confession of faith and religious affiliation. They are, he proposed, independent of *all* confessions of faith and religious affiliations; they are phenomenological analyses of "the thing itself," the thing of ethics. The Other—that thing of ethics—is not a Judaic or even a religious phenomenon. And if religion in general and Judaism in particular agree on the significance and manifestation of ethics, that is because they have caught sight of something in the thing itself rather than because philosophy is an apology for religion or doctrine. To avoid confusion, and in addition to protesting, Levinas chose different publishers for his philosophical writings from those he chose for his Jewish ones. Although several fascinating footnotes in *Otherwise than Being* hint at an unwritten commentary Levinas kept to himself, in the philosophical corpus he generally avoided discussion of Jewish sources, lest they be mistaken for "proof texts," as if a text could prove anything about ethics itself.[1] In principle, even though Levinas was a practicing and learned Jew, he claimed to write *as* a philosopher and asked to be read as one.

It was Gabriel Marcel, as one of the examiners of Levinas's *doctorat d'État, Totality and Infinity*, who was perhaps the first to make the "alarming comment": "Why do you always say 'the Other' when you know that the term exists in the biblical tradition as 'the neighbor'?"[2] We do not know how Levinas responded to his Christian interlocutor; one imagines a slight wink or a wry smile, an unstated acknowledgment of a Judeo-Christian fidelity that philosophers, especially Parisian ones, ought to share only in secret. Ricoeur, another Christian philosopher, likewise thought Levinas was concealing his Judaism in his philosophical cloak.

There are no quotations from the Bible—except one or two maybe—in *Totality and Infinity*. It's Plato. It's Descartes. And when he reads in Plato that the idea of the Good is beyond Being, he is thinking of the unpronounceable Name, and he makes a kind of short-circuit that is never named as such. That the Unsayable and the Good of Plato are superimposed at a point that itself cannot be named, is something that I sense to be very deeply buried, something profoundly dissimulated and always said indirectly.[3]

Two of France's leading Christian thinkers, then, suggested that Levinas secretes his Judaism amid his philosophy. Other Christian thinkers outside France, along with Jewish thinkers in the United States and Israel, agree that Levinas's philosophy is intimately if not entirely bound to his Judaism.[4] And while these commentators regard Levinas's secret Judaism as making an important contribution to contemporary philosophy, several notable philosophers regard the religious element as a fatal flaw or even a bluff, behind which stands an antiphilosophical rhetoric of blind faith, dogmatism, and piety.

Neither Philosophy

Sometimes such critics protest at the generally religious thrust to Levinas's thought; at other times they imply the problem lies in its specifically Judaic character. Almost always the argument has the following form: Levinas's ethics is based on a metadivision between the categories of the

Other and the Same. He himself locates ethics, Judaism, and revelation in the category of the Other, while he places reason, history, and ontology in the realm of the Same. By his own lights, then, there is an alienation or a "diremption," as Gillian Rose calls it, between the spirit of ethics and the world of reflective, deliberative action in which this so-called "ethics" is determined as action, politics, and law.[5] Where Levinas sees ethics as the blind spot of philosophy, a point at which philosophy cannot see itself seeing the world, these philosophers contend that his version of ethics actually blinds philosophy by imposing the sense of an exteriority invisible to the light of consciousness and reason. In Judith Butler's estimation, Levinas's account of ethics involves "a demand that is *not* open to interpretation" and is therefore no more or less "uncritical and unthinking than an acquiescence to an ungrounded authoritarian law."[6] On the basis of a similar appraisal Dominique Janicaud concluded that "such a dogmatism could only be religious."[7] What Levinas calls "ethics" would belong to the realm of faith, indeed, to a particular type of faith set apart from reason or thought. Alain Badiou concurs:

Lévinas's enterprise . . . is entirely bound up with a religious axiom; to believe that we can separate what Lévinas's thought unites is to betray the intimate movement of this thought, its subjective rigor. In truth, Lévinas has no philosophy—not even philosophy as the "servant" of theology. Rather, this is philosophy (in the Greek sense of the word) *annulled* by theology, itself no longer theology (the terminology is still too Greek, and presumes proximity to the divine via the identity and predicates of God) but, precisely, an ethics. . . . To put it crudely: Lévinas's enterprise serves to remind us, with extraordinary insistence, that every effort to turn ethics into the principle of thought and action is essentially religious. We might say that Lévinas is the coherent and inventive thinker of an assumption that no academic exercise of veiling or abstraction can obscure: distanced from its Greek usage (according to which it is clearly subordinated to the theoretical), and taken in general, ethics is a category of pious discourse.[8]

While this condemnation of the "essentially religious" element in Levinas's ethics is indeterminately labeled, within the context of modern European philosophy in general and of Badiou's work in particular it is evidently aimed at a specific religion in which theory is allegedly subordinated to Law—namely, Judaism. Beginning with Benedict Spinoza, a formidable tradition argues for the incompatibility between Judaism, as Law, and the philosophical task of formulating a universal ethics. Spinoza was the first to cast Judaism as Law devoid of reason, a view wholeheartedly adopted by Immanuel Kant, who went so far as to declare that "Judaism is really not a religion at all" but "a collection of mere statutory laws." In this view Judaism makes no rational or even moral demands. On the contrary, the positivism of Jewish Law is "directed to absolutely nothing but outer observance" and animated by purely instrumental concerns, namely, the preservation of the political association of its members.[9] To achieve this merely instrumental, political goal—what might today be called the identitarian function of Jewish Law—Judaism, in this view, established a theocracy and made use of coercive techniques, especially earthly rewards and punishments, rather than determining its laws according to the rationality of conscience and notions of rational morality. The claim, as made by Badiou, Butler, Janicaud, and Rose, that Levinas's thought amounts to a pious and dogmatic assertion of nonrational Law recapitulates the modern philosophical critique, instituted by Spinoza and adopted by Kant, of the nonphilosophical character of Judaism as such.

It is Spinoza's canonizing interpretation of Judaism, then, that needs to be questioned. The case he made for Judaism's alleged disparagement of philosophical reasoning was largely based on an interpretation of Moses Maimonides.[10] Spinoza attributed to Maimonides the view that a person who adopts universal religious and moral laws (which the rabbinic tradition knows as the seven Noahide Laws) because of his own rational convictions rather than his obedience to revelation is not counted among the righteous or even among the sages of the nations.[11] Without acquiescing to revealed, nonrational Law, not only righteousness but also wisdom would count for nothing. What counts in Judaism, according to this view, is only obedience. Even Maimonides, the greatest representative of philosophical Judaism, would have regarded Judaism as essentially opposed to morality and the exercise of unfettered reason. Judaism would accommodate ethics only by subordinating it to the suprarational transcendence of revealed divine Law. The status and legitimacy of ethics within Judaism would therefore in principle be not only heteronomous but, indeed, antirational. Such is the image of Judaism that Spinoza introduced into modern philosophy.

In addition to the prevalence of this antiphilosophical image of Judaism among eminent modern philosophers, such a view has been defended by leading Jewish thinkers, usually by interpreting Maimonides in the way Spinoza did. Employing the exact same schema but reversing the values, neo-Orthodox Jewish thinkers such as Yeshayahu Leibowitz, Marvin Fox, and Benny Levy laud the value of heteronomous, revealed law over the pretensions of philosophical reasoning. Prominent detractors and leading exponents of Judaism are thus in accord: where there is Judaism there can be no philosophy proper since Judaism subordinates the autonomous capacity of reasoning to the dictates of the nonrationally given Law (Badiou's critique of Levinas *in nuce*). That the Law has been *given* is understood by neo-Orthodox Jewish thinkers as a sign of its priority over philosophy, whereas modern philosophers, adopting the same schema, dismiss it as but metaphysical posturing or historico-juridical positivism that carries no philosophical weight and therefore makes no moral claim whatsoever. Unsurprisingly, from the point of view of this Protestant-cum-Jewish tradition the only truly philosophical Jew is "a non-Jewish Jew" such as Spinoza, be he the heretic who prized reason over revelation or the hero who anticipates the solution to the Jewish Question: Jews without Judaism.

Ironically, this tradition was given its illustrious philosophical life because of what is likely a corrupt text. Whereas the printed edition of the text of Maimonides that Spinoza cites says that a person who acts ethically on account of reason alone "is neither a foreign resident nor one of the righteous gentiles nor [ולא, *ve'lo*] one of their wise men," other manuscripts have it that such a person "*is* [אלא, *ela*] one of their wise men."[12] The implications of this minor maculation are significant, for on the corrected reading Maimonides would in fact be legitimating and even honoring the independent wisdom inherent in moral reasoning. Such an interpretation would also cohere much better with his overall approach, as several scholars have argued.[13] On the basis of an uncertain text and an unconvincing interpretation of Maimonides, Spinoza thereby installed in the heart of modern philosophy the view that Judaism holds only heteronomous law in esteem and is thus essentially opposed to moral philosophy.[14]

Unfortunately Levinas himself, especially in his early period, was prone to characterize Judaism in opposition to philosophy and to that extent gave himself over to this tradition, as if Judaism has reasons that reason itself cannot know.[15] This much seems to follow from the metadivision he posits between the Same and the Other and all that falls under their respective signs. Truth and goodness, knowledge and peace, philosophy and prophecy, "totality" and "infinity" are all conjunctively associated without any dialectical or conceptual passage that would allow for their effective synthesis or deployment. Rose lamented this "broken middle" that leaves postmodern philosophy "rended not mended." In her view, this diremption between morality and political law leaves the postmodern thinker with an impotent, broken heart filled with pure intentions. Levinas's Judaic invocation of the transcendence of ethics would not merely assent to an oppositional contrast between reason and revelation but would amplify it to hitherto untold extremes, since the ethical revelation is opposed to phenomenology as such, outside every datum of consciousness, every adventure of the mind, and every experience, including religious experience.[16] The task for philosophy would be merely to yield to the ethical burden of "the Other"; reason would be nothing but the instrumental technique for administering the revelation of ethics and the just society would be the one that knows how to use reason to enforce the heteronomous authority of ethics. No wonder philosophers like Badiou, Butler, Janicaud, and Rose have discerned a radically antiphilosophical gesture in Levinas's work, with all the implications this entails: authoritarianism, piety, dogmatism, recourse to traditionalism, positivism, and communitarian, identitarian politics.

I would add that the image of Levinas as a postmodern *'oseh nefashot* (Gen. 12:5), a maker of poststructuralist souls, and a *ba'al teshuva*, a master of post-Holocaust return and repentance, confirms this estimation. In the wake of the failure of Christian and philosophical enlightenments to realize universality without exterminating difference, it became a matter of affirming brute difference as a mode of resistance. The tremendous emphasis Levinas gives to the ethical value of difference and otherness contributed in no small measure to a positive affirmation of Judaism as the other of philosophy.[17] In an incisive analysis, Jeffrey Kosky took issue with those commentators who sought to lay claim to Levinas as a Jewish thinker somehow speaking from outside philosophy. As he correctly observes, the Judaizing interpretation of Levinas would "confirm a reading which forms the basis of what others count as an objection," namely, that Levinas is imposing religious dogma in place of phenomenological openness to ethics itself. Judaizing Levinas in this way "plays into the hands of his critics by giving them more on which to base the accusation of a theological hijacking of phenomenology." Moreover, since this interpretation of Levinas affirms the religiously determined character of his work by calling it "Jewish," it leads to an impasse. Levinas's philosophy could be affirmed only within a tradition of faith and should therefore rightly be rejected by anyone who stands outside that tradition. Kosky is entirely correct to point to a mirroring of these two interpretative camps, the one affirming the religious element of Levinas's thought as a Judaic alternative to philosophy, the other denouncing it as recourse to revelation, piety, and dogmatism. In my view this mirroring goes back to Spinoza and Kant and the covert alliance we find between their views about Judaism and the views of neo-Orthodox Jewish thinkers. Reading Levinas's account of ethics Judaically would risk repeating and radicalizing the antiphilosophical image of both Levinas and Judaism.[18]

Nor Judaism

In his illuminating and rigorous historical study of the origins of Levinas's thought, Samuel Moyn argues that the reverse can also be shown. Far from being Jewish, "it is ultimately impossible to understand the shape of Levinas's intersubjective theory except as a secularization of a trans-confessional, but originally Protestant, theology of encounter with the divine."[19] Moyn shows how the Jewish philosopher forged most of his enduring concepts in the cauldron of a largely Protestant interwar philosophical milieu. It is Søren Kierkegaard, Rudolf Otto, and, indirectly, Karl Barth who provide Levinas with the theological concepts he eventually fashions into "ethics." Levinas's notion of the transcendence of the face is a secular version of Otto's "wholly other," whereas his account of the ethical self modifies Kierkegaard's argument by contending that it is through the ethical relation to the other, rather than through the theological relation to God, that a critique of philosophy is realized in the guise of subjectivity. In Moyn's account, it turns out that what is essentially religious in Levinas's thought is *not even Jewish* but derives from his "invention" of a Judaism modeled on Protestant existential theology, suitably secularized.[20] In Moyn's words:

Levinas boldly imagined Judaism within philosophy and in a way that made it compatible with a striking and compelling, but idiosyncratic, personal and controversial philosophical vision—a vision therefore dependent on his philosophical formation and historical age rather than inherited or discovered independently of it. . . . For this reason it is mistaken to believe that a traditional (especially a Talmudic) upbringing inoculated him against Heidegger's thought specifically or European philosophy in general and laid the foundations of his mature identity. Recent scholarship, in other words, has too quickly mistaken Levinas's claim to authenticity with authenticity itself and blithely accepted his own rereading of the Jewish tradition.[21]

Before explaining what I think is wrong with Moyn's interpretation I would like to introduce a similar concern, first voiced by Robert Gibbs and more recently amplified into vigorous criticism by Leora Batnitzky. In his pioneering and still valuable study, Gibbs pointed to what he called a "confusion" in Levinas's work. Commenting on Levinas's description of his own project as a kind of "translation" between Hebrew and Greek, Gibbs worried that if such a project is successful, indeed, if it is even conceivable, then it would make the original—the Hebrew or the Judaic basis of Levinas's thought—redundant. If Levinas's philosophy is based on phenomenological analyses that stand independently of Judaism, then why rely on Judaism to develop them? Judaism would be redundant, since philosophy has enough of its own resources to make the claims Levinas asserts. Instead of a productive rapport between Judaism and philosophy, the project of rendering Hebrew wisdom into a philosophical language would be tantamount to idolatry, as if the philosophical mind could capture the transcendence of revelation. In Gibbs's words:

If we could draw upon, for example, Plato's "Good beyond Being," or even Kant's "Primacy of Practical Reason," we might find resources in the "Greek" tradition. It is just this issue that seems to confuse Levinas. . . . [H]as Levinas preserved in method what he established in content? Has the translation project itself not "sold out" to the "Greek"? The very first question in the debate following Levinas's commentary on the Septuagint passages cited the other Rabbinic texts comparing that translation to the Golden Calf![22]

Batnitzky has recently challenged Levinas on similar grounds: "Levinas purports to overcome a totalizing image of philosophy by way of the disruption that comes from revelation, but his fusion of philosophy and revelation, of Athens and Jerusalem, ends by making revelation irrelevant if not redundant to the truth of philosophy."[23] Gibbs and Batnitzky, like Moyn, raise a crucial issue, not only for the interpretation of Levinas but also for the consideration of the very idea of a philosophy of Judaism. For example, when Maimonides claims that the angels referred to in scripture are, in truth, causal agents that Aristotle calls separate intellects, we are prompted, like Gibbs and Batnitzky, to ask, But who then needs angels? Are not scripture and tradition redundant sources of knowledge if all they do is confirm the independent inquiries of philosophy? The crucial thing to see is that the conceptual problem raised by Gibbs and Batnitzky fits the very mold presupposed by Moyn's historical reconstruction. In Moyn's view Levinas invented his own idiosyncratic Judaism, "so much so that he began to retroject the philosophical considerations of his age . . . into some of the foundational documents of the Jewish tradition."[24] The conceptual concerns of Gibbs and Batnitzky would thus seem to be confirmed by Moyn's historical reconstruction of the real (Protestant) sources of Levinas's "Jewish" philosophy.[25]

This disjunctive picture of the relation between Levinas's ethics and Judaism is isomorphic to the philosophical critique of Judaism from Spinoza to Badiou. On the basis of a *common theological assumption* one group asserts that Levinas has no philosophy while the other says he has no Judaism because both agree on the essential: philosophy is not Judaism, for Judaism is based on revelation, taken as the opacity of a transcendent Will commanding a particular law, essentially incompatible with the transparent universality of reason. To these two positions—neither philosophy, nor Judaism (which are, in fact, one)—this book offers an alternative.

From Authenticity to Allegory

A key to the problem surfaced earlier when Moyn, for example, contested the views of scholars who have "mistaken Levinas's claim to authenticity with authenticity itself." Indeed, Moyn's whole book, so sensitive to the historical dimensions of twentieth-century French thought, is deeply flawed by an almost ahistorical, usually implicit theory about the authentic Jewish tradition onto which Levinas would allegedly be imposing his secularized existential theology. Batnitzky and Gibbs, in different ways, also frame their concerns about Levinas's work in terms of its elision of some authentic Judaic difference. According to Maimonides, however, this is precisely the view of the perplexed.[26] His

Guide of the Perplexed is aimed at ridding Jewish intellectuals of the idea that there is a core to Judaism at variance with philosophical wisdom. The introduction to part 3 of the *Guide of the Perplexed* provides a remarkable critique of the notion that there is any authentic philosophical or theological core to Judaism that would distinguish it from philosophy. This brief introduction appears just as Maimonides is poised to expound on the most exalted and secret of all Jewish beliefs, the Account of the Chariot. As he approaches the very heart of Judaism, its most authentic, secret truth encoded in Ezekiel's vision of the celestial chariot, Maimonides frankly states:

In that which has occurred to me with regard to these matters, I followed conjecture and supposition; no divine revelation has come to me to teach me that the intention in the matter in question was such and such, nor did I receive what I believe in these matters from a teacher. But the texts of the prophetic books and the dicta of the Sages, together with the speculative premises that I possess, showed me that the things are indubitably so and so. Yet it is possible that they are different and that something else is intended. (*Guide*, 416)

Maimonides thus arrives at the core truth of Judaism, the ultimate revealed secret of the Chariot, without revelation or tradition. To be sure, he has "the texts of the prophetic books and the dicta of the Sages," but the point is that their meaning depends entirely on "speculative premises" and "conjecture and supposition," in short, on philosophy.[27] It is tempting to see Maimonides as asserting the priority of philosophy over revelation. Thus, for example, Maimonides famously states that if he had been philosophically convinced that the world was uncreated and existed for all eternity he would have easily interpreted the opening of Genesis accordingly. Indeed, he scoffs at those who think the text of Genesis 1—"In the beginning, when God created the heavens and the earth"—compels him to affirm the doctrine of creation instead of the Aristotelian view of the eternity of the world: "our shunning the affirmation of the eternity of the world is not due to a text figuring in the Torah according to which the world has been produced in time" (*Guide*, II.25, 327). As he wryly remarks, to deny the doctrine of creation would be a much easier interpretative feat than denying the notion that God has a physical form, a task he regards himself as having satisfactorily accomplished. "Nor are the gates of figurative interpretation shut in our faces," he candidly says, so much so that he can freely entertain the possibility that Judaism, indeed the Torah itself, might deny the doctrine of creation and endorse the belief in the eternity of the world. It is therefore not difficult to judge Maimonides, as Moyn and Batnitzky judge Levinas, for subordinating revelation to philosophy through an allegorical reading that forgoes the authentic nonphilosophical Jewish tradition. For such inauthentic allegorization, Maimonides' work was burned in the thirteenth century, even as it was becoming the epitome of authentic Jewish philosophy. These are the stakes, all proportions aside, surrounding the Jewish status of Levinas's work.

In this light, the picture assumed by so many of Levinas's critics looks medieval, recalling the critique of medieval allegory expounded by Gershom Scholem. In his influential view the allegorical method discovers the truths internal to the tradition only if they were first "capable of being discovered outside the sphere of religion" by the independent inquiries of philosophy. Only then can philosophical truth be "projected into the old books by way of allegorical or typological interpretation." For Scholem's medieval philosopher, as for the image of Levinas envisaged by his modern commentators, "The documents of religion are therefore not conceived as expressing a separate and distinct world of religious truth and reality, but rather as giving a simplified description of the relations which exist between the ideas of philosophy."[28] The inevitable question posed to the allegorist is the very question asked of Levinas: does this method not make the revealed tradition redundant? After all, *Totality and Infinity* and *Otherwise than Being* show that one can reach the same "difficult freedom" and the same "religion for adults" without having to study a single page of the Talmud. Levinas says so himself: "Is all this phenomenology inspired by the Bible? I believe it free of it." Or again: "It is not under the authority of the Bible that my thought is placed, but under the thought of phenomenology."[29] Then why study the texts? Why affirm the tradition? Why accept the laws? Why not just do philosophy? Framed like this, Levinas would have to avail himself of the standard medieval retort that there is political and pedagogical value to the revealed tradition, as Sa'adia Gaon, Maimonides, and others emphasized. The allegorist thus makes the text "a mere vehicle of philosophic truth." But this only confirms the criticism, since it amounts to admitting that there is nothing to Judaism but an instrumentalization of philosophy.

It is this that prompted Gibbs to ask, "Has Levinas preserved in method what he established in content?" In other words, having established that there is a particular content called "Judaism," which Levinas attempts to "translate" into philosophical terms, does he not "sell out" to philosophy by giving philosophy the methodological authority to determine the very meaning of "Judaism"? Did Maimonides sell out to philosophy by allowing it to determine the inner secret of Judaism, the Account of the Chariot? The concern seems to be that the uniqueness of Jewish wisdom is sacrificed by its translation into philosophical language. In Gibbs's view, "the question of a remainder in translation, an untranslatable core, has serious implications. Whatever can be translated into 'Greek' could be viewed as what is not truly 'Hebrew.'"[30] Or in Batnitzky's more strident tone, "Levinas does not fully acknowledge the 'otherness' of Judaism"; he "ends by making revelation irrelevant if not redundant to the truth of philosophy"; he is guilty of "uncritically conflating Athens and Jerusalem."[31] Alluding to the problem of allegory in Levinas's work, Derrida already wondered if "the spiraling return of Alexandrian promiscuity" could be staved off.[32]

The choice between authenticity and allegory, however, presents a false *philosophical* dilemma. It makes the unintelligible assumption that Judaism is a conceptual scheme with its own contents (revelation) that are impenetrable to philosophy, and that philosophy provides its own independent scheme (reason) for thinking about the world. Donald Davidson has offered compelling arguments for why the very idea of distinct conceptual schemes makes no sense.[33] I think Davidson's argument works against those who want to reaffirm the distinction between Athens and Jerusalem, if by "distinction" they mean that Judaism asserts certain untranslatable beliefs to which reason cannot accede. Whenever this sort of assertion is maintained, it invariably relies on the supposition of a Judaic belief or truth-content that is simply given and requires no interpretation. This "untranslatable core" (Gibbs) of Judaic "authenticity" (Moyn) and "otherness" (Batnitzky) is then contrasted with the rational beliefs that an unencumbered philosopher might maintain. The idea of an untranslatable authentic content, however, makes no sense, because beliefs necessarily relate to the world and to the beliefs other people have of the world. Beliefs, and semantic systems generally, presuppose a shared world and allow no firm boundaries to divide the world into semantic islands such as "Athens" and "Jerusalem." This was Derrida's point in citing James Joyce's "Jewgreek is greekjew" at the very end of "Violence and Metaphysics." In place of "translation," which fosters the misconception of two separate registers of thought in Levinas's work, we should see his project as one of radical interpretation in which the difference between the domestic "Hebrew" and the foreign "Greek" is a matter of degree and which thus points to the latent philosophical sensibility *within* Judaism itself.[34] It is not a matter of reducing revelation to phenomenology, much less Judaism to some version of French republicanism, but of radically interpreting Jewish texts in accordance with the claims of ethics.[35] Although the metaphor of translation is a traditional and suggestive one, in the end it is misleading, for it suggests that philosophy is one thing and Judaism another. To be sure, the Jewish tradition is much richer than the meaning of any of its texts, and therefore "the seemingly cozy implications of the harmonious interchange between philosophy and revelation" do not suffice to unify "Athens" and "Jerusalem."[36] Nevertheless, the relevant point here is not that Judaism is another name for philosophy but that making the best sense, semantically and morally, out of Jewish texts cannot be done in isolation from the claims of philosophy. As James Diamond says about Maimonides' philosophical midrash, "Revelation is earned, not endowed."[37] That is precisely Maimonides' point in the *Guide* and the method Levinas assumes throughout his work.[38] It is not a matter of collapsing Judaism, or even Jewish texts, into philosophical discourse but of insisting on the constitutive and permanent possibility for radical interpretation of one by the other. Levinas's philosophy is always already the result of a series of interpretations of Judaism, just as his interpretations of Judaism are always already philosophically driven. Moyn is right that Levinas is not translating Hebrew into Greek, but he is wrong in suggesting that he is simply translating Greek into Hebrew.

In place of the disjunction between modern Judaism and philosophy, one could therefore speak, as Daniel Boyarin has done in a different context, of a "partitioning" of Judaism and philosophy accomplished through a "virtual (not actual) conspiracy."[39] Parties with opposing values and agendas, such as atheist philosophers and neo-Orthodox Jews, agree to produce a determination of Judaism that authorizes their respective— indeed, antithetical—claims, that Judaism is the authentic custodian of a revelation given without the consent of reason—*torah* as positivist *nomos*—whereas philosophy is the exercise of reason liberated from absolute givens, pure *logos*. This act of partitioning is symbolized by the transformation, or conversion, of the blessed Spinoza from Jew to philosopher, replete with all the regalia of excommunication (from Judaism), canonization (into philosophy), and veneration: "Thought must begin by placing itself at the standpoint of Spinozism; to be a follower of Spinoza is the essential commencement of all philosophy."[40]

Partitioning of Judaism and philosophy by modern philosophers, neo-Orthodox Jewish thinkers, and leading commentators on Levinas thus concerns not only the question of how to read Levinas but also the broader issue of how to understand the very idea of Jewish philosophy. The alternative I am proposing in no way denies the philosophical provenance of Levinas's thought in interwar France. My claim is not that Levinas injected Judaism into philosophy, as Moyn rightly denies, but that one cannot look at his thought as in any way separating Judaism from philosophy. Levinas's thought is indeed constructed out of non-Jewish theological and philosophical sources, but this in no way compromises its Judaic character. The dilemma between authenticity and allegory is a false one, based on a misconceived relationship between Judaic thinking and philosophy. There is no Judaism *and* philosophy, no *between* Athens *and* Jerusalem. That sort of a picture distorts our perception of Levinas's work, of much of the history of Jewish thought, and of the very idea of a modern philosophy of Judaism. What Levinas provides, rather, is a philosophy of Judaism without *and* or *between*.

On the Very Idea of a Philosophy of Judaism: The Heideggerian Debt

One might object that this sort of approach is at odds with Levinas's own views regarding ethics and Judaism. Levinas is one of the few modern philosophers to argue vigorously that ethical judgment is exercised over history and not simply within history. All his efforts seek to provide a moral alternative to the ubiquitous reductionisms of modern Western philosophy. It is precisely through an allegedly ahistorical interruption of historical time that the ethical commandment of the Other is revealed. Levinas himself thus places Judaism and ethics outside history and beyond the reach of the philosophical reductionism at work in modern ontology and historicism. The problem is that this ahistorical ethical revelation of the Other obviously does not resemble the historical character of Judaism but transforms it into something radically new, an ostensibly secular and universal moral phenomenology. It turns out, then, that Levinas's ahistorical view of Judaism is based on a decidedly historical interpretative innovation and is therefore "in sharp tension with [his] attempt to move philosophy and ethics beyond historicism."[41]

My response to this problem, which I apply throughout this book, is to reject the ahistoricist horn of the dilemma or, rather, to recast it. Levinas is certainly not a reductive historicist, but he is also not an ahistorical metaphysician, as he would often have us think; he is a hermeneutical thinker. The Other who interrupts history *cannot be separated* from the hermeneutic fabric of this philosophy and *does not transcend* its textual horizons. Such an assumption can only be borne out as a reasonable conclusion by the end of this book by demonstrating, as I hope to do, that Levinas's philosophy is produced through a reading of the Jewish textual tradition and not, as he sometimes claims, through a traditionless phenomenological description of ethics itself. Contrary to his stated position, invariably formulated as a defense against the charge that his work is not properly philosophical, Levinas does not simply describe the phenomenological situation of ethics but constructs a phenomenological interpretation of Judaism. The Other is not a pure interruption or revelation, and the trace or trail of the Other leads to the Judaic tradition within which Levinas philosophizes.

The hermeneutical assumptions governing my reading of the Judaic character of Levinas's philosophy are above all indebted to Martin Heidegger, for it was he who made the idea of philosophy as hermeneutics possible. He showed that philosophy itself is situated within a tradition that determines the very horizons of thought and that philosophy is determined from the ground up by the interpretative character of thought itself. It is with Heidegger that Western philosophy disburdens itself of the ideal of an independent, atemporal field of knowledge (the "metaphysics of presence") that the philosopher could cognize from his view from nowhere. It is in *Being and Time* that the epistemological ideal of attaining metaphysical knowledge of the objective truth of being is first rigorously overcome.

Such an admission entails two points of immediate relevance. First, Levinas's effort to describe an essential intuition of the other as such, without history, context, or presupposition, would already have been foreclosed by Heidegger from as early as 1919: "The excessive liberties taken recently by many phenomenologists in their use of essential intuition appear in a very dubious light and are hardly in line with the 'openness' and 'devotion' to the things themselves."[42] Heidegger's first deviation from the Husserlian method is to insist that there is no access to the thing itself unless one pays attention not only to those eidetic horizons folded within consciousness but also to the material horizon within which it appears (the body, culture, history, language, and so on). As Heidegger says, "[W]hat is thus necessary is a radical kind of deconstruction and reconstruction, i.e., *a genuine confrontation with the history that we ourselves 'are.'*" It is here that Heidegger first led phenomenology from what Levinas ironically called merely a "theory of intuition" to concrete "interpretative intuitions" in which the truth of appearances is reckoned in light of the material history that we ourselves are. The "essential intuition" of the Other that Levinas describes as interrupting history would be an "excessive liberty" that is "very dubious" from the perspective of the "history that we ourselves are." This line of thinking leads directly to the fundamental modification of Husserl's eidetic phenomenology that Heidegger proposed in *Being and Time*: "The meaning of phenomenological description as a method lies in *interpretation.*"[43] There is no way to provide an unmediated, unhistorical relation with a phenomenon, much less the phenomena of other people, without practicing a merely abstract and theoretical phenomenology.[44]

But if Levinas's excessive liberty in describing the Other beyond history is thereby foreclosed, which is what Derrida argued in "Violence and Metaphysics," we are led to a second, even more important point. As Heidegger declares in the text from 1919: "This confrontation [with the history that we ourselves 'are'] would be something that is enacted within the very meaning of philosophizing. In the end, it is just this precisely oriented detour and the type of roundabout understanding enacted in it that make up *the* path to the things themselves."[45] Far from jettisoning philosophy, disclosing the history that we ourselves are is the very means of discovering the phenomenon itself. Heidegger's critique of Levinas would be that the *Ding an sich* of ethics, the Other, demands an "oriented detour" through its interpretative presuppositions. By exploring the interpretative presuppositions of "ethics" I therefore undertake a Heideggerian reading of Levinas's philosophy by way of an oriented detour through Judaism. For the roundabout route to the Other passes through the interpretative history of the heritage of this thinking—"Judaism" and, in some sense, "Judeo-Christianity," for lack of better words—which is both the history in which ethics is concealed and revealed and the history that we ourselves are.[46] Heidegger is thus at once the archnemesis of Levinas's work and the one who establishes its *philosophical* legitimacy. Only by legitimizing the hermeneutical and, in this case, Judaic dimensions of Levinas's work can the charge of dogmatism be overcome. By reading Levinas hermeneutically, without the false idea of a pure intuition and an ahistorical description of the Other, what strikes readers such as Janicaud, Badiou, and Butler as dogmatism or piety is reconceived as an interpretative accomplishment of the concrete, historical phenomenon of ethics. And it is Heidegger who provides the basis for an understanding of Levinas's work that is properly philosophical and Judaic.[47] This points less to a paradox than to a profound debt and a painful irony constitutive of the complex relation between Levinas and Heidegger.

Marlène Zarader has explored this complex debt with consummate skill. Her conclusion is that "just as Lévinas may perhaps not always recognize all that approximates him to certain structures of Heidegger's thought, so too Heidegger—in a much more radical manner—does not always recognize what he owes to the [Hebraic] sources from which Lévinas's work comes."[48] Although Heidegger's critique of metaphysics is presented as a return to pre-Socratic Greek thinking, Zarader shows how this return is made only by silently borrowing, at every step, from the Hebraic heritage. The standard contrast between Levinas's critique of ontology and its correlative return to Judaism, and Heidegger's critique of metaphysics and its correlative return to the Greeks, is "brought about within strikingly similar structures." Zarader thus proposes that Heidegger is the thinker who, more than any other, "*restored* to Western thought the determinations central to the Hebraic universe," even as it is he who, more than any other, "effaced it from thought and, more broadly, from the West itself."[49] In what sense does Heidegger covertly and even inadvertently Judaize philosophy? In notions, for example, that time is not a homogenous sequence of nows but is tensed toward an unforeseeable event, that words are not merely signs but bear the presence of things themselves, that thinking is not foremost logic and representation but thanking and memory, that truth is not correspondence but revelation and concealment, that poetry is best understood as prophecy and prayer, and that thought is saturated with interpretation so that philosophy itself is an endless hermeneutic—or midrash. At almost every point that Heidegger turns away from metaphysics and epistemology he pivots on the Hebraic heritage, even as he himself never thought this through.

As Zarader pithily concludes, "I am not doubting that such experiences *might* be attributed to the Greeks' unthought, to that which they had not thought. I have simply sought to show that these experiences were present elsewhere. In clear terms, I in no way assert that these experiences could not be found, between the lines, among the Greeks. I am simply recalling that they were set down, in letters black on white, among the Jews."[50]

This brings us to a position exactly opposed to that voiced by Badiou, Butler, Janicaud, and Rose, for whom the religious element in Levinas's thought is a fatal flaw. The best way to read the recourse Levinas's work makes to religion is not in terms of an appeal to the Other as absolutely, dogmatically revealed, as both critics and disciples contend, but in terms of hermeneutical experience: the Other is experienced exegetically. The problematic status of Levinas's thought derives not from its philosophical claims annulled by the dogmatic imposition of revelation but from the fact that these claims are not explicitly presented as midrash, which is a process of continuously reconstructing revelation and thus simultaneously deconstructing the idea of its pure givenness and transmission. It is midrash that enables a new experience of the history that we ourselves are, even as it is Heidegger who argued that this is "the very meaning of philosophizing" after metaphysics. Thus the Judaic element in Levinas's thought is not what disqualifies it from attaining the rank of philosophy proper but, when made suitably explicit, is what becomes the key to its post-metaphysical philosophical dignity—phenomenology as midrash. Far from positing the Other as given without interpretation, Levinas's account of ethics and of the commanding voice of the Other is interpretatively saturated. What Levinas calls ethics is the exegetically constructed experience of another human being as it signifies within the horizon of our tradition-infused philosophical imagination. The crucial point here, and throughout this book, is not to worry (too much) that this picture of ethics is not "realist" enough, as if the other were suddenly reduced to a sign in the text. Texts have no more priority than people, and much less value. The point, rather, is the impossibility of separating our experience of the one from significant traces of the other. Levinas was not unaware of the profoundly, abysmally textual character of his ethics:

Every contesting and interruption of this power of discourse is at once related by the discourse. . . . In relating the interruption of discourse or my being ravished by it, I retie its thread. . . . And are we not at this very moment in the process of barring up the exit which our whole essay is attempting, thus encircling our position from all sides? The exceptional words by which the trace of the past and the extravagance of the approach are said—One, God—become terms, rejoin the vocabulary, and are put at the disposal of philosophers instead of unseating philosophical language. Their very explosions are recounted. . . . Thus signifies the inextricable equivocality woven by language. (OB, 169/ AE, 215)

In Levinas's view, at least as expressed in his later work, his words are not referential in a simple way. "Ethics" in no way refers to the Other directly, without passing through the text, as if there were some unmediated access to the moral meaning presented in the face. As Derrida observes, what Levinas calls "ethics" is a knot "not only of the Saying with the Said, but of Writing to the Said and of Saying to the written."[51] The burden of Derrida's second essay on Levinas, "At This Very Moment in This Work Here I Am," is to show how Levinas's work operates "by weaving together the interruptions" of discourse to produce an account of ethics constituted out of broken texts.[52] This is what the midrashic imagination has always done. What Levinas calls "ethics" takes shape within the horizon of *écriture*, writing, and especially *Écriture*, Scripture.[53] The language of tradition, which metaphysical realism regards as a ladder that can be kicked away once true knowledge has been attained, is here thought, with Levinas, Heidegger, and Derrida, as the very way of doing philosophy. That is why it is not a question of philosophy *or* tradition but of *tradition as philosophy*. In Levinas's words, "This account [of ethics] is itself without end and without continuity, that is, goes from one to the other, *is a tradition*. It thereby renews itself. New meanings arise in its meaning, and their exegesis is an unfolding, or history before all historiography" (OB, 169/AE, 215; my emphasis). Philosophy and ethics, then, as midrash; and midrash as a way of rejoining the disruptions that constitute this tradition from the outset.[54] This in no way amounts to asserting some textual idealism but to acknowledging that the language in which obligation is given is always already laced with a textual heritage that Levinas discerned and deployed anew.

Gibbs was therefore right that Levinas was confused, but for the wrong reason. Rather than establishing Judaism in content but failing to do so in method, Levinas should have said that he was establishing Judaism in method but not in content. For the content of Judaism is whatever the method yields. And this method, the method of Judaism, if you like, is called midrash. Much more than an exegetical tradition, midrash is the way Jewish thinkers have reread their tradition in order to reconceive their world. The modus operandi of Jewish thought as such that it reconfigures its ever-changing boundaries and populates them with new thoughts woven of old texts.

Accordingly, ethics is not the passive reception of an absolute given, that mystical face of the Other, but a construction wrought from the ongoing relationship between moral experience and tradition. It is by embracing the midrashic character of this ethics that we desublimate its gestural ethereality and harness its political mettle. Only by seeing ethics as the product of an emboldened philosophical interpretation can its apolitical, introverted, or anemic condition be overcome (see Chapter 6). In this view it is not simply that Levinas's work extends from ethics to politics but that it never was apolitical precisely because it was never merely ethical; it was always religious, Judaic, and theologico-politically "communitarian" in a quite disrupted, entirely open sense. Exposing Levinas's account of ethics as a philosophy of Judaism will therefore go some way to reconceiving its latent political theology and its implications for related issues such as Israeli-Palestinian relations. For if we can get to the Other only by way of hermeneutical philosophy then we are compelled to respond to each other according to the way we receive tradition. In this way the religious dimension of Levinas's thought, understood as midrash rather than prophecy or revelation, becomes the solution rather than the outstanding problem of his philosophy.

A Shared Midrash:
Levinas, Paul, and the *Logia* Entrusted to the Jews

In what remains one of the best commentaries on Levinas and Judaism, Susan Handelman remarked "that Levinas's philosophy is a kind of 'letter to the Gentiles.'"[55] Handelman did not develop the thought, but it is worth pursuing. As is known, Levinas, like Paul, gambles on the word "Israel," for it must be from the outset that the revelation—in this case, of ethics—be addressed to anyone prepared to respond to it, regardless of their "identity." "The essential thing," remarked Levinas, is "the invitation to *think*" issued by the documents of Judaism rather than their appropriation by one group or another.[56] Levinas's philosophy of Judaism is only tangentially related to Jewishness, his or anyone else's, even as it is deeply planted in the living heritage of Judaic thinking.[57] Such an invitation to think issued by the heritage of Judaism is not addressed to any particular group or restricted to any particular reception. It is a matter of an "ex-appropriation" of revelation, as Derrida often called it. In Levinas's words: "Poured into the common patrimony of humanity, the idea no longer belongs to you. In the final analysis, the idea has no origin. Of what one has, it is least private; a world where one communicates by means of ideas is a world of equals."[58]

But if Levinas thinks that the deposits of revelation are only philosophically relevant when ex-appropriated—"the idea no longer belongs to you"—there follows the inevitable question, first posed by Judaism's greatest ex-appropriator: "Then what advantage has the Jew? Or what is the value of circumcision?" (Rom. 3:1). If, as Levinas and Paul think, the purpose of revelation points beyond the observance of the Law, does this not render the Law an obstacle to the fulfillment of the Word? Should the Law not be discarded in light of the new epiphanic event, whether that event is called Christ or the Other? Paul's views have of course been traditionally understood in just this supersessionist way, as though Paul preaches against the Law as such. In answer to the question, "What is the value of circumcision?" which Paul rhetorically posed to the Romans,[59] the answer is dourly taken from his letter to the Galatians: "For neither circumcision counts for anything nor uncircumcision" (Gal. 6:15a). This view is vigorously contested among recent scholars who have developed the so-called "New Perspective on Paul."[60] According to this view, the apostle to the Gentiles does not come to invalidate the law *for the Jews* but only to preach the promise of faith in Christ for the Gentiles as he discerns it in the Torah.[61] Consider Paul's own answer, in Romans: "Then what advantage has the Jew? Or what is the value of circumcision? Much, in every way. For in the first place the Jews were entrusted [*episteuthēsan*] with the oracles [*logia*] of God" (3:1–2).

The same structure of preserving the law for the Jews while applying its promise to the Gentiles can also be found in Levinas. For the Jewish apostle to the Gentiles as for the Jewish philosopher to the Gentiles, the *logia* entrusted to the Jews, their revelations and commentaries, are the vehicle for a proclamation addressed to everyone or, rather, to anyone prepared to respond to them. This new proclamation issued on the basis of an interpreted event—for Paul, the risen Christ; for Levinas, the face of the Other—implies neither the adoption of Jewish law by Gentiles nor its abolition for Jews. The new proclamation includes Jews and Gentiles without abrogating the law that marks their difference. What Alan Segal says of Paul's "universalization" of Judaism would then equally apply to Levinas's new ethics: "It does not nullify Torah, although it does make totally volitional one's adherence to the *special* laws of Judaism."[62] Levinas's position on the relationship between Israel, its law, and the Gentiles recalls Paul's in Romans: "Is the law sin? By no means! . . . I ask, then, has God rejected his people [Israel]? By no means! I myself am an Israelite, a descendant of Abraham, a member of the tribe of Benjamin. God has not rejected his people whom he foreknew" (Rom. 7:7, 11:1–2).

Paul's position (at least in *Romans*), like Levinas's, is that the radically new event that is upon us *fulfills* the promise of the covenant of Abraham. The *Christusereignis* for Paul, like the *Anderereignis* for Levinas, precipitates those *logia* entrusted to the Jews into an open address to anyone prepared to listen, harnessing their sense without renouncing Jewish law or custom. In keeping with the terms of their respective missions, Levinas's philosophical works, like Paul's letters, are primarily addressed to Gentiles. But in a Talmudic reading addressed to Jews, delivered in March 1969 and occasioned by the topic "Youth and Revolution in Jewish Consciousness"—in the wake of June 1967 and May 1968—Levinas provides a Pauline interpretation of the advent of the Other experienced by Abraham:

Let us recall the biblical and Talmudic tradition relating to Abraham. Father of believers? [This was Paul's view.] Certainly. But above all one who knew how to receive and feed men. . . . Abraham must have taken the three passersby for three Bedouins, for three nomads from the Negev Desert—three Arabs . . . [t]he heirs of Abraham—men to whom their ancestor bequeathed a difficult tradition of duties toward the other man. . . . So defined, the heirs of Abraham are of all nations: any man truly man is no doubt of the line of Abraham.[63]

In other words, "not all who are descended from Israel belong to Israel, and not all are children of Abraham because they are his descendants . . . but the children of the promise are reckoned as descendants" (Rom. 9:6–8). For Levinas, of course, scripture fulfills its promise to the Gentiles not through faith but through obligation. The different content of the promise, however, counts less than the common midrashic ex-appropriation of *logia* entrusted to the Jews—hence Levinas's deliberately polysemous use of the term "Israel." Like Paul, he continues to endorse the validity of a historical and even biological determination of "Israel," while simultaneously liberating the term from its restrictive application to descendants of the tribe. It is not a matter of supplanting Israel of the flesh but of supplementing it by radical interpretation. "Israel" now *also* designates *anyone* who stands under the new covenant of ethics, Jew or Greek, male or female, free or slave. For Paul, this "new creation" is called "the Israel of God" (Gal. 16:15–16). For Levinas, ethical Israel is "a moral category rather than a historical fact."[64] In another provocative, Paulinist remark, he proclaims: "Israel—or the humanity of the Human."[65] Levinas's fundamental move, like Paul's, is to ex-appropriate the Torah of the Jews through a midrash addressed to anyone responsive to it, which thereby creates a new addressee of the message entrusted to the Jews. This new Israel in no way invalidates, much less terminates, "Jewish identity" or its constitutive relationship to law, ritual, and memory.

Hilary Putnam thus aptly refers to "Levinas's mission to the Gentiles."[66] Less precise is his view that "Levinas is universalizing Judaism," since it is more a matter of sharing the ethical sense of the *logia* of the Jews with anyone than of applying it to everyone without regard for their particular points of view. More perplexing is Putnam's conclusion: "He [Levinas] isn't trying to emulate St. Paul."[67] Perhaps he is not *trying* to emulate the apostle to the Gentiles, but he is surely doing so. Putnam's attempt to disanalogize Levinas and Paul only highlights their proximity. Levinas, he claims, is distinguished from Paul because he does not want to convert the Gentiles to the law but to teach them "the fundamental commandment which Rabbi Hillel the Elder gave in two famous forms: 'Love mankind' and 'What is hateful to you do not do to your fellow man; this is the whole Torah, the rest is commentary.'"[68] But this disanalogy involves a mistake and an irony. The mistake is to think that Paul's universalizing of Judaism sought to convert the Gentiles to the law. (A more common mistake goes the other way: Paul sought to abrogate the law for Jews and Gentiles alike. It is this belief that the New Perspective on Paul overturns.) The irony is that it is precisely Paul who teaches the fundamental commandment of love attributed to Hillel: "Owe no one anything, except to love one another: for the one who loves another has fulfilled the law. . . .

Love does no wrong to a neighbor, therefore, love is the fulfilling of the law" (Rom. 13:8–10). Jacob Taubes provides an interesting if overstated comment on this passage:

This is a highly polemical text, polemical against Jesus. Because from the Gospels we know the dual commandment. Jesus is asked: What is the most important commandment? And he says, You shall love your Lord with all your strength and your soul and your might, and after this follows: Love your neighbor as yourself. Paul doesn't issue a dual commandment . . . it is the love not of the Lord, but of the neighbor that is the focus here. No dual commandment, but rather *one* commandment. I regard this as an absolutely revolutionary act.[69]

And of course it is Levinas, more than anyone in the history of philosophical theology, who has insisted on precisely this point: "Everything I know of God and everything I can hear of His word and reasonably say to Him must find an ethical expression."[70] Or again: "Ethics is not simply the corollary of the religious but is, of itself, the element in which religious transcendence receives its original meaning."[71]

For Levinas, then, *verus Israel* designates the new ethical subject, the one who answers to the call of the other. What Badiou says about Paul therefore strikes me as a perfect description of Levinas's engagement with Judaism: "The task Paul [and Levinas] sets for himself is obviously not that of abolishing Jewish particularity, which he constantly acknowledges as the event's principle of historicity, but that of animating it internally by everything of which it is capable relative to the new discourse, and hence the new subject. For Paul [and Levinas], being Jewish in general, and the Book in particular, *can and must be resubjectivated.*"[72]

Levinas, no less than Paul, would agree that *from an ethical perspective* "neither circumcision counts for anything, nor uncircumcision, but a new creation" (Gal. 6:15), which is certainly not to abrogate circumcision for the Jews. The point of this new creation is neither to deny Jews their ongoing "identity" nor to convert the Gentiles to the established Law. In Romans, Paul seems to be responding to those who have already misunderstood his gospel in that way because of his earlier letter to the Galatians:[73] "Do we then overthrow the law by this faith? By no means! [*me genoito*—may it never come to pass!] On the contrary, we uphold the law" (Rom. 3:31). The point, for Paul, is to proclaim the promise of the Torah for all; so too for Levinas it is to expose and disseminate the ethical wisdom of the Torah, as well as the commentaries and historical experiences of the Jews to whom those *logia* were entrusted.

It goes without saying that Jewishness, for Levinas, is a matter of ethical indifference—pure *adiaphora*, as Paul rightly calls it. In Badiou's words, Jewish particularism is "simultaneously extrinsic . . . and compatible" with the new creation of ethics.[74] But it also follows that Levinas's phenomenological works addressed to the Gentiles are midrashic accomplishments, radical interpretations of Jewish texts. *Totality and Infinity* and *Otherwise than Being* are philosophical interpretations of *logia* entrusted to the Jews. Derrida described this sort of midrashic feat as "a nondogmatic doublet of dogma, a philosophical and metaphysical doubtlet, in any case a *thinking* that 'repeats' the possibility of religion without religion." As he rightly says, the *identity* of such a work (Jewish text or not, Levinas as a Jewish thinker or not) "is of limited pertinence," *adiaphora*.[75] As a hermeneutical philosopher, Levinas loves a Torah addressed to all people, not just to the Jews. "Then what becomes of our boasting? It is excluded" (Rom. 3:27).

It remains only to note that the deconstruction of the predicate Israel within the history of Jewish philosophy is not an accomplishment of apostates alone. Maimonides defended the Mishnaic proposition that "all Israelites have a share in the world to come" by identifying the Israelites in this Mishnah with those individuals—Jews or non-Jews—whose intellects are actualized. As Menachem Kellner puts it, for Maimonides "the term 'Israelite' cannot be coextensive with the phrase 'descendants of Abraham, Isaac, and Jacob.'"[76] This split *within* the Jew, as Derrida called it, between the two dimensions of the letter, allegory and literality, is rooted in the ambivalence of the term *torah* itself, which by no means refers only to the particularism, positivism, and literalism of *nomos*.[77] That reductive reading of Torah as pure law, *nomos*, has long plagued Christian and philosophical conceptions of the nature of revelation in the Jewish tradition. But Torah refers to teaching and wisdom as well as law and statute. Indeed, the prominent tradition associating Torah with Wisdom already attests to a native sense for philosophical ex-appropriation. In Jon D. Levenson's words, "Biblical Wisdom teachers provide a solid precedent for the Judaization of later philosophical movements, from Platonism to existentialism."[78] Paul Ricoeur makes a similar point, noting that Wisdom is "the hinge connecting singularity and universality" and therefore, in his view, already foreshadows "contemporary debates concerning the relations of the universal and the historical," or "universality" and "communitarianism."[79] Strictly speaking, Ricoeur should not have equated Wisdom with "universality" because this elides the historico-hermeneutical character of Wisdom itself. The Wisdom of the Torah does not point to its universality but to its capacity to be understood and shared by people outside the immanent historical situation circumscribed by Torah as Law. Wisdom exposes Torah to its immanent excess; it does not establish its validity for everyone at all times and places. It thereby becomes crucial to avoid slipping from an affirmation of "universalism" as a "singular heresy from within," as Badiou rightly describes Pauline universalism, to the position he advocates elsewhere that "from the apostle Paul to Trotsky, including Spinoza, Marx and Freud, Jewish communitarianism has only underpinned creative universalism in so far as there have been new points of rupture with it."[80] Rather, it is a matter of exposing new points of rupture *within* a particular tradition, which is exactly what radical interpretation seeks to do. In contrast to the violence and pretense of universalism, couched in the glorious news that all mankind is one, hermeneutical interventions such as we find in Levinas and Paul expose the immanent excess of received notions and thereby enable new constellations of sense and purpose. Far from simply breaking with Judaism, Levinas is radicalizing an internal tension within the Judaic heritage: Torah not only as *nomos* but also as the anomic or *aggadic* excess of *sophia* and *logos*. Kosky's description of Levinas's Judaism, which could also apply to Pauline Christianity, is therefore preferable to the assertion of the "universalism" of either Levinasian ethics or Pauline Christianity: "If Judaism does appear in this phenomenology, it is a Judaism that thinks or speaks—heretically, hyperbolically, or perhaps heterodoxically—what Judaism has not yet said about *what it has always secretly harbored*."[81] Like Paul, Levinas too "wanted to have it both ways, to understand himself as an apostle in relationship to his Gentile converts but as a loyal son of Israel in relationship to the Jews."[82] Levinas's new philosophical creation of an ethical covenant interprets the Torah for the Gentiles while affirming its meaning and value for Jews. Parallel to the momentous misunderstanding of Romans 10:4, one should see Levinas as proposing that the telos of the *torah* is ethics but not that ethics brings the law to its end (telos).

Two figures, Paul and Heidegger, thus stand out as we approach Levinas's philosophy of Judaism: Paul for proclaiming the message of Judaism to the Gentiles through a radical interpretation of the *logia* of the Jews in light of the new Event, and Heidegger for converting philosophy from meta-physics into hermeneutics and thus establishing the philosophical dignity of the radical interpretation of a heritage of thinking. Combined, Paul and Heidegger pave the way for the non-metaphysical, midrashic philosophy of Judaism to which Levinas's corpus attests. Not until Heidegger was it pos-sible to regard Judaism as a medium for philosophy proper rather than as an allegorical ladder,[83] and not since Paul has such a radical interpretation of Judaism for the Gentiles met with any significant success. Heidegger's Na-zism and the long history of anti-Judaic readings of Paul should not deter us. For then we saw through a glass darkly, but now we see face to face.

Saying Judaism Otherwise

A concrete example illustrates more precisely how Levinas's philoso-phy works as midrash. Anyone who reads Levinas will be struck by his id-iosyncratic and severe vocabulary, brimming with terms that are foreign to the traditional philosophical lexicon and evidently borrowed from another discourse. This trail of more or less covert Judaic terms within Levinas's philosophical corpus has led scholars to assemble various Levinasian sig-nature terms such as "infinity," "separation," "face," "election," "persecu-tion," "hostage," and others and coordinate them with a traditional Jewish vocabulary.[84] This is a perfectly legitimate form of commentary, although somewhat unsatisfying, for the patchwork of Hebrew terms rarely amounts to a philosophical quilt. Let me point to but one example of this sort of co-vert lexicographical exegesis that permeates most of Levinas's philosophi-cal work, the term "saying," *dire*, which is contrasted with "the said," *le dit*. Levinas's claim is that human communication is not reducible to the terms of a functional semantic exchange but that what comes to pass between in-terlocutors relates to the singularity of the person, a point which is of ethi-cal rather than semantic significance. As Simon Critchley remarks, "One might say that the content of my words, their identifiable meaning, is the said, while the saying consists in the fact that these words are being ad-dressed to an interlocutor, at this moment each of you."[85] I would qualify this slightly by noting that the Saying does not happen in the present, or not just in the present, and therefore should not be understood as a purely phenomenological experience. The Saying is, strictly speaking, not an

'Le dire' Hebr. equiv. *lamor* [handwritten annotation]

immediate experience of another person as a speaking subject but the idea of the singularity of the other deduced from the interlocutory situation—a deduction that I wager takes place by way of scripture and tradition.

While the Saying can therefore be explained in secular, purely phenomenological terms, as Critchley does, Levinas's referral of the interlocutory situation from the face to the trace of the other clearly implies that what is heard is a Saying of another Other, the one issuing from the "immemorial past" of scripture: "Speak to the people of Israel, *saying*: . . ." What could be more obvious to a reader of the Bible?[86] That God speaks encapsulates perhaps everything the Abrahamic traditions have opposed to Greek philosophy (as Heidegger, who so wanted to hear "the call of being," should have admitted). Moreover, the word "Saying," *lemor*, functions in the Pentateuch analogously to the way it functions in Levinas's text, as a surrogate for quotation marks. "And YHWH spoke to Moses, *saying*: speak to the people of Israel" can just as well be rendered as: "And YHWH spoke to Moses, 'Speak to the people of Israel.'" The "saying" is not part of the Said but marks the space between the Voice and its addressee. The biblical "saying" has no semantic value but simply signifies the direct form of address. In a Talmudic commentary Levinas wryly relates what his teacher Chouchani taught him about this word: "A prestigious master I had after the Liberation used to claim to be able to give one hundred and twenty different interpretations of this phrase [*lemor*, Saying] whose plain meaning, however, is devoid of mystery. He revealed only one to me." Levinas confesses that he has "tried to guess a second" and that "one hundred and eighteen other significations of the verse remain to be discovered. My master carried them to his grave."[87]

To be sure, one could claim that Levinas's notion of *le dire*, which is plainly ethical and possibly even secular, merely "invents" its Judaic patronage. And yet even this fable Levinas tells of his Talmudic master seems to be modeled on the tradition of R. Eliezer, the outstanding Talmudic sage who was teacher to the extraordinarily inventive Rabbi Akiva and who, like Chouchani, went to his grave carrying three hundred, and some say even three thousand, untold Laws.[88] More to the point is the way Levinas inscribes both interpretations of *lemor* that he and Chouchani have divulged (or "invented," as critics would have it) into *Otherwise than Being*. Chouchani's interpretation of the word hinges on breaking the word apart, so that the *le'* is read privatively, as in *lo*: "translating *lemor* by 'so as not to say.' . . . The unspoken is necessary, so that listening remains a way of thinking; or it is necessary for the word to be also unspoken, so that truth (or the Word of God) does not consume those who listen."[89] In *Otherwise than Being* we find precisely this inventive exegesis of *lemor* presented as phenomenology. There, the Saying is formulated in terms of "ambivalence" for "it is experienced by . . . crossing over its own contestation" (OB, 154/ AE, 196). Chouchani's midrashic reading of *lemor* as *lo/lemor* has found its way into Levinas's philosophy as the Unsaying that every Saying bears within itself. So too Levinas's own explicitly "Jewish" or "confessional" exegesis resurfaces in his philosophical work: "In my own reading of this verse, *lemor* would signify 'in order to say': 'Say to the people of Israel in order for them to speak'; teach them sufficiently in depth for them to begin to speak, for them *to hear at the point of speaking*."[90] This notion is also carried directly into the philosophical corpus inasmuch as the Saying is defined there as the pure responsiveness of the ethical self to the singularity of the Other: "as a sign given to the other . . . without having anything to identify myself with but the sound of my voice or the figure of my gesture—the saying itself" (OB, 149/AE, 190). Instead of prioritizing the Jewish *or* the philosophical, revelation *or* phenomenology, what we have is a hermeneutical circle of midrashic moral experience.

I will not propose further lexicographical correlations between the philosophical and the Judaic in Levinas's corpus, despite the crucial and plentiful terms that could be counted on. My claim is not that there are isolated Judaic threads in Levinas's philosophical text but that there is an intricate Judaic pattern. Levinas's philosophy is a tent for Japhet, and this book is an attempt to discern its midrashic design. His major midrashic accomplishment transforms the Judaic theologoumenon of "creation" into a complex philosophical narrative. Creation is a pervasive metaphor Levinas uses to understand ethics, and although the trope itself is, of course, by no means only Judaic, I will argue that several distinctly Judaic accounts of creation inform his thought. Consider the crucial and well-known rabbinic text, Mishnah Sanhedrin 4:5 (BT Sanhedrin 37a).[91] In the context of a law concerning the procedure for warning witnesses who have come to testify in a case of a capital offense, we read:

How did they exhort witnesses testifying in capital cases? They brought them in and admonished them: "Perhaps you will speak from supposition, and from hearsay, evidence from the mouth of a witness," or "We heard it from the mouth of a witness," or "We heard it from the mouth of a trustworthy person"; or "Perhaps you do not know that afterwards we will test you by inquiry and examination." (Mishnah Sanhedrin 4:5)

Interesting as the details of these instructions to the witness are, their legal complexity, which the Gemara addresses, cannot detain us. It is the moral exhortation accompanying the law that concerns us:

Know that capital cases are not as monetary suits: in monetary suits—a person may give his property and effect atonement; in capital cases—his blood and the blood of his offspring depend on him until the end of the world, for we find concerning Cain who killed his brother, it is written, "the bloods of your brother cry" (Gen. 4:10); it does not say, "your brother's blood" but "bloods"—his blood and the blood of his offspring. (Mishnah Sanhedrin 4:5)

The Mishnah provides an explanation for why capital offenses require additional stringencies for the admissibility of evidence. The reason goes back to Cain, who is said to have killed not only Abel but also all that would come of Abel. This is because the collective noun "blood" is written in the grammatical plural. After a brief additional interpretation the Mishnah resumes its primary course:

[A] Therefore man was created uniquely, to teach you that whoever destroys a single soul of Israel, Scripture accounts it as if he had destroyed a full world; and whoever saves one soul of Israel, Scripture accounts it as if he had saved a full world. [B] And for the sake of peace among men, that one should not say to his fellow, "My father is greater than yours"; and that heretics should not say, "There are many powers in Heaven." [C] Again, to declare the greatness of the Holy One, blessed be He, for man stamps out many coins with one die, and they are all alike, but the King, the King of kings, the Holy One, blessed be He, stamped each man with the seal of Adam, and not one of them is like his fellow. Therefore each and every one is obliged to say, "For my sake the world was created." [D] And lest you say, "What do we need with this trouble?" Has it not already been said, "he being a witness, whether he has seen or known, if he does not speak [he shall bear his iniquity (Lev. 5:1)]." [E] And should you say, "What need is there for us to be responsible for the blood of this one?" Surely it is said, "And when the wicked perish, there is joy" (Prov. 11:10).

Every component of this text recurs in *Totality and Infinity*, and by no means in a haphazard fashion. In [B], for example, the Mishnah links the notion of one God with the idea of one humanity. But it is precisely not a matter of becoming one through a universal anthropology or doxology but, as [C] explains, here it is a matter of a peace that preserves the difference inscribed in each human being as an image of God, as if the impress or trace of God is the face of the Other. The idea is indispensable to Levinas's account of ethics. In his view it is not enough to have an abstract moral conception of persons, as Kantian and utilitarian morality suppose, because ethical responsiveness must attend to the uniqueness of the other. Accordingly, in [C], humanity is thought of as a fraternity constituted through relations of difference, bonded by their difference as unique images of God. *Totality and Infinity* provides extensive analyses for rethinking the notion of fraternity along these very lines:[92]

When taken to be like a genus that unites individuals the essence of society is lost sight of. . . . But the human community instituted by language, where the interlocutors remain absolutely separated, does not constitute the unity of genus. It is stated as a kinship of men. That all men are brothers is not explained by their resemblance, nor by a common cause of which they would be the effect, like medals which refer to the same die that struck them. Paternity is not reducible to causality. . . . Human fraternity has then two aspects: it involves the commonness of a father, as though the commonness of race would not bring together enough. Society must be a fraternal community to be commensurate with the straightforwardness, the primary proximity, in which the face presents itself to my welcome. Monotheism signifies this human kinship.[93]

Throughout this passage, Levinas clearly has in mind the rabbinic interpretation of Cain and Abel from the Mishnah cited earlier.[94] The point is not that Levinas has borrowed from the Mishnah without citing his references but that he has integrated the fundamental idea expressed by the Mishnah, an idea that is in fact a platitude in the Judaic moral tradition, into the substance of his phenomenology of ethical significance of human difference and the sense of fraternity that it implies. Other parts of the Mishnah are also important. Thus [D] describes responsibility for the suffering of another person as an undeclinable witnessing, with the implication that any attempt to disavow one's position as ethical witness amounts to assuming the position of Cain. [E] concludes with a problem familiar to all readers of Levinas. If the injunction of ethics is absolute but the criminal himself bears the image of God, surely it is preferable to avoid having the blood of the accused on one's hands by refusing to be witness on behalf of the victim? The resolution of the Mishnah, which expiates the witnesses for the blood of the capital offender, is less crucial than the decidedly Levinasian logic it seeks to address. A related Mishnah stating that a court that "carries out an execution once in seven years is called murderous" (Makkot 1:10) makes it clear that the issue for these rabbis, as for Levinas, is not so much the concrete application of these laws but the moral sensitivity they cultivate.[95]

But did the Mishnah come only "to teach you that whoever destroys a single soul *of Israel,* Scripture accounts it as if he had destroyed a full world"? As we have seen, for Levinas this sort of restricted interpretation of the term "Israel" as it applies to the subject of ethics is out of the question. Strikingly, parallel versions of this same Mishnah omit "of Israel," and E. E. Urbach demonstrated that such manuscripts are in all likelihood original, as indeed we find in Maimonides' twelfth-century commentary to the text.[96] "Israel" should therefore be put under erasure, or rather, erased. The expropriative use of this Mishnah in the pages of *Totality and Infinity* is thus all the more apposite. The example is instructive because it shows how historical and source-critical scholarship can aid as tools for constructing a philosophical interpretation out of the sources of a tradition and thus perhaps alleviate the concern that we or Levinas are inauthentically "inventing" Judaism. Levinas did not employ such critical-historical methods. He and many of his readers generally advocate an ahistorical approach both to ethics and to Judaism. But just as the ahistorical view of ethics is in truth pervasively hermeneutical and, in that respect, historical, so too an ahistorical account of Judaism is best illuminated by a critical hermeneutic that is cognizant of historical variation within the "transcendence" of revelation, and, indeed, of the historicity of transcendence as such. What we lose in piety is far outweighed not only by intellectual honesty but also, in this case, by the appreciation we gain of the midrashic creativity of both Judaism and Levinas's "ethics" and of our interpretative implication in their respective meanings. The remainder of this book seeks to present the text of Levinas's new creation of ethics by way of its midrashic texture.

2

From Chaos to Creation

THE GENESIS OF ETHICS

"Lovers of YHWH, despise evil!"
—Psalms 97:10

Rav said . . . in customary practice, when a king of flesh and blood builds a palace
on sewers, dung, and garbage, if someone comes and says, "This palace is built on
sewers, dung, and garbage," does he not pronounce it defective? So too, if someone
comes and says, "This world was created out of chaos and waste [*tohu wa'bohu*],"
does he not pronounce it defective? Rabbi Huna said in the name of Bar Qappara:
Indeed if the thing was not written in Scripture it would be impossible to say it!
"In the beginning God created heaven and earth"—Out of what?— "the earth was
chaos and waste [*tohu wa'bohu*]."
—Genesis Rabbah 1:5

Hamm: "Use your head, can't you, use your head, you're on earth, there's no cure
for that!"
—Samuel Beckett, *Endgame*

Phenomenology of Creation: *Endzeit gleicht Urzeit*

Shortly after returning from his five-year captivity in a German
POW camp—during which his parents, brothers, and extended family
in Lithuania were slain by the Nazis and his wife and daughter hid in the
monastery of Saint Vincent de Paul in the surrounds of Orléans—Levinas

wrote an extraordinary phenomenological essay that laid the foundation for all his later thought.[1] Years after, he remarked that this essay, *From Existence to the Existent* (1947), contains "the kernel of all I would say later."[2] The central idea of the essay is Levinas's much-discussed notion of "*there is* existence," what he calls *il y a*, literally, "there is." Like Hegel's *Phenomenology of Spirit*, which Levinas read during captivity, the works produced after World War II sought to explain concrete social institutions (including personal identity, the family, the home, the State, objectivity, and others) by descriptively reconstructing their genesis in experience. *Totality and Infinity* (1961) extended this argument further by adding phenomenological detail to the original sketch of how it is that these social institutions that constitute our world are "produced" or "accomplished."[3] Levinas's concern, at this stage of his thinking, was to provide a genetic phenomenology, that is, an account of how concrete phenomena are generated out of experience itself. As the title of the 1947 book suggests, Levinas is here endeavoring a phenomenological reconstruction of the movement *from* existence in general *to* particular things or "existents."[4] It is the movement from existence in its generality toward existents in their particularity that endows ethics with its privileged status of first philosophy, for Levinas's claim is that existence is particularized through ethics. As he put it to François Poiré, "My effort in *Existence and Existents* consists in investigating the experience of the exit from this anonymous 'nonsense.'"[5] Levinas's three major works from 1946 to 1961 all propose that the intelligibility, objectivity, and order of the actual world are produced *from out of* a chaos of indeterminate existence, that seeing phenomena in this light highlights their ontological fragility and vulnerability, and, above all, that the production of intelligible phenomena is a moral accomplishment.

In this chapter I argue that Levinas's description of the passage from the mere indeterminacy of existence to the actual world of existents is best understood as a phenomenological iteration of the account of creation in the opening chapters of Genesis. What Levinas calls the "hypostasis" or "separation" of the subject as a particular existent is a phenomenological transposition of the creation of the world through speech and action. Like the biblical narrative, Levinas describes a separation (*havdalah*) from indeterminate existence (*tohu wa'bohu*) that is presupposed by the idea of an orderly and good world. Levinas's "linear narrative," as Paul Davies incisively called it, reiterates the biblical account of the creation of the world.[6]

I should say at the outset that although I see Levinas's early works as re-capitulating the biblical, especially the Priestly, account of creation, these works themselves reserve the term "creation" for a different purpose. As we will see in Chapter 3, Levinas generally employs the term "creation" for his anthropology; whereas I am pointing to the cosmogonic or genetic story he tells of the creation of the world, the way it is "produced" or "accomplished," as he prefers to say.[7] For the purposes of this chapter, then, I am not referring to Levinas's use of the term "creation," which we will examine in Chapter 3, but to the implicit creation narrative that *Totality and Infinity* calls the "production" or "accomplishment" of the world, what I have referred to as the genetic phenomenology found throughout his first period of thought.[8] *Endzeit gleicht Urzeit* thus not only describes the eschatological repetition of the original feat of creation, a feat we shall explore in this chapter, but also describes Levinas's phenomenological midrash, which appears at the *Endzeit* of metaphysical theology, when the *Urzeit* of biblical thought can again be appreciated by philosophers.

Levinas's phenomenological repetition of the event of creation is, of course, not a chronological or empirical account but a transcendental one that aims at making explicit what we already take for granted, for example, our embodied individuality, the stable identity of objects, our sense of transcending ourselves through objective knowledge, and much more. My claim is that Levinas's rich descriptions of our prereflective access to ordinary phenomena operate within the horizon of the opening chapters of Genesis. We are led to the ordinary thing itself of phenomenological description by appeal to prereflective experience; at the very same time this description operates within the logic of Genesis 1. Reading Levinas's early phenomenology as a hermeneutical application of the opening chapters of Genesis does not contradict its appeal to experience but illuminates the phenomenological inspiration of the biblical text itself and the textual horizon of basic moral consciousness.

Creation from Chaos

Like the creation narrative in Genesis 1, Levinas's phenomenological recapitulation of it is at odds with the metaphysical doctrine of *creatio ex nihilo*. As Jon D. Levenson says: "Two and a half millennia of Western theology have made it easy to forget that throughout the Ancient Near Eastern world, including Israel, *the point of creation is not the production of matter out of nothing, but rather the emergence of a stable community in a benevolent and life-sustaining order."*[9] This depiction of ancient Near Eastern cosmogony perfectly describes what Levinas means by the "production" of a social world from the chaos of *il y a* existence. Both the biblical and the Levinasian views of creation portray the world as formed from out of a chaotic existence of mythic proportions. Creation is not a given but a fragile accomplishment that can revert to chaos. Just as "the point of creation is . . . the emergence of a stable community in a benevolent and life-sustaining order," so, too, Levinas's point is to show "how the particular and the personal" emerge from *il y a* existence to form an ordered moral world (TI, 26/ TeI, xiv). In both accounts, the dark underside of creation, its indeterminate formlessness, can obtrude and even overwhelm the ordered world and thereby plunge the good of creation back into the turmoil of mere existence. Indeed, this is precisely what happens in the time of Noah:

All the fountains of the great deep [*těhôm*] burst apart,
And the floodgates of the sky broke open.
          (Gen. 7:11)

As Levenson says, with the coming of the Deluge "creation has been reversed," which is exactly what Levinas meant by describing the *il y a* as "existence without a world."[10] In the reversal of creation, evil manifests as the annulment of all difference and distinction, *de les existants à l'existence*, a rewinding of the light and the goodness of creation back to the primeval elemental state of the unformed and void [*tohu wa'bohu*], the darkness [*ḥoshekh*], the abyss [*těhôm*], and the water that existed prior to the spirit (literally, the wind) and speech of God. The alternative to a created world is not the abstract philosophical concept of nothing or nothingness but a radically deformed, de-created world of *tohu wa'bohu* or *il y a* existence.[11] Levinas's first publication after his experience of the Destruction was called "Il y a" (1946). In it he asks us to imagine the total abrogation of every moral point of view. His claim is that such an abrogation would bring an end to the very idea of an intelligible world:

Let us imagine all beings, things and persons reverting to nothingness. . . . The anonymous current of being invades, submerges every subject, person or thing.

. . . We could say that the night is the very experience of the *there is* [*il y a*], if the term experience were not inapplicable to a situation which involves the total exclusion of light. . . . There is no longer *this* or *that*; there is not "something." . . . There is no discourse. Nothing responds to us, but this silence. . . . *There is*, in general, without it mattering what there is, without our being able to fix a substantive to this term. *There is* is an impersonal form, like in it rains, or it is warm. Its anonymity is essential. . . . It is no longer a world.[12]

My suggestion is that the *il y a* is a phenomenological interpretation of the famous elements in Genesis 1:2 that are already there before the act of creation: the *tohu wa'bohu*, variously translated as the "unformed and void," "a formless waste," or "welter and waste";[13] the *těhôm*, usually rendered as "the deep"; and the less semantically troubling but no less ontologically obtruding "darkness" and "water" that pre-exist the creative word. As Levenson says, "Genesis 1:2 thus describes the 'world,' if we may call it that, just before the cosmogony began."[14] Levinas's language for describing the *il y a* is strikingly resonant of these primordial elements; the *il y a*, he tells us, is "the existential density of the void itself," a "darkness . . . which would play itself out even if there were nothing."[15] In 1981 Levinas finally made the reference explicit: "In the absolute emptiness that one can imagine *before creation*—there is [*il y a*]."[16]

This notion of a chaos preceding creation, for Levinas as for Genesis 1, provides a moral rather than a natural account of the origins of the world. "There is no physics in metaphysics," quips Levinas in the course of presenting his phenomenology of creation.[17] Israel Knohl makes a similar point with respect to Genesis 1: "Creation is really a claim about primordial evil."[18] (The clamoring over "creation science" is oxymoronic; the biblical accounts of creation belong to the order of moral theology, not natural theology.) To hold that evil is uncreated and present in the chaos of unformed, indeterminate existence is to affirm that the goodness of the created world consists of its particularities and inherent distinctions and that all value resides in the singularity of phenomena. It is precisely this singularity that is jettisoned by reverting from creation to the indeterminate *tohu wa'bohu* or *il y a* existence. Both the Priestly author and Levinas regard evil not as a lack but as the neutralization of the goodness of creation that takes place when the singularity of things and, above all, of persons is revoked. By way of speech, creation introduces singularity and therefore multiplicity to the indeterminacy of mere existence. Creation is the governing trope of a moral narrative whose purpose is to make explicit that we make sense of the world only because a moral perspective has already been "accomplished." To say that the world is created is not to provide a theory of natural origins but to affirm that pure, brute being has undergone a moral genesis that transforms chaos into order. This "hypostasis," as Levinas calls it, whereby a moral point of view is engendered amid the chaos of mere existence, implies that the condition for an intelligible world is the ethical event of creation: Creation as first philosophy.

This account of creation involves a rejection of the dichotomy between ontology and ethics. Creation *is* good, and its opposite—mere existence without perspective or distinction, without separation or individuation—is evil. As Levenson says, "The world is good; the chaos that it replaces or suppresses is evil."[19] The phenomenology of creation contends that facts cannot be separated from values; creation is the original "entanglement" of ontology and ethics.[20] Facts require *points of view* in order to make any sense at all, and points of view suppose particularities, persons, and purposes.

The *il y a* describes the menacing possibility of a radically de-created world, without bearings or dimensions, without particulars or persons—a world become mere existence, impersonal, neutral, anonymous, and utterly indifferent to particular existents. This indeterminate and chaotic existence must be overcome if an intelligible world is to take shape, and Levinas's idea is that this forming of intelligibility is a moral act of hypostasis in which indeterminate existence particularizes in the form of discrete existents: "Against the anarchy of the *there is* the existent is produced, a subject of what can happen, an origin and commencement, a power" (TI, 281/TeI, 257).

Although Levinas did not specify, in 1946, that this "existence without a world" described the Destruction that had just raged through Europe (was it not obvious?), in later years he left no doubt that the threat of an ontologically degenerate world was not just phenomenological fancy but historical actuality. As he wrote in his autobiographical "Signature," "*There is* [*Il y a*]—impersonally—like *it is raining* or *it is night*. None of the generosity which the German term '*es gibt*' is said to contain revealed itself between 1933–1945. This must be said! Enlightenment and meaning dawn only with the existents rising up and establishing themselves in this horrible neutrality of the *there is*."[21] In a personal, reflective essay written in 1966, twenty years after the "resumption of civilization," Levinas refers to the "total chaos" of a world "fallen apart," "as if being itself had been suspended" during the Destruction.[22] The suspension of the basic institutions of civilization plunged the world into the primordial evil of mere existence—"a world put in question by Hitler's triumphs."[23] The description of the *il y a* should therefore be seen as Levinas's philosophical testimony to the Destruction that overwhelmed European Jewry, much like Jeremiah's prophetic testimony to the first Destruction:

I look at the earth,
It is unformed and void [*tohu wa'bohu*];
At the skies,
And their light is gone.
I look at the mountains,
They are quaking;
And all the hills are rocking.
I look: no one is left [*eyn ha'adam*],
And all the birds of the sky have fled [*nadadu*].
(Jer. 4:23–35)

Jeremiah compares the carnage of the destruction and exile of his time to the reversion of the world to "chaos primeval," as John Bright translates *tohu wa'bohu*.[24] The *il y a* is a phenomenological articulation of this myth of a world stripped of all benevolence, and reduced to an elemental state that is absolutely indifferent and therefore hostile to particularities of value, such as persons. As Richard Bernstein says, "Levinas' entire philosophical project can best be understood as an *ethical* response to evil."[25] This is because Levinas regards evil not as privation but as ontologically real. He first conjured the *il y a* precisely "to contest the idea that evil is defect."[26] *Il y a* therefore expresses the persistent reality of evil: a world in which light, order, distinction, and thus goodness are overwhelmed by the menace of indifferent existence. The created world is not one in which evil is illusory and can therefore be eliminated by virtue of true knowledge. Evil cannot be dissipated because it manifests as the excess of hostile existence *within* the world.[27] The world is therefore always at risk of degenerating into elemental indifference. The created world, unlike elemental existence, must accordingly be actively sustained and regenerated. Levinas's distinct contribution is to have shown how ethics creates and regenerates the world.

The phenomenology of creation from chaos begins with an acknowledgment of the contingency of the world, a sense that the constitution of
the world is vulnerable, that it could be radically otherwise, deformed or
even de-created. In particular it emphasizes the sense that the world is
often not as it ought to be, that there is "a rift between the rational order
and events."[28] Like the Priestly biblical author, Levinas does not think of
the creation of the world as indicating that *everything* was created, for that
would either dignify and justify evil as a created phenomenon or deny its
concrete reality. Levinas's moral realism rejects that sort of metaphysical
theodicy, which was just as far from most biblical minds. Rather, the Parisian and the Priestly authors contend that the good work of creation takes
place against a persistent threat of evil and is therefore vulnerable to degenerating into the immorality of mere existence. The best way to understand Levinas's ontology of evil is as a phenomenological account of the
fragility of the goodness of the world, in other words, a phenomenology
of creation on indeterminate evil, and thus as a philosophical midrash on
the Priestly account of creation in Genesis.

Myth and the End of Metaphysics

By invoking a realm of existence without a world, Levinas was con-
juring a noema with no object and an experience with no subject and
therefore going beyond the strictures of phenomenology, as he frankly admitted. With the *il y a*, he said, "we find ourselves at a level of investigation that can no longer qualify as experience. And if phenomenology is
only a method of radical experience, we will find ourselves beyond phenomenology."[29] Indeed, by comparing the *il y a* to Cratylus's river, where
even the law of noncontradiction does not apply since here nothing can
even be identified as itself, he was in some sense placing his analyses outside the bounds of philosophy. He even wondered if "an existing without
existents is only a word."[30] Is the *il y a*, then, just a myth, in the pejorative
sense given to "myth" in most modern philosophical accounts? Levinas initially denied this. It was to a certain truth in literature and art that he ap-
pealed—to Macbeth and Hoffmann, Rodin and Rimbaud, and above all
to Blanchot—in order to intimate an "experience" of total worldlessness.
By attesting to the *il y a* through literature and art Levinas was able to claim

that although the thought, strictly speaking, went beyond the limits of experience it was nevertheless "stripped of mythological overtones."[31] But when the argument was repeated in *Totality and Infinity* he acknowledged that the horrible presentiment of a world devoid of all light and logic, a world without *logos*, was in fact mythos: "Existence without existent, the impersonal par excellence . . . must be called mythical. The nocturnal prolongation of the element is the reign of mythical gods" (TI, 142/TeI, 116). And of course this account of the elemental *il y a* employs characteristic features of myth: it relates our primordial origins to a presentiment or a memory beyond ordinary consciousness; it orients history through a dramatic structure that moves from a Beginning toward an End (*from* existence *to* the existent); and it explains the essential difference between the world as it is and the world as it ought to be.[32] This recourse to myth recalls Hegel's appeal to "a mythology of reason," from a manifesto discovered and published by Franz Rosenzweig: "Monotheism of reason and the heart, polytheism of imagination and art, this is what we require! . . . We must have a new mythology, but this mythology must stand in the service of ideas, it must become a mythology of reason."[33]

Just as Hegel proposed, Levinas's mythological account of evil stands in the service of his moral rationalism and realism. The point, then, is not to deny the mythic dimension in Levinas's phenomenology but to understand its particular significance and the role it plays in his thought. The mythic idea of primordial formlessness can, of course, also be found in the *Timaeus*. As is well known, Jewish and Christian thinkers often read Plato's myth in light of Genesis.[34] Levinas was surely intentionally extending this tradition when he alluded in one breath to the *tohu wa'bohu* and the *khora* in reflecting on the Holocaust: "We returned to the desert . . . we returned to a space-receptacle."[35] Like Philo and Gersonides, Levinas reads the *tohu* of Genesis and Jeremiah and the *khora* of the *Timaeus* together to account for a world formed *ex hylus* rather than created ex nihilo. The mythic dimension of Levinas's phenomenology of creation will become important when I consider the political implications of his mythology of reason later in this chapter. But having approached the proper provenance of Levinas's ontology of evil in the biblical myth of creation from the *tohu wa'bohu*, we should first contemplate its distinctive mythological contours.

As is well known, the Bible records several mythic accounts of creation, comparable and in many respects parallel to other ancient Near

Eastern cosmogonies describing the formation of the world as a process that restrains and combats primordial evil. The famous "combat myths" interspersed in the Bible relate a primordial *Chaoskampf*, in which creation results from the victory of God in his battle against the evil gods of chaos and destruction.

O God [*Elohim*], my King from of old [*mikedem*],
who brings deliverance throughout the land;
it was You who drove back Sea [*Yāmm*][36] with Your might,
who smashed the heads of the monsters [*taninim*] in the waters;
it was You who crushed the heads of Leviathan,
who left him as food for the denizens of the desert;
it was You who released springs and torrents, who made mighty rivers run dry;
the day is Yours, the night also;
it was You who set in place the orb of the sun;
You fixed all the boundaries of the earth;
summer and winter—You made them.
   (Ps. 74:12–17)

The psalm describes a primordial battle between Elohim and his elemental adversaries. Sea, *Yāmm*, is the proper name of the ocean god who, in Canaanite mythology, is defeated by the god Baal. The psalm records the ancient Israelite myth according to which Elohim tamed Sea and defeated Leviathan and the *taninim*, the primeval oceanic monsters, in order to create the world. To understand the myth of Genesis 1, which is also Levinas's myth, we have to consider the fundamental difference between its account of creation and the ones we read in the combat myths, for biblical scholars since Günkel have understood that Genesis 1 polemicizes against these alternative cosmogonic myths.

The difference between Genesis 1 and the combat myths is best grasped by appreciating their similar dualistic schema. Both accounts of creation agree on the fundamental point: God does not create primordial evil but opposes it. Just as God did not create the evil adversaries against whom he battles for the sake of creation in the psalm, in Genesis 1 he does not create the primordial elements that form the background to his creative word. This ontogenetic dualism reflects the *moral dualism*, which is a reflex of the *moral realism*, of these biblical authors, that is to say that they confront evil, injustice, and superfluous suffering without evasion, denial, or justification and that their faith in a God who is good and just does not blind them to the concrete moral reality of this world in which evil persists. They are less concerned with a metaphysical concept of divine omnipotence than with the idea of an absolutely good and just God. They therefore propose that all God made was good but that evil was not created. As Genesis puts it, "And God saw *all that He had made,* and found it very good" (Gen. 1:31), which Knohl urges us to understand as follows: "Evil was not made by God. It predated the Creation in Genesis 1."[37]

The moral dualism and moral realism underpinning the account of creation from chaos is also found in a famous passage from Isaiah in which the prophet bewails the evil and injustice besieging Zion in cosmogonic terms. God's benevolent creation has proven vulnerable to what Levinas called "the reign of mythical gods," the gods of the chaotic, oceanic abyss who are ontologically independent of God. The prophet therefore calls on God to renew his creative power by once again waging battle against those primordial evil elements.

Awake, awake, clothe yourself with splendor,
O arm of the LORD!
Awake as in days of old [*kedem*],
As in former ages!
It was you who hacked Rahab in pieces,
That pierced the Dragon [*tannin*].
It was you that dried up Sea [*Yāmm*],
The waters of the great Deep [*těhôm*];
That made the abysses of Sea
A road the redeemed might walk.
   (Isa. 51:9–10)

The prophetic cry to "awake, awake," strives to reactivate the benevolent power that can combat evil in order to transform the chaos of historical reality, which has degenerated to mere existence, back into the goodness of a world, "a road the redeemed might walk." Faith in the goodness of God and creation does not dampen the prophet's outrage at injustice, evil, and chaos. It is not by accident that both Isaiah 51:9–11 and Psalm 74:11–17 are surrounded by verses that describe rampant suffering and triumphant evil. For it is precisely this moral realism, without the evasions of theodicy, that provokes the prophet to call for a renewal of the benevolent power for creation. As Levenson puts it, "The psalmist refuses to deny the evidence of his senses in the name of faith, to pretend that there is some higher or inner world in which these horrific events are unknown."[38] In place of theodicy, the prophet protests at injustice and reminds God of the moral order constitutive of the act of creation. For most biblical authors it is not a matter of justifying evil by attributing it to God or *Heilsgeschichte* but of calling on God to end it.

Levinas likewise formulates ethics as an appeal, indeed, as a call to "awaken" our often dormant powers to prevent the world from reverting to elemental evil. Like these biblical authors, he is adamant that creation is good and that evil is simply evil and should therefore be defeated. This moral dualism, in which creation is affirmed without theodicy, explains Levinas's recourse to a mythic ontological dualism (the difference between *il y a* existence and the world). It is, moreover, a post-metaphysical phenomenological midrash that refuses to see evil from a "higher perspective" that would somehow justify suffering. In affirming what he calls "the end of theodicy," he thereby rejoins its immemorial biblical past (*yemei kedem*).[39] Unlike the metaphysicians who either deny evil reality by regarding it as a mere error that would vanish on seeing the truth or else justify it within a larger ontotheological project, the mythic notion affirms the reality of evil and suffering in order to denounce and combat it. Levinas's notion of the *il y a* provides a mythology of post-metaphysical reason that stands in the service of an ethical view of the world, just as the biblical myths provide a pre-metaphysical mythology in the service of a similar view of the goodness of the world. Evil and suffering are not meaningful or justified but call for a reactivation of the force of the good. To say that suffering is "useless," as Levinas does, is to say that there is no theological panorama in which superfluous suffering makes good sense and that all there is to do with evil is to put an end to it.

Levinas's myth of the *il y a* thus belongs to the epoch of post-metaphysical theology. At the heart of his moral dualism, which many Jewish monotheists share, lies an acknowledgment that if the three cords to the problem of theodicy—that suffering exists, that God is benevolent, and that God is omnipotent—cannot be maintained all at the same time then it had better be the notion of omnipotence that is cut. Indeed, the very problem of theodicy derives from a decidedly metaphysical notion of God as an absolute and actualized power that lacks for nothing and is therefore the ultimate, efficient cause of everything, including evil. It was Martin

Heidegger who proposed that the epoch of metaphysics is determined by the definition imposed on God as the ultimate causal ground of Being, as *causa sui*.[40] Jean-Luc Marion has argued that Heidegger's rejection of metaphysics amounts to "a relief for theology," both a reinforcement and a respite for theology, because it circumscribes *the concept* of God in terms of causality and thus allows us to approach God differently.[41] In his words, "metaphysics indeed constructs for itself an apprehension of the transcendence of God, but under the figure simply of efficiency, of the cause, and of the foundation. Such an apprehension can claim legitimacy only on condition of also recognising its limits."[42] Marion's critique of metaphysical theology allows us to think of *creation without the concept of God as absolute causal ground of all that is.* Levinas's account of creation from chaos marks just such a break with metaphysical theology and its enthrallment to the idea of God as absolute causality. The doctrine of *creatio ex nihilo* is the preeminent expression of the metaphysical concept of God as cause of all being, whereas the mythological dualism we have considered denies this doctrine, for it proposes that God is not the cause of evil but that the elemental agents of evil are external and hostile to the divine creative power. It is through myth that God's power is dissociated from the concept of absolute causality, for myth articulates the multiplicity of irreconcilable forces and allows for the idea that not everything that exists is good. Myth is the medium of the *drama* of omnipotence, just as metaphysics is the medium of its *concept*. The myth of the *il y a*, like the myth of Genesis 1, overcomes the pairing of creation and causality in one concept by dramatizing their relation in the time of narrative, in which ethical life is lived, rather than in the frozen time of immutable metaphysical concepts. The point is well illustrated in Psalm 82, in which it is precisely a matter of dramatizing the mythic agon between Elohim and other gods in "the divine assembly." The psalmist calls on God to arise and establish justice in the face of the clamoring disregard for "the wretched and the orphan," "the lowly and the poor." The psalm implies that "God's mastery is not complete and that the demise of the dark forces in opposition to him lies in the uncertain future."[43] The metaphysical notion of divine omnipotence, which inevitably regards goodness and justice as fully actualized in God, fails to capture what both myth and moral experience make clear, namely, that our world bespeaks the fragility of goodness. For their part, Heidegger and Marion, following Ludwig Feuerbach and Friedrich

Nietzsche, interpret the so-called death of God as referring to the death of a specifically metaphysical picture of God as *causa sui* (René Descartes) or moral *concept* (Immanuel Kant).[44] But for Levinas, as for many in the Jewish tradition, God's causal and moral powers are not metaphysical concepts but moments in the temporal structure of life in the world. The causality and morality of God are not metaphysical concepts but moments within the drama of history that allow us to perceive the injustice in the actual world. It is not therefore a matter of setting aside the idea of a moral God because such a concept is incorrigibly metaphysical, as Heidegger and Marion think, but of responding to the idea of god as a moral call constituting the very passage of created, historical time. It is that call that Levinas, like the prophets of yore, sought to awaken in us from the beginning to the end of his career. His "ethical monotheism" has this mythic call in mind and not some bygone metaphysical concept of God's actualized potency and goodness. Levinas's ethics temporalizes a call addressed to our historical condition in which the actual world—creation—is utterly morally corruptible.

If this account of mythic evil repeats ancient Jewish views, it is nevertheless atypical among modern Jewish thinkers. The great influence of Maimonides and Kant on modern Jewish philosophy, from Moses Mendelssohn to Hermann Cohen, has generally led to a disavowal of myth. To be sure, Rosenzweig and Martin Buber were more sympathetic to myth,[45] but only Levinas, deploying the method of phenomenology, develops a robust myth of the world as morally created ("produced" or "accomplished"). For him, the very terms of our culture—the value of human life, the objectivity of discourse, the passage of time, the validity of political institutions, and so on—emerge from the drama of formative ethical events at the *Urzeit*: the awakening of a moral subject from the chaos of the *il y a*, the establishment of a covenantal relationship with other people, and the recurrent task of suppressing mere existence for the sake of this moral world. In this respect Levinas's myth picks up many of the most ornate threads of rabbinic mythology, such as a view of creation against the status quo ante of an *Urwelt* in which all moral distinctions, and therefore all ontological or natural distinctions, are dissolved. As Michael Fishbane has shown, rabbinic literature extends the biblical myths by developing its own mythic account of "episodes involving the upsurge of the primordial waters in historical time."[46]

And yet, although Levinas's account of ontological evil is firmly indebted to traditional Jewish mythology, it is, for all that, no less a secular accomplishment. It appeals neither to God nor to the biblical or rabbinic traditions as much as to our secular regard for the difference between the world as it is and the world as it ought to be, our secular hatred of the suffering of innocents, and our secular understanding of our precarious but undeniable power to ameliorate such suffering. The question of how evil can exist in a world created by a wholly benevolent and omnipotent God becomes, with Levinas, a question of the responsibility each of us takes for combating the excesses of evil in our world by respecting the other in her particularity and difference, for that is what sustains "creation" within the moral void of elemental existence.[47] Levinas is thus attuned to an essentially secular understanding of ethical experience, and at the same time he is reiterating a biblical and rabbinic view of the reality of evil that calls for the reactivation of the power to create a good world.

The Transcendence of Evil and the Goodness of the World

We can now much better understand what Levinas means when he says, for example, "The law of evil is the law of being. Evil is, in this sense, very powerful."[48] Such sentiments are not uncommonly found in Levinas, for in his view there is something malign in merely being. For this reason Phillip Blond accuses Levinas of "essentially Manichaean prejudices" based on "an idolatrous opposition of God to His creatures."[49] Blond charges Levinas with promulgating a modern form of gnosticism that severely contrasts the goodness of the Other with the evil of the phenomenal world. In his words, "This antagonistic opposition is deeply idolatrous and flawed because it departs from the phenomenal relation that actually pertains between God and His creatures. . . . Phenomenology refuses to understand or even see that Saint Thomas Aquinas was right, that God as pure act is pure actuality."[50] Despite the sanctimonious tone, Blond's concern should be addressed, for it alerts us to a predictable but mistaken interpretation of Levinas. What Blond means by the "relation that actually pertains between God and His creatures" is the familiar metaphysical doctrine that God is the absolute cause of all being. It follows that if one could only see evil from the right perspective (theodicy or *Heilsgeschichte*) one would see that in truth all being is good. But there are crucial flaws to this critique of Levinas that show Blond to be mesmerized by metaphysical theology and even (idolatrously?) captivated by a concept of God as absolute *cause* and thereby to have entirely missed Levinas's point. But the fact that even an astute reader such as Michel Haar can make a similar claim—"Levinas's polemic against Being actually falls into Manicheism"—suggests that something is awry.[51] Haar, however, does not see the theological argument that Levinas is secularizing, just as Blond sees only a Christian metaphysical critique of it. Both misinterpret Levinas by overlooking or misunderstanding the particular theology of creation at work in his phenomenology. Whereas in the light of the biblical creation theology we have considered, Levinas's argument appears as entirely opposed to a Manichaean or gnostic hatred of creation.

The point is to see that Levinas does not oppose the goodness of God to the evil of the world but opposes the goodness of the world, as created morally, to the evil of merely existing uncreatedly and amorally. Despite the premium *Totality and Infinity* places on "the transcendence of the Other," it is not there but in *Being and Time* that we find the gnostic idea of a forsaken world, as Hans Jonas brilliantly argued.[52] For Heidegger, the opposition between inauthenticity and authenticity cuts across being *as a whole*, for the self is from the outset and unto death constrained by the horizon of the everyday inauthentic world. The only escape from inauthentic everyday life is to resolutely flee into the authenticity of selfhood. In that respect, authenticity is a modern mode of *gnosis* that regards the everyday as the forsaken space into which we are "thrown." Levinas's entire thought is driven by his view of Heidegger as presenting a polar choice between the inauthenticity of everyday sociality and the gnostic nullity of authentic "mineness." Ironically, it is Levinas who resolutely stands against gnosticism and nihilism precisely by accepting one of Heidegger's most important insights, which is that the meaning of being is from the outset social, normative, and purposive. Whereas Heidegger took this to mean that ethics is simply "idle talk" (*Gerede*) into which we have but "fallen" and is therefore devoid of authentic meaning, for Levinas it signified that one could not even speak of authenticity without first acknowledging one's debt and gratitude to everyday ethical life. Heidegger demeans everyday ethical life because it is not an authentic experience of being, but Levinas emphasizes that everyday ethical life, life in a world understood as created, is what gives being to its meaning in the first place. In phenomenologically recovering the account of creation in Genesis 1 by passing from mythos to *logos* (from existence to existents), Levinas shows that establishing a moral relationship with existents in their particularity marks the very opening of the meaning of being in the world. Such an opening is the event of creation.

Recall that Levinas's idea, as I've been interpreting it, is that creation takes place *within* existence; it is the emergence of a particular moral point of view that enables meaning to arise from the indeterminacy of pure existing. Levinas's idea that existence is evil amounts to saying that when the world is stripped of ethics, values, and normative purposes, the very possibility of meaning, as such, collapses. When *From Existence to the Existent* was first published, it appeared with a band around the cover that read: "where it is not a matter of anxiety." The critique of Heidegger essentially says that the anxious disclosure of authentic finitude abandons an ethical point of view only at the cost of abandoning intelligibility as such. That this may not be a critique of Heidegger as much as a qualification or, as I think, a difference in emphasis is not our current concern, which is to explain why Levinas's view of being as evil is neither Manichaean nor gnostic, as is not uncommonly asserted. This is because the evil of being is simply the mythic ontological underside of the goodness of creation. When Levinas says that pure existence is evil he means precisely the opposite of the idea that *the world* is evil. What he means, rather, is that when the world is stripped of all ethical points of view, one does not get to "phenomena themselves" or to "existence itself" but, on the contrary, one loses all perspective and is reduced to absolute meaninglessness. Levinas is thus urging us to think along the lines that Hilary Putnam has proposed in his arguments that scientific knowledge, factual claims, and even the notion of an "object" are all determined normatively and, indeed, ethically, since without values to guide empirical research there would be no way of saying or even thinking all the things we do say and think about the world.[53] The *il y a* suggests that a world without values "is" a world without facts, or is not a world at all but a sheer chaos of indeterminate existing. To be sure, Levinas is saying not only that ontology is determined by "norms," the way a scientific theory is determined by consistency and elegance, but also that ontology is from the outset *ethical*, for the indeterminacy of mere existence is rendered meaningful only by assuming the

perspective of a *person* with a *particular* moral point of view. That is why
existing *without a world* is evil and why the world, which is created from
the chaos of pure existing, is intrinsically bound to the good. To imagine
being without regard for the values human beings make of it is to imagine a neutral existence in which everything we care for—not just people
or pets, but also phenomena in general and even scientific theories—is
plunged into inconsequence and indeterminacy. From *any* perspective,
such neutrality is evil, and, unless we want to conjure the old ontotheological idea of thinking without a point of view, we had better accept that
our world cannot be neutralized of ethics. That is why creation is good,
while pure existing is evil—not evil because it aims at me specifically, or
at us humans generally, but because in this imaginary, mythic neutralization of the ethical structure of the world, all meaning collapses, no objects can be picked out in their particularity, no values can be asserted,
and no facts ascertained. The notion that there could be meaning without ethics betrays a metaphysical longing for facts without values, and it
takes a countermyth, such as that of the *il y a* or Genesis 1, to show us
that such pure existing is not possible for us ethical creatures. The Manichaean objection thus mistakes Levinas for hating the world when his
pronouncement that "being is evil" is in truth an affirmation that nothing merely exists, because the world is created ethically, that is to say, constituted intelligibly on account of ethical norms, purposes, and points of
view. This is precisely the opposite of gnosticism, for whereas the gnostic
Creator creates an evil world and reserves a spiritual truth for those who
can absent themselves from the world, according to both Genesis 1 and
early Levinas it is the created world that is good and the transcendence
of worldhood that is evil. Captivated by a metaphysical theology according to which *everything* is powered by God as an external, permanent, and
absolute cause of all beings and being, including evil, Blond does not see
that Levinas neither ascribes evil to God's causal power nor denies the existence of evil but calls on us to take responsibility for evil by continu-
ally re-creating our moral world in the face of the fragility of creation and
the persistence of evil. I therefore cannot agree with John D. Caputo's attempted defense of Levinas's "unfortunate tendency to describe being or
existence as 'evil'" by an interpretative qualification that suggests that "all
things are made good from something that is innocent of good or evil."[54]
Levinas's point is precisely that there is no such thing as an innocent on-

tology, no neutral facts of existence, for the very idea of neutral existence collapses the normative structure of intelligibility.

Levinas thus secularizes the idea of creation but maintains its original ethical sense. A similar view has been proposed by Adi Ophir in avowedly secular terms. "Evil," he says, "has no meaning other than the ever-changing, open-ended ensemble of superfluous evils and the order of their social production."[55] Evil is "an inevitable aspect of Being" that is never negated but only reframed within a new configuration of superfluous evils.[56] To offer my own examples: disasters such as the Boxing Day Tsunami, Hurricane Katrina, and the cyclone that devastated Burma were all in some sense natural events of pure "being" entirely morally neutral. But these events of pure being are experienced from the outset in terms of their moral assault on particular human beings. Moreover, the suffering undergone as a result of these purely elemental events includes superfluous evils brought about by human action, governments, individuals, scientific communities, and so forth. Levinas's account of the world as an ethical creation floating on a sea of evil provides a way of understanding the intrinsically moral character of such "natural" events. Creation is always a matter of responding to the evil that can never be totally overcome because it inheres in existence itself. Ethics reveals concealed ways of experiencing evil anew in order to contest it once again. Ophir puts it this way: "Evil is Being in excess, Being that has lost its measure. However, Being has no measure, except where there is an ethical point of view to delimit it, to endow it with its proper measure, to relate violence and destruction to those who produce and distribute them and to those who undergo them."[57] This is precisely the secular project we find in Levinas's notion of creation, which enframes the evil of *il y a* existence. Ophir again: "Evil is a storm of meaninglessness, formless violence that precedes ethical values and in fact endows them with their proper task: to let a certain aspect of Evil appear only in order to conceal the overwhelming excess that constitutes it. Ethics may thus be described as an appropriation and forgetfulness of Evil."[58] This is a superb description of what I take Levinas's creation narrative to be accomplishing, namely, an account of the indispensable but always incomplete process of adopting an ethical point of view to provide *some* shelter against the overwhelming, persistent violence of evil. One could even substitute "creation" for Ophir's use of the word "ethics" and replace "il y a" or "tohu wa'bohu" with his use of "Evil":

creation is a way of enframing the evil of *il y a* existence. Creation lets a certain aspect of *tohu wa'bohu* appear only in order to conceal its excesses. Creation is an appropriation and forgetfulness of the *tohu wa'bohu*.

To be sure, the adoption of such a point of view is not much, and everyone does it, but Levinas's point is that this is how we make sense of the world, by beginning with ethics, even if moral life can only ever reframe evil time and again. There is no other salvation in Levinas's creation narrative than the genesis and regeneration of an ethical world out of the chaos of evil. Paul Ricoeur expressed this perfectly in his commentary on the dualistic myths of good and evil that we have been considering. Since the reality of moral dualism cannot be overcome, *"salvation is identical with creation itself;* the act that founds the world is at the same time the liberating act."[59] Creation *delivers* one from the horrible intimation of worldless existence, and ethics is the continuous task of re-creating the world by reframing ineliminable evil. It bears noting that although *Otherwise than Being* modifies Levinas's early work in a decisive way, the *il y a* returns at the *end* of that work. The *il y a* must come at the end of *Otherwise than Being*, for the very reason it appeared at the beginning of *Totality and Infinity*: The later argument supposes no act of creation and eschews the method of transcendental genetic phenomenology, as we shall see later in this book. For the time being, I note only that in *Otherwise than Being* the *il y a* is no longer an originary point of departure, the chaos preceding creation, and yet this work continues to envisage the fundamental difference between mere existing and the goodness of creation. Here, ethics no longer sets out to "accomplish" a world, but it continues to be a "deliverance" from the evil of depersonalized chaos: "the ethical deliverance of the self through substitution for the other" that keeps "the anonymous rustling of the *there is*" at bay (OB, 164/AE, 209). Silvano Petrosino is therefore entirely justified in explicating the idea of "otherwise than being" *as* creation.[60] For creation is the rendering of mere being otherwise, a rendering in which goodness and glory break through the indifferent neutrality of pure being.

Although Putnam suggestively labeled Levinas a "moral perfectionist" because he regards ethics as an "infinite" task,[61] it is equally the case that Levinas is a *moral minimalist*, because he also thinks that there is no way to escape ethics, since the minimal conditions for intelligibility are already ethical. I would therefore propose that it is not only saintly figures like Moses or Abraham who provide Levinas with a sense of ethics—

although that is undoubtedly the case—but also ordinary folk like Noah, perhaps the quintessential figure of the modern moral subject. "Noah was a righteous man, blameless *in his generation*" (Gen. 6:9), and as every schoolchild knows, the point is that Noah's moral stature is entirely relative to the immorality of his contemporaries. Noah builds a frame to shut out Evil. And although he succeeds in providing some shelter from the meaningless violence of the bursting *tĕhôm* that is released, in Genesis 7:11, from the reservoir in which it was placed in Genesis 1, he does so only by feigning deafness to the whole of humanity save his family. "Outside of here it's death," says Beckett's Hamm, whom we can identify metonymically with Noah through his son Ham.[62] Faced with torrential evil, Noah, like modern moral subjects, creates a sanctuary on the face of the abyss, as the whole of creation was originally meant to be. Although Noah's minimal morality is not much, it remains the case that "no ethics can exhaust Evil; at any particular moment it enframes *only some* of the existing evils and lets only *some* of its victims come into presence and assume a voice of their own."[63] We modern moral subjects are all children of Noah, like Beckett's Hamm in *Endgame*, almost entirely deaf to those currently plunged into excessive evil. "There's something dripping in my head," said Hamm. But although Hamm, like Noah, reminds us of our paltry moral lives, the point is also to insist that this minimal morality reflects our actual world, in which evil is excessive, perennial, and insurmountable, and in which it is not a matter of overcoming evil but of constantly renewing and reframing our exposure to it. In Hamm's words, "You're on earth, there's no cure for that!" Children of Noah—like Beckett's Hamm and the rest of us modern moral subjects—reframe the goodness of the world plank by plank while the superfluities of evil never cease flooding in, dripping in our heads. If ethics is an infinite task and, in that respect, Levinas is a moral perfectionist, this is largely because for him the presence of evil and superfluous suffering is the ineliminable background to the constant work of creation.

Mythic Evil and Political Theology

Thus far I have run two dualistic idioms of creation from chaos together, namely, the account in Genesis 1, which Levinas reiterates, in which speech or *logos* drives evil away, and the *Chaoskampf* versions, according to which evil is violently defeated in military battle. These two idioms share the view that evil is uncreated and thus primordial and that creation works against evil to render mere existence into a moral world. On the basis of this similarity we can point to the crucial difference between Genesis 1 and the combat myths in order to better grasp their respective political theologies. Since Levinas follows the Priestly myths rather than those of *Chaoskampf*, our analysis will also enable us to understand the political vectors of Levinas's phenomenology of creation. Interpreting "ethics" within the horizon of biblical theology thus foregrounds the theologico-political character of Levinas's work in a manner usually obscured by the depoliticizing refrain of "politics after." We have seen that these accounts of creation share the basic idea that the creation of a good world takes place by opposing evil. Therefore the crucial question is: how to oppose evil? According to the combat myths, creation is founded on spectacular militant violence, whereas for Genesis 1 and Levinas it is founded on the power of words. In his recent study of Jewish myth, Michael Fishbane proposes a useful terminology for this division of the myths, calling the latter a "*logos* model" of creation and the former an "*agon* model."[64] The two myths can likewise be distinguished by their conceptions of evil, with the logos model regarding evil as passive and the agon model viewing evil as actively destructive and thus personified in the gods, as we saw in Psalm 74 and Isaiah 51. Recall Psalm 74, cited earlier in this chapter. There, Elohim creates the world by vanquishing his adversaries in military battle, "smashing" Leviathan and "crushing" *Yāmm* (Sea), forcibly controlling the chaotic waters by releasing torrents and making mighty rivers run dry, and positioning the sun in its place.[65] In stark contrast, Genesis 1 disciplines and separates the elements through speech (*logos*) alone. The difference between these two accounts of creation is all the more significant when these myths are extended to the political and historical plane, as is inevitably the case. Ricoeur alerts us to the decisive issue:

The structure of the [combat] myth permits us to anticipate what may be called a theology of the Holy War. If the King represents the god who overcomes chaos, the Enemy should represent the forces of evil in our history and his insolence should represent a resurgence of the ancient chaos. . . . I see the ultimate outcome of this type of myth in a theology of war founded on the identification of the Enemy with the powers that the god has vanquished and continues to vanquish in the drama of creation. Through the [ritual and historical] mediation of the king, the drama of creation becomes significant for the whole history of mankind, and particularly for all of that aspect of human life which is characterised by combat. In other words, the mythological type of the drama of creation is marked by the *King-Enemy* relation, which becomes the political relation *par excellence*. This phenomenological filiation is fundamental, for it introduces us through the myth to the problem of political evil.[66]

The combat myths imply a drama of creation replayed throughout history in the perpetual war of Good versus Evil. The historical application of the myth of primordial combat becomes the history and anticipation of militant apocalypse. It implies a history of perpetual war that comes to a halt only at the eschaton when the Evil Enemy is definitively annihilated. Yet in the myth of Genesis 1, as in Levinas's myth, evil is radically depersonalized. There never was an Enemy who will resurface throughout history. Genesis 1 relates "creation without opposition" and deliberately distinguishes its mythic ontology of evil from the combat myths.[67] Notably, historians agree that the combat myths (intra- and para-biblical) chronologically precede the writing of Genesis 1, which lends credence to the view that the Priestly Torah is revising, contesting, and, in some measure, demythologizing the rival account. Knohl concisely points to the significant difference between the two myths: "Unlike the combat myth, the Priestly account of Creation depicts no struggle between the forces of good and evil. The evil elements are entirely passive. God creates the world peacefully, without any struggle or war."[68] The Priestly Torah makes this point in several salient ways. First, it narrates creation as a verbal act rather than as a military battle. Second, it depersonalizes, deanimates, or demythologizes the primordial evil elements, most famously by transforming the goddess *tiamat* into the passive and impersonal *tĕhôm*, Abyss, or Deep. Third, it explicitly specifies that the primeval aquatic monsters, the *taninim* who feature so prominently in the combat myths, were *created* by God on the fifth day: "And God created [*wa'ybra*] the great sea monsters [*ha-taninim*]" (Gen. 1:21). Unlike the combat myths, in which the beastly foe is uncreated and persistently menacing, a god contesting the reign of God, the Priestly Torah demotes the great mythic sea monsters to the rank of mere creatures. Accordingly, although the Priestly and Levinasian accounts regard evil as uncreated and ineliminable, they do not imagine evil as a mighty Enemy who can be approached only in battle. For them, the opposition to evil is figured not militarily but verbally. The war on evil has become a discursive battle ("communicative action"?), and the goal of creation is not military victory but enlightenment.[69]

It is therefore not surprising that here we approach Kant's notion of "radical evil" that can be curtailed only by (the *logos* of) the moral law. While Kant's idea is often seen as a secularized version of original sin, I think it is more like the rabbinic *yetzer ha'rah* (evil impulse), for it affirms the fundamental fragility and corruptibility of the will while simultaneously insisting that human beings *can, provisionally,* triumph over evil because freedom is given them in the form of the Law. It is not that grace overcomes radical evil but that an always temporary, fragile grace is accomplished through moral action. The work of creation stays evil and thereby allows for moments of grace. To say that evil is radical, for Kant as for Levinas, is neither to arm oneself for perpetual war nor to sublimate evil by faith in grace but to understand ethics as *the work of grace* that provisionally keeps evil at bay, since the work is never done.[70] In Kant's words, "When it is said, Man is created good, this can mean nothing more than: He is created *for good* and the original *predisposition* is good; not that, thereby, he is already actually good, but rather brings it about that he becomes good or evil."[71] I suggest that Genesis 1 is the original site in which radical evil is acknowledged so as to be contested by *logos* rather than agon, a view that Kant first secularized and that later Kantians, including Levinas and Jürgen Habermas, repeat in their quite different ways (*logos* as revealed in the face or reasoned through discourse).[72] This view is closer to the rabbinic account of radical evil than to the Augustinian one. For the rabbis, the evil impulse is never eliminated, at least not in this world, but it can be curtailed by the proper use of *logos*, which they identified with Torah.[73] Indeed, the biblical Priestly and later rabbinic understandings of the holiness of the Torah ascribe to it the preeminent role in combating ontological evil and thereby preserving the goodness of creation. The famous platonic midrash from the opening of Genesis Rabbah, in which God looks into the Torah to create the world, is developed in a later collection into the idea that every jot and tittle of the Torah, every shape of its every grapheme and the celebrated spacing of its fiery black letters on fiery white parchment, have "sealed the sea Okeanos, so that it may not go forth and submerge the world." As the midrash reasons, "With it [the *torah*] He conquered [*kabash*] the Abyss [*Těhôm*], so that it would not flood the world."[74] In Fishbane's words, the rabbis understand the Torah as "the instrument that leads to the restraint and containment of the antagonistic sea—a striking triumph of *logos* over watery waste."[75] (It may even be, according to Fishbane's original and tantalizing suggestion, that the homage to love at the end of the Song of Songs is an expression of a similar view of how to respond to evil: "Love is as strong as death . . . mighty waters cannot quench love" [Song of Sg. 8:6–7]. Death and deluge, which I have equated with indeterminate *il y a* existence, are here contrasted not with speech or Torah but with love.[76] Note, though, that love is not stronger than death, as biblical finitude constantly acknowledges, but that it can sometimes be as strong as death and can therefore resist and reframe the persistence and excesses of evil.)

Needless to say, both the *agon* model and the *logos* model of creation from chaos are still at work in contemporary political discourse, in which the method of combating evil is regularly put in terms of the use of "hard power" and "soft power."[77] The drama of creation is thus extended to contemporary agonistic political discourse under slogans such as the "axis of evil" and the "clash of civilizations" whose apocalyptic eschatology goes all the way back, for example, to the vision in Isaiah 27:1 of a day when YWHW "will slay the Dragon [*tannin*] of the Sea," or to Revelation 21:1, which envisages a time when "the sea was no more," or, most appositely, to the extraordinary depiction in the Qumran War Scroll of the enemies of the righteous as "*desiring* chaos and waste," *le'tohu u'lewohu tshukatam* (1QM 17:4).[78] In contrast, the *logos* myth relies on the soft power of the word, analogous to the enlightenment project of a rational consensus that would be reached under ideal conditions of freedom, deliberation, and communication. It surely implies a "weakening" of the myth, as Gianni Vattimo might call it, although it asserts the need for soft power to control the elemental evil, which now figures less as a personified Enemy than as an effect of miscommunication and the conflict of interests. Although Levinas is much closer to the *logos* model than to the agon model, it is crucial to see how he qualifies his use of *logos* for political purposes. In brief, for Levinas, it is not the case that there is only one *logos*, not even ideally, for the *logos* in question is not reason but speech. The *logos* is not merely secularized, as we find in other Kantian thinkers, but also pluralized because what matters is less its content than its locus in a particular speaker, a face that speaks. It is not the rationality of the *logos* that combats evil but its ethical substance in multiple voices. Levinas's *logos* has the *form of a voice*, as it were, like a face, rather than the form of reason, as Kantianism supposes.[79] Accordingly, when we say that the *Endzeit* recapitulates the *Urzeit* we should not restrict our understanding of this to mean that the telos of creation must repeat *either* the primordial agon of polytheism *or* the primordial univocal *logos* of monotheism. According to Levinas, the eschatology of peace, the *Endzeit* of creation from chaos, is neither total war (the war of good versus evil) nor universal enlightenment (the horizon of rational consensus). "Peace," he suggests, "cannot be identified with the end of combats that cease for want of combatants, by the defeat of some and the victory of others, that is, with cemeteries or future universal empires" (TI, 306/TeI, 283). Rather, an eschatology of peace consists of multiple *voices* that retain their distinct moral claims and perspectives: "The face to face is a final and irreducible relation which no concept could cover without the thinker who thinks that concept finding himself forthwith before a new interlocutor; it makes possible the pluralism of society" (TI, 291/TeI, 267). The creation narrative of *Totality and Infinity* therefore comes to an end by contrasting the peace of "an impersonal reason" with the peace of the "pluralism" of concrete, speaking persons (TI, 306/TeI, 283). This is but a sketch of the implicit political theology in Levinas's account of creation. Its purpose has not been to provide a political theory but to indicate how, in Riceour's salient words, "the drama of creation . . . becomes the political relation *par excellence*." Reading Levinas's genetic myth of the *il y a* as a phenomenological account of creation from chaos highlights its proximity to and distance from other secularized political theologies.

Monotheism and Moral Dualism

The ontology and the persistence of evil is not a gnostic rejection of the world. It does, however, imply a certain moral dualism that metaphysical monotheism has long sought to overcome by uniting good and evil in a unified concept of God as absolute causal ground. In contrast, the creation theology I have been proposing understands the notion of divine power as referring not to the all-encompassing "omnipotence" of God but to God's power for the goodness of creation, which is vulnerable. In Levenson's words, divine power is "often fragile, in continual need of reactivation and reassertion, and at times, as in the laments, painfully distant."[80] As Ricoeur observes, this notion of divine power is "iconoclastic" with respect to the static concepts of metaphysical theology.[81] To quote Levenson again: "The absolute sovereignty of the God of Israel is not a simple given in the Hebrew Bible."[82] Derrida or Caputo might have said that God is unconditioned but not sovereign.[83] What status does this moral dualism and the limits it places on the notion of divine power have within Jewish intellectual history?

Gerhard May showed that the countervailing view of God as absolutely sovereign creator of everything, encapsulated in the doctrine of *creatio ex nihilo*, enters the Judeo-Christian tradition in the middle of the second century through Christian apologists such as Tatian and heresiologists such as Irenaeus.[84] Responding to the challenge of gnostics and philosophers, Christian thinkers introduced the doctrine of *creatio ex nihilo* into their reading of scripture and thereby established its authority for later Western thinkers.[85] Out of the *Kulturkampf* between early Christianity and its gnostic and philosophical rivals—in other words, with hardly any regard for Judaism—the concept of divine omnipotence, of absolute freedom and power, attained the rank of a philosophical and theological doctrine within the church. Maren Niehoff recently argued that the doctrine of *creatio ex nihilo* attributed to Rabban Gamaliel II, the leader of nascent rabbinic Judaism in the last decades of the first century, is in fact the view of a later redactor writing within the linguistic and ideological milieu of Christian theology at the beginning of the fifth century.[86] This is a bold argument, because the view of Rabban Gamaliel II is the chief example, and arguably the only unequivocal evidence, for early rabbinic belief in *creatio ex nihilo*. Niehoff's argument, then, suggests that the earliest and most celebrated rabbinic view advocating *creatio ex nihilo* is a response to Christianity formulated approximately three hundred years after its attribution. In contrast, another noted rabbinic interpretation of Genesis 1:2 (which forms the epigraph to this chapter), that of the second-century sage Bar Qappara, regards the primordial elements as malignant "dung" that lies beneath the created world and was there before the work of creation.[87] As May already concluded, "The Jewish theology of antiquity did not bring its conception of creation to the unambiguous conceptual form of the *creatio ex nihilo*, while on the Christian side this happened after a relatively short period of debate with philosophical ontology."[88]

Medieval rabbinic Judaism preserves this ambiguity. No lesser authorities than Rashi, Abraham Ibn Ezra, and Gersonides adopt the view that God's creative act in the book of Genesis takes place in relation to the primordial elements that already exist.[89] Maimonides' view on creation, which we will discuss further in Chapter 3, has been the cause célèbre of disputes from the thirteenth to the twentieth centuries, but at the very least it must be said that Maimonides allowed for legitimate alternatives to *creatio ex nihilo* and perhaps even espoused one himself.[90] To be sure, medieval exponents of Jewish dogma who followed Maimonides embraced the doctrine of ex nihilo. Their efforts began in earnest, however, more than two hundred years after Maimonides and are largely restricted to fifteenth-century Sephardic authorities.[91] From the point of view of the history of Jewish ideas, then, *creatio ex nihilo* is neither universal nor indispensable.

Accordingly, in breaking with the metaphysical view of God as absolute cause of all being, Levinas is hardly breaking with the tradition of Jewish philosophy. By contrast, *creatio ex nihilo* is fundamental to the most kabbalistic thinkers, who tended to unite the duality of good and evil within the one divine emanation.[92] Levinas was opposed to the unitive mystical speculation of the Kabbalah, no doubt because of his hatred of theodicy. In his view, the desire to unify good and evil within one ultimate concept, as the Kabbalah invariably does, is both metaphysically and morally mistaken. Elliot Wolfson's recent exploration of kabbalistic morality begins by problematizing the relation between mysticism and morality in exactly such terms:

If, however, mystical experience truly embraces a form of non-dual consciousness, as a number of scholars have surmised, then in such a state of mind, or mindlessness as the case may be, the regulative dichotomy so basic to ethical discretion would seemingly be transcended and the very foundation for ethical decisions undermined. . . . Then mysticism seemingly would preclude morality, as the unitive consciousness attained by the mystic is a form of abstraction that not only collapses binaries that appear to be essential for moral discernment, but also dissolves the concrete separateness of persons, which alone guarantees the alterity of the other. . . . Mystical consciousness may in fact subvert the basic structure of worldhood necessary to legitimate moral behaviour.[93]

Levinas could not have said it better. I therefore find it surprising that several scholars have delved into Isaac Luria's monistic Kabbalah to uncover what Oona Eisenstadt calls "the premodern sources of Levinas's postmodernism." Eisenstadt and Catherine Chalier, taking their lead from Charles Mopsik, see Levinas's account of creation as a type of post-Lurianic Kabbalah. Although some of the correspondences they discern are indeed suggestive—for example, that Levinas's "trace of the infinite" evokes the *reshimu* or traces of the Infinite dispersed amid the created remains of Its contracted Infinity—the comparison is on the whole misplaced. Lurianic Kabbalah explains evil by inscribing it in the primordial creative act, whereas Levinas denies that evil has any creative value or that it can be sanctified at all.[94] Levinas and Luria cannot be reconciled because Luria is a monist for whom the cause of all being and the end of all being are one, whereas Levinas is a monotheistic moral dualist for whom evil is separate and other than God.[95] Unlike the view that regards evil as caused by God and therefore somehow serving a useful purpose, Levinas's phenomenology recapitulates a non-metaphysical moral realism, amply attested to in biblical, rabbinic, and medieval Judaism, according to which good and evil are "non-integratable."

I therefore find myself at once in accord with much of what Catherine Keller says in her pioneering constructivist creation theology and yet disagreeing with her conclusion. Her idea, with which I agree, is that we get rid of *creatio ex nihilo*, with its fantasy of total power, dominion, and control. But she also argues that we surmount the dualism of good and evil, which in my view inscribes the very metaphysics she has rejected back into her project. Rather than opposing the goodness of creation to the evil of chaotic existing, Keller urges us to affirm the chaos. In her view, Genesis 1:2 "reinstates the primal creative sea, not as itself good-natured or personal, yet as the source of the 'good' natures in which Elohim delights."[96] Unlike the dominant history of theology that has denied and denounced the primal elements of chaos, Keller proposes a "těhômophilic" reading that reclaims them: "To love the sea monsters and their chaos-matrix is consonant with affirming their 'goodness' within the context of the whole. It doesn't make them safe or cute. They also get poetically 're-buked,' i.e. bounded, held back, so that the orders of creation may emerge; so that any creative work may be wrested, as it must be in all our creations, from chaos. But this tradition cannot be reconciled with the identification of chaos and its wild creatures as *evil*."[97]

Even though Keller vigorously argues against the doctrine of *creatio ex nihilo,* which she thinks derives from a masculine and metaphysical fantasy of total domination, she also contests the position I have defended for two reasons. First, she rejects the ascription of evil to the *těhôm* because she sees this as an insidiously misogynist gesture that repeats the "gender politics of the Bronze Age" by establishing an opposition between the good male God and the evil female chaos.[98] Second, she rejects the "primordial dualism" that I find in Levinas and in many other Jewish sources. Keller's critique of Karl Barth picks up on both these features, and, here, as elsewhere, Barth and Levinas are extremely close.[99] In light of these concerns, Keller proposes a Christian process theology in which Elohim and the *těhôm* "co-create" the cosmos, thus at once celebrating the feminine face of the deep and overcoming the dualism.

But there are two problems with this move that warrant us preferring Levinas's solution. First, Keller's constructive theology, attractive as it may be, is based on avoiding the decisive evidence that the *těhôm* is explicitly opposed to the creative act. Keller ignores, for example, the prominent return of the *těhôm* in Genesis 7:11, in which the unambiguously destructive event of the Deluge can be viewed only as opposed to creation and in no sense in partnership with it. Keller's view that the *těhôm* is a partner in creation cannot be supported by this and other cases in which its obtrusion (whether as the chaos of the Deep or the barrenness of the desert) *contrasts* with the goodness of creation as constituted by the variety and plurality of creatures. I therefore find it hermeneutically unpersuasive to propose that the *těhôm* should be understood "not as the evil, but as the active potentiality *for both good and evil.*"[100] If, for the biblical authors, the chaos and its monstrous agents are not evil, why do they consistently decry the appearance of these beasts, call for their destruction, and ritualize the desire to separate from the impurity they introduce into creation?[101]

The exegetical point is less important than the substantive one, however. Is not to affirm the goodness of the elements "within the context of the whole" to overlook the basic phenomenological dualism of moral life? Is not this process theology in the end another exercise in theodicy? Keller is concerned that an affirmation of moral dualism denigrates the beauty and joy associated with the chaotic elements. But if *Totality and Infinity* indeed provides an implicit creation theology in which the goodness of creation is consistently contrasted with the evil of mere existence, then this concern is misplaced. Section II of *Totality and*

Infinity is devoted to rich and affirmative descriptions of the *jouissance* of elemental life, the way we are nourished and live from the elements—a "love of life" that is "the primordial positivity of enjoyment, perfectly innocent" (TI, 145/TeI, 118–19). Happiness is a hot bath, the winter sun, and wind in one's hair. This enjoyment of the elements, however, must not obscure the fact that such an affirmation can be made only *within the order of creation*, once good and evil have been *separated*. A tsunami or a cyclone can never be good, can never be affirmed within the context of the whole, not even by calling it "sublime." Faced with the Great Lisbon Earthquake, Voltaire was right in deriding Leibniz's idea that ours is "the best of all possible worlds," which it had to be if God had caused everything to come into being. And no amount of process theology, not even one that affirms the intellectually liberating effects of the Lisbon earthquake, will ever reveal that disaster to have been a good thing, or even a neutral thing, within some new and enlarged context. The reason we take pleasure in the elements and find them beautiful, good, and useful is because we do so within a moral context in which good and evil (superfluous suffering) are separate and "non-integratable," as Levinas put it. We can love and affirm the chaos of the *tĕhôm*, the elements, and the darkness only once they have been subordinated to a moral context in which superfluous suffering is unambiguously regarded as evil. This point is made by a rabbinic midrash that reflects on the moment when the work of creation was completed: "The heavens and the earth were finished, and all their array" (Gen. 2:1). Rabbi Hama compares this verse to another from Proverbs:

Rabbi Hama b. Haninah opened [by comparing the verse from Genesis to a verse from Proverbs]: "The dross having been separated from the silver, a vessel emerged for the smith" (Prov. 25:4). Said R. Eliezer: This can be compared to a bathtub that was full of water in which there were two delightful plates [*dyuskusim na'im*]. So long as the water was full, the artistry on the plates could not be seen. But when the drain opened and the water removed from the bathtub the artistry on the plates became visible. In this way, every time the *tohu wa'bohu* is in the world the artistry of the heavens and the earth is not seen. But when the *tohu wa'bohu* is uprooted from the world the artistry of the heavens becomes visible—"a vessel emerged for the smith"—and their production was complete: "The heavens and the earth were finished."[102]

This midrash elegantly expresses the sense in which the watery chaos of *tohu wa'bohu* is the evil excess that prevents one from delighting in creation. The excess of chaos plunges creation into an abyss in which there is no perspective, neither up nor down, neither good nor bad. Without doubt there is luster to the heavens and a glistening to the earth, but the point is that these become visible and valuable *only as long* as the elements are subordinated to a moral context. In affirming the elemental *tohu* as a partner in creation, we effectively lose sight of the ever-changing but never-to-be-overcome difference between good and evil. The midrash just cited highlights the fact that the beauty and goodness of the world depend on the subordination of the chaotic waters. Keller offers marvelous analyses of fascinating material, but in the end she must either sanitize evil or use it for a higher purpose, whereas all we should do is get rid of it. Needless to say, by affirming the dualism of good and evil I do not at all mean to identify evil with some particular being or other, much less with some eternal enemy, as can frequently happen in such a schema.[103] That this was also Levinas's view is clear from his description of the *il y a* as "the impersonal par excellence." The evil we experience as superfluous suffering is constantly repositioned against the goodness of creation and continuously reframed by ontological and human design. Ethics is therefore the continuous re-creation of the goodness of life in opposition to the always-changing yet nonintegratable reality of evil.

Creation as Covenant

Evil persists. The task of theology should not be to justify evil but to respond to it. In Levinas's view, such a response takes place by reawakening to the covenantal structure of creation, for covenant is precisely a moral bond stronger than the pressures of merely existing. Curiously, Levinas does not remark on the fact that this very point is made in a Talmudic passage, BT Shabbat 88a–b, that plays a major role in his understanding of covenant. In this passage, Resh Lakish says: "If Israel accepts the Torah, you will continue to exist; if not, I will bring you back to chaos [*tohu wa'bohu*]."[104] This text explicitly proposes that without covenant there is only the *there is* of murmuring, meaningless existing. In accepting the terms of our covenantal bond we sustain creation. In this sense, perhaps, ethics is a type of theurgy, for it is quite literally the case that *reality depends on responsibility.*[105] Covenantal faithfulness (to the other) sustains the goodness of the world and wards off the persistent threat of evil. As R. J. Zvi Werblowsky says, "The stability of nature is itself the result of a covenant."[106] And Levinas's celebrated idea that "ethics precedes ontology" is therefore best understood in terms of the covenantal structure of creation. To be sure, Levinas secularizes the relation between chaos, creation, and covenantal faith in a way that neither presupposes nor even requires an idea of God. But the fact that the Bible can be imitated in a secular guise through a phenomenological interpretation of the goodness of the world as the ultimate horizon of meaning attests not to a breach with the tradition but to its fecundity. If one substitutes secular pronouns for those that refer to God, Levenson's description of how covenant sustains creation perfectly describes Levinas's account of ethics: "Between creation and chaos, life and death, there stands . . . only *our* covenantal faithfulness. . . . Here again the endurance and stability of nature is not intrinsic; it is only a corollary of *our* faithfulness. Should *we* in *our* freedom choose to dishonor *our* covenantal pledge, the created order would vanish. Humanity's only hope is that *we* will spurn that option. . . . Creation has become a corollary of covenant."[107] Of course, for the biblical author the burden of the Noahide covenant is borne by God, not by human beings. After the Flood, it is His unilateral covenantal pledge that secures creation from further deluge. Levinas will have none of that. For him, the covenant of creation is a claim based entirely on the human condition. Divine causality, fluctuating and elusive as it is, has become human responsibility.

One could even say that the ancient view that covenant sustains creation is an exemplary modern idea. Because ours is an age of extreme technological and environmental culpability, the "theological" idea that covenant sustains creation is realized in the modern "secular" age more than at any previous time. As Judith Shklar argues, human beings are today responsible even for what has hitherto appeared as an "act of God."[108] The distinction between natural disasters ("misfortune") and human evil ("injustice") today holds no water, to use a těhômic pun, for so-called natural disasters are created, compounded, or else immeasurably reduced by political action. Creation has *in fact* become a corollary of our covenantal political responsibility. To overstate the point only slightly: there are no natural disasters in the modern world, only injustices. This is not just because we indirectly "cause" acts of God through environmental mismanagement but also because our responses to natural disasters overwhelmingly determine the extent to which they will have been misfortunes or injustices. What matters for Levinas is not whether this structure of ontological culpability is called secular or religious but that the covenantal structure of creation is acknowledged.

Biblical authors, of course, knew no distinction between natural and supernatural disasters, and although we moderns pride ourselves on over-coming such primitive beliefs, in an interesting way we have returned to the biblical position in an inverted form. For today we, too, lack almost all means of distinguishing between natural and moral violence and we, too, no longer uphold a firm distinction between facts and values. This applies in epistemology as in ethics: just as the meaning of being is determined from the ground up by ethical norms, so too our responsibilities determine the boundary between misfortune and injustice. Whereas the idea of creation as covenant at first blush appears anthropocentric in the extreme, even egocentric, and belies the "natural attitude" to ontology, I think we can adopt it for philosophical reasons that have nothing to do with the Judaic tradition. Such a view is in accordance with Shklar's critique of the distinction between misfortune and injustice, but also with the pragmatic normative ontology that has been defended from many quarters in recent years.[109] Post-metaphysical philosophy recapitulates in a nontrivial way the pre-metaphysical traditions of the Bible, in which pure being was set aside for the sake of the moral meaning of life as such. *Endzeit gleicht Urzeit.*

Ethics in the Image of God

ANTHROPOLOGY EX NIHILO

> and at times when
> only the void [*das Nichts*] stood between us we got
> all the way to each other.
> —Paul Celan

Davar Acher: Creation from Chaos and *Creatio ex Nihilo*

In this chapter I explore another sustained midrashic account of creation we find throughout Levinas's first major period of work. The preceding chapter argued that Levinas offers an implicit account of the creation of an ethical world *ex hylus* on the basis of an intimation of the mythic evil of mere existence. According to this account, the idea of an intelligible world is based on the adoption of a moral point of view that ascribes value to particular beings. Intelligibility is produced—created—through our moral covenant with one another. Facts are already evaluatively determined because of our orientation as persons with respect to one another, by means of the moral, epistemological, and functional goals we provide each other. Distinctions we make between fact and value, misfortune and injustice, are all based on the degree of responsibility or responsiveness we render each other. The world, as created, is a moral covenant. This

midrashic transformation of divine causality into human responsibility involves an important correlate, namely, the elevation of moral agency to a
point at which it can exercise freedom from the chaos of brute existence.
It is here that Levinas's view of the transcendence of ethics emerges—the
transcendence of the other, but also what it calls for, the "difficult freedom"
or the transcending moral agency of the self. In this chapter I argue that
Levinas develops this notion of the transcendence of ethics by transforming another trope of creation, that of *creatio ex nihilo*. This chapter, then,
discerns another midrashic thread to Levinas's implicit creation theology.
There are, accordingly, two accounts of creation in Levinas's early works
that are entwined but not reducible to each other. These correlate with the
two axes of his thought, the horizontal or "linear" axis of creation from
chaos that narrates historical time and the vertical or metaphysical axis of
creation ex nihilo that interrupts it. Together these axes produce what Levinas called "the curvature of intersubjective space" (TI, 291/TeI, 267). Like
the celebrated *davar acher* of the midrash, creation affords us another angle
of exploration, as another matter, another word, and another interpretation of the same trope—this time as *creatio ex nihilo* rather than *ex hylus*.

Once again I stress that the Judaic hermeneutic at work in Levinas's thought does not compromise its philosophical claims or provenance. Levinas's midrashic account of *creatio ex nihilo* is, as we shall see,
deeply and avowedly indebted to Immanuel Kant, who provides him with
the moral and conceptual resources to read the Judaic tradition against the
grain of the moral reductionism of contemporary ontology. Like Kant,
Levinas sought to provide a "metaphysics of morals" that outlined the philosophical grounds of the sense of obligation. Both thinkers derive moral
freedom and responsibility from the primary fact of a categorical imperative. The great difference between them is that Levinas regards the fact of
obligation as presented in the face of the Other whereas for Kant it is given
in the form of Reason.[1] Moreover, both thinkers derive their respective
views by secularizing and philosophically interpreting their own religious
heritage.[2] Levinas, like many modern Jewish thinkers, regarded Kantianism with natural religious affinity, as if they shared a kindred conception
of religious and moral life. As Maimonides had incorporated Aristotle,
Levinas incorporated Kant. In both cases, the epochal philosopher had
brought to light what Judaism had long secretly known. In modern times
this concerned the pure unrepresentability of God and, more importantly,

the concrete transcendence of the Law and the "absolutely inexplicable" postulate of human freedom it compels us to accept.[3] Given Levinas's interest in interpreting Judaism in an age of critical reason—his complex engagement with Hegel and Heidegger, the influence of interwar Protestant theology on his thinking, his sympathy to a Kantianism that beholds the categorical imperative in the sublime presence of "the Other" (integrating all three *Critiques* in one moral phenomenology), and his personal passion issuing from the Holocaust and Judaism generally—he naturally turned to the greatest exponent of critical Judaic reasoning before him, Moses Maimonides. In particular, he turned to the medieval thinker's affirmation of divine freedom to lay the grounds for his theologico-political interpretation of Judaism. Although Levinas regarded Judaism as less a "political theology" than a "moral theology," clearly he and Maimonides were equally concerned with the normative force of Judaism outside the narrow sphere of "religion": Judaism as a motivating force for action generally, for mobilizing and organizing the polis (for Maimonides), or for anarchically mobilizing the ethical self (for Levinas) in response to transcendence. Not least, then, is the fact that Levinas and Maimonides gather their respective thoughts on freedom and transcendence under the sign of *creatio ex nihilo*.

Levinas and Maimonides on Creation as Freedom, or Escape from Being

The absence of Maimonides in all of Levinas's "strictly philosophical" works is conspicuous, for already in 1935 he had invoked Maimonides' defense of *creatio ex nihilo* to mount a political critique. In that year the twenty-eight-year-old Levinas published a brief column for *Paix et Droit*, the journal of the Alliance Israélite Universelle, in which he decried the demagoguery besieging Europe and defended, in its place, what he characterized as a Judeo-Christian opposition to the political and ideological forces at sway in the 1930s. Levinas proposed that contemporary politics was in a state of "pagan" captivation with the immutable order of things and the natural destiny of peoples—ideas that Judaism, with its faith in moral possibilities transcending the natural and political order, contested. This three-page exercise in philosophical journalism should be seen in the context of the young Levinas's work. In the preceding year, 1934, he had published one of his first pieces of philosophy *engagé,* "Some Reflections on the Philosophy of Hitlerism," and in 1935 his earliest original philosophical essay also appeared, "De l'évasion." It is not surprising that these early thoughts coalesce around similar themes, even though they are addressed to quite different readerships, those of philosophers and Jewish educators. The most noticeable overlap in these works appears in the defense of freedom that the young Levinas endeavors to make against what he calls, in his philosophical essay, "the brutal fact of being that assaults this freedom."[4] As is often the case, Levinas's Jewish-journalistic article makes the political stakes of his phenomenological argument explicit. The means of "escape" that Levinas the young philosopher sought from the "the fatality" of being is elucidated by Levinas the young Jewish thinker as "the folly or the faith of Israel."[5] In both cases Levinas is referring to what at that time he affirmed, no doubt overstating the matter in the face of Hitlerism, as "man's absolute freedom with respect to the world and to the possibilities which invite his action" that Nazism reduced to the "concept of human destiny."[6] Moreover, already in 1934 we find the beginnings of what developed into an ever more adamant critique of Heidegger, who stands behind "the philosophy of Hitlerism," in whatever distorted form, and who stands accused of reducing ethics to the authentic destiny of the *Volk.* This theme of the transcendence of freedom—an "escape" (*evasion*) from Heidegger and Hitler, not yet called "ethics" and already associated with the name Maimonides, became a constant feature of Levinas's Jewish and general philosophy; a clear path arcs from his 1935 publications through *De l'existence à l'existent* (1947) to *Totality and Infinity* (1961), just as there is a consistent trajectory from these early thoughts on Jewish faith to the essays collected in *Difficult Freedom* (1963).

What is surprising is that we all but lose sight of the Great Eagle in Levinas's corpus. Why is that? One would have thought Levinas would have returned time and again to Maimonides, the greatest, most revered, and most influential of all Jewish philosophers, if he could prove compatible with Levinas's own views, as was already the case in 1935. Did Levinas change his mind and come to disagree more profoundly with Maimonides?[7] At any rate, Levinas's early reflections on Maimonides, although doubtless more edifying than scholarly, evince an acute appreciation of the philosophical potency of the *Guide of the Perplexed.* For the young Levinas the decisive contribution of the *Guide* lay in Maimonides' lengthy discussion of whether the world was created or eternal, since this discussion bore the burden of philosophically articulating the possibility of freedom—primarily God's freedom, but also, by imitation, human freedom too. Aristotle had argued that the cosmos was ordered according to invariant laws of causality and that all the elements and species, indeed, the cosmos as such, was *necessarily* entailed by the perfect nature of metaphysical reality. This claim implied that the world had not been generated at a particular moment in time but was eternal.[8] If the elements and the species were all derived from the perfectly spherical rotations of the spheres there could no more be an origin to the world than there could be a beginning to any perfect circle. By contrast, belief in creation allows for the possibility of a free will external to the undeviating laws of nature and their necessary causal relations. Citing and commenting on *Guide* II.17, in which Maimonides defends creation, or rather, the *possibility* of a creative act prior to the establishment of laws of natural necessity, Levinas writes:

> The solution proposed by Maimonides is perhaps the essence of his work. It consists in distinguishing between the universe that is already created, submitting it to the irrefutable logic of Aristotle, and the very creation of that universe, which eludes him. . . . The conditions for the world as a whole should not be confounded with the laws regulating things inside the world. The worker needs matter. But God does not work. He is a creator. Let us be liberated from our intellectual habits imprisoned in a world *already made* and we shall understand creation.[9]

According to the young Levinas, Maimonides' defense of creation over eternity is tantamount to an acknowledgment of freedom within the limits of human knowledge. This early interpretation of the *Guide* is in accord with its dominant reception by Jewish and Christian philosophers ever since the thirteenth century. Although some radical interpreters of Maimonides argued that he concealed his true Aristotelian belief in the eternity of the world, most thought that he believed the world was created ex nihilo before the establishment of unchanging laws of nature.[10] Samuel Ibn Tibbon, the influential translator of the *Guide* into Hebrew, and others who followed him, espoused the radical, esoteric, Aristotelian (Averroistic) view, revived in the twentieth century by Leo Strauss (who gave it an atheistic spin). Samuel's son Moshe Ibn Tibbon, however, advocated the moderate and dominant view, which Levinas also espouses. As

Levinas puts it, "The conditions for the world as a whole should not be confounded with the laws regulating things inside the world."[11]

This moderate interpretation of the *Guide of the Perplexed* was of great consequence for Christian theology too. Heated medieval disputes over the eternity of the world raged through the University of Paris in the 1270s, and during these disputes Maimonides' view that there is a line that reason cannot cross between the science of nature and the science of theology enjoyed a central and typically contradictory fate. At first it was embraced by Franciscans, most notably Bonaventure, who wished to defend the Christian faith against the natural philosophy of Aristotle and invoked Maimonides to argue for the superiority of faith over reason. But following the condemnation of 1270 issued by the bishop of Paris, Maimonides' view became a mainstay of the opposing side. Members of the arts faculty, notably Siger of Brabant and Boethius of Dacia, now relied on the distinction proposed by the venerable Rabbi Moyses to argue that their Averroistic interpretation of Aristotle was no threat to Christian belief. Drawing on Maimonides, they distinguished between the disciplines of *scientiae naturalis* and *christianae fidei* to claim that although philosophy held sway within the arts faculty it posed no risk to theology, which was, they contended, a separate discipline. Thomas Aquinas occupied a position between these two groups, although he was closer to the philosophers. Relying on the very passages from Maimonides' *Dux dubitantium* that impressed Levinas, Aquinas defended the use of philosophy against the Franciscans, while at the same time denouncing its abuse by the more radical artists.[12]

Aquinas thus stands exactly where Maimonides was positioned by his moderate Jewish interpreters, including the young Levinas, where philosophy is granted free and independent legitimacy but does not sovereignly determine truth, since theological revelation exceeds the bounds of speculation.[13] Scholars have noted that Maimonides and Aquinas provide a proto-Kantian position, since their views neither subordinate philosophy to faith nor reduce faith to philosophy but mark the limits of philosophical reasoning in order to make room for faith. According to Shlomo Pines, there is a direct line from Maimonides through Aquinas to Kant's *Critique of Pure Reason*, inasmuch as the antinomies of pure reason make way for faith by recapitulating what might be called "the antinomy of creation and eternity."[14] The young Levinas certainly saw it this way. In defending the possibility of creation without claiming to philosophically demonstrate its validity he remarked that Maimonides "glimpsed what one calls, six centuries later, the critique of pure reason."[15] For early Levinas, then, the decisive merit of the *Guide* consists in its exoteric defense of the belief in creation based on the postulate, not the proof, of God's freedom and transcendence with respect to the already existing laws and structures of nature. According to this view, Kant's argument for human freedom provides an anthropological recapitulation of Maimonides' argument for divine freedom. In both cases it is not a matter of proving freedom so much as of combining the *normative necessity* of adopting it with the *logical possibility* of defending it.

Creation or the Eternullity of the World: Levinas and Maimonides contra Heidegger and Aristotle

When Levinas adopted a moderate Maimonidean defense of creation against the logic of eternity—which is the logic of necessity, the denial of freedom, and the inability to escape the structures of ontology—he was arguing against Heidegger in a way that parallels his predecessor's disputes against Aristotelian interpretations of the Torah and Maimonides. Let me spell out this perhaps unobvious claim. The major moral and theological challenge of *Being and Time* can be understood as a revival of the argument for the eternity of the world, while Levinas's critique of Heidegger can be seen as a Maimonidean revival of the defense of creation. The decisive point at which Maimonides opposes Aristotle revolves around the question of necessity versus freedom, and this question is repeated in the dispute between Levinas and Heidegger, with Levinas playing the moderate Maimonidean who defends the idea of moral freedom and Heidegger cast as the radicalized Aristotelian for whom possibilities in the world are pre-established (*Geworfen*) and who therefore rejects the very idea of moral freedom. We can see this more clearly if we bring into focus a reading of Heidegger as an Aristotelian. My claim is that Levinas's critique of Heidegger's account of the ontological primacy of the everyday world imitates the critique made by Maimonides of Aristotle's view of the eternity of the world.

Heidegger's profound debt to Aristotle goes back to the period culminating in *Being and Time* (1927), during which Heidegger delivered several seminars on Aristotle (1922–1925). Recent scholarship has demonstrated that Aristotle's work is the main source behind Heidegger's momentous

breakthroughs from this period, such as his disengagement of the phenomenon of truth from the structure of the proposition and his ontologiz-
ing of human action as the ground of understanding in general.[16] Another
crucial, if twisted, line leading from the *Nicomachean Ethics* to *Being and
Time* involves the transposition of *phronesis,* Aristotle's account of practical wisdom, into the circumspect practices of everyday life that Heidegger
regarded as constitutive of the meaning of being. Stanley Rosen, however,
has argued that the Aristotelian basis of the philosophical innovations of
Being and Time should not blind us to the desiccation that Aristotelian
ethics suffers in Heidegger's hands. In his view, "the transformation of *phronesis* into fundamental ontology is based on the transformation of Aristotelian ethical virtue into authenticity and the transformation of happiness
into anxiety in the face of death."[17] In brief, the reduction of phronesis to
the ontological horizon of everyday life empties it of all ethical content by
consigning its public and deliberative character to the realm of inauthentic
idle talk and reducing its teleological concern for happiness to the anxiety
of finitude disclosed in the "blink of an eye" (*Augenblick*).[18] To this formidable list of Heidegger's "translations" of Aristotle—his phenomenological
reduction of truth to nonpropositional disclosure, of *phronesis* to everyday
praxis, and of virtue to an authentic *Augenblick*—I want to add a Heideggerian transposition of the belief in the eternity of the world. I suggest that
the ontology of everydayness, of "being always already in-the-world," can
be viewed, from a certain perspective (namely, the perspective of moral
theology), as a phenomenological account of the eternity of the world.
Levinas's response to Heidegger, which largely assumes the vantage point
of moral theology, thus appears as a translation of the medieval defense of
creation against the belief in the eternity of the world. In particular, two
principal aspects to this "translation" of the medieval debate over the eternity of the world stand out.

Responsibility in Everyday Life

According to Heidegger, the everyday world always ontologically and
conditions everything that takes place within it. Just as Aristotle assumed
we cannot philosophize about the world before the *given* structures that
determine it, Heidegger denied that there is any meaning to being outside its "always already" given structures. In *On Generation and Corruption*

(I.3, II.1–3) Aristotle rejects the idea of an absolute genesis of the elements and establishes the famous principle that "nothing can come to be out of not-being." On this basis the idea of *genesis* is reformulated by Aristotle such that it no longer indicates a new beginning so much as the qualitative transformation of eternal elements by way of association and dissociation. Aristotelian cosmology maintains that the elements, structures, and laws of nature are not to be explained by way of generation but by principles of privation inherent in the continuum of matter and the universal structures that organize it.[19] According to Maimonides, Aristotle's view is that "first matter is not subject in its essence to generation and passing-away, but that various forms succeed each other in it in such a way that it divests itself of one form and assumes another. He [Aristotle] thinks furthermore that this whole higher and lower order cannot be corrupted and abolished, that no innovation can take place in it that is not according to its nature . . . and that all that exists has been brought into existence, in the state in which it is at present" (*Guide* II.13, 284).

In one sense this Aristotelian position is exactly opposed to Heidegger's breakthrough. Where Aristotle regards the structures of *nature* as given, Heidegger argued that the idea of the objectivity of nature is a contingent determination made within the givens of the historicity of being. The idea of the cosmos is mondialized by Heidegger by being historicized within the horizons of the everyday world. The implication of Heidegger's view is that there is no eternal structure of nature, which is precisely what Aristotle asserts. But this disagreement masks a more general agreement, which is that *whatever* the structures of ontology are they are always already *given* as such. As Kenneth Seeskin says of Aristotle, "All that exists has been brought into existence *in the form in which it is as present*."[20] It matters less that for Aristotle these structures form the material substratum and the heavenly spheres, just the sort of extra-mundane ontology Heidegger rejects, whereas for the latter such givens exist within the world and its contingent horizons of everydayness. In a paradoxical way, the "historicity of being" is, for Heidegger, ahistorically and, in that sense, eternally given in the existential structures of the everyday world. As Habermas said, "With his steady focus on *the invariant structures of Dasein*, Heidegger from the start cuts off the road from historicity to real history."[21] It took thinkers like Thomas Kuhn and Michel Foucault to overcome this great flaw in Heidegger's philosophy by augmenting historicity with an account of historical genealogy. Others, especially Jean-Luc Nancy, have responded to the same problem from another angle by redescribing Heidegger's ahistorical givens in terms of their *coming into presence*, whereas Hannah Arendt produced the idea of "natality" to recover the loss of freedom that happened when the subject became *Dasein*. These emphases on genealogy, birth, and natality, with their echoes of genesis and creation, are in part responses to the fact that *Being and Time* takes historicity and everydayness as simply given; we are "thrown" into them and they, it seems, are simply *there*, ready to provide us with the horizon of our possibilities. This has the effect of treating the everyday world, or the horizon of everydayness, as the eternal given that nothing precedes and no possibility exceeds. From very early on, Levinas was highly critical of the notion of "thrownness" in Heidegger, which he saw as reducing the experience of obligation to that of conforming to the conventions of everydayness and therefore simultaneously ignoring the uniqueness of the other while derogating freedom and responsibility.[22]

Aristotle also argued for the eternal givenness of the world, although from an entirely different perspective. For our purposes, the most relevant of his several arguments for the eternity of the world is the argument from the perfect circular motion of the heavens. Belief in the perfectly circular rotation of the heavens led Aristotle to think that the world must be eternal. He argued that since perfection lacks nothing, is self-sufficient and not subject to external causal influence, it cannot be initiated by anything outside its own existence. It follows that the movement of the heavens must be eternal.[23] As Friedrich Solmsen comments, Aristotle's "new mathematical concept of perfection" introduced a "new religious feeling for the divinity of the Cosmos" based on "the one eternal circular movement."[24] By the time of the medieval Arabic Aristotelian milieu of Maimonides, this view had evolved into an account of the emanation of the material cosmos as a *necessary* process implied by the very being of God.[25] It was precisely this account of divinity as necessity that Maimonides challenged in the *Guide of the Perplexed*. Notably, he did so neither because he rejected the metaphysics underlying Aristotle's belief in eternity nor because of the apparent assertion in Genesis 1 that the world was created. In Maimonides' view, Aristotle's belief in the eternity of the world was to be rejected not on the grounds of philosophical demonstration or of the literal word of the Bible but on account of its ethico-political implications (*Guide*, II.25, 327–28).

He prefers the doctrine of creation for moral reasons rather than metaphysical or exegetical ones, for without belief in creation the very basis of political and religious authority is undermined:

> The belief in eternity the way Aristotle sees it—that is, the belief according to which the world exists in virtue of necessity, that no nature changes at all, and that the customary course of events cannot be modified with regard to anything—destroys the Law in its principle, necessarily gives the lie to every miracle, and reduces to inanity all the hopes and threats that the Law has held out. (*Guide*, II.25, 327–28)

Since belief in eternity stands for a deity who is immobile and a cosmos regulated by necessary laws and structures, it undermines the very idea of divine free will and with it the logic of divine intervention, be it for deliverance or retribution. Maimonides' defense of creation thus has less to do with "theoretical" reasoning, as Kant might have said, than with practical reasoning. In his view, belief in creation was to be preferred and eternity to be rejected because the latter was "more harmful" (*Guide*, II.22, 320). Because of this practical consideration he opposed belief in the eternity of the world, for "in this opinion is contained the destruction of the foundation of the Law" (*Guide*, II.23, 321). Creation, for Maimonides, is an ethico-political doctrine more than a speculative or scientific claim. Creation is a postulate of practical reasoning, of the theologico-political kind. In Maimonides' view, belief in creation is a correlate of the transcendence of divine freedom, or simply another way of expressing that very idea. The doctrine of creation thus underpins the whole project of political theology. It is the fundamental postulate resulting from the practical interests of theology. If, for the biblical and rabbinic authors we considered in Chapter 2, creation *ex hylus* was a response to the moral problem of evil, for Maimonides creation ex nihilo is a response to the political problem of law and order, freedom and culpability.

As I have been suggesting, Maimonides' gesture anticipates Kant's initial method. It was Kant who formalized the argument that the freedom of the will can be neither proved nor disproved but that it must be affirmed on the basis of the practical interests of reason. Since morality requires freedom, while reason is unable to demonstrate or refute it, a rational person ought to *assume* that she is free so as to take responsibility for her actions. "Ought" implies "can," or, in the rabbinic dictum cited as the epigraph to *Difficult Freedom*, "freedom on tablets of stone." Like Pines, Seeskin is prepared to assert that Kant's response to the antinomy of freedom "clearly derives from Maimonides."[26] He has in mind remarks such as this: "Regarding the question whether the heavens are generated or eternal, neither of the two contrary opinions could be demonstrated" (*Guide*, II.22, 320). At any rate, Kant and Maimonides agree that the only way to talk in a thick moral language—for example, by talking about responsibility, guilt, forgiveness, cruelty, kindness, conscience, and culpability—is by assuming the freedom of moral agents with respect to the world in which they are constituted and the situations into which they are thrown.

This brings us back to Heidegger. His view of the everyday world as always already given reduces ethical obligations to contingent norms based on impersonal ontological structures for which no one is ultimately responsible. It thereby transposes the theological problem of creation and eternity to the plane of transcendental anthropology. What for Maimonides was a problem with Aristotle's denial of God's freedom in the face of the eternity of the world became a problem of Heidegger's denial of personal freedom, agency, culpability, and conscience in light of the always already given and determining structures of an impersonal everyday world. Levinas's close friend Maurice Blanchot expressed this perfectly in his unmistakably Heideggerian review of Henri Lefebvre's *Critique de la vie quotidienne*:

The idea of creation is inadmissible when it is a matter of accounting for existence as it is borne by the everyday. . . . The everyday is our portion of eternity: the eternullity of which Laforgue speaks. The Lord's prayer, in this way, would be secretly impious: give us our daily bread, give us to live according to the daily existence that leaves no place for a relation between Creator and creature. Everyday man is the most atheist of men. He is such that no God whatsoever could stand in relation to him. And thus one understands how the man in the street escapes all authority, be it political, moral, or religious.[27]

Blanchot's point is that the dailiness of existence, the daily bread of which the Lord's Prayer speaks, has become the modern experience of everyday life borne without reference to origins or transcendence and is thus severed from the idea of a Creator. The primacy of the everyday in the ontology of *Being and Time* raises the specter of eternity and recalls the Judeo-Christian Averroist Aristotelians who denied the doctrine of creation. Levinas, like Maimonides before him, followed "the philosopher" only to the point at which he undermines the very possibility of freedom and thereby "destroys the Law in its principle." In 1935, when Levinas implored that we "be liberated from our intellectual habits imprisoned in a world *already made* [his emphasis] and we shall understand creation" ("The Contemporary Relevance of Maimonides," 93), he was not only explicating Maimonides' critique of eternity in the name of transcendence and freedom but also alluding to the freedom of an escape from the "always already" existing "eternullity" of the everyday world. To be sure, the perfection of Aristotelian eternity must be contrasted with the drone of everyday eternullity, as Blanchot's evocative reflection reminds us. For while Aristotle introduced a new religious conception of divine perfection, Heidegger disclosed being not as it rotated perfectly and therefore eternally around a divine center but in the eternullity of "the pallid lack of mood which dominates the 'grey everyday'" (*Being and Time*, 345). Yet, from the perspective of moral theology the problem with eternity (that is, the lack of divine freedom) is isomorphic with the problem of the eternullity of the everyday world (that is, it eliminates human freedom). Neither eternity nor eternullity is ever initiated or created. They both lack what Arendt called "natality," which defines the *bios politikos* as "the capacity of beginning something anew, that is, of acting."[28] Levinas is similarly motivated in his argument against Heidegger. Creation becomes a trope for the human capacity to act freely within a worldly context and thus to activate the transcendence of ethics within the immanence of being. In reducing the locus of the *vita activa* to *das Man-selbst*, Heidegger subordinated the moral and political agency of individuals to the impersonal forces of everyday being and even denied that it was intelligible to individuate action on the basis of moral agency, for the latter has no real ontological ground. Instead of personal responsibility for what one does, Heidegger saw only the problem of authentically coming to terms with the groundlessness of who one is. With this we arrive at the second feature of the repetition of the medieval dispute over the eternity of the world that we find in Levinas's critique of Heidegger.

Particularity in Everyday Life

For medieval Aristotelians, belief in the eternity of the world provided an explanation of the necessity of laws governing species, but it could not explain why this particular event took place or that particular detail was a certain way. This gap in the Aristotelian apparatus, which See-skin calls the problem of *particularization*, was grasped by Maimonides as a great flaw in Aristotle's cosmology.[29] The problem came to a head for medieval Aristotelians when their cosmology failed to explain the *particular* motions of the heavenly bodies as successfully as the Ptolemaic system did. The point may seem somewhat incidental today, except that Maimonides' argument for the transcendence of divine free will was leveraged by his regard for the significance of *particular* entities, which Aristotle's general principles, precisely those that implied belief in eternity, could not explain. Maimonides insisted that the decisive question was not, Why is there something rather than nothing? but, Why is there *this* thing rather than *that* thing? And this question, he argued, cannot be answered without invoking a principle of freedom at work in nature. Belief in creation is thus a response to the fact of contingency, the fact that existence is not wholly determined by invariant laws and structures but involves the particulars of desire. David Burrell explains Maimonides' position: "To know what really exists will be to know it in its individuality and not as instantiating a species."[30] Levinas is similarly concerned with the problem of particularization as it emerges in ethical life, and above all as it emerges within what Heidegger called the "undifferentiated" or "indifferent" givenness of the everyday life, which determines the entire ontological problematic of "everydayness" from the opening of *Being and Time*:

At the outset of our analysis it is particularly important that Dasein should not be Interpreted with the differentiated character [*Differenz*] of some definite way of existing, but that it should be uncovered [*aufgedeckt*] in the undifferentiated character which it has proximally and for the most part [*zunächt und zumeist*]. This undifferentiated character of Dasein's everydayness is *not nothing*, but a positive phenomenal characteristic of this entity. Out of this kind of Being—and back into it again—is all existing, such as it is. We call this everyday undifferentiated character of Dasein "*averageness*" [*Durchschnittlichkeit*]. (*Being and Time*, 69/SZ, 43)[31]

It is this undifferentiated character of everydayness that is the object of Levinas's critique of Heidegger. His major objection to Heidegger is that ethics attests to the concrete particularity of the other in everyday life. The point requires some further elaboration. The result will show, I think, that we have all the more reason to see Levinas's critique of Heidegger as a repetition of Maimonides' critique of Aristotle. Heidegger argued that the undifferentiated character of everyday life implied that human existence was fundamentally inauthentic because it was from the outset disindividuated and homogenized by the public structures of being. Even the private pangs of moral conscience were, in his view, not properly (or "ontologically") one's own: "this 'public conscience'—what else is it than the voice of the 'they'?" (*Being and Time*, 323/SZ, 278). Moral conscience properly disclosed thus reveals its own "nullity," although in Heidegger's view that is not such a bad thing because, in any case, moral conscience is "ontologically suspect" anyway (*Being and Time*, 335/SZ, 289). By contrast, in the truthful experience of conscience, in which one hears the true call of being, "the '*they*' collapses" and one is left without the noisy clamor of public moral platitudes (*Being and Time*, 317/SZ, 273). The crucial point here is that guilt and conscience are eviscerated of all moral significance because from the outset Heidegger has determined that ethics belongs to the realm of the undifferentiated and inauthentic modes of everyday life.

Moreover, it has not often been noted that in the crucial §59 of *Being and Time* Heidegger explicitly associates his damning depiction of moral conscience with a distinctly Judaic outlook. At first we are told that moral conscience is a "tranquilizing" mode of self-assurance involving mental "balancing" acts that are nothing more than "warning" bells rung by the internalized "they"; moral conscience therefore tells one nothing about one's true situation. Heidegger then baptizes this tranquilization of conscience "Pharisaism," which objectifies conscience and thereby does no justice to its true character as care for the situation. He then adds "the idea of moral *law*" to the list of misinterpretations of moral conscience and thus explicitly likens Kant to a Pharisee who mistakenly conceives of Dasein as a subject with rules, values, and norms that stand as objects to it regardless of the fluidity of its situation. Before moving on to the positive disclosure of the call of conscience Heidegger adds one final barb, once again urging us to be rid of our self-afflicted "Pharisaism" that leads us to mistake Dasein for a "'household' whose indebtedness simply needs to be balanced off in an orderly manner so that the Self may stand 'by' as a disinterested spectator while these Experiences run their course" (*Being and Time*, §59). From this vigorous strike at moral conscience we learn a great deal, not least that Heidegger has Kantian *Moralität* in mind when he attacks the calculus and law of conscience and that he associates this Kantianism with Pharisaism. There is even an echo of Paul's critique of the Law in this attack on Kantian Pharisaism, as if any attempt to formalize the spirit of ethical conscience by following a law was itself the cause of sin, or inauthenticity, manifest as the ontological illusion of guilty pangs of conscience. Nothing less than abrogating the moral law, by dying to being, will allow for authentic Dasein; authenticity thus reigns not under the old dispensation of metaphysical morality but under the new spirit of ontology. It was this demoralization of conscience, and especially Heidegger's interpretation of conscience as undifferentiated and disindividuating "Pharisaism," that Levinas challenged by showing how "the Other" is a singular locus of ethical authority addressed to and soliciting the nonformalizable uniqueness of the self as ethical respondent.

Levinas's argument, then, is that Heidegger overlooked something that belongs to the "primordial" level of conscience, namely, its regard for the particularity of the other, from whence conscience receives its singular moral imperatives that cannot be reduced to conventions and platitudes. Heidegger's account of the morality of everydayness claims to map conscience completely onto the averaged-out, leveled-down, undifferentiated, and inauthentic norms of everydayness without any ethical remainder. He assumes that moral conscience simply repeats the "indifferent modes that characterize everyday, average Being-with-one-another" (*Being and Time*, 158/SZ, 121). But Levinas's point is that social ontology is always from the outset characterized by the singular voices and particular characteristics of other people. To reduce these particularities to the glib conventions of public morality is to miss the fact that conscience aims not at the undifferentiated mass of people or at impersonal conventions to which "one" is obliged but at the particularities of the other. From this perspective, Levinas's critique of Heidegger again resembles Maimonides' critique of Aristotle. Like Maimonides, Levinas's challenge to the philosopher is based on his vigilant regard for particularities that escape the philosopher's understanding. Just as Maimonides invokes a principle of volition in order to explain the contingency of particulars and thus rejects the abstract philosophical view of an eternal world, so too Levinas refuses to abstract the manifest particularity of the other revealed in everyday ethical life. From Levinas's perspective, only blindness or cruelty allows Heidegger to regard moral conscience as a ruse of the common mind; in truth, conscience is a relation to the particularities of the other, to faces and circumstances that are not reducible to rules or conventions. The seat of one's own conscience is the face of the other, an ethical intuition of the singularity of the other that does not correlate with a formal moral principle, a psychological calculus, or a public convention—conscience without consciousness, as one might say in French. To reduce this conscience to the glib protocols of public morality is to overlook its basic modality and thereby gravely misinterpret the phenomenon of "having a conscience." Heidegger's mistake lies not in his critique of the "ontologically suspect" notion of a public conscience but in the complete correlation he proposes between true conscience and the average, inauthentic morality of everydayness. Nancy makes a similar argument in his rethinking of the fundamental *existentiale* of *das Man*, the "one" as punctuated by the multiple singularities that constitute "being-with" from the outset. In his words, "Heidegger confuses the everyday with the undifferentiated, the anonymous, and the statistical. These are no less important, but they can only constitute themselves in relation to the differentiated singularity that the *everyday* already is by itself: each day, each time, day to day. One cannot affirm that the meaning of Being must express itself starting from everydayness and then begin by neglecting the general differentiation of the everyday, its constantly renewed rupture, its intimate discord, its polymorphy and its polyphony, its relief and its variety."[32] In place of the indifference of conventions and social roles and the priority of *das Man-selbst*, Nancy concentrates on the variety and strangeness of people and the resultant impossibility of acceding to the average and ordinary undifferentiatedness of everyday social relations. Notably, Nancy also maintains that in place of the notion of "thrownness" we should redeploy the idea of *creatio ex nihilo* in order to account for how the origin of sense preserves and continuously renews the singularity of beings.[33]

Two points, then, correlate Maimonides' critique of Aristotle with Levinas's critique of Heidegger. The perfection of Aristotle's God excluded the basic presupposition of divine freedom and left unexplained the particular contingencies of cosmology. Maimonides' pragmatic assent to belief in the creation of the world affirmed, within a critically circumscribed account of theological reasoning, the possibility of the freedom and particularization of the divine will. For Maimonides, this pragmatic assent to the doctrine of creation implies that providence, miracles, reward and punishment—in short, the conceptual apparatus of political theology—are all possible and therefore usable. This debate is repeated, perhaps with even higher stakes, in the dispute between Heidegger and Levinas. Heidegger's description of the everyday world envisaged the human being without the freedom to take a moral stand against the tides of history and without a conscience that responds to the ethical particularities of others encountered in everyday life. For this reason, as Blanchot put it, Dasein "escapes all authority, be it political, moral, or religious" (*The Infinite Conversation*, 245). In defending creation against the eternullity of the everyday world, Levinas repeats the two most important features of Maimonides' defense of creation, freedom and particularization, which are joined in "ethics," that is to say, in the difficult freedom to respond to the particularity of the other. Maimonides' belief in creation as a pragmatically more preferable doctrine than that of the eternity of the world is thus repeated by Levinas in his anthropological defense of creation. Let us now turn to Levinas's text for confirmation of this reading.

The Ethics of *Creatio ex Nihilo* in *Totality and Infinity*

Although there is no mention of Maimonides in *Totality and Infinity*, I have been arguing that the critique of Heidegger throughout that book is continuous with the Maimonidean axiology of creation proposed by Levinas in 1935. This continuity can be seen in Conclusion 4 to *Totality and Infinity* (called, quite simply, "Creation"), in which Levinas employs the notion of *creatio ex nihilo* for the very reasons we have considered—to affirm the transcendence of freedom and the desire for particularity that render human life irreducibly ethical.

To affirm origin from nothing by creation is to contest the prior community of all things within eternity, from which philosophical thought, guided by ontology, makes things arise as from a common matrix. The absolute gap of separation which transcendence implies could not be better expressed than by the term creation, in which the kinship of beings among themselves is affirmed, but at the same time their radical heterogeneity also, their reciprocal exteriority coming from nothingness. One may speak of creation to characterize entities situated in the transcendence that does not close over into a totality. (TI, 293/TeI, 269)[34]

Levinas is harnessing the logic of Maimonides' defense of creation that in his youth he made explicit. Even if Samuel Moyn is right to contend that in the 1930s there was no hint of the secularization of transcendence that was to mark Levinas's major works after World War II, once the secularized concepts turn up we cannot help but trace them back to their theological and, indeed, distinctly Judaic provenance.[35] Creation now belongs to the order of moral phenomenology rather than that of metaphysical theology, but despite this secularization it serves a strikingly similar purpose and carries remarkably congruent values as it did for Maimonides: to account for the value of particularity and to defend the possibility of a finite freedom that outstrips "the prior community of all things within eternity." In another formulation Levinas writes: "The idea of creation *ex nihilo* expresses a multiplicity not united into a totality; the creature is an existence which indeed does depend on an other, but not as a part that is separated from it. Creation *ex nihilo* breaks with system, posits a being outside of every system, that is, there where its freedom is possible" (TI, 104/TeI, 78). Indeed, throughout *Totality and Infinity* the trope of *creatio ex nihilo* is deployed to suggest a sense of the transcendence of the human, both irreducible to the general conditions and semantics of its appearing and freely able to rise above them by responding to the face of the other. *Creatio ex nihilo* thus refers to the capacity of the moral self to act not merely on the basis of external causes but by preserving a distance, that of the *nihil*, within itself, whereby it can take responsibility for what it causes. Once again, then, we have a resoundingly "secular" interpretation of creation that, to paraphrase Celan, takes place in the void between us and through which we get all the way to each other. For Levinas, *creatio ex nihilo* is presented in the "expression" of the particularity of the other (the face, the voice, and the mortality of the other) and in the "difficult freedom" of responsibility in everyday life. The sense of everyday life is therefore not merely given but *gifted*, since it always refers us to the personal and the singular whereby our freedom is awakened.

Creatio ex nihilo renders Maimonides' theological critique of Aristotle into a modern philosophical anthropology by refiguring freedom, transcendence, agency, and particularity. Accordingly, although we glimpse only shadows of the Great Eagle in *Totality and Infinity*, there is reason to think that the Maimonideanism Levinas defended in his youth permeated his account of ethics as "metaphysical desire." From "The Contemporary Relevance of Maimonides" in 1935 to *Totality and Infinity* in 1961, the argument for human freedom and the moral significance of the uniqueness of the other are consistently advanced by prizing creation over eternity. The contours of Levinas's argument with Heidegger are shaped in terms of Maimonides' critique of Aristotle. Theology has again become anthropology. According to this Kantian, anthropological, "secular" reading of Maimonides, the meaning and possibility of ethics is revealed through critique of the limits of philosophical understanding, a limit not respected by Heidegger's reduction of being-as-a-whole to the alternatives of everyday indifference or an amoral authentic disclosure of finitude. A similar interpretation of Maimonides has been defended, independently of Levinas and the post-Heideggerian context in which he philosophized, by leading Maimonidean scholars such as Seeskin and David Hartman. Hartman, for example, opens his "covenantal anthropology" by invoking Maimonides' belief in God's "independence and freedom," a belief embedded in the latter's defense of *creatio ex nihilo*, as we have seen. On the basis of the idea that human beings are in the image of God, Hartman argues for "the unique ontological status of the human being as one who can transcend necessity and act within a context of freedom."[36] But neither Hartman nor Seeskin contends with Heidegger, although he is arguably "the philosopher" of modernity, as was Aristotle in medieval times. To that extent, Levinas's phenomenology of *creatio ex nihilo* assumes the Maimonidean task of defending, within philosophical modernity, all that destroys the Law in its principle.

Embodying Metaphysics

Levinas's ethical *imitatio* of the Maimonidean account of the transcendence of freedom and the particulars of desire makes no claim about God. Rather, it provides an account of ethical life in the image of God, whether YHWH exists or not, according to the phenomenological sense of the world as a moral creation. The idea of God is suspended in a phenomenological *epoché* that allows the meaning of creation to present itself within the horizon of moral experience. The two great themes of Maimonidean creation theology, the transcendence and the particularization of the Will, now constitute ethical life. Ethics is therefore a secular embodiment of *imitatio dei*. Although this is evidently a transgressive interpretation of "Judaism," in a way Levinas is more faithful than Maimonides to the biblical and rabbinic traditions because he eschews the abstractions of Maimonidean metaphysical theology and restores the pre-metaphysical, embodied sense of *imago dei* (*tzelem elohim*) and imitatio dei (*hidamut la'el*). Even though Levinas secularizes the divine image, his secularization is at least faithful to the embodied character of the image as it presented itself to pre-metaphysical Judaic traditions. In contrast, Maimonides interpreted the image of God as referring only to the actualized intellect and on that basis maintained that failure to actualize one's intellect deprived one of being called in the image of God. In his words:

> You know that whoever is not endowed with this form [of the image of God as the intellect *in actu*[37]], whose signification we have explained, is not a man, but an animal having the shape and configuration of man. Such a being, however, has a faculty to cause various kinds of harm and to produce evils that is not possessed by the other animals. For he applies the capacities for thought and perception, which were to prepare him to achieve a perfection that he has not achieved, to all kinds of machinations entailing evils and occasioning and engendering all kinds of harm. Accordingly, he is, as it were, a thing resembling man or imitating him. (*Guide* I.7, 33)

Maimonides' metaphysical view of the *imago dei* as an intellectual faculty even leads him to overturn the prohibition on murder in cases in which it is politically expedient for the ruler to do so. People who have not actualized their intellects have not attained the status of being in the image of God and have therefore "been relegated to the rank of the individuals of all the other species of animals: 'He is like the beasts that speak not'" [Ps. 49:13, 21] (*Guide*, III.18, 475).[38] Whereas the biblical and rabbinic prohibitions on murder derive from values borne by *the human body as image of God*, for Maimonides the image of God is a purely incorporeal faculty.[39] As Yair Lorberbaum has shown, since the body, according to Maimonides, indicates nothing of God's holiness and transcendence, it becomes subject to all the instrumental considerations of the ruler and presents no limit to the legitimate exercise of power in the name of God. "For this reason," says Maimonides, in the continuation of the passage just cited, "it is a light thing to kill them, and has been even enjoined because of its utility." From a certain moral perspective, Maimonides is more like Heidegger than Levinas, since he also thinks that ultimate truth renders ethics null and void. Where Heidegger *reduces* ethics to the truth of being authentically disclosed, Maimonides *abstracts* from ethics to the truths of metaphysics apprehended only by intellects *in actu.*[40] It is not surprising, then, that despite his debt to Maimonides, Levinas is deeply ambivalent toward his great medieval predecessor.

This ambivalence is spelled out at the far end of Levinas's career, fifty years after his first reflections on Maimonides, in an interview with Françoise Armengaud in 1985. This is the only other substantive discussion of Maimonides we find in Levinas's published work, besides the 1935 piece of philosophical journalism, in addition to which we have only desultory comments. Whereas in this interview Levinas acknowledges the monumental status of Maimonides in the Jewish tradition—"Who in their right mind would question the existence of Mont Blanc?"[41]—he hesitates considerably since Maimonides belongs to "the great philosophical tradition that finds intelligibility, rationality and meaning in knowledge. In Maimonides, spirituality is essentially knowledge: knowledge in which being is present to the mind."[42] Maimonides indeed understood the ultimate union a human might attain with God in terms of "knowledge and drawing near through apprehension" (*Guide* I.18, 44), Levinas, like Franz Rosenzweig, favored the view of Judah Halevi, according to which proximity to transcendence was less an intellectual accomplishment than a social one.[43] In Levinas's view, knowledge is inferior to "terms like 'association' (*hithabrut*) and 'proximity' (*hitqarvut*). It is as if these social meanings of 'the relation' did not indicate a deficiency in knowledge, some least bad approximations of knowledge, but were, rather, possessed of their own, sovereign positivity."[44] Having laid claim to an anthropological application of Maimonides' theology of creation, Levinas refuses its epistemological intellectualism in order to recover the ethical character of the image of God. In doing so he returns to the biblical and rabbinic positions that Maimonides had subordinated to the goal of knowing God.

Ethics in the Image of God

Two features of the biblical and rabbinic accounts of the body as image of God stand out in relation to Levinas's ethical secularization, namely, their entailing the prohibition on murder and the imperative to be fruitful and multiply. The idea of being created in the image of God is mentioned only three times in the Jewish Bible. On the first and most famous occasion, in Genesis 1:27, humanity is proclaimed the image of God, whereupon immediately "God blessed them and God said to them: 'Be fruitful and multiply, fill the earth and master it'" (1:28). Indeed, the image of God is always linked to the blessings and obligations of fecundity. When Noah steps out of the ark and creation is resumed after the chaos of the Deluge, the theologoumenon of the image of God is reiterated, although this time with the addition of the prohibition on murder:

> Whoever sheds the blood of man,
> By man shall his blood be shed;
> For in His image
> Did God make human.
> Be fruitful, then, and multiply.
> (Gen. 9:6–7a)

The prohibition of murder is now inserted into the proclamation of the *imago dei*, establishing murder not only as a crime but also as a fundamental desecration. This logic works only insofar as it is the body, as that which can be murdered, that constitutes the image of God. Ancient Jewish authors eschewed a dualism of body and soul. Because they regarded the human body as the site of the sacred image of God, they reasoned that murder is the first and most egregious desecration. As Moshe Greenberg established, murder is seen in the Bible as an incommensurable violation that cannot be recompensed by economic exchange precisely because the murdered person is an image of the incommensurable God.[45] Biblical and rabbinic laws pertaining to capital punishment can therefore be understood only by postulating that the human body attests to the image of God. This emphasis on the body leads Michael Fishbane to translate *tzelem elohim* (*imago dei*) as "the visage of God."[46] Levinas's formulations must be heard with this non-metaphysical understanding of the image, or visage, of God in mind: "The Other . . . resembles God" (TI, 293/TeI, 269); "This infinity . . . is his face, is the primordial *expression*, is the first word: 'you shall not commit murder'" (TI, 199/TeI, 173).[47] Levinas's emphasis on the difference between murder and other forms of destruction thereby renders the bodily image of God into secular terms:

The face [*visage*], still a thing among things, breaks through the form that nevertheless delimits it. This means concretely: the face speaks to me and thereby invites me to a relation incommensurate with a power exercised. . . . Neither the destruction of things, nor the hunt, nor the extermination of living beings aims at a face, which is not of the world. . . . Murder alone lays claim to total negation. . . . Murder exercises a power over what escapes power. It is still a power, for the face expresses itself in the sensible, but already impotency, because the face rends the sensible. The alterity that is expressed in the face provides the unique "matter" possible for total negation. . . . The Other is the sole being I can wish to kill. (TI, 198/TeI, 172)

Or in the words of Rabbi Akiva, "Whoever spills blood, such a one annuls the divine likeness [*d'muth*]."[48] The crucial point, for Levinas as for the biblical and rabbinic traditions, is that murder "annuls the divine likeness" because the divine likeness is borne by the materiality of the body of the other.

This account of the bodily image of God entails not only the prohibition on murder but also the commandment to "be fruitful and multiply." Indeed, the two motifs are explicitly linked on the three occasions they are mentioned in Genesis 1, 5, and 9. This explains why Rabbi Akiva's view that murder annuls the divine image is immediately followed by another interpretation in the name of Ben-Azzai: "Whoever does not engage in reproductive sexual relations sheds blood and annuls the divine likeness, since it says: 'for in the image of God he made humanity,' and it says: 'and you be fruitful and multiply.'"[49] For Ben-Azzai, failure to procreate corporeally constitutes a denial of the divine image, just as murder did for Rabbi Akiva. Strange as it might seem, this is confirmed by the third and final explicit mention of the image of God in the Bible. In the genealogical record of Adam given in Genesis 5:1–3, we are first reminded that humanity "was created in the likeness of God, male and female He created them," and then, surprisingly, that Adam "begot a son in his likeness and after his image." This implies that human fecundity, to use Levinas's term, is the very means by which the image of God is itself, quite literally, reproduced and regenerated.[50] The remarkable account of "fecundity" that governs the temporalizing structure of *Totality and Infinity* should also be understood as a modern interpretation of *imitatio dei*, of striving for transcendence and for "likeness" to God by being fruitful and multiplying. By contrast, Maimonides, who denied that murder was an assault on the divine image because the image of God is present only in the actualized intellect, rejected the idea of a corporeally procreative divine image and therefore interpreted procreation as an obligation to engender intellectual disciples (*Guide*, I.7, 32–33). Levinas therefore clearly sides with the non-metaphysical biblical and rabbinic view of ethics in the bodily image of God. His ubiquitous deployment of the biblical postulate of humanity in the image of God recovers the fundamental sense of the human body as icon of God, locus of incommensurate value that entails the prohibition on murder and the obligations of fecundity. The original ethical implications of the doctrine of the image of God are conserved by Levinas, although not by Maimonides, even as they are secularized. Levinas's phenomenological transposition of the *imago dei* into an account of the prohibition on murder and the significance of fecundity thus advances Alon Goshen-Gottstein's programmatic announcement that "the liberation of rabbinic theology from the reins of medieval theology is still underway."[51] In reclaiming the bodily visage of God under the sign of ethics by emphasizing the prohibition on murder and the desire for fecundity that it entails, Levinas at once secularizes a Judaic account of the image of God and liberates it from medieval metaphysics. Moreover, Levinas's interpretation of ethics in the bodily image of God provides the narrative structure for *Totality and Infinity* as a whole.

The Purpose of Creation: "Eschatology Without Hope"

The main argument of *Totality and Infinity* concludes by recalling the great myth of creation from chaos: "Against the anarchy of the *there is* the existent is produced, a subject of what can happen, an origin and commencement, a power" (TI, 281/TeI, 257). In Chapter 2 we saw that Levinas's account of creation from chaos prizes the logos model rather than the agon model. Creation from the evil of merely existing takes place through speech and involves no necessary combat. Creation is established over the abyss not by virtue of the "impersonal reason" of Enlightenment thinking but by a *logos* oriented toward "the pluralism of society" expressed in the concrete particularity of speaking persons—*logos* as "a relation that starts from an I and goes to the other" in which each self "will remain a personal I" (TI, 306/TeI, 283). Creation from chaos thus becomes concretely historical without resorting to an agonistic "clash of civilizations" or the discursive triumph of Enlightenment *logos*. Creation ensures "the convergence of morality and reality" (TI, 306/TeI, 283) by attending to new claims, new perspectives, and new voices that others continuously introduce into the world. The weak messianic force of creation, to borrow Walter Benjamin's famous phrase, consists in our capacity to continuously reshape the chaos of mere existence into a world that respects the particularity of the other—as body, voice, and claim rather than as impersonal reason. Levinas's eschatology of peace, the telos of the work of creation, consists of a pluralist society of speakers in which different views and claims are respected and in which dissensus is valued above the ideal of rational consensus. Levinas calls this desire for creation, this desire for a good world, "fecundity," since fecundity attests to the desire for others who transcend my finite horizon.

> Fecundity is to be set up as an ontological category. In a situation such as paternity the return of the I to the self, which is set forth in the monist concept of the identical subject, is found to be completely modified. The son is not only my work, like a poem or an object, nor is he my property. Neither the categories of power nor those of knowledge describe my relation with the child. The fecundity of the I is neither a cause nor a domination. I do not have my child; I am my child. Paternity is a relation with a stranger who while being Other ("And you shall say to yourself, 'who can have borne me these? I was bereaved and barren . . .'" Isaiah 49) *is* me, a relation of the I with a self which is yet not me. In this "I am" being is no longer Eleatic unity. In existing itself there is a multiplicity and a transcendence. In this transcendence the I is not swept away, since the son is not me; and yet I *am* my son. The fecundity of the I is its very transcendence. (TI, 277/TeI, 254)[52]

Despite the gender bias of Levinas's position, which slides from the neutral "fecundity" to "paternity" and "the son," I want to salvage the notion of fecundity as a *model* for ethics in the secular image of God. An interesting point remains, I think, despite the serious problems of Levinas's apparent naturalization of the family, his essentializing of the erotic in heterosexual terms, and his glorifying of the father and the son, for which he has been rightly censured.[53] Think of the "ontological category" of fecundity as a diachronic relation with another person who matters to you in her particularity, according to how she will one day express her own embodied needs and desires. By turning to fecundity instead of the history of nations or states Levinas reminds us that the future we work for does not consist of the abstract values we make of people envisaged as equal citizens or rational agents but of particular others, embodied persons, whose enjoyment and suffering of life matter to us because of their singular character. This view provides an alternative to Hegelianism, according to which the personalism of the family is but a stage in the unfolding of reason that is overcome and elevated but also depersonalized by civil society. In envisaging an eschatological peace as the purpose of creation, what is important for Levinas is to sustain the singular, embodied, and unpredictable character of the other whose horizons exceed one's own sense of the possible. He therefore boldly, if problematically, asserts that the ethical desire for the particularity of the other is "concretized in the marvel of the family" (TI, 306/TeI, 283). However, the family is but *a phenomenological model* for the ultimate term of our desire.[54] It attests to a desire for the goodness and well-being of each particular person in a manner that exceeds the impersonal logic of statist reasoning. Levinas therefore concludes that "the family . . . identifies itself outside the State, even if the State reserves a framework for it" (TI, 306/TeI, 283). The family is a model for how love and the desire for goodness are oriented toward particular persons. The fecundity of ethical time is thus the key to the teleological structure of *Totality and Infinity.* This fecundity attests to the desire for the particularity of the other that goes further than the will to knowledge, which abstracts from the singular, goes beyond the quest for authenticity, which forecloses the significance of a future belonging to someone else, and rises above the anonymous values of the State. As Levinas says, "To act without entering the Promised Land . . . to renounce being the contemporary of the triumph of one's work is to envisage this triumph in a *time without me,* to aim at this world without me, to aim at a time beyond the horizon of my time, in an eschatology without hope for oneself, or in a liberation from my time."[55]

With the interpretation of fecundity as the eschatological desire for the "pluralism of society," ethics is rendered as the secular embodiment of the image of God. Time itself unfolds according to the purpose of creation, which ethical life imitates. Creation calls one to welcome and give voice to what sounds from beyond one's horizon by respecting the incommensurability of the other and by fruitfully multiplying distinct voices.[56] The image of God—expressed in the prohibition of murder and the fecundity of ethical desire—is a trope for the orientation of historical life toward a "new interlocutor" who transcends the present and all its possibilities

(TI, 291/TeI, 267).[57] The eschatological movement of Levinas's creation narrative reaches its denouement with an extraordinary interpretation of resurrection of the body.

> The death sentence does not approach as an end of being, but as an unknown, which as such suspends power. Resurrection constitutes the principle event of time. There is therefore no continuity in being. Time is discontinuous; one instant does not come out of another without interruption, by an ecstasy. In continuation the instant meets its death, and resuscitates; death and resurrection constitute time. But such a formal structure presupposes the relation of the I with the Other and, at its basis, fecundity across the discontinuous which constitutes time. (TI, 284/TeI, 260)

Resurrection of the body, perhaps the most bizarre of all Judeo-Christian concepts and one that caused philosophically minded theologians such as Maimonides and Aquinas no small discomfort, has been secularized by Levinas as the fecundity of time. What is interesting about resurrection of the body is that it refuses to dissociate the ultimate purpose of creation from the horizon of embodied reality. Instead of separating the soul from the body, the idea of resurrection insists that the orientation of creation toward an ideal moral reality remains concerned with particular physical bodies, bodies that matter. Once again Levinas's phenomenological myth overcomes the distance that metaphysical theology has placed between us and the ancients. Ethics is life in the image of God. The moral self is a creator charged with the difficult freedom of producing a good world and keeping the evil of mere existing at bay. Creation is the continuous work of responding to particular voices and respecting their embodied visage. Its ultimate term is the concrete corporeality of others beyond my field of possibility, persons whom one reaches only by transcending oneself through the fecundity of ethical time.

Messianic Naturalism and the Transcendence of the World to Come

Levinas's emphasis on the bodily image of God marks a rejection of Maimonidean metaphysics. Nevertheless, the distance between their respective anthropologies is bridged by the fact that it was Maimonides who made possible Levinas's secularized eschatology. For it was Maimonides, before Levinas, who first naturalized Jewish messianism and at the same time oriented history toward the idea of the infinite. In Maimonides' view, "the messianic days" are entirely continuous with all other natural and historical phenomena. The messianic age has nothing of the supernatural to it and is marked by no miraculous transformations of nature. It portends no apocalyptic war and does not bring time to an end. As he says in the crucial and famous concluding chapters of the *Mishneh Torah*: "Do not think that King Messiah will have to perform signs and wonders, bring anything new into being, revive the dead, or do similar things. It is not so."[58] And shortly after: "Let no one think that in the days of the Messiah any of the laws of nature will be set aside, or any innovation be introduced into creation. The world will follow its normal course [*olam keminhagoh noheg*]."[59] Levinas endorses this "rationalist sobriety" that Maimonides introduced into Jewish messianism and would surely have relished Maimonides' poignant remark that what distinguishes the messianic age from the premessianic period is only that each person will "earn a comfortable living in a legitimate way."[60]

And yet Maimonides' naturalized messianic age merely paves the way for achieving the intellectual aspirations of metaphysical religion. The accomplishment of a messianic age is the material precondition for establishing a civil society in which knowledge can be pursued and attained on a mass scale. His messianic naturalism thus serves a view of Judaism as an enlightenment project in which "the earth shall be full of the *knowledge* of the Lord, as the waters cover the sea."[61] Maimonides therefore makes a fundamental distinction between messianic naturalism, which he calls the messianic age (*yemei hámashiach*), and eschatological intellectualism, which he calls the world to come (*olam ha'bah*). The former transpires on the historical plane and in accordance with all the laws of nature, whereas the latter is a vertical axis intersecting natural history only in the minds of men. It is the latter, of course, that Levinas rejects, for in his view the attainment of metaphysical knowledge "certainly does not absorb all that waiting for the Messiah means for Jewish sensibility."[62] But although Levinas absolutely rejects Maimonides' view of the world to come as a state of knowing, his messianic idea still sounds like an ethical reworking of Maimonides' position.[63] Like Maimonides, Levinas sees the linear narrative of political history as curved by transcendence, now figured as the ethical claims of the other that intervene like a vertical axis on the conscience of historical agents. Levinas's view of history therefore correlates with Maimonides'; they both regard history as the site of unceasing and irredeemable strife interrupted only by invisible traces of a world to come. This eschatological world is always still to come—for Maimonides because there is an infinity of knowledge that can never be realized *in actu* by a human mind and for Levinas because infinity is ethically presented in faces still to come. As Levinas says, "Of peace there can be only an eschatology" (TI, 24/TeI, xii). What *Totality and Infinity* calls an "eschatology of messianic peace" is an ethical alternative to Maimonides' "eschatology of truth," in which society is wholly oriented to "bringing about the happiness of contemplation" (TI, 22/TeI, x). But this alternative is indebted to Maimonides for its central conviction that the world to come bears on life vertically, *within* historical experience, and that this interruption of transcendence marks the very duration of time.

This explains Levinas's faltering attitude toward Maimonides. Although he rejects Maimonides' view that the ultimate purpose of creation is to perfect the intellect, his account of ethics is indebted to Maimonides for many of its salient features, including the argument that everyday ethical life is constituted by an escape from mere being and regard for the moral particularity of the other. Levinas weaves these Maimonidean views into an account of ethics in the image of God even as he distances himself from Maimonides' dualist anthropology by taking the prohibition on murder at face value and corporeally interpreting the fecundity of time. Indeed, the idea of transcendence as a trace of the world to come within historical time is quintessentially Maimonidean.

Totality and Infinity is a midrash comprised of philosophical interpretations of biblical, rabbinic, and Maimonidean threads. Ethics secularizes the process of creation from chaos and imitates life in the image of God, whether or not he exists.

From Moral Creators to Ethical Creatures: Levinas's *Kehre*

> Cloud and darkness surround Him,
> Righteousness and justice are the foundations of His throne.
> —Psalms 97:2

> Enough of those glorious imitations of a creator!
> —Levinas, *Proper Names*

The Deformation of Ethics and the Defacement of the Other

Levinas's work undergoes a dramatic movement in his later period that can be emblematically marked by the epigraphs to this interlude. Whereas *Totality and Infinity* provides a foundational account of righteousness and justice, in *Otherwise than Being* ethics is enveloped in clouds and darkness. Everyone who has read Levinas will have noted the transformation that besets his vocabulary as it evolves from one magnum opus to the next. Consider the following examples. Whereas in *Totality and Infinity* ethics was thought of as "desire," in *Otherwise than Being* it is figured as "persecution." Whereas the earlier work describes ethics as oriented toward a "messianic" future and "an eschatology of peace," the later work situates ethics in an "immemorial past" that is "testimony" to a "trauma." Whereas "paternity" was once the metaphor for establishing an ethical relation with a particular person still to come, "maternity" now figures as a metaphor for how the self bears the other inside itself. This palpable shift—or *Kehre*—dates from the years immediately following the publication of *Totality and Infinity*.[1] Sometimes it makes ethics seem grotesque—ethics is now an "obsession," a "persecution," the condition of a "hostage." At other times it enables ethics to speak in the very name of love. This unity of love and trauma that marks Levinas's later work owes itself to a new account of ethics as bondage and infatuation, as the sickness of love that *Otherwise than Being*, like many mystical texts in the Judeo-Christian tradition, procures from the Song of Songs (OB, 198/AE, 181). The mutation is significant enough to warrant us talking of Levinas 1 and Levinas 2, a terminological distinction I will employ for the remainder of this book.[2] If each Levinas presents "a picture" of ethics, to use a Wittgensteinianism, then each picture is strikingly different; indeed, from the perspective of the other, each appears fundamentally distorted.

The distance between Levinas 1 and Levinas 2 can be measured by observing that in *Totality and Infinity* the self enjoys an ontological independence that enables it to exercise free will by responding to the other and thereby transcend its natural solipsism. In *Otherwise than Being*, however, the self is constituted in its deepest recesses entirely by virtue of the other. *Totality and Infinity* is subtitled *An Essay on Exteriority*, but *Otherwise than Being* is a meditation on the other *within*, often called "the other *in* the same." Accordingly, whereas *Totality and Infinity* conceives of ethics as an encounter with the "presence of the face," an other who is "separate," in *Otherwise than Being* it is a matter of "the non-phenomenality of the face" that is "never present" because it precedes and, indeed, constitutes self-identity. This transformation of ethics is clearly marked by the difference between the ethical subject who *hosts* the Other, "the subject is a host" (TI, 299/TeI, 276), and the one who is *hostage* to the other, "a subject is a hostage" (OB, 112/AE, 143). For Levinas 2, ethics is no longer a matter of an encounter with vulnerable strangers but of obligations that run counter to one's very sense of oneself as an individual. There is no longer any possibility of being "at home with oneself," of a "self-referential" "egoism" that is "independent" and "free" and therefore "welcomes" the Other, as *Totality and Infinity* consistently maintained.[3] On the contrary, Levinas 2 critiques

Levinas 1, for there never was a time when the self was ontologically or phenomenologically independent: "To take hold of oneself for a present of welcome is already to take one's distance, and miss the neighbor" (OB, 88/ AE, 110). Hence the disturbing ethical language of "persecution" and "traumatization," of subjectivity rent by the other before it has come into its "ownmost" self. *Otherwise than Being* seeks to establish that there is no self without ethical bondage: "I am 'in myself' through the others" (OB, 112/ AE, 143) and "I exist through the other and for the other, . . . having-the-other-in-one's-skin" (OB, 114/AE, 145).

Perhaps the most significant effect of the deformation of ethics in Levinas's later work is the defacement of the Other. For Levinas 1, the other was a figure of vulnerability, exemplified by "the widow, the orphan," and, above all, "the stranger," who are all asymmetrically related to the "imperial" "egoist" self. The crucial point here is the causal relation. It is *because* of the phenomenological asymmetry between the self and the other that ethics makes its claim: *because* the other is destitute I am obligated (TI, 215/TeI, 190). Levinas 1 still *derives* ethical obligations from phenomenological experience, as if obligation could be read off the face of the other. In contrast, Levinas 2 abandons the attempt to base ethics on a descriptive account of the character of the other.[4] In *Otherwise than Being* it is no longer a matter of an ethical response to those one regards as good, poor, deserving, or needy. Ethics is now radicalized in the form of obligations that do not depend on sympathy, intuition, or even the appearance of the other. Indeed, for Levinas 2 ethical obligation is no longer derived from moral experience at all. As he remarkably puts it: "The ethical language we have resorted to does not arise out of a special moral experience, independent of the description hitherto elaborated. The ethical situation of responsibility is not comprehensible on the basis of ethics. . . . The tropes of ethical language are found to be adequate for certain structures of the description: for the sense of the approach in its contrast with knowing, the face in contrast with a phenomenon" (OB, 120/AE, 154–55). For later Levinas, obligation does not derive from an experience of the face of the other and is not a function of the moral character of the other. Rather, obligation imposes itself "prior to consciousness, an implication, a being caught up in fraternity" (OB, 82–83/AE, 104), or simply on account of "proximity." *Why* does mere fraternity or proximity suffice to oblige me? No answer can be given that appeals to a reason outside the relationship, for Levinas's point is that I am myself only by virtue of the other. It is not the character of the other but our inextricable codependence that obliges me, since each one "is" only in relation to others. To fail ethically is to fail oneself. But ethics no longer describes an experience. It indicates a structure of obligation, dependence, and implication that cannot be abrogated. It no longer matters if the other is a widow or an orphan, for now the point is that one is already caught up ethically, indebted and obliged, regardless of how the other appears. Accordingly, "the Other" is disfigured, indeed, defaced. Whereas formerly ethics was generated by the desire for the Other, now it hinges on obligations arising from the *undesirability* of the other, who gnaws at me despite my disinclinations. As Levinas 2 says, "In a sense nothing is more burdensome than a neighbor. Is not this desired one the undesirable itself? The neighbor who could not leave me indifferent, the undesirable desired one, has *not revealed* to desire the ways of access to him" (OB, 88/AE, 110). Whereas *Totality and Infinity* regards the *stranger* as the ultimate term of the ethical desire to create a hospitable world, *Otherwise than Being* views the other as an intrusive *neighbor* who has lodged himself inside one's own sphere of selfhood.[5] Ethics is no longer an epiphany of the vulnerability on the face of a stranger but the intrusion of an unwanted neighbor, one who won't go away, who keeps you up at night, who disrupts your peaceful domicile. Note that in the preceding citation Levinas signals that revelation, previously figured as the manifestation or expression of the face, is no longer an adequate category for thinking ethics, since ethics signifies without appearing. It follows that the theological hermeneutic appropriate for understanding Levinas's later thought must be modified in at least two fundamental ways. First, ethics can no longer avail itself of the tropes of metaphysical theology such as we described them in Chapter 3, for it is no longer based on a free and independent moral creator responding to the particularity of the other. The theological hermeneutic Levinas employs in his later work eschews the metaphysical tradition that regards transcendence as exteriority, separation, freedom, and independence. Levinas 2 thus develops a non-metaphysical secularized theology. Second, ethics no longer appears through the positivity of revelation expressed in the face/presence of the Other but through the negativity of the absence or trace of an encounter with the thing of ethics itself. Levinas thus turns from positive theology to negative theology. Whereas *Totality and Infinity* secularized the tropes of positive, metaphysical theology, *Otherwise than Being* is a work of secular, post-metaphysical, negative theology.

Transcendence Without Metaphysics

Levinas 2 repudiates metaphysics, whereas Levinas 1 advocated for it in two principal ways. First, metaphysics designated the separate, transcendent, independent, exalted presence of the Other, "beyond being" and "invisible" but nevertheless given positively, even positivistically, through a pure voice that issues an intrinsic, immediate moral commandment. Second, *Totality and Infinity* assumes the metaphysical notion of a moral subject free to exercise its ethical desire for the other. According to both the subject of desire (the moral ego) and the object of desire (the Other), *Totality and Infinity* is a work of secularized metaphysical theology. Now, this position is vulnerable to the critique of metaphysics underway from Hegel and Nietzsche to Heidegger, as Jacques Derrida brilliantly demonstrated in "Violence and Metaphysics." Levinas 2 acknowledges this and for that reason redoubles his effort to provide a post-Heideggerian account of ethics. Ethics is not expressed in the givenness of the moral presence of the face to a free will belonging to a separate subject but is always concealed and revealed within the structures of implication that bind us to another and thereby sustain the sense of the world. Unlike Levinas 1, Levinas 2 thinks it impossible to "escape" from being to get a clear moral point of view that transcends the plane of history and the evil of mere being. Ethics is refigured as the "exposure" to the other in the very inwardness and passivity of the self. Ethics now takes place not in relation to a separate other but in the interstices of "senescence" and "sensibility," "before the intervention of a cause, before the appearance of the other," as a "gestation of the other in the same," and even "writhing in the tight dimensions of pain" (OB, 75/AE, 95). The severe and relentless quality of *Otherwise than Being* results from this new sense of ethics as the bondage of self and other. The moral subject prized by *Totality and Infinity* is no longer enjoined to relate the freedom of its will to the other, regarded as separate and transcendent, but to awaken to the priority of debts and obligations that precede and even constitute its own self-identity. The subject is always already subjected. For

Levinas 2, ethics does not bridge the separation between self and other but traces the ethical fibers, indeed, the moral knot, at the innermost recesses of self-understanding and self-identity. As Levinas puts it in one of his more moderate formulations:

Responsibility for another is not an accident that happens to a subject, but precedes essence in it, has not awaited freedom, in which a commitment to another would have been made. I have not done anything and I have already been accused—persecuted. . . . Responsibility in obsession is a responsibility of the ego for what the ego has not wished, that is, for the others. . . . I exist through the other and for the other, but without this being alienation: I am inspired. This inspiration is the psyche. The psyche can signify this alterity in the same without alienation in the form of incarnation, as being-in-one's-skin, having-the-other-in-one's-skin. (OB, 114–15/AE, 146)

The self is now exposed from the outset and thus responsible in the very passivity of its being, like the maternal body. This leads Levinas to describe ethics with new metaphors. Ethical subjectivity is a "trauma" and a "wound," a "persecuting obsession" and a "hostage." What happened to "metaphysics"? It is consigned to the tradition of methodological egoism and therefore abandoned: "Far from marking a point of departure, the intentional subject refers to the unity of transcendental apperception itself issued from a whole metaphysical tradition" (OB, 82/AE, 103). What of the "separation" between the self and the other that dominated the analyses of *Totality and Infinity*? It has become "the trace of *separation* in the form of inwardness, and of the one-for-the-other in the form of responsibility" (OB, 79/AE, 100). Even "the face" has made way for the "trace" of the other that is no longer present to experience but signifies through an "immemorial past" of exposure prior to identity. Examples could be multiplied: from transcendence to incarnation, from agency to passivity, from separation to implication, from the father to the mother, from the future to the past, and, crucially, from the stranger to the neighbor and from the moral creator to the ethical creature. Unlike the moral subject, the ethical creature is exposed to the other prior to its own self-identification. The other lives "in me and in the midst of my very identification" (OB, 125/AE, 160), before the subject can assume its moral commitments and accomplish a moral world, in short, before creation. This passivity of responsibility renders the ethical self a creature rather than a creator. As Levinas says, "the oneself is a creature, but an orphan by birth or an atheist no doubt ignorant of its Creator, for it knew it would again be taking up its commencement" (OB, 105/AE, 133). The metaphysics of creation is now regarded as a fantasy of power, separation, and autonomy. To become an ethical creature is to dispel oneself of the fantasy of being a moral creator responsible for one's free acts. The metaphysics of creation—ex nihilo and ex hylus—is thus cast aside.

We have been accustomed to reason in the name of the freedom of the ego—as though I had witnessed the creation of the world, and as though I could only have been in charge of a world that would have issued out of my free will. These are presumptions of philosophers, presumptions of idealists! Or evasions of irresponsible ones. That is what Scripture reproaches Job for. He would have known how to explain his miseries if they could have devolved from his faults! But he never wished evil! His false friends think like he does: in a meaningful world one cannot be held to answer when one has not done anything. Job then must have forgotten his faults! (OB, 122/AE, 156)

The transcendental moral subject of *Totality and Infinity*, with its ex nihilo powers, values, and freedoms, is now derided as both a phenomenological fallacy and an evasion of responsibility. Like Job at the onset of his affliction, the moral subject longs for a correlation between agency and culpability, which Levinas now dismisses as an evasion of the passivity of responsibility characteristic of idealism and liberalism. In the end, Levinas 2, like Job after the tempest, "recants and relents, being but dust and ashes" (Job 42:6). Ethics is no longer in the image of God. It no longer presumes the freedom of a separate subject to desire goodness so as to create a moral world. Can the idea of creation, rooted in the transcendence of the will, still be affirmed? Levinas is no longer sure: "In the concept of creation *ex nihilo*, if it is not a pure nonsense, there is the concept of a passivity that does not revert into an assumption. The self as a creature is conceived in a passivity more passive still than the passivity of matter, that is, prior to the virtual coinciding of a term with itself. The oneself has to be conceived outside of all substantial coinciding of self with self" (OB, 113–14/AE, 145).

Levinas 2 thus completely revises the notion of creation. Where there was a moral creator charged with producing a good world in the face of the evil of mere existing—ethics in the image of God—there is now the ethical creature, captivated and entwined and having no choice in the matter of ethics. Creation is no longer the work of a separate, independent, and free subject who is able to "enter" into a moral covenant of creation. Rather, Levinas now says, "this freedom enveloped in a responsibility which it does not succeed in shouldering is the way of being a creature, the unlimited passivity of a self, the unconditionality of a self" (OB, 195n13/AE, 140n13). Ethics is no longer the creative desire for the good but the deposition of the will, a passive exposure to the undesirable other whose authoritative sense can be neither disburdened nor discharged. *Otherwise than Being* thus concludes with a meditation on the breath, that most creaturely activity, operating below and before the great philosophical hope for a subject able to create a moral world. In place of the moral creator, we have the inspired creature, for "in breathing I already open myself to my subjection to the whole of the invisible other" (OB, 181/AE, 228). With no interiority of its own, "the subject could be a lung at the bottom of its substance . . . a subjectivity that suffers and offers itself before taking a foothold in being" (OB, 180/AE, 227). Accordingly, it is no longer a matter of the transcendence of the other, for "to free oneself by breathing from closure in oneself already presupposes this beyond" (OB, 180/AE, 227). The biosociality of the self consists in the incorporation of the other into the immanence of the flesh, like a lung: "An openness of the self to the other, which is not a conditioning or a foundation of oneself in some principle . . . *breathing is transcendence in the form of opening up*" (OB, 180/AE, 227; my emphasis).

This turn in Levinas's itinerary thus involves a fundamental modification of the notion of "transcendence" that was so important to his earlier account of ethics. Levinas 1 sought to *reverse* Heidegger's breakthrough from the subject to Dasein by reasserting the integrity of the subject as an independent moral agent. In 1947 he claimed to "repudiate the Heideggerian conception that views solitude in the midst of a prior relationship with the other."[6] But in 1974 his point was to account for one's exposure to the other *before* the dawn of one's own "personal identity," and thus precisely to account for the self "in the midst of a prior relationship with the other." Accordingly, if the "transcendence of the other" first designated a metaphysical height of separation, it is now an exposure to the anteriority of the claim of the other, a claim heard before one properly becomes oneself. For Levinas 2, then, transcendence designates the immemorial exposure of the self to the other, before and within its "self": "transcendence in the form of opening up." Notably, this corresponds with early Heidegger's usage of the term "transcendence."

Transcendere means to step over; the transcendens, the transcendent, is *that which oversteps as such* and not that toward which I step over. . . . The Dasein itself oversteps in its being and thus is exactly *not the immanent* . . . it is a being which in its being is out *beyond* itself. The epekeina belongs to the Dasein's own most peculiar structure of being. . . . Transcendence is even the presupposition for the Dasein's having the character of a self. The *selfhood* of the Dasein *is founded on its transcendence,* and the Dasein is not first an ego-self which then oversteps something or other. . . . The Dasein does not exist at first in some mysterious way so as then to accomplish the step beyond itself to others or to the extant things. Existence, instead, always already means to step beyond or, better, having stepped beyond.[7]

Otherwise than Being is therefore closer to early Heidegger than was *Totality and Infinity.* Levinas 2 regards ethics as the very attestation of a critique of transcendental subjectivism, and it was in *Being and Time* that the foundations of transcendental subjectivism were first overturned. I return later to the complex question of Levinas's relation to Heidegger. For now, it will suffice to note that there is even greater proximity between later Levinas and early Heidegger than there is between Levinas 1 and early Heidegger. In *Otherwise than Being,* the primary target is the tradition of transcendental and methodological solipsism, from Descartes to Husserl, and this critique is Heideggerian in inspiration. We will return to the proximity between later Levinas and early Heidegger after I explore the Judaic elements of Levinas's later philosophy.

But for the moment my concern is to locate Levinas's *Kehre* within a philosophy of Judaism. Having abandoned the central ideas of ethics in the image of God, Levinas wonders if he has arrived at "animality" rather than ethics (OB, 181/AE, 228). This he denies by proposing that "human breathing" extends the biological function to "absolute expiration, in the kiss of God," in which the ethical creature bears witness to "the inspiration by the other, an inspiration that is already expiration, that 'rends the soul!'" (OB, 181–82/AE, 229). A note to this remark references a "parable" of "the sages of Israel" describing how Moses died "on the mouth of God" (Deut. 34:5; 'al pi YHWH, interpreted hyperliterally rather than in the idiomatic sense of "according to the word of God").[8] Behind Levinas's new ethical language of the inspiration of the other—"the longest breath there

is, spirit" (OB, 182/AE, 229)—we hear echoes of mystical and martyrological exegetical traditions in which inspiration of the One becomes the soul's
expiration and self-abandonment. The bearing of these traditions on the
argument of *Otherwise than Being* far exceeds the paucity of direct citation,
since the majority of the book's analyses are devoted to critiques of various
philosophical positions (idealism, transcendental subjectivism, and epistemological foundationalism, among others). Indeed, the claim of Levinas 2 is that *ethics cannot be said* and therefore requires an unconcealment
glimpsed by way of critique. The "third way" of ethics is not so much the
positing of another philosophical position as the attestation of a critique
of philosophical method. Such an attestation can in principle be glimpsed
only in a "saying" that is never equal to what is "said." Apophatic traditions such as those of mystical and martyrological testimonies are thus *exemplary* precedents for the unconcealment of ethics within philosophical
discourse, indeed, more exemplary than the traditions of Western moral
philosophy that themselves, according to Levinas, betray the saying of ethics by making it said.[9]

To be sure, this deformation of ethics and this defacement of the
other serve the same purpose as Levinas's earlier work, namely, to show
that ethics provides the ultimate sense to everyday philosophical and religious life. The goal of *Totality and Infinity*—"to know whether we are not
duped by morality" (TI, 21/TeI, ix)—is precisely the same as that of *Otherwise than Being*, which concludes by declaring that ethics "is not a barter
of the duped" (OB, 184/AE, 232). Despite the seismic shift in his thinking,
the goal is the same. Throughout, Levinas is working midrashically by distorting the theologically given so as to preserve its normative force. With
this midrashic horizon in view, one can see that the movement from *Totality and Infinity* to *Otherwise than Being* corresponds to the passage from
Judaic metaphysics to a Judaic theology without metaphysics, or from positive Jewish theology to a Jewish *via eminentia*.

Otherwise than Being as Secular Apophasis

It is an arduous climb through a difficult work, its author admitting
to a certain "breathlessness" that he was trying to account for. *Otherwise
than Being* seeks to accomplish a presentation of the ethics of selfhood, but

it develops in a paradoxical manner that prevents us from assigning the ethical witness with substantive selfhood of its own. The ethical self is but a witness to the other; it comes to itself only after the other has "appeared," although one can no longer speak strictly of an appearing or manifestation, for the witness itself is only borne of the appearance and therefore cannot be said to "be there" before the call of the other. The ethical creature testifies itself in response to the other. It does not testify to itself but testifies itself as the one who responds. Levinas is explicit about this: "I find the order in my response itself, which, as a sign given to the neighbor, as a 'here I am,' brings me out of invisibility, out of the shadow in which my responsibility could have been evaded. This saying belongs to the very glory of which it bears witness" (OB, 150/AE, 191). What Levinas now calls "ethics" no longer refers to the phenomenological situation of experiencing the moral presence of the other but designates the impossibility of avoiding the originary exposure to the Other. As he says, "the order has not been the cause of my response, not even in a question that would have preceded it in a dialogue" (OB, 150/AE, 191). Eric Santner reaches a similar position from a quite different trajectory: "'Creature' is not so much the name of a determinate state of being as the signifier of an ongoing *exposure*, of being caught up in the process of *becoming creature* through the dictates of divine alterity."[10] Levinas's new "ethical language" strives to account for the anteriority of obligation over identity and thus of obligations accrued without experience, without fault or choice, in the very passage or the awakening of the self to itself. One is beholden to the other before one beholds her particular attributes.

The central idea is that of "illeity," the third person *singular* whose anteriority and absence enjoin me to respond without presenting or revealing itself. Illeity designates the necessarily absent other, absent not because he happens not to be present when he could be or because he is abstract and is therefore known without presenting himself. Rather, illeity is the absence implied by the uniqueness of the other, since uniqueness transcends knowledge and negation. Ethics is the response one makes to this impossibility of experiencing the uniqueness of the other, an impossibility that can no more be ignored than comprehended. This negative phenomenology is explicitly indebted to Neoplatonic traditions of the One beyond conceptualization, a tradition that admittedly cuts across pagan and

Abrahamic theology and that Levinas knew primarily through the work of Plotinus and the Jewish Neoplatonic tradition.

In "The Trace of the Other," a decisive essay written in 1963 that constitutes the turning point from *Totality and Infinity* to *Otherwise than Being*, he referred to the first deduction of Plato's *Parmenides* (137e–142a) and its elaboration by Plotinus (*Enneads* 5:5) in order to develop a phenomenology of the other that can be encountered only as the trace of uniqueness.[11] Characteristically, Levinas secularizes this negative theology or, rather, anthropologizes it: "Can the question of the divinity of the One God be put as the question of the humanity of man is put?" (OB, 193n36/ AE, 124n36). This is the question that *Otherwise than Being* explores at every turn of the *via eminentia* it charts "beyond being." The Neoplatonic distinction between the One beyond being and being one becomes, for Levinas, the difference between ethics as such and all that is said about it. Moses de Leon, the principal author of the *Zohar*, the central text of the Kabbalah, already indicated the possibility of an anthropological application of negative theology, as did Meister Eckhart at a similar time.

Arouse yourself to contemplate, to focus thought, for God is the annihilation of all thoughts, uncontainable by any concept. Indeed, since no one can contain God at all, it is called Nothingness, *Ayin*. This is the secret of the verse, "Wisdom comes into being out of nothingness" (Job 28:12). Anything sealed and concealed, totally unknown to anyone, is called *ayin*, meaning that no one knows anything about it. Similarly, no one knows anything at all about the human soul; she stands in the status of nothingness, *ayin*, as it is written: "The superiority of the human over the beast is *ayin* [nothing]" (Eccles. 3:19). By means of this soul, the human being ascends higher than all other creatures and attains the glory of *Ayin*, nothingness.[12]

By means of an ingenious hyperliteral exegesis, humanity is distinguished from the beasts by *ayin*, that is, literally, by nothing. Because of the human capacity to abandon itself, to abnegate identity by the excess of negation it bears in its soul, it distinguishes itself from the beasts. Whereas Ecclesiastes plainly says that there is "nothing" that makes humans superior to beasts, the mystical Neoplatonist says that this nothing, this immanent surplus of negation that makes humans other to themselves and to one another, constitutes our distinct creatureliness. Levinas's later work is a sustained exercise—a spiritual exercise, as Pierre Hadot called this sort of philosophical work—in apophatic anthropology. In Chapter 4, I explain why Levinas regards this exposure of creatureliness as a distinctly *ethical* event, although Santner's account of it in political terms is equally apt: "Human beings are not just creatures among other creatures but are in some sense *more creaturely* than other creatures by virtue of an excess that is produced in the space of the political and that, paradoxically, accounts for their 'humanity.'"[13]

Levinas was not reading de Leon's *Shekel Hakodesh*. We know, however, that he was a keen admirer of *Keter Malkhut*, the much-acclaimed Neoplatonic poem often read as part of the liturgy of the Jewish New Year.[14] The poem was composed by Solomon Ibn Gabirol, the famous eleventh-century poet from Saragossa who also authored the *Fons Vitae*, a Neoplatonic work widely studied by medieval Christian thinkers. Although it deploys an acutely intertextual idiom of biblical and rabbinic Hebrew, *Keter Malkhut* conveys a Neoplatonic sense of divinity that seeks to transcend historical and even religious particularism. The poem is therefore an important precedent for Levinas's own Neoplatonic "Hebrew humanism." In it the poet addresses himself to the indescribable "One":

You are one, but not one that can be grasped or counted,
for with You there is no variety and no variation,
neither description nor nomination.

You are one, yet reason fails to limit or delimit You,
therefore I will guard my way
lest my words lead me astray.[15]

Nothing can be properly thought or said about the One, so the poet speaks *to*. Poetry is language as pure address and response, language negating its own predicative substance, a Saying without a Said. One thinks of the poetry of Paul Celan and his now-famous address, "The Meridian," in which poetry is said to take "creaturely paths" toward an "encounter" between "this 'wholly Other' and an 'other' which is not far removed, which is very near."[16] And of Celan's words, cited by Levinas: "I cannot see any basic difference between a handshake and a poem." As Levinas comments: "A singular de-substantiation of the *I*! To make oneself completely into a sign, perhaps that is it. Enough of those glorious imitations of a creator!"[17]

Levinas was probably also familiar with Bahya Ibn Pakuda's *Hovot Halevavot, Duties of the Heart*, a popular work that introduced the notion of the trace into the Jewish apophatic tradition in the eleventh century.

You should exert your soul and oblige it to become acquainted with the true nature of our Creator from the point of view of his traces, not from the point of view of his essence. For he is as close as can be from the point of view of his traces and as distant as can be from the point of view of imagining or conceptualizing his essence and form, for he has absolutely no existence in our intuitive mind from these perspectives, according to what we have explained. So if you arrive at excluding him from your intuitive mind and senses as if he has no existence, and find him from the point of view of his traces, as if he is inseparable from you, that is the furthest reach of knowledge that the prophet encouraged in you, saying, "you shall know today and place on your heart that the Lord is God (in the heaven above and in the earth beneath)" (Deut. 4:39).[18]

Ibn Pakuda's account of creation as the trace of the One beyond being clearly echoes the passage from *Enneads* 5:5 that Levinas cited in "The Trace of the Other." But Levinas did not cite de Leon or Ibn Gabirol or Ibn Pakuda. He referred to Exodus 33 to illustrate the Neoplatonic notion of revelation approached through a trace. Here, Moses, seeking to behold the glory of God, is given to see only the ways, or traces, of transcendence. This seminal text has received numerous significant interpretations, though none more famous than Maimonides' in *Guide of the Perplexed*. Moreover, Maimonides' interpretation of Exodus 33 belongs precisely to a sequence of chapters devoted to the negation and transcendence of positive theology, including the very metaphysical theology to which he was otherwise committed. Thus, although Levinas's language of the trace undoubtedly resonates with various Neoplatonic elements of Jewish mysticism and Kabbalah, as several scholars have observed, it is Maimonidean negative theology that provides the most obvious point of departure for an analysis of his Jewish negative theology. It is therefore to a very different Maimonides—a Maimonides without the metaphysics of creation—that we now turn to explore the *via eminentia* of the ethical creature of *Otherwise than Being*.

Ethical Negative Theology

> Can the question of the divinity of the One God be put as the question of the humanity of man is put?
> —Emmanuel Levinas, *Otherwise than Being, or Beyond Essence*

Maimonides Without Metaphysics

Levinas had good reason to be wary of the metaphysical intellectualism of Maimonides, for whom proximity to God was tantamount to "drawing near through apprehension" (*Guide* I.18, 44). Yet in 1935 he had already acknowledged that there was a different way of approaching Maimonides' text. His Kantian interpretation of Maimonides' preference for creation over eternity resurfaced throughout his phenomenological rendering of ethics in the image of God, Levinas repeatedly asserted the proposition that Maimonides "glimpsed what one calls, six centuries later, the critique of pure reason" even as he repudiated the master's metaphysical intellectualism.[1] For example: "We know since Maimonides that all that is said of God in Judaism *signifies* through human *praxis*."[2] Although on this occasion he did not elaborate, Levinas is clearly pointing to the practical implications of Maimonidean negative theology. Fifty years after his first reflections on Maimonides, he finally notes how his ethical project rejoins Maimonides at precisely the point at which negative theology gives way to moral life:

In Maimonides himself, to whom rational knowledge of God, metaphysical knowledge, is the supreme good of the human person (and, precisely, an inalienable good, exalting the self in its own happiness, a good that "profits yourself alone" [*Guide* III.54]), everything culminates in the formulation of the negative attributes. But the possibility of this knowledge is maintained as the ethical behavior of good-will (*hesed*), judgment (*mishpat*) and fairness (*tsedeqah*), as "for the other." The imitation of God! The love of one's neighbor is at the summit of a life devoted to supreme knowledge. This is a remarkable reversal, unless we are to question the sincerity of this teacher, suggesting that he may have spoken otherwise than he thought, to avoid unsettling pious minds.[3]

If Levinas was critical of Maimonidean metaphysics, here he suggests that Maimonides' radical version of the *via negativa* might provide a critique of metaphysical knowledge and thereby open a passage from intellectualism to ethics. And, of course, the idea that a critique of intellectualism and epistemology might lead philosophy back to the primacy and ultimacy of ethics was precisely the task Levinas set for himself with respect to the history of Western philosophy. The possibility of reading Maimonides without metaphysics, which Levinas here acknowledges, thus converges with his own lifelong project of critiquing philosophical intellectualism in the name of ethics. This is not to say that Levinas's account of ethics as critique is derived from Maimonides. On the contrary, for most of Levinas's career the Great Eagle marked but the edge of one of his many circles. The frequency of Levinas's explicit engagement with Maimonides, however, is less important than their striking agreement, at least on a certain interpretation of Maimonides, on the decisive passage from metaphysics to praxis via the negation of positive (theological) attributes.

Such an interpretation was advanced by Shlomo Pines, the eminent French-Israeli scholar who translated the *Guide* into English. Pines's influential interpretations of the *Guide* amount to a reading of Maimonides as eschewing *all* metaphysical knowledge and therefore as regarding theology as an essentially practical, in fact political, discourse geared to imitating the actions by which God "governs" the world without making any claim to knowing God. Writing in 1979, Pines argued that because of Maimonides' view of the limits of the human intellect there could be no way, within this philosophy of religion, to cross from the radical negative theology developed in the *Guide* to positive metaphysical knowledge. Pines argued this despite the fact that Maimonides constantly states that the purpose of religious life is the attainment of true knowledge of God. But this view, the human intellect does not, for Maimonides, draw near to God through apprehension but only to traces of God as manifest in natural events. The only relation that obtains between human beings and God is that of *imitation* of God's *actions*, not apprehension of or union with God's essence. *Imitatio dei* applies our knowledge of God's governing actions of the world to the sphere of political governance while forgoing every claim to knowledge of God's true essence. Maimonides' resort to *imitatio dei* thus highlights the gap between human knowledge and divine reality and, at the same time, reframes the ultimate purpose of the quest for transcendence in terms of political life. In Pines's words:

The only positive knowledge of God of which man is capable is knowledge of the attributes of action, and this leads and ought to lead to a sort of political activity which is the highest perfection of man. The practical way of life, the *bios praktikos*, is superior to the theoretical. . . . If, to use the Platonic image, man, because of the nature of his cognitive faculty, is unable, or able only to a limited extent, to leave the cave, as Maimonides . . . appears to hold, the superiority of the theoretical life may appear as less than evident. Both Kant and Maimonides, the first outspokenly and the second partly by implication, have tried to show that because of the limitations of his mind man is incapable of intellecting some of the main objects of the traditional metaphysics. There may be a correlation between this fact and the tendency of both philosophers and also of al-Farabi to accord primacy to the life of action.[4]

Pines's interpretation hinges on the very last sentence of the *Guide*, in which "the perfection of man that may be glorified . . . after he has achieved this apprehension, will always have in view loving kindness, righteousness and judgment, through assimilation to His actions" (III.54, 638). Despite Maimonides' ubiquitous intellectualism, the ultimate purpose of Judaism, knowledge of God, leads back to the *bios praktikos*. This is precisely what Levinas referred to as the "remarkable reversal" at the end of the *Guide*.

To be sure, such an interpretation is not without difficulties. One cannot simply discount the contemplative ideal and the concrete possibility of attaining metaphysical knowledge from Maimonides' work, since these determine its most basic design.[5] We have seen that Levinas remains ambivalent toward Maimonidean intellectualism for just this reason.[6] Unlike Pines, however, Levinas never imagined himself as providing a resolution to the tension between metaphysical knowledge and practical life in Maimonides' corpus. On the contrary, he was seeking a *philosophical* interpretation of the history of philosophy rather than a critical-historical one. As he said in his 1935 essay on Maimonides, "The truly philosophical aspect of a philosophy measures itself by its contemporary relevance. The purest homage that can be given to it consists in blending it with current concerns."[7] What sort of current concerns? In the milieu of philosophical modernity, perplexity lies less in the contradictions between scripture and metaphysics, as it did for the medievals, than in metaphysics itself, in the contradiction between the finitude of modern wisdom and the claim to eternal knowledge. As a guide for today's perplexed, Levinas will therefore maintain, as Pines and more recent scholars have also argued, that Maimonidean intellectualism is subject to radical self-negation that leads beyond metaphysics. Like Pines, Levinas thinks that the Maimonidean passage beyond metaphysics leads to the *bios praktikos*, although for him that means ethical life rather than political leadership: "The knowledge of God which we can have and which is expressed, according to Maimonides, in the form of negative attributes, receives a positive meaning from the moral 'God is merciful,' which means: 'Be merciful like Him.' The attributes of God are not given in the indicative but in the imperative. The knowledge of God comes to us like a commandment, like a *Mitzvah*. To know God is to know what must be done."[8]

Even so, if philological concerns can be accommodated, within reason, by hermeneutical imperatives, the claim that negative theology leads to ethics nevertheless gives rise to its own conceptual and interpretative problems. For if one follows the path of Maimonidean negative theology and denies the possibility of metaphysical knowledge, how is it that one thereby approaches *ethics*? Indeed, alternative, compelling interpretations propose that Maimonides' negative theology leads not to ethics but to intellectual apprehension that cannot be verbally articulated but is nonetheless an authentic experience of God's presence,[9] or at least an elusive, fragmentary experience of the divine reality that "appears, flashes, and then is hidden again" (*Guide*, Introduction, 8).[10] Either way, the *via negativa* arrives at God and not, as I am suggesting, at ethics. Others maintain that Maimonides' negative theology leads to the construction of rational symbols pointing to the unfathomable perfection of God, and this view also subordinates ethics to the theosophy it recuperates at the symbolic level.[11] A fourth view denies that Maimonides' radical negative theology rescues knowledge from the errors of anthropomorphism and metaphysics, be it through the recovery of intuitive, fragmentary, or symbolic knowledge, and yet stops short of emphasizing the ethical implications of negative theology. In this account, Maimonides is fundamentally skeptical about all claims to knowledge of God; the purpose of the *via negativa* is not to attain non-metaphysical knowledge but simply to discipline the mind in order to perfect the rational nature of man as far as possible.[12] Given these alternative interpretations, are we entitled to assert that negative theology yields practical and indeed specifically ethical sense? If knowledge of God is impossible, as the radical reading of Maimonides and the standard reading of Levinas maintain, then does not the significance of God simply vanish? Can negative theology have a practical sense that distinguishes it from atheism? I want to suggest that Levinas and Maimonides provide a common set of answers to this question by providing three theses on the ethical significance of negative theology.[13]

Negative Theology Works in Practice but Not in Theory

Levinas provides us with an important answer to the difficult question of why negative theology leads to *ethics* rather than, say, to silence or skepticism. In his view transcendence lives up to its name only when refracted through ethics. As he puts it: "Transcendence owes it to itself to interrupt its own demonstration" (OB, 152/AE, 194). Transcendence *depends* on the insertion of ethics into religious life. Only through an ethical interruption of the desire for God can true transcendence be maintained. Ethics refracts transcendence through the prism of social life and thereby enables its infinite, ungraspable passage. Like Pines and others who adopt the view that Maimonides is ultimately skeptical about knowledge of God, Levinas finds this refractory logic in the "remarkable reversal" at the end of the *Guide* that suggests a way beyond the quietism of contemplative union with divine Intelligence. For where God is thought as Intellect, divine transcendence is necessarily homologous or at least analogous to the human intellect, as Maimonides generally maintains (e.g., *Guide* I.68, I.72, III.51). But elsewhere, and precisely as a result of the process of negative theology, the isomorphism between the metaphysical self and the metaphysical deity is decisively rejected by Maimonides (especially in *Guide* I.59, III.20). The otherness of God exceeds the apprehension of "God" by the intellect, just as the otherness of the Other is not revealed through knowledge or concepts. The negation of theosophy tells one nothing about God: "The attributes of negation do not give us knowledge in any respect whatever" but "conduct the mind toward the utmost reach that man may attain in the apprehension of Him" (*Guide* I.58, 135). Indeed, for Maimonides, unlike Thomas Aquinas, "the utmost reach" implies no partial or analogical knowledge of God's essence.[14] Negation is categorical, as when "we say of a wall that it is not endowed with sight" (I.58, 136). Knowledge of God is a category mistake, for the structure of knowledge—based on definitions, essential attributes, accidental attributes, predicates, and relations—fails when it comes to the absolutely simple, unique, and incomparable unity of God (I.50–52, 58).

Since knowledge of God's essence is impossible, Maimonides argues that the purpose of negative theology is to imitate God's *actions*: "For the utmost in virtue of man is to become like unto Him, may He be exalted, as far as he is able; which means that we should make our actions like unto His" (I.54, 128). These actions have a moral and political valence because of *our* experience and *our attribution* of moral predicates to natural events—the "grace" of the rain or the "wrath" of an earthquake—but tell us nothing about God. Maimonides thus shifts the goal of theology from apprehension to moral and political action. No longer does theology lead to knowledge of God but to the actions that express grace, justice, wrath, and so forth in accordance with the political exigencies of maintaining a harmonious and flourishing society. According to Maimonides, the *via negativa* leads from the impossibility of knowing God's essence to the attribution of moral predicates to natural events that supply a model for the practice of theology, and this practice is the ultimate way in which one "knows" God, a way that knowingly bears no relation to the essence and truth of God. The transcendence of YHWH is thus honored by turning away from the unknowable divine essence to the known *traces* of God attributed to natural events and expressed in political action. Only by turning away from God can negative theology preserve the transcendence proper to it.

Like the Maimonidean practice of imitating the attributes of action, the Levinasian practice of ethics requires the absolute negation of the knowledge of God—"to the point of absence."[15] In a lecture delivered in 1974 following the publication of *Otherwise than Being*, Levinas explained how the negation of knowledge of transcendence leads to moral practice, a point he had already discerned in the "remarkable reversal" at the end of the *Guide of the Perplexed*:

In order that disinterestedness be possible in desire, in order that the desire beyond being not be an absorption, the desirable (or God) must remain separated within desire: near, yet different—which is, moreover, the very meaning of the word "holy." This is possible only if the desirable commands me to what is undesirable, only if he commands me to the undesirable *par excellence*: to the *other person*. . . . Here we find the notion of a love without eros. . . . In this reversal and this referral of the desirable to the nondesirable, in this strange mission commanding the approach of the other person, God is torn out of the objectivity of presence and out of being. He is no longer an object or an interlocutor in a dialogue. His distancing or his transcendence turns into my responsibility: the nonerotic *par excellence*.[16]

To keep transcendence in play, theology must turn away from the object of its desire. Ethics interrupts the desire for God and thereby maintains transcendence. Transcendence is not given in any positive sense, not even in the immediate appearance of a face, but refers to an ethical trace we attribute to "Il," just as Maimonides argued that all we can know of God signifies through the ethical traces or moral effects of creation. Transcendence is never given, never positive, neither when the intellect actualizes itself in cognition (as Maimonidean metaphysics mantains) nor when the face is presented to intuition (as the metaphysics of Levinas 1 assumed), because transcendence has no essential properties or predicates that can be perceived or intuited as such. Alluding as much to Maimonides' famous interpretation as to the biblical text on which it is based, Levinas proposes his negative formulation: "He shows himself only by his trace, as is said in Exodus 33. . . . It is through this illeity . . . that being has a sense [*sens*]. A sense which is not a finality. For there is no end, no term."[17] For both Levinas and Maimonides there is an ineluctable passage, from the limits of knowledge to the practice of acknowledgment.

Transcendence is not given as a concept but as what Levinas called *sens*, an orientation rather than an apprehension of meaning.[18] Or as Maimonides said: "For this reason, we give the gist of the notion and give the mind the correct direction toward the true reality of the matter when we say one but not through oneness" (*Guide* I.57, 133). Negation, then, leads to transcendence as an orientation, a *sens* given in the absence of *significa-tion*, an indirection or detour of meaning that does not relate the subject of desire to its transcendent "object" but orients one toward transcendence by another way, by way of the other. By contrast, when transcendence is a concept that signifies directly to the subject, then what is apprehended is not God but merely the "God" of metaphysics, just as, for Levinas, one misses the other when one approaches her conceptually and descriptively. Holding fast to transcendence requires a critique of the very idea that the intellect is adequate to the term of ultimate desire. For Maimonides this implies that negative theology is a critique of theosophy and a rejection of the correlation between YHWH and the human intellect. For Levinas, the excess of transcendence means that the way of ethics involves a critique not only of epistemology but also of everything that is "said," even within the discourse of moral philosophy said, about the other. Ethical negative theology is as much a critique of epistemology as of moral philosophy, if moral philosophy is a discipline that thinks *about* others in order to generate rules or values for action. More like a prayer or a poem, ethical negative theology works by speaking to the other without speaking about the other. Ethical negative theology works in practice but not in theory.

Negative Theology Is Always a Practice of Humility

Levinas's Maimonides moves from the desire to approach "God" through knowledge to the experience of unknowing the sense of God. What, then, can be learned from negative theology? Maimonides' answer, which Levinas repeats in his own way, is that the experience of unknowing leads to, and obliges us to, humility: "Glory then to Him who is such that when the intellects contemplate His essence, their apprehension turns into incapacity; and when they contemplate the proceeding of His actions from His will, their knowledge turns into ignorance; and when the tongues aspire to magnify Him by means of attributive qualifications, all eloquence turns into weariness and incapacity!" (*Guide* I.58, 137). Ethical negative theology is a spiritual exercise that negates knowledge so as to acknowledge the Other. It *gives* the sense of the finitude and partiality of knowledge. This humility is *the starting point* for every post-metaphysical ethic that forgoes the certainties of deductions based on pure reason, essentialist psychology, and universal principles. In demanding that we accept our own partiality and finitude by acknowledging that we have no access to the essence or truth of the other, negative theology leads directly to an ethics of humility.

This explains why humility is the most conspicuous deviation Maimonides makes from the Aristotelian tradition of cultivating intermediate virtues. For Aristotle, humility is a vice or an error resulting from deeming oneself less worthy than one truly is.[19] But Maimonides, for all his Aristotelianism, takes the opposite view. For him, humility is a supererogatory virtue that should be practiced in extremis and not according to the doctrine of the mean. In *Hilkhot De'ot* II.3 he says that "there are some dispositions in regard to which a man is forbidden to accustom himself to the mean. They must be shunned to the extreme. Such a disposition is pride (*govah lev*). The right way in this regard is not to be merely humble (*anav*), but to be humble-minded (*sh'fal ruakh*) and lowly (*nemukha*) of spirit to the utmost."[20] What is most striking about Maimonides' view is that he regards the virtue of humility, which characterizes the *hasid*, or pious person, as more valuable than the virtue of the wise person, the *hakham*, who cultivates the intermediate position between humility and vanity.[21] The reason for this disparity between wisdom and piety is that the wise person, as Aristotle maintained, cultivates the intermediate virtue of self-respect or pride in relation to his social status, whereas the pious person is humble in the extreme because she relates her moral standing to God. As Daniel Frank has shown, this explains why Moses is the exemplar of humility for Maimonides, whereas Aristotle would have regarded Moses' humility as a mistaken conception of the pride due to him as the honorable leader of the people. In Maimonides' anti-Aristotelian view of humility, "God, not man, is the author of the moral law, and as a result of this ethical theocentricism the Mosaic stance toward God was one of extreme humility. . . . Moses, the [humble] *hasid*, stands revealed as the polar opposite of the Aristotelian *megalopsychos* [the proudly virtuous person]. . . . Aristotle's vice becomes Maimonides' outstanding virtue."[22]

Frank provides a cogent articulation of Maimonides' view of the virtue of humility, but he falls short of explaining it. My suggestion is that the virtue of humility depends on the practice of negative theology. The emphasis Maimonides gives to humility over wisdom results from the negation of the metaphysical view of human beings and God. According to the metaphysical reading of Maimonides, the human intellect is isomorphic with divine reality and capable of cognizing the Active Intellect of God. Maimonidean intellectualism thus elevates human beings as somehow analogous, through the intellect, to the divine reality. But the virtue of humility implies a sense of being "lowly of spirit," and this sense is logically dependent on the rupture of the analogy between divine and human intellects that only negative theology accomplishes. This is why negative theology inherently implies a practice of humility. Negative theology provides a critique of the metaphysical correlation between human intellect and divine reality and thereby prizes humility over wisdom. Humility is to Maimonides' theological account of the virtues what negative theology is to his metaphysics. Humility is the negative theological virtue par excellence.

The point is brought out in an important development in Maimonidean ethics resulting, I believe, from the increasing significance he ascribes to negative theology in his later thought. In Maimonides' earlier legal corpus, he had described the task of *imitatio dei* as the process of imitating God's positive moral attributes in order to cultivate one's soul. The soul is here regarded as the moral character of a person; it is the locus of moral action that should not be confused with the various acts issuing from it. Following Aristotle and al-Farabi, Maimonides proposed that one should cultivate intermediate dispositions, intermediate states of the soul, by understanding and following the ways of God.[23] These "ways," according to the rabbinic tradition accepted by Maimonides, include mercy, compassion, and so forth.[24] But in the *Guide*, which was written later, Maimonides places far greater emphasis on his view that God does not truly have moral attributes and therefore does not really have a moral character. Maimonides' account of negative theology radically separates God's ways from the essence of God. Negative theology establishes that YHWH has no moral attributes, intermediate or otherwise, even as it enjoins us to act "as if" God did. It follows, as Herbert Davidson argues, that "genuinely to walk in God's ways should entail not the cultivation of intermediate or any other psychological characteristics, but the extirpation of psychological characteristics."[25] To *imitate* God is therefore no longer to cultivate one's moral character but to negate the very idea of oneself as having essential psychological attributes.

The anthropological ideal thus dramatically shifts from Maimonides' legal works to the *Guide*. Whereas formerly the virtuous person cultivated moral habits by imitating the moral characteristics of God, now the very idea that God has moral character is negated. Imitation of

God is therefore no longer a matter of cultivating one's moral character but of negating the very idea of self. Here is Davidson again: "Just as God does not act from intermediate characteristics or any other psychological characteristics, man should perform acts that spring from no psychological characteristics, intermediate or otherwise. . . . Man will walk in God's ways by performing acts as God does, not through intermediate, or any other psychological characteristics, but wholly dispassionately."[26] Instead of cultivating moral character or personhood the ideal now is to overcome oneself entirely, for the attributes of the self, even one's moral attributes, in no way imitate divine reality. The surpassing of metaphysics by negative theology is thus accompanied by an apophasis of the self, or a negative anthropology. The intellect that formerly cognized "God" as its metaphysical correlate gives way to the trace of oneself oriented toward an unknowable God. In Davidson's view, this shift from cultivation of character to abnegation of self is based on the view expressed in the *Guide* that God is "pure intellect and consequently has neither intermediate, nor any other, psychological characteristics."[27] In my view, however, it is not the radicalized intellectualism but the radicalized negative theology that drives Maimonides from an ethics that imitates God's ways to an ethics that imitates God's transcendence with respect to all action and virtue. It is because imitation has become negation that the theological significance of character is subordinated to the task of overcoming oneself, or becoming un-self-ish (or "dis-inter-ested," as Levinas frequently put it). It is not the pure intellect that overwhelms the moral self but the dazzling excess of the unknowable one that manifests through negation: "God, may he be exalted, cannot be apprehended by the intellects" but "apprehension of Him consists in the inability to attain the ultimate term in apprehending Him. Thus all the philosophers say: We are dazzled by His beauty, and He is hidden from us because of the intensity with which He becomes manifest, just as the sun is hidden to eyes that are too weak to apprehend it" (*Guide* I.59, 139).[28] By way of negation, the self and therefore the cultivated moral character are plunged into the dazzling darkness of unknowing rather than the light of the intellect. Imitation of God is a practice of negative anthropology; to become like God amounts to an endless task of becoming unlike, of denying all essential attributes, and of contesting the very idea of one's essential self.[29] For Maimonides, the task of imitating a God beyond being, intellect, and attributes is converted into the task of becoming disinterested, un-self-ish "to the utmost possibility."

Levinas's view corresponds in an unexpected way to the two stages of Maimonides' account. For Levinas 1, ethics begins with the "hypostasis" of the moral subject and the cultivation of a moral self who is able to reach out, open itself, and welcome the other by acting the host. But one can play the host and welcome the other only when the bounds of one's own domain are fairly well established. This is Levinas's view throughout *Totality and Infinity*, in which the subject is described as a "self-referential" "egoism" who is a "host." For Levinas 1, then, as for Maimonides in his legal works, ethics is based on the integrity of the moral subject as a locus of moral attributes accomplished through *imitatio dei*.

But in *Otherwise than Being* Levinas radicalizes his argument, just as Maimonides did in his later philosophical work. The shift is from a metaphysical account of humility to the humbling of metaphysics, from the subject as host to the subject as hostage. Humility is no longer a matter of opening oneself to the other but of acknowledging that there is no real self except by way of the other, an other who is essentially unknowable. Subjectivity is "an undoing of the substantial nucleus of the ego . . . which does not leave any place of refuge, any chance to slip away" (OB, 141/AE, 181). As was the case for Maimonides, Levinas's later work is a radical exercise in negative anthropology. Levinas calls this apophasis of the self an "obsession," a "folly," and "sick." Like Maimonides, he refers this obsessive sickness that consumes the soul to the Song of Songs 5:8, "I am sick with love."[30] Ethical negative theology is the practice of exposing oneself to the claim of the other in a way that hollows out one's own claim on oneself. Accordingly, as Levinas says, "one can no longer say what the ego or the I is. From now on one has to speak in the first person . . . in a recurrence which empties me of all consistency" (OB, 82/AE, 103). From this follows a "dis-interestedness" in the extimacy of subjectivity, a "de-posing or de-situating of the ego" that "has the form of a corporeal life devoted to expression and to giving. It is devoted, and does not devote itself: it is a self despite itself, in incarnation, where it is the very possibility of offering, suffering and trauma" (OB, 50/AE, 65). Anthropological apophasis, the becoming un-self-ish of subjectivity, is, for Levinas and Maimonides, the only ultimate attestation of religious life.[31]

Only Ethical Negative Theology by Name

Why does the apophasis of subjectivity imply an "*ethical* language"?[32] After all, Levinas insists that it "does not arise out of a special moral experience" (OB, 120/AE, 154) and presents itself "before the bipolarity of good and evil" (OB, 122/AE, 157). Why, then, "ethics"? I have suggested that negative theology is a practice, specifically an apophatic practice of humility to the point of "a coring out [*dénucléation*] of my substantiality" (OB, 181/AE, 228). These are surely normative implications of negative theology, but why should this practice be called "ethics" rather than, say, politics or mysticism? Levinas's answer is not always convincing. "The tropes of ethical language," he tells us, "are found to be adequate for certain structures of the description" (OB, 120/AE, 154). Where once we had concrete moral phenomenology, now we have "tropes" referring oneself to that which is "not only outside all intuition, but outside of all thematization, even that of symbolism" (OB, 150/AE, 191–92). But why then is this language *ethical*?

Although Levinas no longer resorts to a special ethical experience of the presence/face of the other, he nevertheless has a way of justifying the ethical appellation of the apophasis of subjectivity he describes. Faced with the problem of relating the discourse of radical negative theology to ordinary language without attributing definition, essence, predication, or relation to transcendence, Levinas, like Maimonides, concentrates on the apophatic significance of the proper name. In both their accounts the proper name provides a "rigid designator," to borrow Saul Kripke's well-known term, to anchor apophatic discourse in the real of an indescribable referent. Ethical negative theology thus culminates in a reduction to the proper name.

For Maimonides, the proper name of God, YHWH, is the *only* positive theological data we have. Everything said of YHWH is subject to negation (*Guide* I.56). Actions ascribed to YHWH are merely metaphysical constructs that relate to our limited concept of "God" rather than to any true likeness to YHWH. As Maimonides pointedly remarks, "would that I knew accordingly whence the likeness could come so that the divine and the human attributes could be comprised in the same definition and be used in a univocal sense, as these people believe" (I.56, 131). Concepts that analogize God by means of human attributes—as all the positive theologies assume—are, for Maimonides, nothing but metaphysical idols in our minds that in truth do not refer to YHWH and should therefore be negated. Maimonides extends this radical negation of all predicates to the derivative names of YHWH—Shekhinah (Presence), Makom (Omnipresent), Elohim (God), and so on. These derivative names should be understood as compressed descriptions of actions *we attribute* to YHWH rather than of anything about YHWH's true reality. Such names evidently encode various descriptions of YHWH, descriptions which, when decoded, cannot be taken literally or even analogically. For example, the name Shekhinah refers to the attribute we ascribe to YHWH of dwelling immanently, Makom to our ideal of a spatio-temporal predicate ("omnipresence"), and Elohim to the action of judging in accordance with our conception of what an ideal judge does. But for Maimonides these names have no more descriptive accuracy than the name Rock, which is also used to refer to YHWH. Although one can call YHWH by the name Rock, as scripture often does, this is a purely equivocal use of words that points to no true or essential description of YHWH (*Guide* I.16, 42). *Mutatis mutandis* for names such as Shekhinah, Makom, Elohim, and all the others. In no way whatsoever do such names *describe* YHWH's true reality, as if the truth of YHWH is to dwell, extend throughout space-time, or judge (I.63). In Maimonides' words:

All names are derivative or are used equivocally, as *Rock* and others similar to it. He, may He be exalted, has no *name* [*shem*] that is not derivative except the *name having four letters* [*shem ben 'arba oti'ot*], which is the *articulated name* [*shem hameforash*, i.e., YHWH]. This name is not indicative of an attribute but of simple existence and nothing else. Now absolute existence implies that He shall always be, I mean He who is necessarily existent. Understand the point at which this discourse has finally arrived. (*Guide* I.63, 156)

The divine names are, in truth, descriptions and must therefore be categorically negated, save the proper name YHWH, which alone refers to the true reality to which theological language aims. This is because the proper name has no semantic value—"is not indicative of an attribute"— but merely *designates* the thing itself: YHWH. Unlike a common noun that can be described predicatively, a proper name designates its referent without describing it in any way, neither through the imaginative faculty nor through the rational faculty. As a proper name, YHWH designates God without describing "God" at all, just as all proper names designate their referents. God's proper name "means" as much as any proper name, exactly nothing, for proper names are not exchangeable for any set of descriptions, no matter how precise.[33] On the contrary, the priority goes the other way. As Kripke showed, descriptive attributes refer to a proper name through a causal chain of transmission. Reference to the phenomenon, to "that" which is named, is established entirely by the "initial baptism," the first point at which *that* is named, whatever it is and whatever it will become. A proper name designates an identity without imputing any descriptive essence to it at all. After the name is given, one knows that one is talking about *that* thing as long as one establishes a causal or historical relationship with the initial baptism, regardless of whether one can describe that thing at all or understands the intentions of its original use as it was given at the initial baptism. As Kripke put it, "Our reference depends not just on what we think ourselves, but on other people in the community, the history of how the name reached one, and things like that. It is by following such a history that one gets to the reference."[34] Everything therefore depends on the original giving of the proper name, for it fixes the reference to *that*, whatever will subsequently be said about it, including errors. In fact, errors, false descriptions of that which bears the proper name, are mistaken descriptions that nevertheless *succeed* in attributing their false content to *that* thing named at the initial baptism.

Positive theology, in Maimonides' view, works just this way. Positive descriptions of YHWH are all categorically mistaken. "Rock," "Presence," "Compassionate," and so forth do not truly *describe* YHWH in any sense. But they successfully *refer to* YHWH, to that which was initially named as such, as long as there is historical continuity between the use of these descriptive appellations and the original designation of *that* as YHWH. The reduction of theology to the proper Name implies a nondescriptive realism established by an initial event of direct acquaintance. The descriptive accuracy of subsequent theological language is less important than the historical continuity with the initial event of direct acquaintance. Moshe Halbertal and Avishai Margalit were the first to note how Kripke's account of proper names resembles Maimonides' view of the role of the Name in legitimizing all theological language. As they saw, "the crucial question here is what guarantees the reference of the tetragrammaton in the first place, and the answer is Moses. He is the direct link in the sense that his knowledge was not mediated by descriptions. Moses' relationship with God does not guarantee any supernatural propositional knowledge [i.e., metaphysics], but it guarantees that the name by which God 'revealed' himself to Moses has a reference. And from Moses the name was passed on by the chain of tradition."[35] Once established, it is less important that descriptions of the named phenomenon succeed or fail than that they refer, through a causal chain of transmission, to *that* which was initially designated by the name. Maimonides thinks that in the case of YHWH, who essentially eludes our descriptive capacities, the descriptions will all be categorically mistaken. Nevertheless, although categorically mistaken *as descriptions* of YWHW (as if YHWH really did "dwell," and so on), they *successfully refer* to YHWH, as long as these erroneous descriptions can be causally connected to the baptismal moment when the Name was first fixed. In the biblical narrative, such an event is marked by the historical occasion when the proper name of YHWH is revealed to Moses alone. This happens in Exodus 6:2–3: "God spoke to Moses and said to him, 'I am YHWH. I appeared to Abraham, Isaac, and Jacob as El Shaddai, *but I did not make known to them My name YHWH*'" (Exod. 6:2–3). Henceforth, successful reference to "God" depends not on the descriptive accuracy of the theological language but on establishing a causal, historical connection to the occasion when YHWH first made known "his" Name. Descriptive theological language, including all the derivative names, is from now on entirely dependent on whether or not they refer to that which was designated as YHWH to Moses. In other words, it is not because "God" *is* compassionate and gracious that one can say "YHWH is compassionate and gracious" but because these loose and, strictly speaking, erroneous descriptions *refer* to YHWH, *whatever* the true nature of YHWH really is. Without the primacy of the Name no description would successfully refer to God. But the fact that God has a proper name, for Maimonides, means that everything *said* about "God"—that "He" "is" "great," "good," "wise," and even "living" or "existing"—is truly said *about God*. Indeed, for Maimonides such descriptions are pure homonyms with respect to the true reality of YHWH. But even if such descriptions are categorically mistaken, the point is that they are mistaken about the right thing, namely, YHWH, and can therefore be used effectively, if cautiously, in certain pragmatic contexts, such as prayer, oath taking, exhortation, and exegesis. Without the primacy of the proper name, one would have merely the most marvelous descriptions that refer to nothing real. The rigid designation established by the proper name ensures that the negation of theological language about "God" draws one closer *to YHWH*; via negation we approach the nonsemantic referent of YHWH. Maimonidean negative theology thus rejects every description of "God" while successfully referring these negations to YHWH.

Because of the direct, nonsemantic, nondescriptive, non-metaphysical acquaintance that only Moses has with YHWH, the rest of us are able to use religious language properly, even if we cannot know whether our descriptions correspond to the true essence of YHWH. Therefore, according to Maimonides, all prophetic authority derives from and refers back to Moses' unique acquaintance with God. It follows that any putatively prophetic or revealed experience that breaks with Mosaic authority ipso facto delegitimizes itself, since Moses alone establishes the legitimate use of theological language by ostension, or direct acquaintance with YHWH.[36] Maimonides' radical negation of theological descriptivism demands a fundamental reliance on an unbroken chain of transmission, a living tradition, from Moses to Moses Maimonides. This is not simply a dogmatic claim about the authority of tradition but a philosophical means of establishing the legitimacy of the imprecise and even categorically mistaken theological language of religious life, liturgy, and law on the basis of Moses' direct acquaintance with YHWH. Without a tradition going back to the giving of the Name to Moses, negative theology would only undermine the possibility of religious language. But on the basis of the giving of the Name and the ensuing causal-historical tradition, negative theology simultaneously critiques the positive language of theological descriptivism and legitimates its multiple uses in everyday life. As Jean-Luc Marion has said in an analogous context, the theology of the Name is "no longer predicative (whether this means predicating an affirmation or a negation) but purely pragmatic. It is no longer a matter of naming or attributing something to something but rather of aiming in the direction of . . . , of relating to . . . , of comporting oneself towards . . . , of reckoning with . . . —in short, of dealing with. . . ."[37] Since there is no way of describing what the Name names, the decisive thing is to maintain the pragmatic sense of the Name that leads from the initial occasion of when it was given to our use of it. Metaphysics thus gives way to the pragmatics of naming and therefore enables hermeneutical theology, in which multiple and even contradictory interpretations retain their pragmatic validity through historical transmission of the Name.

Like Maimonides, Levinas regards all theological language except the proper name as incapable of describing what it presumes to talk about: "Language about God rings false or becomes myth, that is, can never be taken literally" (OB, 197/AE, 155n25). Levinas makes it clear that the language of positive theology, including words such as "divinity," "transcendence," and "exists," is descriptively incongruous with the unique and inconceivable reality it feigns to describe. He too proposes a reduction of the theological language of description to its pragmatic commencement as a proper name that "makes the word God be pronounced, without letting 'divinity' be said. That would be absurd, as though God were an essence" (OB, 162/AE, 206). In this profoundly Maimonidean view, the word "God" itself would not describe anything at all, or at least nothing but our metaphysical idols, unless it referred to the *nonsemantic Real* of the Name. This Maimonideanism is expressed in an essay Levinas wrote on the "The Name of God According to a Few Talmudic Texts," in which he writes that "the Hebrew terms of the Old Testament that we are led to translate by God, or *Deus*, or *Theos*, are proper names according to the wishes of the Talmud. The name of God is always said to be a proper name in the Scriptures. The word God would be absent from the Hebrew language! A fine consequence of monotheism in which there exists neither a divine species nor a generic word to designate it."[38] That this interpretation of Talmudic and biblical usage of the divine names is decidedly Maimonidean becomes evident in a splendid slip Levinas seems to have made in reading the opening of Maimonides' *Mishneh Torah*. His essay continues:

The first book of the famous Tractate in which Maimonides, in the twelfth century, summarizes and systematizes the Talmud, begins in fact as follows: "The foundation of all foundations and the pillar of wisdom consists in knowing that the Name exists and that it is the first being." The word designating the divinity is precisely the word Name, a generic term in relation to which the different names of God are individuals. . . . The term thus names—and this is quite remarkable— a mode of being or a beyond being rather than a quiddity.

Levinas has lucidly summarized the Maimonidean theology of the proper name that we explicated above. But he has done so by reading *shm* (שם) as "Name," whereas all other interpreters read Maimonides to be saying that "the pillar of wisdom consists in knowing that *there is a being* and that it is the first being," that is, not as *shem* but as *sham*. Both Samuel Ibn Tibbon and Joseph Karo specify that although *shm* should be vocalized openly, as *sham*, meaning "there," it should not be taken literally to mean that there is a "place" in which God resides, but that Maimonides is importing a standard Arabic term for "existence" into Hebrew. Levinas, however, unwittingly reads the opening of the *Mishneh Torah* as designating "God" by the Name, *shem*, rather than as an entity that is "there," *sham*, thus substituting the philologically correct ontological reading of *shm* with an interpretation driven by his non-metaphysical negative theology of the proper name. This is a creative misreading I have not come across elsewhere and that can be explained only by privileging Maimonides' negative theology of the proper Name over Maimonidean metaphysics. But the crucial point is that the passage from the negation of theology to the truth of the proper Name provides Levinas with the primary argument of *Otherwise than Being*, which is that the negation of ontology leads to the *eminentia* of the proper ethical name.

The Claim of the Name

As with the reduction of metaphysical theology to the proper Name, so Levinas 2 reduces the metaphysical significance of the face/presence of the other to its proper name. We are now in a position to understand how it is that ethics signifies without an experience of the other and why negative anthropology is intrinsically ethical. According to Levinas 2, the ethical claim issues not from the face of the other, that is, not from the presence of the other as vulnerable, widowed, orphaned, or any other asymmetrical predicate, but from the name of the other. The tropes of this transformation lead us from the positive phenomenology of *Totality and Infinity* to the negative phenomenology of *Otherwise than Being*. Ethics is no longer revealed in the Presence of the Face (*panim*) but in the name bearing the trace and absence of the other. The emphasis on the name in place of the face results from the Maimonidean view that "this name is not indicative of an attribute but of simple existence and nothing else" (*Guide* I.63, 156). It is the uniqueness of the other that matters for Levinas 2, not any particular attributes he or she might have. Indeed, only by negating the positive ideas one has of the other can one accede to the uniqueness signified by the proper name. Such a uniqueness can be signified only by the proper name, since phenomenological descriptions always refer to general predicates that never correlate with the uniqueness of the other. The reduction of the other to the proper name strips the other of all descriptive attributes precisely in order to approach his or her uniqueness:

> Perhaps the names of persons whose *saying* signifies a face—proper names, in the middle of all these common names and commonplaces—can resist the dissolution of sense [*sens*] and help us to speak. Perhaps they will enable us to divine, behind the downfall of discourse, the end of a certain *intelligibility* but the dawning of a new one. What is coming to a close may be a rationality tied *exclusively* to the being that is sustained by words, the *Said* of the Saying, the Said of conveying fields of knowledge and truths in the form of unchanging identities.[39]

The ethical "saying," suggests Levinas, resists the attribution of descriptions to the other by attending to the uniqueness to which the proper name refers. Levinas effectively articulates the negative anthropology implied by Maimonides' theology of the Name. Ethics, like negative theology, hollows out substantive nouns (*noms*) and the false identities they institute in order to approach the uniqueness of persons as bearers of proper names (*noms*). The tortuous practice of critical philosophy that Levinas 2 practiced with such severe rigor was devoted to negating the discursive fixtures of meaning. This was no slide into nihilism, or, rather, it passes through nihilism toward the ethical substance of language as such, a reduction of meaning (*signification*) to sense (*sens*) in order to approach proper names (*noms*) that are not nouns (*noms*). This is what Levinas means to accomplish in the reduction of the Said to the Saying. It is because of this critical function played by philosophy that it, like negative theology, "is the wisdom of love at the service of love" (OB, 162/AE, 206–7). The shift from a descriptive account of the other to the saying of proper names determines the entire logic of *Otherwise than Being*. This can go unnoticed because of the French homonym *nom*, which has confounded readers and translators who are not attentive to the negative theology of the proper name it trades on. Levinas's extensive (Maimonidean) use of *nom* points to a sense in which human beings are not substances with fixed identities that can be described like common nouns but are individuated singularly like proper names—without essential attributes and unconvertible into a set of descriptions. The epigraph to *Otherwise than Being* attests to this ambivalence in the *nom* by "translating" a general description of "victims of the same hatred of the other" into the proper names of the members of Levinas's family who perished in the Holocaust. This is an example of a "reduction to the saying" that works by moving from a description of the other to proper names that silently say what is at stake by their own feeble testimony, which never correlates with positive descriptions, not even the descriptions of moral discourse. At the other end of this extraordinary work of almost pure apophasis, *Otherwise than Being* concludes with a remark that confirms that everything is geared toward an apophatic approach to the singularity of the other borne by the name:

In this work which does not seek to restore any ruined concept, the destitution and the desituating of the subject do not remain without signification: after the death of a certain god inhabiting the world behind the scenes, the substitution of the hostage discovers the trace, unpronounceable inscription, of what, always already past, always "he," does not enter into any present, to which are suited not the nouns designating beings, or the verbs in which their essence resounds, but that which, as a pronoun, marks with its seal all that a name can convey. (OB, 185/AE, 233)[40]

Like Maimonides, Levinas reduces discourse from nouns (or essences) to verbs (or actions) and finally to an approach to the proper name. Despite the absence of metaphysical positivity, both discern the trace of transcendence in a pragmatic response to the proper name of the other. Ethical negative theology is the avowed response to proper names that designate the "realism" of the other in a nonessentialist, nondescriptivist, non-metaphysical sense. It is at once a realist and nonessentialist approach to the other since it refers to a uniqueness whose "essential" predicates change over time, and therefore one who cannot be correlated with a description or its negation, one without essence, one only in name. This is a *realism without positivism* that attests to the singularity of the other without asserting that this singularity is an objectively given essence. Neither the affirmation of the presence of the other ("Authority is not somewhere, where a look could go seek it, like an idol, or assume it, like a logos" [OB, 150/AE, 191]) nor the negation of the other ("Negativity, still correlative with being, will not be enough to signify the *other than being*" [OB, 9/AE, 10]), the "reduction from the said to the saying" indicates the sense of proper names, a "third way" or *via eminentia* of approaching the uniqueness of the other. Ethical negative theology is this strictly pragmatic approach to the other, beyond affirmation and negation.[41] It is a response to one designated without description, designated as a proper name, and thus one who assigns me to myself without attributing me with substance or lack, myself as "a unicity withdrawing from essence" (OB, 8/AE, 10). For Levinas, then, the theological problem of reconciling human language with divine reality corresponds to the moral problem of reconciling philosophical language with ethical experience. As he says, "the problem of transcendence and of God and the problem of subjectivity irreducible to essence, irreducible to essential immanence, go together" (OB, 17/AE, 20).

*

The ethical creature is the one exposed to the name of the other. Proper names assign us to creatures in their singularity, and therefore define us, we who bear and use names, as exemplary ethical creatures, despite ourselves. Like Eric Santner's account of creaturely life, the ethical creature who is exposed to the name of the other implies "a specifically human way of finding oneself caught in the midst of antagonisms in and of the political field."[42] Here too the dimension of creatureliness relates to the secularization of "the laws of normative Judaism" that have become "opaque rules" for modern subjects, much like Franz Kafka's characters who were faced with laws with which they could "no longer identify even if they did not fully cease to feel addressed by them."[43] But one must be careful not to forget that the modern experience of normative laws that retain "validity but no significance," as Gershom Scholem put it, is not only the experience of the *anonymous* institution of law carried over from the sacred to the profane but also the loss and dispersal of the experience of the Other as the source and authority of the Law, the Other whose Name can now perhaps be heard only as an echo of the name of the other. The proper name is the locus of sense without signification, of orientation and address without presence or essence. Santner is right, then, that the "dimension of creaturely life is an ongoing and passionate subjection not to a Creator God or even to a sovereign whose legitimacy is figured on the model of the Creator but to an agency, a master's discourse, that has been attenuated and dispersed across a field of relays and points of contact that no longer cohere, even in fantasy, as a consistent 'other' of possible address and redress."[44] But this dispersal of creatureliness across the field of modern secular life is not just an experience of the anonymity of the law; it is also and at the same time an exposure to the name of the other. I would even suggest that the biopolitical dimension of creaturely life gets a grip on us *only* because we are implicated with one another ethically, exposed to each other's names, to the sense we have of each other as unique under historical circumstances in which uniqueness has validity but no signification, since we use proper names but no longer signify proper essences. The ethical creature is thus what remains of the otherwise tired and abstract concept of "humanity." "Can the question of the divinity of the One God be put as the question of the humanity of man is put?" (OB, 193n36/AE, 124n36). If we take names at face value, then yes.

Glory to the Name

Levinas's account of ethics is often rightly regarded as a remnant of humanism. But is the anthropocentric interpretation of Levinas, which Levinas himself espoused, the ultimate sense of the reduction of the other to the proper name? If the ethical creature is an exposure to the name of the other, is it ultimately an exposure to other humans? A similar problem arises in Maimonides' theology of the proper name. The reduction of affirmative and negative predicates to the Name liberates religious language from metaphysics only by chaining it to traditions issuing from Moses. Is there, then, no other access to "God"? Although Maimonides suggests there is no way to approach "God" save the Name, he provides an opening, or a supplement, that is also instructive for our interpretation of Levinas.

In part 1, chapter 64 of the *Guide of the Perplexed*, which follows the chapter in which Maimonides posits the Name as the only viable approach to YHWH, his position is complicated in a decisive way. In brief, Maimonides proposes that *kavod* (glory) provides a supplementary way of approaching the truth and essence of God.[45] Maimonides begins by reiterating that the Name YHWH is "sometimes intended to signify His essence and true reality" (*Guide* I.64, 156). This restates the conclusion of the preceding chapter (I.63), which established his Millian/Kripkean view (explicated earlier), according to which the Name, unlike all descriptive accounts of "God," including those of metaphysical theology, designates without describing. YHWH is not a metaphorical, analogical, or symbolic way of speaking about "God" but a pragmatic way of referring to God. Maimonides now adds a crucial supplement: there is *another name* for this unspeakable "essence and true reality" of YHWH, and it is called glory, *kavod.* Maimonides explains: "This expression [YHWH] is sometimes intended to signify His essence and true reality, may He be exalted, as when he [Moses] says, *Show me, I pray Thee, Thy glory* [Exod. 33:18], and was answered: *For man shall not see me and live* [Exod. 33:20]. This answer indicates that the *glory* that is spoken of here is His essence, and that his saying *Thy glory* is by way of honoring Him, in the same way as we have made clear with regard to his saying: *And they shall say to me: What is His name?* [Exod. 3:13]" (*Guide* I.64, 156–57). Remarkably, Maimonides seems to regard glory not simply as a derivative name that would in truth be but another homonym that refers to YHWH pragmatically without gaining purchase on the essential reality of YHWH. Rather, "the glory that is spoken of here is His essence," just as the name YHWH signifies "His essence and true reality." How is this possible? Was not the proper name YHWH the only way of signifying the essence of God? After all, Maimonides argued that even predicates such as "exist" and "living" should not be understood as referring to the essence of YHWH since such terms are merely homonymous when used to refer to God. How, then, can glory signify His essence?

Earlier in the same chapter Maimonides had said that "the glory of Y.H.V.H. is sometimes intended to signify the created light" (I.64, 156). This has led commentators to posit a clear distinction between the "essence and true reality" of YHWH and that of glory, since the latter refers to the created light and not to the essence of YHWH.[46] But we just saw that Maimonides also says that glory sometimes refers not to the created light but to the "essence and true reality" of YHWH. The citation of Exodus 33:18 is marshaled to propose that when Moses asked to see the glory he was *not* asking to see the created light but to see YHWH, the one who says about himself that "no man shall see me and live." As Maimonides explains, "This answer indicates that the *glory that is spoken of here is His essence*" (I.64, 157; my emphasis). Unlike all the other descriptions attributed to YHWH, glory is singled out as "sometimes" referring to the essence— not to "God," then, but to God, to YHWH. Glory is therefore not another metaphorical description or an attribute of YHWH but more like another proper name for God, since it provides another way of referring to the true essence and reality of YHWH.[47] Glory is not simply another loose way of talking about "God," and it is not shorthand, like the derivative names of YHWH, for a set of metaphysical descriptions of God. Rather, since it sometimes refers to the "essence and true reality" of YHWH, glory attests to God in a literal but non-metaphysical sense, as the Name itself does. A cleavage thus emerges within the Maimonidean referential apparatus that now indicates an alternative way of referring to God independently of the name of YHWH. This cleavage—both binding and dividing—means that one can no longer restrict the proper use of theological language to traditions issuing from the proper Name, for glory properly attests to God in its own way. Although Maimonides privileges the Name as a way of approaching God without the fallacies of description or their mere negation, glory provides another way for the non-metaphorical and non-metaphysical God to reveal itself in the cosmos at large.

Glory is sometimes intended to signify the honoring of Him, may He be exalted, by all men. In fact all that is other than God, may He be exalted, honors Him, for the true way of honoring Him consists in apprehending His greatness. Thus everybody who apprehends His greatness and His perfection, honors Him according to the extent of his apprehension. Man in particular honors Him by speeches so that he indicates thereby that which he has apprehended by his intellect and communicates it to others. Those beings that have no apprehension, as for instance the minerals, also as it were honor God through the fact that by their very nature they are indicative of the power and wisdom of Him who brought them into existence. For this induces him who considers them to honor God, either by means of articulate utterance or without it if speech is not permitted him. The Hebrew language gives itself latitude in that it applies to this notion the term *saying* [*amira'*]. Accordingly it is said of that which is devoid of apprehension that it praises God. Thus Scripture says: *All my bones shall say, Lord, who is like unto Thee* [Ps. 35:1]; whereby it conveys that the bones necessitate this belief, as though they put it into speech, for they too make this known. It is in view of this notion being named *glory* that it is said, *The whole earth is full of His glory* [Isa. 6:3], this being equivalent to the dictum, *And the earth is full of His praise* [Hab. 3:3], for praise is called *glory*. Thus it is said: *Give glory to the Lord your God* [Jer. 13:16] and it is said: *And in His temple all say: Glory* [Ps. 29:9]. This occurs frequently. Understand then likewise the equivocality with reference to *glory* and interpret the latter in every passage in accordance with the context. You shall thus be saved from great difficulty. (*Guide* I. 64, 157)

If YHWH designates the God without being, beyond predication and negation, to which Moses acceded when the Name was given to him, glory declaims, through bones and minerals, that to which YHWH also refers. If the *via negativa* leads from metaphysics to the Name, glory indicates the *via eminentia* of another way. Glory refers, "sometimes," to the essence and true reality of YHWH. Every subsequent attempt to speak properly of God is therefore cleaved by the choice between the looseness of a theological language whose legitimacy is entirely dependent on its causal-historical relation to the unique Name (the way of Maimonidean orthodoxy) and the language of glory spoken "by means of articulate utterance or without it," by humans who apprehend and communicate it or by those who "have no apprehension, as for instance the minerals," and, indeed, "the whole earth" (the way of Maimonidean heterodoxy). For example, when the minerals praise YHWH by "saying" themselves gloriously, they do not use the proper Name. But neither do they simply indicate a metaphorical and metaphysical account of God's power and wisdom, for glory is not a metaphor but the "essence and true reality" of God. Glory is not a derivative name referring back to YHWH but constitutes the original impropriety of the proper Name. Glory disperses the true reality of God, beyond being and negation, encapsulated by the Name. No less than the Name, glory exceeds the descriptive and conceptual resources of ordinary language and experience because it bears the true reality of God, without metaphor or metaphysics. Like the Name, glory indicates the truth of God beyond the limits of both intellect and imagination. Neither the Name nor the glory is the object of perception or intellection, but for opposite reasons. Whereas the Name designates the true reality of God because it empties the idea of "God" of all semantic content, glory indicates it with an abundance of sense that neither reason nor the imagination can contain: a "perpetual, dazzling light the overflow of which illumines all that is dark—in accordance with what is said in the prophetic parables: *And the earth did shine with His glory* [Ezek. 43:2]" (*Guide* III.9, 437). If the Name accedes to the non-metaphoricity and non-metaphysicality of God because it successfully refers while being perfectly empty of meaning, glory accedes to the Real in the mode of superabundance. The name is sense emptied of significance, whereas glory is the excess of sense over significance.[48] Neither the Name nor the glory belongs to the order of cognition or of perception. To encounter the Name is to belong to the order of tradition, that is, to the causal-historical chain relating back to the initial baptism, and to encounter the glory is to forgo the categories of consciousness by yielding to its blinding and bedazzling phenomenality. As Marion puts it, "The gaze cannot any longer sustain a light that bedazzles and burns. . . . Thus the glory of the visible weighs down with all it has."[49] Spinoza also identified this surplus of particulars (knowledge of the third kind) as a "love or blessedness" that is "in the Bible, called Glory, and not undeservedly."[50] Thus, glory, like the Name, is to be honored and acknowledged rather than known. What is crucial is the "saying," which honors with either praise or silence, rather than the limitations of cognition or imagination.[51]

The problem posed earlier was that Maimonides appears to liberate God from ontology by a reduction of predication and negation to the Name in a manner that restricts access to the God beyond being to traditions issuing from Moses. The subsequent analysis proposed that Maimonides acknowledges a supplementary way of access to the true reality of God attested by glory. It remains to show that Levinas's work can likewise be divided into an orthodox interpretation that maintains that the one approached in the name is exclusively another human and a heterodoxical interpretation according to which the reduction to the name is not an exclusively human affair. Such a division is attested in what Levinas calls the "*ambiguity* of the order that orders to me the neighbor who obsesses me" (OB, 162/AE, 206; my emphasis). This ambiguity is intrinsic to the language of ethical negative theology. On the first reading, ethical negative theology leads to a reduction to the proper name of the other, to an immemorial exposure of the ethical creature to proper names of other human beings. The "fission of the ultimate substantiality of the ego" (OB, 144/AE, 183) takes place prior to self-identity while abandoning the one who remains, the ethical self, to responsiveness to the uniqueness of the other *person*. But the ambiguity of this "fission of the ego unto me" (OB, 185/AE, 233) cannot be contained. Because the fissure takes place prior to self-identity ("In it I could not arise soon enough to be there on time" [OB, 162/AE, 206]) there is no knowing if the name that exposes one to the dimension of ethical creatureliness is the name of another person or perhaps some other name. In the fissure of self-identity that precedes consciousness, the real referent of the proper name that solicits my response is abandoned to my response. As Levinas puts it: "Its transcendence . . . does not come to pass save through the subject that confesses or contests it. Here there is an inversion of order: *the revelation is made by him that receives it*, by the inspired subject whose inspiration, alterity in the same, is the subjectivity or psyche of the subject. The revelation of the beyond being is perhaps indeed but a word, but this 'perhaps' belongs to an ambiguity in which the anarchy of the Infinite resists the univocity of an originary or a principle" (OB, 156/AE, 200; my emphasis). This profound ambiguity in the exposure generating the self as an ethical creature implies *the dependence of the name on the response.*[52] Who is the other? Which other? What name? Levinas's answer is that there is ambiguity all the way down, and therefore only the response will determine the answer to such questions: "It is the coming of the order to which I am subjected before hearing it, or which I hear in my own saying. It is an august command, but one that does not constrain or dominate and leave me outside of any correlation with its source. . . . Thus the saying that comes to me is my own word" (OB, 150/AE, 194). Thus the name that comes to me belongs to the other to whom I give myself, whoever that other will have been.

What is remarkable is that Levinas, like Maimonides, says that "these ambiguities . . . belong *to the glory* of the Infinite" (OB, 152/AE, 196; my emphasis). A few pages earlier he suggested that "Glory is but the other face of the passivity of the subject. . . . The glory of the Infinite is the anarchic identity of the subject flushed out without being able to slip away" (OB, 144/AE, 183). Like the Maimonidean notion of glory that I have explicated, for Levinas the exposure to glory also leads to a certain abandonment *to* the name that is also an abandonment *of* the name, for the name gives itself excessively, to the point of giving priority to the response over its own referentiality. The glory of the name is that it glorifies itself by giving the self to itself. But this means that glory conceals the essence of the name in order to let the response do its work of naming. As Levinas puts it, "The Infinite does not appear to him that bears witness to it. On the contrary the witness belongs to the very glory of the Infinite. It is by the voice of the witness that the glory of the Infinite is glorified" (OB, 146/AE, 185). The ambiguity of the name results from this impossibility of acceding to its referent, if indeed it has one, and the impossibility of escaping it. It is this abandonment of and to the name that Levinas calls glory, as Jewish negative theologians before him have likewise done. What is above all crucial for Levinas is that the abandonment of the name also assigns me to it. Ethical negative theology is therefore a matter of binding me to the other, whichever other, in abandon.

Ethical negative theology is a pragmatic response to the other, not a theory. Its response is always one of humility, not of the false modesty of an inverted egoism but of the coring out of the ego itself, its surrendering to an exposure to the other borne "deeper inside" itself than its own self. The moral creator must become an ethical creature, caught in the throngs of names to which it must respond without freedom, separation, or independence, as the pure one-for-the-other of responsiveness. It is a glorification—of the Name, of the other, and of other names, for it is the ever-renewed abandonment one makes of oneself responsively.

Secularizing the Covenant

THE ETHICS OF FAITH

> The sentence in which God gets mixed in with words is not "I believe in God."
> —Emmanuel Levinas, *Basic Philosophical Writings*

Beyond Belief

I have been arguing that what Levinas calls "ethics" is best understood not as a secularized philosophy of religion in general but as a secularized moral theology of Judaism in particular.[1] In this chapter I argue that the term "religion" itself, in Levinas's philosophical writings, is hermeneutically drawn from a specifically Judaic understanding of the term. The specifically Judaic loom from which Levinas spins his philosophical cloth does not compromise its philosophical consistency. What matters philosophically is not the putative neutrality or universality of this thought but its essential openness to anyone responsive to it. If Levinas begins with Judaism, it is always in order to interpret a claim addressed to *anyone*: "to the Jew first and also to the Greek" (Rom. 1:16).

There is no question that from early on religion and ethics were entwined in Levinas's philosophy. In 1951 he had already made use of the doubtful etymology of "religion" as deriving from "ligature," a bind that ties together.[2] In his view religion ties us together ethically without regard for the positive representations we have of one another. Re*ligion* would be a society stitched with ob*ligation,* a word that indeed derives from the act of binding. It is not the contents of faith but the fabric of normative relations that matters to Levinas, and these relations he characterizes as religious while attempting to remove all theological postulates. Theology belongs to the old metaphysics that must be bracketed by the phenomenological reduction of meaning to the concrete life of consciousness, but this consciousness itself is caught in a web of obligations, in concrete religious life. In this way Levinas pushes positive theology aside with one hand while embracing religion with the other; theology, we might say, is metaphysics whereas religion is our hermeneutical situation. In his later period he reaffirms this view: "Theological language destroys the religious situation of transcendence" (OB, 197/AE, 155). For whereas the "language of God rings false or becomes myth, that is, can never be taken literally," the ethical bond itself "is religion, exceeding the psychology of faith and of the loss of faith."[3] The term "religion," as Levinas deploys it for over forty years, suggests a binding force of obligation that spans the void of modern nihilism and antifoundationalism—religion without theology.

It is not difficult to see Levinas's preference for religion over theology in terms of the celebrated Jewish predilection for practical over theoretical life. Whereas a church billboard on the road to my university declares that "Christianity begins where religion ends," the very opposite is espoused by exponents of Jewish "orthopraxy": Judaism is regarded as a pure practice of religious obligation without spiritual or metaphysical dogma. Levinas remarked on this point in a discussion with Christian colleagues:

The Christians attach great importance to what they call faith, mystery, sacrament. Here is an anecdote on that subject. Hannah Arendt, not long before she died, told the following story on French radio. When she was a child in her native Konigsberg, one day she said to the rabbi who was teaching her religion: "You know, I have lost my faith." And the rabbi responded: "Who's asking you for it?" The response was typical. What matters is not "faith," but "doing." Doing, which means moral behavior, of course, but also the performance of ritual. Moreover, are believing and doing different things? What does believing mean? What is faith made of? Words, ideas? Convictions? What do we believe with? With the whole body! With all my bones (*Psalm* 35:10)! What the rabbi meant was: "Doing good is the act of belief itself." That is my conclusion.[4]

But this conclusion can yield at least two interpretations, each expounded by Levinas on different occasions. First, the preference for the practical implies an absence of credo and a pluralism of "theologies" that removes "any dogmatic pretension from the general idea which this word ['theology'] harbours."⁵ Levinas lauds this pluralism, according to which "no Credo brings together or orientates the reading of the texts. . . . In Judaism, the formulation of articles of faith is a late philosophical or theological genre. It does not appear until the Middle Ages."⁶ Levinas thus adopts an orthopraxical view of Judaism's nondogmatic normativity.⁷

A second interpretation of the preference for religion over theology is more controversial. Purified of dogma, the orthopraxical account of Judaism is sometimes closer to a certain atheism than any number of theisms and theologies, even when it continues to express loyalty to traditional religious praxis. As Levinas puts it, "Faith purged of myth, the monotheist faith, itself implies metaphysical atheism" (TI, 77/TeI, 50). Other influential modern Jewish thinkers have made similar arguments. Abraham Isaac Kook offered a dialectical and mystical defense of the view according to which the negation of theology, or atheism, converges with the truth of Judaism: "There is no difference between conceptualised faith and denial of God. Both of them do not give the truth because everything that a person grasps in a positive way is negated in light of the divine truth."⁸ For Kook, however, the atheistic critique of the platitudes of belief does not so much suspend theology in order to abide in the pure practice of religion, as Levinas proposes, but raises faith to a higher level of mystical knowledge: "Atheism has a temporary legitimacy, because it is needed to purge the foulness that has attached itself to religion . . . to extirpate the dross that obscures from man the true light of godliness."⁹ In contrast to Kook, religion, for Levinas, results in no theological knowledge whatsoever; atheism is thus not a "temporary" denial but a perennial religious imperative aimed at avoiding the idolatry of all concepts of God, including the mystical "true light of godliness." Levinas, then, is closer to Yeshayahu Leibowitz, whose radicalized Maimonidean negative theology contests not only false beliefs but *belief as such*, since belief by definition reduces God to a concept and is therefore tantamount to idolatry.¹⁰ As Jean-Luc Marion has superbly shown, insofar as belief implies a determined concept of "God" it can only fall short of God.¹¹ To approach God one must therefore move beyond belief, whether by receiving the saturated phenomenon of revelation (Kook, Marion), prioritizing religious praxis over theological cognition (Leibowitz), or doing both by responding to the Other (Levinas). A critique of belief and thus a deep affinity with a certain nonfoundational atheism is intrinsic to the anti-idolatrous aspirations of religious service. In denying this and that concept of God, the atheist joins forces with the negative theologian to help rid religion of internal idolatries. As late as 1986, Levinas refuses to resort to theology since he is entirely interested in the noncognitive religious situation of obligation, "without evoking creation, omnipotence, rewards, and promises." But then comes the qualification: "We have been reproached for ignoring theology; and we do not here contest the necessity for a recovery. . . . We think, however, that theological recuperation comes after the glimpse of holiness, which is primary."[12]

However, can theology be completely expunged from religious life, even from a purified life of religious observation, without degenerating into mindless behavioralism? Why commit to these or those practices if one believes in nothing? How can one determine the meaning of that "glimpse of holiness, which is primary," without resorting to the positivist "myth of the given"? It is not only a matter of acknowledging the role of interpretation and all that it involves—clerical authorities, canonization, polemic, and so forth—in determining the meaning of "the glimpse of holiness," but also conceding that if religious praxis is to be a mode of *action* rather than merely of behavior, it must include belief. This is because belief is constitutive of the notion of action, in the sense that action involves reasoned and normative considerations. The hatred of belief, which poses as a sovereign negative theology in charge of demolishing our conceptual idols, becomes, at its perverse extremity, an idolatrous slavishness to rigid religious behaviorism, which is precisely Badiou's charge against Levinas. Without any content to faith, the practice of religion fetishizes the givens of tradition, disregards the cognitive dimensions of faith, and ignores the deliberative, interpretative, and evaluative processes of determining religious action. In the end, then, even a religion without theology must come to terms with the content, values, and aims of religious praxis.

A Covenant of Faith

The preceding chapters have hopefully established that the recovery of Jewish theology that Levinas wanted to defer was in fact at work from the outset. *Totality and Infinity* is a secularized phenomenological tapestry of Jewish creation theologies: creation from chaos, *creatio ex nihilo*, creation

in the image of God. *Otherwise than Being* rejects the metaphysical supposi-
tions of creation theology in favor of the ethical creature, as we will further
see, but its method of apophatic anthropology is equally indebted to a post-
metaphysical, secularized Maimonidean account of humility, glory, and the
unique sense of the proper name. I now want to propose that the critique
of religious *belief* that enables Levinas to construct ethics on the model of
religion without theology is itself best understood as a recovery of a non-
epistemological, that is to say, phenomenological account of Jewish *faith*.
For the sake of illustrating Levinas's phenomenology of Judaism, I therefore
distinguish between "belief" and "faith," as did Wilfred Cantwell Smith.[13]

Belief is usually regarded as a propositional attitude or a mental state
in relation to an object in which a subject thinks that something is the
case. Clearly, Levinas is not urging us to believe in the other in the sense
of believing that "other minds" exist.[14] Is he perhaps trying to persuade
us to adopt certain beliefs "about" the other, for example, about the holiness of the other? This is closer, although Levinas denies that ethics involves correlating one's mental attitudes with predicates attributed to the
other. It is therefore tempting to say that the relation to the other is not
a matter of belief at all. And yet Levinas calls it a religious relation and,
as we have seen, he makes use of a type of critical a/theological language.
The problem lies not so much, or not only, with Levinas's unusual descriptions of religion but with the narrow construal of religious belief in
the modern epistemological period.[15] I propose to put this common but
pointedly modern notion of belief aside for the moment—that is, to put
aside the notion of belief as a psychological disposition to regard something as being the case or being true—in order to explore its basis outside
the mind. The two essential features of modern belief, that it is a mental
disposition and that it has propositional content that regards something as
being true or false (or being the case or not being the case) independently
of us, are conspicuously marginal in both ancient and contemporary nonfoundational accounts of faith. I therefore want to suggest that a post-
metaphysical account of belief such as we find in Levinas dovetails with
the pre-metaphysical meaning of faith. Not unlike Martin Heidegger's recourse to the pre-Socratics, or Marion's explorations of a Christian mysticism outside the confines of metaphysics, what we find in Levinas is an
ethics of faith that points beyond modern epistemology to the earliest articulations of Jewish *emunah*.

Levinas's critique of a propositional account of religious belief, like so much of the rest of his thinking, thus has two main sources, Heidegger and Judaism. Like Heidegger, Levinas regards the sphere of the mental, in which beliefs and representations reside, as derivative of the concrete social situation. Contrary to the metaphysical and largely Christian picture of religion as a set of beliefs or symbolic meanings about God that regulate the universe,[16] Levinas regards religion as a set of historical and normative practices that are themselves the ground, or the glue, for faith. The question of faith and even the very idea of God is not equivalent to the problem of religious belief as it arises in modern epistemology or the philosophy of religion: "The sentence in which God gets mixed in with words is not 'I believe in God.'"[17] The grounds for belief lie outside the mind of an individual in the normative interstices of sociality and history. Levinas's ethics of faith is thus diametrically opposed to W. K. Clifford's "ethics of belief," according to which an individual should assent only to what he can know for himself.[18] Levinas rejects both the individualism and the cognitivism of such an ethics of belief. He is concerned with a type of faith that is fundamentally social and nonindividualistic: "*Believe* is not a verb to be employed in the first person singular. Nobody can really say *I believe*—or *I do not believe*, for that matter—that God exists. The existence of God is not a question of an individual soul's uttering logical syllogisms. It cannot be proved. The existence of God, the *Sein Gottes*, is sacred history itself, the sacredness of man's relation to man through which God may pass. God's existence is the story of his revelation in biblical history."[19] That is to say, the social and historical are the milieu in which God makes sense. This milieu is the substance of faith, whereas the language of belief is merely a component of this faithful substance. What is important is to use the word "God" properly, but belief is not a privileged way of doing that. On the contrary, the language of God is rooted in social narratives and a shared history, as well as in performative occasions of prayer and ritual. The language of belief is derivative of the pragmatics of those assertions we are entitled to make about God in the social context of our religious condition. The propositional contents of beliefs, even of true beliefs, are not basic to the viability of God-talk but are what Heidegger called a "deficient mode" of relating to their "object," or what Wittgenstein and Rosenzweig might have called "pathological."[20] To isolate those beliefs and enumerate them as a set of assertions about the world is of course possible, but when this

ipens beliefs are deployed in their thinnest, most useless, and least plau-
_____e fashion. But if Levinas is reclaiming the noncognitivism at the basis
of religious life, then what he offers is not so much a religion deprived of
theology but an ethical interpretation of faith.

The idea that faith is inseparable from action goes back to Abraham. As Kenneth Seeskin points out: "It is not just that Abraham had a
high opinion of God but that he recognised His authority *and could be
counted on to obey it*. It is noteworthy, in this connection, that *emunah* is
sometimes translated as 'faith' and sometimes as 'faithful.' I would venture to say that from the standpoint of traditional Judaism, there is no
difference between them. The idea is that the man of faith is reliable.
Much the same is true of the original meaning of *faith* in English. . . .
Loyalty is above all an action-oriented concept. . . . It is no surprise, then,
that the Jewish understanding of faith finds its natural expression in the
notion of *covenant*. . . . It follows that for Judaism there is no conflict between faith and work."[21] To say, then, that someone is faithful is to say
that she is a person who exhibits or can be counted on to exhibit loyalty.
The notion that *emunah* involves loyalty in practice is decisive. To say
that Abraham's faith can be described as the belief that God is such and
such (e.g., existent or holy, good or reliable) is to miss something crucial
in the nature of Abraham's faith, namely, that it attaches itself to God *no
matter how God is described*. That is the whole point of the story of the
Akedah, the binding of Isaac. Abraham's faith is *in* God regardless of any
belief *that* God will be or act according to certain descriptions. This is
the crucial importance of the *personal* language of monotheism, which attaches to the *Who* of God regardless of the *What*. Similarly, Levinas's ethics of faith is not a belief *that* the other is such and such but a faithfulness
to the other: "The invoked is not what I comprehend: *he is not under a
category*. He is the one to whom I speak—he has only a reference to himself; he has no quiddity" (TI, 69/TeI, 41; see also TI, 64–70/TeI, 35–42).
The decisive character of this type of faith, then, is not the propositions
it affirms or denies but the loyalty or faithfulness it displays in action.
Without the act, or the readiness to act, we could not say, for example,
that Abraham "had" faith. This explains why God, too, is sometimes described as *el emunah*, a God of faith, which evidently does not mean that
God has faith but that God is faithful.[22]

This sense of faith as involving loyalty and dependability in action is underpinned by the range of meanings associated with the Hebrew word *emunah*, which can be translated equally as "faith," "belief," or "trust." Many of these meanings are markedly close to the Latin *fides* and, indeed, to the Greek *pistis*. In contrast, however, modern accounts of belief as a psychological disposition to regard an object as true or false have almost entirely dissociated it from its actional orientation and from its attachment to persons or personalities. In what might be called an epistemologization of faith, beliefs have come to be oriented toward truths, falsehoods, and states of affairs. I do not propose to reverse the mistake by severing faith from knowledge and truth, and so I will presently return to the problem of the veracity of faith. But my argument will be that truth itself shows a different face once we have a better picture of faith. For now, consider the range of the Hebrew *emunah*. Moshe Halbertal provides a useful sketch: "The source of the verb "to believe" [*le'ha'amin*] is in the giving of trust in relation to security [*bit'ahon*]. It is therefore not surprising that in the language of Scripture and in Hebrew generally one finds within the semantic field of belief [*emunah*] the "craftsman" [*omen*] whose work is to be trusted; the "nurse" or "midwife" [*omenet*], to whom the baby is entrusted; and "training" or "practice" [*imun*] whereby the practitioner acquires skill."[23] Note the emphasis on skill, practice, and dependability among the words related to belief. A couple of other valued members of the semantic family can be introduced. The adjective "loyal," *ne'eman*, should be mentioned, as well as *Amen*, the response one makes to confirm a prayer or assert the truth of what someone, usually someone else, says. The family resemblance between all these terms, as with the Latin *fides—fiduciary, fidelity, confidence*—lies in what we might today call trust. To believe and be believable is first of all to trust and be trustworthy; to "have" faith is to be faithful.

Significantly, the genealogy of the modern concept of "belief" is entwined with the genealogy of modern views about "truth." The latter is rooted in the ethical, legal, and, above all, personal sense of the Old English "trothe" (e.g., betroth). According to Richard Firth Green, our modern notion of truth as validity, independent of subjective or even human factors, is the result of a prolonged separation, in legal and evidentiary matters, of the accuracy of evidence from the testimony of witnesses. Before this separation, the "trothe" lay in the evidence of the witnesses, who were either reliable or not. But as evidence and witness were pried apart, testimony became a matter of trust while truth was rendered as accuracy.[24] In this regard it is notable that the Hebrew for "truth," *emet,* is simply a feminine form of *amen,* so that in Hebrew, as in Old English, truth and trust belong together. The historical and conceptual link between truth and trust must be kept in mind because in many respects it is similar to the relation between epistemic belief and covenantal faith. By contrast, the modern view of belief has been dissociated from its original attachment to the problematic trustworthiness of persons.

Among Jews it is of course Moses Maimonides who holds most of the responsibility for installing the imperative to believe in certain theological propositions within the heart of Judaism. In his view "belief is the affirmation that what has been represented is outside the mind just as it is in the mind."[25] But this view of belief as "warranted assertability," as it is called today, was of only limited success within post-Maimonidean Judaism. At the end of the fifteenth century, Isaac Abravanel could still urge readers of the *Guide of the Perplexed* to reconsider Maimonides' position: "But I have not found in the Holy Scriptures that *'Emunah* is said of a thing comprehended by thought and speculation, as being synonymous with knowledge and comprehension."[26] Moreover, even within the *Guide* the epistemic notion of belief is subject to sustained deconstruction, as we have seen. It is precisely in the chapters following I.51, in which belief is defined purely cognitively, that Maimonides develops his radical negative theology and thus effectively proves that cognition of God, and therefore belief, is structurally impossible. There is reason to think, then, that defining belief in terms of "certain knowledge," as Maimonides does in I.51, is a preliminary and provisional step and by no means a final accounting of *emunah.*

Accordingly, in asking about belief there are sound reasons for asking not only "*what* do you believe?" and "what do you take for true?" but also, indeed above all, "*who* do you trust?" Levinas's work helps us appreciate the etymological and historical roots of truth in the deep, dark recesses of trust; it also makes the more contentious philosophical claim that belief is still, today, derived from a phenomenological hermeneutic of faith. Such an analysis might allow us to avert a good deal of misunderstanding of religious belief that happens by misconstruing it in unduly cognitive terms. The phenomenology of trust that Levinas provides breaks with the epistemological tradition and brings us closer than we moderns have been for a long time to the original senses of *emunah*. The point can be illustrated by a well-known rabbinic anecdote:

> Our sages taught: It happened that a gentile came before Shammai and said, "How many Torot do you have?" He replied, "Two, the Written Torah and the Oral Torah." The man said, "I believe you (*ma'aminkha*) about the Written Torah, but I don't believe you (*eini ma'aminkah*) about the Oral Torah. Convert me so that I can learn the Written Torah [only]." He [Shammai] rebuked him and sent him away angrily. He came before Hillel, who converted him. On the first day he said to him, "*aleph, bet, gimel, dalet.*" The next day he reversed them. He [the man] said to him, "But yesterday didn't you teach it to me this way!" He [Hillel] said to him, "Have you not relied [*samakht*] on me? So rely on me also with regard to the Oral [Torah]!"[27]

The convert believes in the Written Torah, believes in Revelation. Presumably he is disposed to regard it as bearing truth, although he is not prepared to trust its rabbinic custodians. He wants theological truth without religion; belief without trust. Hillel's lesson teaches that there is no truth to revelation without trust in tradition. This is the same lesson Edmund Husserl derives in his "Origin of Geometry," which Derrida so brilliantly emphasized. Even formal, ideal objects, such as the geometric properties of a triangle, depend on the material and contingent a priori conditions of history.[28] Samuel Wheeler has compared this priority attributed to the Oral Torah (that is to say, to tradition) over the Written Torah to the semantic externalism of several philosophers, such as Derrida, Davidson, Heidegger, and the later Wittgenstein, whose views have in recent years become more proximate than was formerly imagined. As he puts it, the "Rabbis seem to have had views about language and truth that makes truth contingent on social decision but nonetheless objective."[29] I would put it slightly differently—for the Rabbis, truth is contingent on the sharing of interpreted beliefs—but the point essentially stands. Hillel and Levinas surely belong to this group for whom the social conditions for truth always presuppose relationships of trust with persons. Levinas is explicit: "To seek truth, I have already established a relationship with a face which can guarantee itself, whose epiphany itself is somehow a word of honor. Every language as an exchange of verbal signs refers already to this primordial word of honor. . . . Deceit and veracity already presuppose the absolute authenticity of the face" (TI, 202/TeI, 177). Modifying Descartes's argument from the

Third Meditation, Levinas argues that subjective knowledge can avoid the infinite regress of skepticism only if it acknowledges the trust it has already given the other. Descartes's methodological doubt is emblematic of the epistemological transformation of faith into belief in modernity. For Descartes, personal loyalty and practical reliability are subordinated to an inquiry into the truth values of impersonal states of affairs. Although he is far from alone in the endeavor, for Levinas the task is to reanimate the question of the truth of belief by returning it to the elements of sociality and speech, trust and testimony, which originally characterized faith. His modification of Descartes's Third Meditation, such that it is the Other who guarantees the veracity of my doubtful experiences, is aimed at recovering the moral faith that has been subordinated to epistemic belief. As Wittgenstein remarked, "*The basic form* of our game must be one in which there is no such thing as doubt."[30] Or again: "A language game is only possible if one trusts [*verlässt*] something (I did not say 'can trust something')."[31] The web of belief is itself enveloped by a web of trust. In Levinas's Judaically informed view, this thought of Wittgenstein's is tantamount to "the impossibility of a world without religion."[32]

Before Good and Evil: Covenant and *Caritas*

Seeskin alerted us to another important aspect of faith, namely, that its inseparability from action is what characterizes it as covenantal faith. Faith and works are not merely compatible but are inseparable, and this inseparability is called covenant. This is further reason why Levinas's "ethics" ought to be understood as a secularized account of covenantal faithfulness. When we take faith in its pre-propositional, covenantal sense, with the primacy it accords to socio-historical relations and normative action, Levinas's entire project looks like an ethical interpretation of faith. Moreover, we gain a valuable perspective on religious belief when we view it from the secularized standpoint of ethics, because then the hermeneutical substance of the faith underlying religious belief shows its face. This will presently allow us to revisit, from this ethico-hermeneutical perspective, the question of the truth of religious belief.

Before doing so, however, let us explore two notable features of the covenant of faith that will prepare the way for a recovery of the problem of truth as it arises both in Judaism and in Levinas's secularized, ethical interpretation of it. We have seen that the idea of covenant involves a loyalty that does not depend on the sort of properties borne by the Other. Covenantal faith means that such loyalty goes beyond the moral character of the other, beyond the question of whether the other is good or not, deserving or unworthy. Ethics becomes covenantal when it acknowledges obligations that are not contracted and cannot be abrogated. This position is emphasized by later Levinas far more than by early Levinas. For Levinas's ethics is based not on the character or qualities of the other, not on the idea of the rational nature of the other, and not even on empathy with the destitution of the other. No description of the other justifies my obligations but, on the contrary, obligation constitutes the field in which justification takes place. That is why for Levinas 2 the point is that even in cases in which the other appears as hostile or morally reprehensible, the covenantal bond—ethics—cannot be severed. Indeed, it is *only* when the other appears in this way that covenantal faith is exercised and made explicit, as the trials of Abraham attest. In that case, as with Job, the otherness of God assumes a malevolent face, murderous and persecuting, and faith is credited to the person who does not relinquish trust that God will come around.[33] The hallmarks of covenantal faith are therefore loyalty and disinterestedness. The trial motif in monotheistic faith asks one to accept a will running counter to one's own interests, a malevolent will, which exposes a loyalty to the Other no matter what He or She does. It is this notion of ethics as covenantal faith, extending to the malevolence of the Other, that stands behind the shocking "ethical language" that Levinas 2 develops. In his view, ethics—or, as we can now properly call it, the ethics of covenantal faith—is an "obsession," "persecution," "trauma," and "hostage." Some critics have been puzzled, others outraged at this moral vocabulary, asking why such a pathological condition should be regarded as a moral one. But this is because Levinas is figuring, or disfiguring, ethics in terms of covenantal faith, as a bond that does not depend on, even as it hopes for, the benevolence of the other.

The second feature of the covenantal ethics of Levinas 2 is its passivity or choicelessness. Later Levinas regards the ethical relation as prior to the freedom of the will, which is exactly how we should understand covenantal faith. One is not free to desist from trusting, to desist from this bond with the other, even if one can and, indeed, one ought to work within such trust by shaping it in various ways. Covenantal faith is not contractual. It is not like a contractual arrangement among liberal individuals in which parties freely enter into a mutually obligating relationship and in which the validity and value of that relationship depend on the freedom of the parties to enter it. Rather, in the case of the covenant, as Jon D. Levenson says, "the wrong choice results in nothing short of death."[34] That is exactly the sort of covenantal faith Levinas is talking about. As in "ethics," so it is in the covenant—exit amounts to an abrogation of life. Within covenantal faith there is no such thing as life prior to moral life, for life itself always already implies ethics. The idea harks back to Deuteronomy: "See, I have set before you this day life and good, death and evil. . . . I call heaven and earth to witness against you this day, that I have set before you life and death, blessing and curse; therefore choose life, that you and your descendants may live" (Deut. 30:15, 19). Covenant is hardly a matter of choice. The alternative is between life, which is good, and death and evil. To decline the covenant is not merely to abstain from entering into a moral contract but to refuse the good of life itself. This makes covenant hardly a matter of choice or of the exercise of a will freely assuming commitments. Levinas 2, whose aim is to describe the ethicality of subjectivity rather than any set of particular values or actions, likewise insists that ethics is not based on commitment, decision, choice, or free will: "The condition of being hostage is not chosen; if there had been a choice, the subject would have kept his as-for-me, and the exits found in inner life. But this subjectivity, his very psyche, is for the other, his very bearing independence consists in supporting the other, expiating for him. . . . The one-for-the-other is not a commitment" (OB, 136/AE, 173–74). The ethics of faith, the covenant, depends neither on the moral character of the Other nor on the choice or commitment to enter it. Commenting on the locus classicus in rabbinic literature that reiterates this covenantal structure, in which God is portrayed as holding Mount Sinai over the people of Israel and offering the "choice" of Torah or death, Levinas asks: "Is it certain, though, that the Israelites spoke against all logic and all reasonable reason? Maybe they expressed their trust [*confiance*]. Through trust in him who speaks, we promise to obey the very origin of trust prior to all examination. Nothing is less paradoxical, except the very origin of trust prior to all examination."[35]

   The accusation leveled against Levinas, that this ethics is violent, coercive, and devoid of moral content,[36] is thus mitigated by considering the phenomenological priority of trust in concrete life. Levinas's answer to the liberal objection is to appeal to the covenantal condition of life itself. Without this bond to the other, and despite its manifest risks, there could be no human life, no rationality or understanding, and no good or evil. As Putnam comments, "Without ethics one cannot even enter into the world."[37] It is only in the light of the Other that we see light. Accordingly, Levinas's sense of ethics does not contest Nietzsche's insight that ordinary goods and evils are in so many ways contingent, unstable, and reversible. But rather than rising to an ethics beyond conventional good and evil, Levinas emphasizes the way we are caught up with ethics before good and evil, before ethics has been determined in terms of rules, laws, or values: "If ethical terms arise in our discourse, before the terms freedom and non-freedom, it is because before the bipolarity of good and evil presented to choice, the subject finds himself committed to the Good in the very passivity of supporting" (OB, 122/AE, 157). This is important to recall, for the "responsibility" that Levinas preaches can easily be misunderstood as a call for order moralistically imposed within the banalities of ordinary political discourse.[38] But by situating "responsibility" *before* conventional good and evil, Levinas is making an entirely different claim, which goes to the constitution of the self *as* ethical response. "Responseability" for the other *is* the very identity of the self, one that belies the idea of a substantive subject that "has" obligations that can be discharged like items on a shopping list and then left innocently alone. Maurice Blanchot caught sight of this apophatic quality of ethical subjectivity, which "causes me to disappear in the infinite movement of service where I am only temporarily singular and a simulacrum of unity," "a me without selfhood."[39]

Moreover, the distinction between the good as the object of moral experience—goods and evils that one encounters in the world, such as values or actions, individuals or regimes—and the Good of the bond between self and other is the very condition for intelligibility. It is what gives sense to life and therefore to moral experience, much like Heidegger's distinction between being and beings. The covenant of ethics is "immemorial" rather than empirical, which means that it is transcendental—ethics is the indispensable condition enabling a meaningful world, although it is precisely not a condition that an individual subject, even idealized, could cognize, much less realize alone. Levinas 2 provides philosophy with the novel idea that there is no adequate explanation or description for the fact of obligation but on the contrary that obligations are the precondition for our capacity to reason. The ethics of faith, covenantal fidelity, is what makes "life" possible. We do not choose or commit to it from the vantage of our separate individuality but live *within* it. As with the covenant, the bonds of ethical subjectivity cannot simply be abrogated but are imposed irrespective of choice or will—"a fraternity that cannot be abrogated, an unimpeachable assignation" (OB, 87/AE, 109–10)—and are thus, as Slavoj Žižek calls it, an "ethical violence."[40] In biblical theology the risk that such ethical violence will degrade into slavery is tempered by the memory and promise of God's redemptive love. But the covenant is still a violation of the fantasy of autonomy and presents an unavoidable risk since there is no exit from it short of the collapse of the created order and no guarantee that the Other will in fact be good.[41] In Levinas's secular version of covenantal faith, the idea is that *we live in trust*, in ordinary but absolutely indispensable, numberless ways. Even as none of us can avoid betrayal and malevolence, everyday life is entirely under the sway of the rule of faith. The point is not merely anthropological or sociological; it is ontological and transcendental, and it names "ethics" as the condition for intelligibility as such.

The hermeneutics of trust precedes the hermeneutics of suspicion and enables it, just as the interpretative principle of charity enables misunderstanding, disagreement, and error.[42] Gianni Vattimo has remarked on how the thoughts of Heidegger and Donald Davidson converge on this point in order to argue, more like Levinas than Heidegger or Davidson, that the interpretative principle of charity has moral and political implications. The principle of charity, according to which one's own capacity for understanding presupposes that one take most of what another speaker says to be rational and coherent, is also an ethical principle of *caritas*.[43] Heidegger alluded to this when he cited Augustine in support of his critique of metaphysical objectivism: "One does not enter into the truth except through charity."[44] It was Levinas, however, who insisted that entering truth through charity is not a neutral hermeneutical principle or a mere semantic necessity but an ethically significant condition that implicates meaning, truth, and understanding in the bonds of obligation. Reversing Aristotle's famous apothegm, Vattimo puts it this way: "*Amica veritas, sed magis amicus Plato.*"[45] But in contrast to Vattimo's Rortian irreverence for objective truth, it seems to me that the better interpretation of the principle of *caritas* does not subordinate the semantic to the ethical but implies that they are two arcs of the one hermeneutical circle, or two mobile moments on the one Möbius strip. At any rate, the reintroduction of the forgotten ethical dimension of hermeneutical charity suggests that it is Levinas who gives Augustine's principle its fullest modern determination. For Augustine, the crucial point about interpretative charity is that it yields the sense of love. As he puts it, "whoever thinks he has understood the divine scriptures or any part of them in such a way that does not build up the twin love of neighbor and God has not understood them at all."[46] For Levinas, as for Vattimo, this principle of scriptural exegesis governs understanding in general. Ethical faith is the very substance of interpretative *caritas*. For Heidegger and Davidson the principle of charity implies that we live *in* truth, but Levinas emphasizes "the other side" of the Möbius band on which interpretation runs, namely, that we live *in* trust. For this reason, too, it is not a matter of "having" faith or leaping into it, for one already abides in the ethical covenant of faith.

The objection that Levinas's ethics is unethical because it does not distinguish between the good other and the evil other is therefore met not by denying the accusation but by yielding to it. Levinas aims to awaken a sense of covenantal faith that constitutes each of us in relation to others—"oneself as one-for-the-other"—rather than to provide objective values or rules that capture the sense of ethics. It is moral prophecy as much as moral philosophy that is at work in Levinas's call for people to "awaken, awaken" to their covenantal condition, for he too is responding to the eclipse of goodness in everyday life.[47] When Levinas's account of covenantal ethical faith is understood as the constitutive condition of the self and its entire horizon of meaning, the moralist's indignant protest at the tyranny of the Other appears as but a liberal objection to our ineliminable interdependence. Levinas's response is therefore to affirm the objection: "Responsibility for another is not an accident that happens to a subject, but precedes essence in it, has not awaited freedom, in which a commitment to another would have been made. I have not done anything and I have been under accusation—persecuted. The ipseity, in the passivity without arche characteristic of identity, is a hostage" (OB, 114/AE, 145). But this traumatic ethical condition implies a tremendous affirmation: "Responsibility for the other, this way of answering without a prior commitment, is human fraternity itself, and it is prior to freedom" (OB, 116/AE, 148). On the extreme republican language of ethics, in which fraternity radically qualifies the principles of liberty and equality ("the self, the persecuted one, is accused beyond his fault before his freedom, and thus in an unavowable innocence"), Levinas is perfectly clear: "One must not conceive it to be in the state of original sin; it is, on the contrary, the original goodness of creation" (OB, 121/AE, 155). This is not to say that one is obliged to every villain who comes one's way or that one should not exercise prudence in one's social and political relationships. Levinas is not appealing to the naïf to deliver himself to every bastard on the scene but is alerting us to the fact that being and knowing are already and always regulated by the ethical response we make of ourselves to the other. Ethics does not demand that one yield to the tyranny of others but to work judiciously within the ethical bonds of sense that, as Jean-Luc Nancy has brilliantly argued, is the *sense we are*.[48] There is no avoiding the ethical covenant, for it is only *in* it and *through* it that we make sense of ourselves, of beings, and of others. Instead of choosing, deciding, committing, or renouncing, it is a matter of tending to these bonds—in our most intimate as in our political relationships—for it is to that ethical covenant that we are entirely abandoned, that is to say, entrusted.

Trust: Heidegger

If Levinas's covenantal ethics is indebted to a Judaic account of the primacy of normative faith over epistemic belief, collateral debt is nevertheless owed to Heidegger.[49] As is well known, perhaps the central concept of *Being and Time*, which Levinas never ceased to regard as the seminal philosophical work of our time, is "care," *Sorge*, which is related to the practical concern with entities (*besorgen*) and everyday social relations with others (*Fürsorge* or solicitude). Care is the fluid in being, what makes beings matter in the various ways they do. Care is the "under" part of understanding, and understanding is the basis for meaning in general and for the disclosure of truth. Care is the prereflective way that entities assume significance within the world by mattering in this or that way. Now, according to Levinas's standard critique, when Heidegger ontologizes care he strips it of all moral connotations and reduces ethics to the impersonal and inauthentic realm of "the one" (*das Man*). But Levinas's strong misreading of Heidegger ignores the positive modes of solicitude explicitly emphasized in the crucial §26 of *Being and Time*. No doubt this interpretation, already in play from the mid-1930s, was guided by knowledge of Heidegger's ontopolitical commitment to the authentic destiny of the Volk.[50] It is therefore particularly noteworthy that despite Levinas's constant polemic against Heidegger, at several key moments he defends his foe against the accusation that *Being and Time* is not concerned with others. Consider, for example, his final reflections on Heidegger from 1987: "The concern-for-being of the human being-there [*Dasein*] also bears the concern for the other man, the care of one for the other. It is not added onto being-there, but is a constitutive articulation of that *Dasein*. A concern for the other man, a care for his food, drink, clothing, health, and shelter. A care which is not belied by the actual solitude of the solitary or the indifference one may feel for one's fellowman, a solitude and indifference that, being deficient modes of the *for-the-other*, confirm it."[51] This sympathy for the way Heidegger attends to the concrete singularity of personal beings in their interrelated phenomenality goes back to Levinas's earliest appraisal of *Being and Time*.[52] But perhaps the most striking example of Levinas's Heideggerianism is attested in his critical remarks on Martin Buber's philosophy of "I and Thou." The problem with Buber, says Levinas, is that the I-Thou relation is described in a merely formal and spiritual way, without regard for the details of the material character of the other as presented in the concrete specificity of its situation. And yet it is only by attending to the specificity of the other that ethical sense manifests.

Buber rises in violent opposition to the Heideggerian notion of *Fürsorge* which, to the German philosopher, would be access to Others. It is certainly not from Heidegger that one should take lessons on the love of man or social justice. But *Fürsorge* as response to an essential destitution accedes to the alterity of the Other. It takes into account that dimension of height and misery through which the very epiphany of others takes place. Misery and poverty are not properties of the Other, but the modes of his or her appearing to me, ways of concerning me, and modes of proximity. One may wonder whether clothing the naked and feeding the hungry do not bring us closer to the neighbor than the rarefied atmosphere in which Buber's Meeting sometimes takes place.[53]

Levinas's usual charge against Heidegger—that Dasein's *Jemeinigkeit*, "mineness," is a solipsistic immanence akin to egoism, or that the authentic moment of the disclosure of being is deaf to the other—is here debunked by Levinas himself. In fact, as Levinas moved beyond his initial attempt in the years following World War II to distance himself from Heidegger, his thought developed in a way that brought him closer to the German philosopher. *Otherwise than Being* is far more Heideggerian than *Totality and Infinity*. In 1961 Levinas was still operating within a contractual notion of ethics that viewed the self as an island of solitude "separated" from the other, and ethics as the way of creating the intersubjective fields of time, objectivity, justice, and so forth. Ethics bridged the distance separating self from other, thus inflecting but essentially preserving the epistemological paradigm that philosophers from Descartes to Husserl affirmed. Like these thinkers, for early Levinas, self and other are thought as separate spheres of consciousness, except that since the "analogical apprehensions" of the transcendental cogito fail to secure intersubjective knowledge, Levinas proposes that the breakthrough comes from the ethical epiphany of the face.[54] Ethics overcomes the natural separation of persons and thereby accomplishes an intersubjective, and thus objective, world. But this recourse to an ontologically independent subject, even if such a subject plays the role of ethical host, is a rejection of Heidegger's breakthrough, which situates the very opening of *Dasein* in its external relations with others. As Levinas 1 put it: "From the start I repudiate the Heideggerian conception that views solitude in the midst of a prior relationship with the other."[55] Accordingly, despite the extraordinary novelty and exquisite descriptions provided by Levinas 1, ethics is still premised on a Cartesian account of the subject's ontological solitude and regarded as the solution to the problem of transcendental subjectivism. Heidegger argued, though, that this premise and the "problems" it generated for philosophers from Descartes to Husserl were, in essence, pseudo-problems: "It is wrong to oppose to objects an isolated ego-subject, without seeing in the Dasein the basic constitution of being-in-the-world; but it is equally wrong to suppose that the problem is seen in principle and progress made toward answering it if the solipsism of the isolated ego is replaced by a solipsism en deux in the I-thou relationship."[56] As *Being and Time* puts it: "Even Dasein's Being-alone is Being-with in the world. The Other can *be missing* only *in* and *for* a Being-with. Being-alone is a deficient mode of Being-with."[57] This is effectively the position adopted by Levinas 2, although he might say rather that being-alone is a deficient mode of being-*for*-the-other. *Totality and Infinity* should therefore be regarded as the last, perhaps the most noble, and certainly one of the most beautiful works of transcendental subjectivism, for thereafter Levinas denies the possibility of being "at home with oneself" as a "self-referential" "egoism" that is "independent" and "free."[58] For Levinas 2, ethics is no longer a matter of "receiving" or "welcoming" the other, as *Totality and Infinity* proposed, for there never was a time when the self was ontologically or phenomenologically independent.

Levinas's *Kehre* therefore led him to a covenantal account of ethics indebted to Judaic notions of faith whose profound proximity to early Heidegger cannot be gainsaid. In Marion's incisive account, the only difference between Levinas 2 and Heidegger 1 is that Levinas *names* the passive and exposed self as a hostage to the Other whereas Dasein is thrown and expelled into Being.[59] Marlène Zarader proposes that the difference between Levinas 2 and Heidegger can be explained only in terms of Levinas's attempt to describe the same phenomena without *neutralizing* their ethical significance under the anonymous name of "being."[60] For in *Being and Time* the very "meaning of being," even in fleeting moments of the authentic disclosure of truth, remains fundamentally social. Levinas himself says so: "When Heidegger formulates *Being-in-the-world, Being-for-death*, and *Being-with-others*, what he adds to our age-old knowledge of our presence in the world, our mortality, our sociality, is that these prepositions *in, for*, and *with* are in the root of the verb 'to be' (as *ex* is in the root of *ex*ist)."[61]

The argument according to which Levinas's "ethics," especially in its later, radicalized mode, is an interpretation of Jewish covenantal faith—passively encumbered, extending beyond the moral character of the other, preceding and enabling the distinction between good and evil, inseparable from action—should therefore be understood to derive as much from Judaism as from Heidegger. Like the covenant of ethics, "care" designates an irrevocable bond of being-with and being-for the other, a fluid bond that constitutes who one is and, indeed, one's entire horizon of intelligibility. Moreover, today we know that Heidegger's ontological interpretation of *Sorge* emerged precisely from forays into *the phenomenology of faith* and, in particular, the phenomenology of trust. This has been thoroughly documented by recent scholarship into Heidegger's formative period. For example, in a comment penned to his 1922 "Introduction" to a book on Aristotle, we find Heidegger explicating the notion of "care" as "the highest form of taking Being in trust."[62] What came to be called "care" in *Being and Time* began as an account of *the bonded fidelity to the social and histori-cal ground of being,* in other words, *a covenant of being.* What seems, with Levinas, to be an archaic account of ethical faithfulness when compared to the modern propositional notion of belief is in fact a Heideggerian inter-pretation of *emunah.* As Derrida said, "The point of departure of *Sein und Zeit* resides in a situation that cannot be radically alien to what is called *faith.* Not religion, to be sure, nor theology, but that which in faith acqui-esces before or beyond all questioning, in the already common experience of a language and of a 'we.'"[63] Heidegger's response to Ernst Troeltsch's epistemic characterization of faith in terms of cognitive beliefs prompted him, as Theodore Kisiel comments, to return to biblical notions of faith: "Citing a passage in the Old Testament which identifies faith with unshak-able trust and secure expectation, he [Heidegger] makes a note to himself to read the psalms of trusting faith."[64] Had Heidegger done so, he would have come across Psalm 31:6.

Into Your hand I entrust (*afkid*) my spirit;
You redeem me, O YHWH, faithful God (*el emet*).

The word translated as faithful is *emet,* which in many contexts, in-cluding modern Hebrew, means "true." Seeskin points out that the Septua-gint renders *el emet* as *theos tes aletheias,* which Brenton translates as "God of truth." He argues that by translating *el emet* as *theos tes aletheias* rather than as "faithful God," the Septuagint and thereafter Christianity effects "a sub-tle shift from a moral quality to an epistemological one."[65] This emboldens Seeskin to contend that the Hellenization of scripture transforms faith from the ethical to the epistemic register. But this interpretation cannot be sus-tained. The difference between *aletheia* as "truth" and *emet* as "trust" does not correlate with the putative difference between Greco-Christian epis-temic belief and Judaic normative faith. Rather, it seems that the notion of faith undergoes this shift from the moral to the epistemological much later, under the pressure of modern concepts of verification and accuracy that stem not from Hellenism but from developments in law and science, when criteria for truth are dramatically depersonalized or "neutralized." This view accords with Smith's historical analysis of the constriction of faith into epis-temic belief in modernity and with his contention that the contrast is not between Christian belief and Jewish faith, as Seeskin, following Buber, sup-poses, but between premodern faith and the modern obsession with depersonalized, verifiable beliefs. It was precisely this modern notion of belief that inspired Heidegger to turn to *aletheia* for an alternative to the epistemological concern for truth as the objective validity of universals, certain propositions, or warranted assertions. Heidegger turned to Aristotle and the pre-Socratics and roundly ignored the many nuanced uses of *aletheia* that can be found in the Septuagint, the New Testament, and the works of the Greek fathers, to say nothing of his complete elision of the Hebrew cognates of *aletheia* that they often translate (*emunah, amen, ne'eman,* and so forth).

Zarader's compelling analysis of Heidegger's debt to the Hebraic tradition could thus perhaps be extended. Instead of the eclipse and apocalypse of YHWH, Heidegger leads us to the concealment (*Verborgenheit*) and unconcealment (*Entborgenheit, Enthülltheit*) of Being, the revelation of Being (*Offenbarkeit*), the withdrawal of Being (*Entzug*), the forgetfulness of Being (*Seinsvergessenheit*), and the forsakenness of Being (*Seinsverlassenheit*). But are these not evidently secularized, almost desperately Hellenized (in fact Germanicized), articulations of the *Hebraica veritas* of the *emet of YWHW*, that covenantal faithfulness that perdures through concealment and revelation, withdrawal and forsakenness? For his part, Levinas opposed neither the secularization nor the Hellenization of the Judaic. It was the *neutralization* of *emunah* under the purely ontological interpretation of *Sorge* and the depersonalization or, worse, the demoralization of *emet* in the guise of *aletheia* that he contested. This contestation therefore involves a re-expropriation of the Judaic in the service of ethics, in other words, a rejudaization of Heidegger's neutralization of and "unavowed debt" to the Hebraic. Levinas's Judaization of phenomenology is not an antiphilosophical gesture so much as a just corrective of Heidegger's phenomenological hermeneutic. In moving from epistemological truth to truth as disclosure, Heidegger revived but veiled the normative force of faith as covenental fidelity to revelation. For Levinas, this irreducibly ethical dimension of faithfulness was revealed through the interpretative actuality of the Judaic heritage. Heidegger had glimpsed this very notion of phenomenological faith in his formative period when he turned from scholastic dogmatism, which at this time he ascribed to the influence of Greek philosophy, to the proto-phenomenological insights of primitive and mystical Christianity.[66] My argument, then, is not meant to suggest that early Heidegger deliberately occludes the Judaic but that, when Levinas proposes a Judaic interpretation of *ethics as faith*, he is repeating the phenomenological hermeneutic begun but quickly abandoned by the young Heidegger, whose infidelity to the phenomenology of faith led him to neutralize and demoralize the fundamental notions of care, truth, and being. This would not have been possible had he remained within a Pauline, Augustinian, or even medieval Christian mystical phenomenological horizon. For what matters for a phenomenological recovery of faith is not whether the faith is Christian, as Heidegger fleetingly appreciated, or Jewish, as Levinas consistently understood, but that this faith, which early Heidegger understood as "the persistent underground of intellectual development," is fundamentally and resolutely ethical.[67] And this is the case whether one calls it "pistis," "fides," or "emunah." Levinas's ethics accomplishes this deneutralization of being through its recovery of the phenomenology of faith.

For post-metaphysical philosophy, as for pre-metaphysical religion, truth and trust belong together. The significant difference between Heidegger and Levinas is that care for being discloses an impersonal, anonymous truth of disclosure, whereas the ethics of faith reveals truth in the name of the other. Great as this difference is, care for being *always* involves others and presupposes their trust, just as Levinas's ethics of faith must incorporate truth, and not only the truth revealed and concealed in the other but also the truths of epistemic belief. For the phenomenology of faith must inevitably, and quite legitimately, concern itself with "the truth content" of religious beliefs.

We can now clarify a problem that has remained in the background, although it besets Levinas's entire ethics, post-metaphysical theology in general, and this book in particular. Does the interpretation of faith as trust make light of the cognitive and propositional contents that undoubtedly constitute religious belief? How can we talk of religious belief without talking about truth, or about what belief takes to be true? Without following the hermeneutical circle or, as I prefer, the Möbius strip leading from faith to belief (religious or otherwise), the ethical covenant would collapse under the weight of its own concretion. The ethics of faith would, as Badiou charged, amount merely to piety, dogmatism, and rigid behavioralism in which philosophy *and* theology have been "annulled" by the "essentially religious" element of Levinas's ethics.[68] Without recovering the capacity for disagreement, error, and deliberation, the primacy accorded to normative social life would leave "ethics" short of the minimum conditions for action, responsibility, and critique and block the passage from faith to belief. This predicament besets not only Levinas's ethics of faith but also a range of related problems concerning religious belief in the modern world. But, as we know, where the danger is, there grows the saving power.

Justified Beliefs, or Corresponsive Truth

The problem of the veracity of religious belief is the same whether one talks about religious beliefs or beliefs generally. According to Levinas, *all* beliefs are derived from the covenantal ethical relation. How, then, are we to justify veridical religious beliefs? How are we warranted to assert their veracity? By deriving veridical beliefs from ethical faithfulness or, to use Bernard Williams's terms, by deriving accuracy from sincerity.[69] Levinas never intended, much less proposed, to throw out the baby of truth with the bathwater of epistemology but rather provided an account that illuminated the ethical face of truth and belief. Although Levinas surely prized ethics over epistemology, the critique of epistemology never amounted to a rejection of the legitimate enterprise of getting beliefs right as much as it explained how such a process might be morally and philosophically justified. One could even say that Levinas was concerned with nothing but *justified belief*, where "justified" refers to ethics rather than epistemology. Just as the "objective" truth of being is always already exposed to ethics, so too ethics is always already disposed to "objectivity."[70] From the perspective of faith, the accuracy of beliefs is an effect of ontology *as* solidarity. The old *correspondence theory* of truth is replaced with an even older *corresponsive account* of truthfulness. Corresponsive is here meant to refer not only to interpersonal relations but also to our corresponsiveness to shared objects encountered in a shared world by means of shared languages. Since the ethics of faith exposes one to the other *within* oneself, it demands the internalization of the "intersubjective" field, to the greatest extent possible. Minimally, this involves acknowledging the veridical nature of belief, that is, that belief is not in fact a "subjective" attitude but analytically implies the capacity to consider the object from another perspective, from which it might turn out to be false. One could not believe anything to be the case without comparing and associating one's own responses to the world with those of other creatures.[71] This Davidsonian interpretation of Levinas's account of belief (if I have correctly understood Davidson) is useful for making good sense of Levinas, that is, for reading him charitably. I am suggesting that the ethical internalization of the other does not leave one blinded by the light of the Other, as some readings of Levinas suggest, but compels one to acknowledge that true beliefs are what we *share* by virtue of our ethical imbrication. The ethics of faith implies modes of objective belief, including religious belief, because it describes precisely the process of subjectivizing the field of intersubjectivity and internalizing the vision and perspective of others into the folds of self-presence. Despite the resemblance to G. W. F. Hegel, this is less of a dialectical accomplishment than a phenomenological accession to the *plurality* of origins of sense given through other people's take on the world.[72] Although Levinas 2 is no doubt modifying Heidegger's groundbreaking account of the social basis of meaning and knowledge in an explicitly ethical direction, his covenantal account of ethics above all affirms the critique of methodological solipsism and epistemological foundationalism made in *Being and Time*. For example, Levinas 2 writes: "Paradoxically enough, thinkers claim to derive communication out of self-coinciding. They do not take seriously the radical reversal, from cognition to solidarity, that communication represents with respect to inward dialogue, to cognition of oneself. . . . The relationship with the other precedes the auto-affection of certainty, to which one always tries to reduce communication" (OB, 118–19/AE, 151–52).[73]

Levinas is noting, as many others have since Heidegger and Wittgenstein, that cognition is first of all an external, social phenomenon and that internal dialogue—including belief—already implies relations with others with whom one shares the world. The point applies to beliefs in general, and religious belief is simply a species of ordinary belief. Accordingly, when Levinas says that "responsibility is what first enables one to catch sight of and conceive of value" (OB, 123/AE, 159), I understand him to mean that "values," which are the moral *beliefs* one has, that is, the moral propositions one is disposed to affirm, are derived from the *faithful responsiveness one makes (of oneself) to the other*. In other words, ethical faith is what enables one to catch sight of and conceive of moral belief. But not only moral belief. For the covenantal faith Levinas exposes is not simply the basis of the moral component of life but of intelligibility in general. Accordingly, covenantal faith enables one to catch sight of and conceive of true belief generally. Far from jettisoning the truth of beliefs, ethics justifies beliefs by accounting for the corresponsiveness of truth itself.

The important point, as Jeff Malpas explains, is that by regarding the intelligibility of one's own psychological makeup as dependent on the priority of communication and shared understanding, one cannot in principle exclude *any* other speaker from making a claim on one's own beliefs. Levinas, like Heidegger, takes this to apply not only to one's psychological constitution and beliefs but also to the very idea of oneself. The contours of *self*-understanding stretch as far as the horizon of the encounter with others, without any a priori limits on *who* the other is or what claims he or she might make. The important point is that *inner sense* "is not a horizon which is exclusively our own, but one that belongs to other speakers also. That overall horizon can only be the horizon of the world as such. But in that case the world—the world-horizon—is not just my world, or even our world, but a world we hold in common with all speakers."[74] In regarding communication as an external relation to the other that has already been internalized or is endlessly being internalized, Levinas must regard *all* speakers as potentially making a claim on the self. As indeed he does.

This is perhaps the great difference between Kierkegaard and Levinas; the former remains a subjective thinker of religion, whereas the latter, for whom subjectivity is stitched with others, accedes to philosophy. Kierkegaard's night of faith remains in the dark, but Levinas's ethical self, who is also constituted faithfully, makes sense of itself by corresponsive communication with the other, with *any* other, within itself and outside itself. The holistic horizon of interpretative charity is both the condition for true beliefs and the avowal of a moral world shared by all speakers. Border lines between religions such as those marked by custom and law in no way obstruct the overlapping of wisdom, the sharing of sense, and the ensuing hermeneutical transformations of theological belief. The history of theology proves this at every turn. This does not imply a teleological horizon of one religion in which all horizons have been fused but an endless process of making sense of ourselves relationally. The very idea of rational religious belief in principle implies an open horizon of claimants. Citing an apothegm from Islamic philosophy, Maimonides instructed Jews to "know the truth from whoever speaks it."[75] As Davidson puts it, "If we cherish rationality, then we are bound to seek discourse with others, for we owe our ability to entertain thoughts and to reason to the society of others, and the better we understand others the better we understand the world and ourselves."[76]

Jewish philosophers expressed a similar view by invoking Deuteronomy 4:6: "For this is your wisdom and your understanding *in the sight of the nations* which shall hear all these statutes and say, 'Surely, that great nation is a wise and discerning people.'" Important medieval interpretations of this verse took it to mean that the wisdom and understanding of Israel depends precisely on "the sight [literally 'eyes'] of the nations," that is to say, on the community's own beliefs making sense in the eyes of other nations. For Bahya Ibn Pakuda and Abraham Ibn Daud these beliefs were of a theological kind pertaining to dogmatics. But Maimonides added the community's scientific beliefs, which he insisted should also be judged "in the eyes of the nations." This led him to modify the method for calculating the lunar calendar in light of the best scientific practice of his day, even though this amounted to an explicit and self-conscious break with the Talmudic tradition. Most strikingly, in addition to philosophical and scientific belief, Maimonides argues that the rationality of Israelite *law* also needs to be seen in the eyes of the nations. As Isadore Twersky noted, this implies that for Maimonides "the reasons [for the laws] must be universally intelligible and persuasive" and, more generally, that "the Torah as a whole is grounded in reason and wisdom."[77] Levinas liked to make a similar point by citing a rabbinic gloss to the preamble to the covenant in Deuteronomy 27, which states: "And you shall write upon the stones all the words of this law very clearly." The Talmud interprets "very clearly" to mean "in seventy languages," signifying all spoken languages and therefore the unrestricted communicability of covenantal faith.[78] Commenting on this passage, Levinas proposes that it heralds the "liberation" and "universalization" of the Jewish covenant.[79] *Totality and Infinity* and *Otherwise than Being* communicate this exegesis.

Ethics therefore has no more need to renounce theology, as Levinas sometimes implied, than phenomenology has the need to repudiate veridical beliefs generally. Prereflective phenomenological faith traces beliefs, just as it traces values, back to their origins in an ethical covenant. The point is not to sacrifice the epistemic objects of belief but to acknowledge that religious beliefs—like all beliefs—are products of fidelity, sincerity, and truthfulness with respect to all that we share ("the world"), which is all that we are, even as the "we" who we are designates differently, or at least unpredictably, on each occasion. For this reason the problem of religious belief can only be answered indexically, with respect to the fragile, porous, mobile "we" that each one of us is.[80] Religious beliefs, as with all beliefs, are products of our corresponsiveness to the world and to each other; they therefore have a human face. And for this reason Levinas reduces truth to testimony—in the phenomenological sense of a reduction that leads back rather than in an eliminationist sense—although it is important to keep in mind that testimony is not a subject's "own" "subjective" point of view but one that incorporates the claims of others. As Levinas puts it, "this reduction always has to be attempted, because of the trace of sincerity that the words themselves bear, and which they owe to saying as witness . . . where, in the midst of the information communicated to another, there signifies also the sign that is given to him of this giving of signs. That is the resonance of every language 'in the name of God,' the inspiration or prophecy of all language" (OB, 194/AE, 152). This tracing of truth back to testimony neither collapses into subjectivism or relativism nor congeals into naturalism or realism.[81] For Levinas, truth does not establish correspondence between facts and mental states or sentences one is warranted in asserting, and it does not merely maximize the coherence or consistency of one's own beliefs with respect to the world. Rather, it demands a responsiveness to the other that is also corresponsive to the nonhuman features of our world. My argument, however, hinges less on any particular account of postfoundational truth, religious or otherwise, than on there being some such plausible account. Or perhaps it hinges on even less: that within the covenant of faith, religious beliefs can and therefore ought to make good sense. To say that the ethics of faith is first philosophy is not to say that it is all of philosophy. Ethics does not abandon belief but draws our attention to the human face of all veridical beliefs, including religious ones.

Levinas's account of religion is therefore not devoid of theology, as Levinas at times implies. To be sure, there is no *metaphysical* theology that stands over and above and independently of the ethical covenant of faith. In Levinas's terms, theology can never be "said" without reduction to the "saying" and without exposure to ethical skepticism. As a consequence we should refuse the still prevalent and quite metaphysical schema that regards belief as the basis of religion.[82] On the contrary, as Levinas insists, the covenant of faith precedes and enables theological belief. Theology is the handmaiden to religion, as truth is to trust and ontology is to ethics. In demanding only the truth of religious belief, the evidence without the witnesses, too many modern critics of religion mistake it for a body of knowledge and a set of claims to transcendent truth that can be separated from its ethical substance. Implicitly, they invariably have an ill-conceived notion of "belief" at work, as if beliefs established one-to-one relationships between mental states and facts, when in truth the very notion of belief implies a web of associated beliefs and, no less importantly, of relationships of trust. When we see religion as first and foremost an ethical covenant rather than an epistemic doctrine, which is how Levinas views it, then the role of religious belief changes significantly. Belief is not what leads one to religion but the propositional content worked out *within* religion. It is indeed the task of theology to work out the truth of religion, but this interpretative theology is precisely the opposite of the "onto-theology" that claims to provide a ground for meaning. Theology is what we do to make sense of religion, but theology depends on covenantal faith rather than on any particular metaphysical view of God or nature. It is therefore not a matter of getting rid of theology, just as there is no getting rid of veridical belief generally. We need to make the best sense out of the faith that binds us. Naturally, then, theological truth will vary from one period to another, from one place to another, from one community to another, and sometimes even from one moment to another. Theological truth is thus provisional, pragmatic, and subject to critical scrutiny, quite like ordinary hermeneutic truth. The objection that this sort of picture describes Jewish theology more accurately than it does other theologies hardly counts, for that is partly the point of saying that Levinas's philosophical account of ethics is Judaic in a nontrivial sense.[83] If the sketch I have provided of the relationship between faith and belief characterizes Jewish theology, I take it that the history of religious ideas establishes its validity for other religions too. This is simply how tradition, which is always transmission and betrayal, lives on. This is what it means to keep the faith. In any case, whether or not Levinas's account of the primacy of faith over belief can be applied outside the Jewish religion, there is no doubt that his secularization of the covenant of the Jews is both indebted to the Judaic heritage of thinking and expropriates it from the Jews. What Levinas calls "ethics," then, is both a secularization and a dejudaization of the covenant of the Jews, but in such a way that preserves and even emphasizes the Judaic dimension of this thinking. These are less paradoxes than simple effects of thinking Judaism philosophically.

The Religious and the Secular: Covenantal A/Theology

Nothing that I have said suggests that the ethics of faith implies belief in God. On the contrary, my argument is that each one "is" his or her own *credo*, his or her own *ani ma'amin*, worked out historically in relation to others. Religious belief has its place here, since it too derives from the covenant of faith that constitutes our ethical creatureliness. But there is nothing in the covenantal structure of the ethics that necessitates religious belief. In my explication of Levinas, atheism is no less a plausible belief system than theism; or we might say that atheism is the theology of the secular. The point is brought out well in an exchange between Umberto Eco and Cardinal Martini, published as *Belief or Nonbelief?* Reflecting on "what underlies some people's impulse toward closeness and solidarity without having recourse to God the Father, Creator of All, and our brother Jesus Christ," the Cardinal provides a hypothesis: "My sense is that what they are more or less expressing is that the other is within us. He is a part of us, whether we love him, hate him, or are indifferent to him."[84] This leads Martini to suggest that secular people are implicit believers, a view I reject and I think Levinas rejects, although I fear my explication of Levinas's ethics of faith might lead some readers to that thought. But Eco's response to the Cardinal illustrates why the relation to the other does not *necessarily* imply religious beliefs, even if it legitimates them. Eco replies:

You too attribute to our virtuous [secular] man the belief that the other is in us. This is not a vague sentimental propensity, but rather a basic condition. As we are taught by the most secular of the social sciences, it is the other, his gaze, that defines us and determines us. Just as we couldn't live without eating or sleeping, we cannot understand who we are without the gaze and reaction of the other. Even those who kill, rape, rob, and violate do so in exceptional moments, and the rest of the time beg love, respect, praise from others. And even from those they humiliate, they ask recognition in the form of fear and submission. Without any such recognition, the new-born abandoned in the forest will not become a human (or else, like Tarzan, he will look for the other in the face of an ape).[85]

Eco rightly insists that the Cardinal's "belief that the other is in us" is a basic condition that entails nothing about "God the Father, Creator of All, and our brother Jesus Christ." Of course there is no reason for the

Cardinal himself, and for others who share his faith, not to make good theological sense of beliefs consistent with such faith. Although the ethical covenant is a form of creaturely life that calls on the name of the other, it does not follow that the creature must call on *the* Name of the Other. The ethical creature therefore may or may not be "religious." Positive religious beliefs—"creation, omnipotence, rewards, and promises," as Levinas puts it—are plausible, but by no means necessary effects of the ethics of faith. For belief to become "a live option," as William James famously called it, there must first be a covenant with those to whom one entrusts oneself. This, I venture, is the best way to understand the vast majority of acts of religious conversion, which are not cognitive deductions based on war-ranted epistemic justification but acts of *caritas, ways of making sense of the love that binds us.* So-called crises of faith work the same way in reverse—not by establishing a new ground for knowledge and belief but by trans-ferring trust from one social horizon to another.[86] It is probably for this reason that theological heresy plays a marginal role in Jewish covenantal consciousness, in contrast to the thunderous ecclesiological heresiologies that arise over issues of authority and loyalty.[87] At least in Judaism, heresy has always been less a matter of theology than of fidelity and community, more of a betrayal of trust than a mistake about the nature of God, and this is no less the case in secularized contexts. The borders of faith, the lines one crosses in conversion or apostasy, are normatively rather than cognitively constructed. Within these borders, religious belief is constrained only by the endless repositories of covenantal faith, tradition, and experience.

In a valuable essay pointing to several important Jewish themes in Levinas's work, Shmuel Trigano commented on "how much the notion of 'covenant,' so central in the biblical text, seems surprisingly missing in Levinas's writings."[88] Trigano is right. The notion of covenant almost never appears explicitly in Levinas's work, neither in his philosophical nor in his confessional writings. This is because covenant is pervasively, if implicitly, everywhere in Levinas's work; it *is* "ethics" itself.

The Ambivalence of Fraternity

ETHICAL POLITICAL THEOLOGY

> "I became a Jew to Jews, so that I might gain Jews . . . to those outside the law I
> became like one outside the law . . . I became weak to the weak."
> —Corinthians 9:20–22

"A time to act for YHWH—violate His Torah!"

Totality and Infinity and *Otherwise than Being* are interpretations of
Judaism addressed to anyone, *sans identité*. In Levinas's interpretation, Judaism has been secularized as a covenant of creatures, an ethical exposure
to the other whose essence can be approached only in name. This is not to
deny that Levinas was fundamentally indebted to European philosophy
and, indeed, to modern Protestant theology, as Samuel Moyn has established. Philosophical midrash interprets Judaism in the best philosophical light and therefore depends on the philosophical milieu of the exegete.
Levinas's midrash is a creative philosophical reconstruction of the meaning
of the Judaic heritage, but not an "invention," as Moyn calls it, for it is Judaism that is here interpreted.[1] In Jeffrey Kosky's words, it is "a Judaism that
thinks or speaks—heretically, hyperbolically, or perhaps heterodoxically—
what Judaism has not yet said about what it has always *secretly* harboured."[2]
This heterodoxical secret is transmitted through a series of exegeses of texts
and tropes regarding the covenantal character of creation.

In the time of the Rabbis, "the account of creation," *ma'aseh bereishit*, was already regarded as a secret that should not be expounded, even in the presence of two people (m. Hag. 2:1).[3] In the twelfth century Maimonides overcame this prohibition against expounding the secrets of Judaism.[4] He disclosed it to *one* disciple, Joseph son of Judah, in the form of an ostensibly private letter, and then disseminated this letter under the title of the *Guide of the Perplexed.* The one thus became anyone.[5] Needless to say, Maimonides was entirely conscious of transgressing the letter of the law. He enumerates several reasons for his disclosure, including a midrash he employs to justify his unrestricted dissemination of Judaism's secret account of creation. Whereas, in context, Psalm 119:126 says that "it is a time to act for YHWH, they have violated His Torah," a rabbinic gloss reads the verse as an injunction, under certain circumstances, to transgress the law for the sake of God: "A time to act for the Name—violate His Torah!"[6] Levinas's interpretation of Judaism's secret account of creation involves a similar interpretative violation for the sake of the proper name, and he too dispersed his interpretation of the secret account of creation in fragments scattered throughout his oeuvre. More importantly, like others before him, he *transformed* the secret of creation through a philosophical midrash of Judaism. As Moshe Halbertal has shown, although the account of creation belongs to the core of Judaic belief, its prima facie esoteric status enabled diverse and contradictory interpretations to attach to it, precisely because the logic of the secret implies the structural incapacity to safeguard its content. The more it is concealed, the less the secret can be guaranteed by appeal to common knowledge. The secret is thus simultaneously the core of Judaism and that part most vulnerable to contestation and transformation. When Levinas discloses the core meaning of Judaism as the covenant of creatures, he too transforms it by making explicit "what Judaism has not yet said about what it has always secretly harboured." He expropriates the *logia* entrusted to the Jews for the sake of the Name.

Such an expropriation, however, is not an allegorization, if by that one means "allegory in the strict sense of the interpretation of the concrete elements of a narrative as signs of a changeless, wholly immaterial ontological being."[7] Alternatively, if we forgo this medieval and metaphysical notion of allegoresis as referring to a realm of ideas beyond historical Judaism and revert to the original sense of *all-egoria* as speaking-otherwise, then Levinas's midrash is indeed an *all-egoria*. Levinas's strictly philosophical works speak Judaism's account of creation otherwise, even to the point of allegorizing "being Jewish," which now refers to obligations accrued by passive exposure to the other. But Levinas does not so much discover ethics outside Judaism and then "retroject" it onto the experience of being Jewish so much as he interprets ethics through a philosophical expropriation of Judaism. The *giluy 'arayot* he commits is a complete union, no doubt illicit for some, of Judaism and philosophy, and therefore also a denuding of Judaism of any particular "Jewish identity" that would foreclose its anarchical availability to anyone with eyes to see and ears to listen.

Although this is an anticlerical and even anarchical interpretation of being Jewish, it does not spiritualize the concrete elements of covenantal faith but embodies them otherwise. It is hard to see how an objection to Levinas's allegoresis of Judaism would not depend on the dubious assertion of a nonallegorical, authentic "true Israel," a determination that only the force of law can establish, and, as we know, not without arbitrariness and brutality. The choice between allegory and authenticity does not correlate to the difference between the spirit and the letter but to the difference between the anarchy of interpretation and the authority of the interpreter. And the space between the anarchy of interpretation and the authority of an interpreter is precisely the space of faith, ethical and religious. The passive exposure of becoming one's own *ani ma'amin*, one's own *credo*, is the working out of the always improper relation between allegory and authenticity. This is not the faith one has, like a belief, but the faith one is, like a covenant. It is the credo or the *ani ma'amin* of one's very own abandonment to the other.

After Judaism, Christianity, and Secularism

"Allegories are, in the realm of thoughts, what ruins are in the realm of things," wrote Walter Benjamin.[8] Levinas's allegoresis of Judaism, the interpretative anarchy he deploys to allow Judaism to be spoken otherwise, comes after the ruin of every definitive form of Jewish orthodoxy and after the ruin of every authoritative determination of "being Jewish," be it clerical or statist. After World War II, when "being Jewish" was mercilessly enforced, Levinas began to interpret the notion philosophically as a category of experience at large, as the stiff-necked subjectivity whose ethical sense is irreducible to the impersonal, neutral, and formal categories of ontology.[9] Three decades later this sense of the passivity of being Jewish, or "election," had evolved into what he now described as the unchosen exposure that constitutes the ethical self, without substantive identity, subjectivity "elected" uniquely as one-for-the-other: "Has not the Good chosen the subject with an election . . . by virtue of which he is unique? A philosopher can give to this election only the signification circumscribed by responsibility for the other" (OB, 122/AE, 157). But Levinas's philosophical articulation, even if conceived on the basis of a secular experience, clearly reworks traditional Jewish accounts of the passivity and solidarity of election. The rabbinic notion of *'arevut* maintains that Israelites are bound not only to one another but even to one another's faults and therefore undergo an "involuntary expiation," as Levinas calls it (OB, 111–25/AE, 141–48). In Leviticus 26:37 we read that "each one shall stumble over another." The rabbis interpret: "This does not merely mean that each one shall stumble over another but that each one shall stumble over the sins of the other— which teaches that each Israelite is a surety for the other."[10] The corporeal election and solidarity of the Jews as one body of faith, substituting and expiating for one another, becomes, in Levinas's new creation, the ethical condition of creatureliness.[11] The (Jewish) body of faith is exposed to, even infected by, "the other." It therefore mutates into a body of ethical faithfulness for humanity at large. The effect is to conceal the ethical significance of the *'arevut* or substitution of the Jews for one another in order to reveal "the astonishing human fraternity" of "the extraordinary and everyday event of my responsibility for the faults or the misfortune of others" (OB, 10/AE, 12). This ethical solidarity transcends identity by preceding it. The other is first and foremost any*one*. In ethics, regarded as our secular, embodied faithfulness to one another and regarded as such through the heritage of Judaism, there is neither Jew nor Greek, neither male nor female.[12]

This philosophical proclamation of Judaism as ethics points neither to the end of "Jewish identity" nor to the "universalism" of Judaism. Rather, Levinas's philosophical text sounds out unheard voices from the textual heritage of his thinking in order to transmit them to *whoever becomes susceptible to hearing*. It makes an appeal, which contingently first strikes those attuned to that heritage of thinking: those Jews or Christians or atheists for whom that heritage constitutes the substance of their moral intuitions.

And of course such an appeal can reach others too, can reach anyone who becomes responsive to it. Levinas's interpretation of Judaism as ethics is an open letter, but its validity depends entirely on those who respond to it, not on some independent universal structure of moral reality. Accordingly, Levinas was pleased to refer to Matthew 25:31–40 to illustrate what he meant by ethics.[13] Indeed, although he generally avoids citing the New Testament explicitly, who could doubt the most profound proximity between what Levinas calls "ethics" and a certain "Christian experience"? Do we not find in the New Testament everything Levinas says about the coming to pass of God through the ethical relation to the other? For example: "No one has ever seen God; if we love one another, God lives in us" (I John 4:12). Does not the "ethical language" of a persecuted subjectivity responsible for the persecuting of the persecutor "translate" the characteristically Christian injunction to love one's enemy?[14] At the very least, Levinas's midrash, although *derived from* the Judaic heritage of thinking through a series of complex, implicit exegeses, *converges with* the plain reading of many of the ethical teachings of the New Testament. The point is not to level undeniable theological differences or ignore historical enmity and identity but to acknowledge a common patrimony in the theological construction of our secular ethics. Perhaps the best example is the one Levinas mentions from Matthew 25:35–36, in which the King praises his subject because "I was hungry and you gave me food . . . I was a stranger and you welcomed me, I was naked and you clothed me." When the King's subjects protest that they have never seen their Lord hungry or a stranger or naked the King replies, "Truly, I say to you, as you did it to one of the least of these my brethren, you did it to me" (40). Levinas no doubt found in Matthew what he also knew from the Talmudic midrash in Sotah 14a: "How can a man walk after God? . . . Just as God clothes the naked (Gen. 3:21), so must you clothe the naked, as God visits the sick (Gen. 18:1) so do you; as God comforts mourners (Gen. 25:11) so must you; as God buries the dead (Deut. 34:6) you must do likewise." Accordingly, we are not surprised that a New Testament scholar glosses Matthew in remarkably Levinasian terms: "In Matthew, service of the neighbor is not just analogous to the service of God, but it is in itself God's service. . . . The service love renders the neighbor is service to the Lord Christ. Here we have ample New Testament warrant for Luther's continuing insistence that Christ himself may be met in the neighbor."[15]

On occasion Levinas was even emboldened to offer a Christolog-ical interpretation of ethics. In 1968, the year he published "Substitu-tion," he delivered a talk at a conference for Catholic intellections titled "A Man-God?" On the one hand, he says, such an idea implies "a descent of the Creator to the level of the Creature; that is to say, an absorption of the most active activity into the passive passivity. On the other hand, the problem includes, as if brought about by this passivity pushed to its ul-timate degree in the Passion, the idea of expiation for others, that is, of a substitution."[16] Christology as "substitution" and, therefore, "ethics" as *imitatio Christi*! Slavoj Žižek is thus right to wonder if the sacrifice and hostage of the ethical self to the other is not the exemplary gesture of Christ—"Was He not the hostage who took the place of all of us and, therefore, exemplarily human ('ecce homo')?"—as long as one denies that this substitution "reconciles" us to each other.[17] By the same token, ac-cording to Levinas, the Christian idea of kenosis, in which transcendence empties itself, taking the form of a servant, and is humbled in human like-ness to the point of death (Phil. 2:7–8), has, according to Levinas, "its full meaning in the religious sensibility of Judaism."[18] Consider the following early rabbinic midrash, provided as exegesis of Deuteronomy 21:23, "for the accursed of God is hanging":

(This is like) two brothers who were identical twins and lived in the same city. One was made king, and the other became a bandit. The king commanded, so they strung him up. Everyone who saw (the dead body) said "The king has been strung up." So the king commanded and they took him down.[19]

This midrash, attributed to Rabbi Meir from the second century, proposes a likeness between the accursed villain hanging on the wood and the king, who is a metaphorical figure for God. The likeness of these twins is, as Alon Goshen-Gottstein says, "purely physical." In fact, since accord-ing to rabbinic law the convicted capital offender was strung up only after execution (by stoning), the corporeal and visible likeness obtains not only between the king and the criminal but between the king and the accursed cadaver, that is, a likeness between the King and the utterly abject human body. The point of this midrash is to explain why the Torah says that the curse or the accursed *of God* is hanging, and it does so by likening the ac-cursed cadaver to the king. Although this midrash seems strikingly Chris-tological, it articulates the rabbinic view of the body as icon of God and not what most Christians understand by incarnation.[20] The (dead) body expresses the divine presence and is therefore iconically "like" the king, but the king has not fully taken on the form of the dead man on the wood.[21] Levinas 1 had already gestured in this direction, since, as we saw, ethics is revealed in the image of God through the prohibition on murdering the iconic face and the fecundity of creative desire. Levinas 2 goes further. The other is now incorporated into ethical subjectivity and therefore haunts the subject in the interstices of bodily self-identification. Subjectivity is "alterity in the same without alienation in the form of incarnation, as being-in-one's-skin, having-the-other-in-one's-skin" (OB, 114–15/AE, 146).[22] Later in the chapter on "Substitution" he remarks that "the absolute passivity of being a creature" is a "*gnawing away at oneself* in responsibility, which is also incarnation" (OB, 121/AE, 155–56). Levinas's most difficult word, "substitution," is thus a secularization of incarnational theologies, although that does not privilege the event of Christ in attesting to the ethical condition of creatureliness. A philosophical midrash, then, that comes after Judaism but also after Christianity.

By deploying a phenomenological interpretation that passes through Judaism and Christianity, Levinas's work effectively secularizes this ethical heritage of thinking, as Kant, for example, had formerly done. The idea of ethics as a covenant of creatures is in fact profoundly secular, even rightly passing for atheistic. It supposes no idea of God, neither positive nor negative. Ethics is the "very rupture that creation operates in being" and yet takes place "prior to both the negation and the affirmation of the divine" (TI, 58/TeI, 29–30). It is the thought of the goodness and glory of creation as depending on a human covenant of creatures that determines this philosophical midrash, a religion of ethics without religion. As Levinas elsewhere explains, "It is up to man to save man: *the divine way of relieving misery is not through God's intervention.* The true correlation between man and God depends on a relation of man to man in which man takes full responsibility, as if there were no God to count on. This state of mind conditions secularism, even modern secularism."[23] Ethics therefore *is* the hermeneutical secularization of Judaism (and Christianity). In other words, Levinas's account of ethics *weakens* the claims of Judaic theology to transcendence by an interpretation that incarnates transcendence in our historical covenant with each other, in precisely the sense that Vattimo proposes with respect to "Christian modernity." Just as hermeneutical Christian modernity removes "all the transcendent, incomprehensible, mysterious and even bizarre features" of Christian revelation, so too does Levinas's hermeneutical secularization of Judaism as ethics—except, of course, that in the case of ethics it is precisely a matter of attending to the incomprehensible, mysterious, and even bizarre features of the other.[24] In this way the account of ethics as the secularization of Judaism distinguishes itself from a reductive secularism. In Levinas's secularized view of Judaism, the prohibition of idolatry retains its ethical force, because the other is unrepresentable and for that very reason encountered as unique, only by name, and therefore requires a pragmatic approach that does not thematize the one to whom it responds. The trace of the One in the proper name of the other demands a response that cannot be converted to knowledge. Ethics is secularism without idolatry, and one can even think of Levinas as a secular prophet of Israel in a manner that retains some of the most characteristic and traditional features of prophecy. For not only was it always the function of classical prophecy to call the people back from idolatry to the ethical core of Israelite religion, but from medieval to modern times, and precisely through the influence of philosophy, Jewish thinkers routinely described their exegetical inspirations and their appeals to new sense in the Torah as acts of prophecy.[25] Levinas's secular prophetic appeal decries the modern moral idolatry of somnolent individualism that leaves one deaf to the suffering of the other. Ethics is an iconoclasm of autonomous liberal individualism that calls for an awakening to the other based on the compassion that "is" the self itself, the self as one-for-the-other. It is a prophetic call to awaken to the covenant of creaturely compassion that constitutes each of us.[26] In this sense ethics comes not only after Judaism and after Christianity but also after secularism.

Levinas's thought therefore cannot be objectively determined in terms of conventional identity discourses, whether Jewish, Christian, or secular. The "identity" of the ethical subject is entirely determined by the one who responds *hineini, me voici,* "here I am." Even if the call of the Other is generated from a philosophy of Judaism, or of Judeo-Christianity, no one but the ethical self can decide if she should "rightly pass" *as* Jew, *as* Christian, or *as* atheist, as Derrida said.[27] The ethical self is awakened through its abandonment to the other, a condition that paradoxically deprives one of conventional identities and substantive selfhood. One "is identified with nothing but the very voice that states and delivers itself" to the other (OB, 143/AE, 182).[28] Ethics is not a matter of securing an identity but of *testifying oneself.* As Levinas says, "the Infinite does not appear to him that bears witness to it. On the contrary the witness belongs to the glory of the Infinite. It is by the voice of the witness that the glory of the Infinite is glorified" (OB, 146/AE, 186). Is the ethical witness "Jewish," "Christian," "secular," or some other determinate form of identity? Ethically, such determinations are *adiaphora.* One testifies oneself ethically, and one passes, rightly and wrongly, with derivative and ethically indifferent names in everyday contexts. To the Jew, Levinas will have come as a Jew, to those outside the law he will have come as one outside the law, and for the secular hermeneutical thinker he will have become weak to the weak.

The Ambivalence of Fraternity: Israel and Idolatry

But this also leads us to the major problem with Levinas's ethical creature, since the reduction it undergoes of identity to responsibility paradoxically abandons the self to itself. Although this reduction effectively marks the deposition of the individual ego and the transcendental subject through its immemorial exposure to the trace of the other, the one who concretely says "here I am" is left alone to answer for the whole of humanity. This "coring out" of all substantial identity—this *dénucléation* "in which the nucleus of the ego is cored out" (OB, 64/AE, 81)—puts ethics itself at great peril, for it seems to abandon ethics to a political vacuum. Ethics risks becoming a political safe haven for the very individualism it set out to overturn. Because the ethical relationship hollows out the political basis on which it arises, critics have denounced Levinas's ethics as nothing but a subjective hole from which all one can do is gesture to injustice without engaging the concrete demands of political life.[29] Levinas tells us that "the Other appears in solidarity with all the others" (TI, 280/TeI, 257) and "is from the first the brother of all the other men" (OB, 158/AE, 201). But is not ethics then attenuated to the point of being merely the attestation of a subjective humanistic conscience? Levinas's frequent recourse from the radical *individuation* of ethics to a platitudinous humanism risks undoing everything he set out to achieve and, ironically, relapsing into mere *individualism.* Ethics would become an affair of the lone individual in relation to all others. The result of this referral of the ethical self to "all" others implies that the differences that constitute others as such would be *neutralized*. Simon Critchley calls this Levinas's "vapid universalism," according to which, in Levinas's words, "my relationship with the other as neighbor gives meaning to my relations with all the others" (OB, 159/AE, 202).[30] Levinas has been mocked for figuring ethics as the intrigue of beautiful souls whose claim to render themselves entirely to the Other inevitably renders unto Caesar what is Caesar's. By dividing the ethical self from its political context, in which there are always constellations of creatures, Levinas risks attenuating the covenant of faith. Is there anything more to the "saying" of the ethical creature than a prayer addressed to the name of the other? Notionally it is a matter of "solidarity with all the others" but concretely it amounts to an exposure of oneself alone. To harness the energy produced through the "fission of the mysterious inwardness of nucleus of the subject" (OB 141/AE, 180) it is necessary that ethics be shared and attested together in concrete political situations. In other words, one cannot be ethically faithful "to the other" without at the same time knowing how to respond together and to which others. The problem is analogous to the imperative of moving from faith to belief. If ethics is not to collapse into a subjective gesture or congeal into the vapid humanistic reflex of subjectivism it must not only operate on the ego but also cooperate with other ethical creatures.

This problem corresponds to the difficulty Heidegger faced when moving from the attestation of authentic Dasein to the possibility of the "cohistoricizing" of a "people," *des Volkes*, a move that many scholars regard as having enabled him to find a way from *Being and Time* to Nazism.[31] Just as Heidegger had to face the question, In what way does authentic finitude not only historicize itself but also cohistoricize itself with others? one must ask Levinas, In what way does the ethical witness concretize itself with others? Does not ethics, in Levinas's sense, necessitate a horizon of concrete others *with* whom the ethical self will have awoken *to* the other? And which others? Without a more or less determined historical horizon of others, can ethics be anything more than subjective individualism and abstract humanism? Levinas is keen to talk about the concretion of the ethical self, the witness exposed to itself through the other, but he is reluctant to concretize ethics through the co-attestation of the self and the identification of particular others necessary for a genuine concrete ethical covenant. Indeed, the whole point of the "new ethics" was to overcome the metaphysical morass of moral universalism and abstract humanism, so the leap from the ethical self to its solidarity with all had better not reproduce a humanistic liberal account of the universal individual.[32] Levinas therefore also had to consider, as did Heidegger before him, how it is that the concrete phenomenological self, as the temporality of a hermeneutical exposure to others, could be understood not only in terms of its own ethical attestation but also in terms of the necessary co-attestation of ethics. This proximity between Heidegger and Levinas extends to the essentials of each man's thought, to the point that even Jacques Rolland, "Levinas's most faithful interpreter" (as Zarader calls him), could not help but remark on the "formally identical" structures of their thinking.[33] Zarader's impressive accomplishment is to have shown that the proximity between Heidegger and Levinas owes itself to the former's unavowed debt to the Judaic heritage and the latter's deliberate forgetting of Heidegger's renewal of a non-metaphysical attention to Being. I will therefore restrict myself to what is perhaps the most demanding dimension of this double disavowal. For if Heidegger unknowingly appropriated a Judaic way of thinking of Being while neutralizing its fundamentally ethical appeal, and Levinas half-knowingly appropriated Heidegger in order to make that very appeal philosophically audible, double disavowal of Judaic and Heideggerian thought knowingly intersect precisely at the point where hermeneutical philosophy becomes political.

Heidegger acknowledged that "primordial historicizing" always implies the cohistoricizing of Dasein, and Levinas must do likewise if the ethical self is to avoid the illusions of subjectivism and the metaphysics of humanism. Moreover, Heidegger acknowledges that the only way to transcend the inauthentic experience of being borne by conventional platitudes and reified values is "*in terms of the heritage* which that resoluteness, as thrown, *takes over*" (*Being and Time*, 435/SZ, 383; emphases in original). Cohistoricizing means that heritage, whatever we make of it, is destiny, the contingent, multifaceted, hermeneutical source of destiny. As Heidegger puts it, "Only in communicating and struggling does the power of destiny become free" (*Being and Time*, 436/SZ, 384). If Levinas is to provide more than an ethical Augenblick, then he too needs to account for the cohistoricizing of the heritage of Judaism that is "ethics." To reveal the power of ethics, *we*, whoever we are that respond to this heritage of thinking, must communicate, struggle with, and cohistoricize our ethical creatureliness.

Given the delicacy of these issues I should say that in my view Heidegger's philosophical recourse to the cohistoricizing of the *Volk* enabled him to endorse Nazism, even though the Nazi ideology of the *Volk* is inconsistent with the political ontology of *Being and Time*, and, indeed, that Heidegger understood this. His resolve for the *Volk* transpired without the metaphysical illusions of biologism and essence. The *Volk* is no doubt an indispensable category in *Being and Time*, made necessary by its eschewal of universalism and the grounding of being in the temporal transcendence of the socio-historical, but it is also essentially incompatible with Nazi ideology because it is not based on any properties that the people have but on "the nonidentity proper to itself as the transcendence of being-with-one-another," as James Phillips ably puts it.[34] It is therefore necessary to resort to *a people* in order to account for the concrete, historical individuation of the self and yet impossible to do so, since there is no way for "people" to gather the groundlessness of being into the unity of a historical project. Although my position will doubtless not satisfy some, I take it that the fact that Heidegger signed on to Nazism shows his readiness to compromise the strictly impossible political ontology of *Being and Time*.

The important point for us, however, is that even if there is no ontology of the *Volk* because "a people," in Phillips's words, "is a rupture of the identifiable,"[35] it is still necessary to account for the cohistoricizing of ethics that has always happened and is always still to come. This is the case no matter how one reads Levinas, but all the more so for the interpretation offered in this book, according to which the phenomenology of "ethics" is always already hermeneutical, indeed, midrashic. There was never a doubt that the one who says *hineini, me voici*, was *always* cohistoricizing *in terms of the heritage* that he or she *takes over*. In saying "me" and thereby testifying to myself without identity, it was always "we" who were speaking through me, we who share this heritage of thinking, whoever we are, as well as those others, now dead, who speak through it.[36] The necessary relation between ethics and politics, for lack of better words, neither assumes nor needs to assume an ontological account of the *Volk*, for there is no such proper account.[37] But it does need to assume, as we have done all along, an impure and inauthentic cohistoricizing of the "we" not only "in" every *me voici* but also *with whom* one communicates and struggles over the destiny of our moral heritage.

Levinas is often reluctant, even elliptical, in facing up to the unavoidable cohistoricizing of ethics. "It is not always easy to be Heideggerian."[38] Nevertheless, just as "Dasein's fateful destiny in and with its 'generation' goes to make up the full authentic historizing of Dasein" (*Being and Time*, 436/SZ, 384–85), so "ethical destiny"[39] requires a fateful cohistoricizing of a heritage that enables the communication and struggle required for "the power of destiny," as Heidegger put it, to "become free" (*Being and Time*, 436/SZ, 384). Howard Caygill has shown that Levinas consistently effects this concrete cohistoricizing of ethics through a notion of "fraternity," which itself appears in several guises.[40] Levinas never abandoned this view of ethics as fraternity, which goes back to his earliest convictions. Indeed, as Caygill astutely observed, fraternity is "the central problem of Levinas's political thought."[41] For Levinas, fraternity materially and historically underwrites of the liberty and equality conferred by the state on all its citizens and is therefore the precondition for a republican state whose ethical raison d'être is to protect the rights of the other. It is important to see that in this assignation of ethical fraternity to republican politics the curved space of ethics is not flattened or neutralized but attests to an ethical relation within the republic that ruptures the identity of its constitutive relations. Ethical fraternity indicates a relation *beyond the state within the state*. In a related context, Žižek has described the disturbance and even the "violence" of ethics that "cuts across the symmetry of equal relations, distorting and displacing them."[42]

I am suggesting that, for Levinas, political fraternity is a necessary supplement to ethical fraternity but is not reducible to it. It is not enough merely to be a cosmopolitan ethical creature in solidarity with all others. This merely deploys the rhetoric of ethics in the service of such global phenomena as capitalism and technology, for the only way that individuals are all connected to one another outside the communication of their heritages of thinking is through such phenomena. This is why ethics cannot be abandoned to the self alone in relation to "all" others but must cohistoricize its heritage. Ethics is therefore inextricable from a certain civic republicanism that is open to the immanent surpluses of the other within the body politic. It is through this effort "to separate rights discourse from its roots in individualism, without, however, lapsing into the fraternal politics of communitarianism,"[43] that Levinas understood the ethical vocation of the liberal state, especially of the French Republic and the State of Israel. This explains his hyperbolic estimation of the significance of the establishment of the State of Israel as "one of the greatest events . . . of all History."[44] But it is important not to be distracted by this hyperbole, for although Levinas gave more attention to the fraternity of the State of Israel than to that of the Republic of France, the argument, with all its associated difficulties, is applicable to all political attempts (French, Israeli, and other civic republicanisms) to safeguard ethics by cohistoricizing the heritage of this thought through communication and struggle. Zionism, like French republicanism and, indeed, like the rights discourse of the West, is, for Levinas, grounded in "ethics," that is to say, in a secularized interpretation of the Judeo-Christian heritage of thinking. Politics has a purpose other than the preservation of the freedoms of the individual, namely, the ethical concern for the other, but this purpose requires a state organized around the heritage of this thinking that would "bring to perfection its monotheistic message."[45] This provocative formulation without doubt refers to Levinas's secularized interpretation of the "monotheistic message," that is, to "ethics." Levinas's account of fraternity therefore has two crucial features. First, political fraternity is the means by which ethics is cohistoricized as a civic republicanism that mobilizes the heritage of its thinking in the name of the other. Levinas's Zionism, his French republicanism, and his civic republicanism generally articulate this view and are therefore consistent with his secular philosophy of Judaism or Judeo-Christianity. France and Israel are merely *examples*, not exceptions or paradigms. In no sense are they privileged over other secular republics based on a heritage of thinking, any heritage of thinking, that points to "ethics."[46] The constant passage between ethical and political fraternity takes place, according to Levinas, in all states whose raison d'être is the rights of the other. Second, in all cases, ethics exceeds and distorts the politics of fraternity. If ethics depends on the cohistoricizing of a heritage in the mode of a republican state it nevertheless distorts and exceeds the state. Ethics is a response within the state to the other, or the name of the other, beyond the state. Let us examine each of these moments in the politics of the philosophy of Judaism that Levinas secularizes as ethics.

There is no doubt that Levinas held high hopes that "the State of Israel . . . finally offers the opportunity to carry out the social law of Judaism" that he understood philosophically as "ethics."[47] In 1951 he was clear about the relationship between the ethics of Judaism and political Zionism. What is important about the State of Israel, he then thought, is "the subordination of the State to its social promises" so that "the political event is already outstripped." The political fraternity giving rise to Zionism is legitimate because it safeguards ethical fraternity. As he puts it, "The contrast is between those who seek to have a State in order to have justice and those who seek justice in order to ensure the survival of the State."[48] In this respect, for Levinas there is no difference between the State of Israel and every other civic republican state. Thirty years later he again argued that the State is necessary "even for going beyond the State," and that "the Law entering the world requires an education, protection, and consequently a history and a State." This is precisely to avoid the criticism I have raised in this section, namely, that ethics is a "facile eloquence of a careless moralism" that renders unto Caesar what is Caesar's.[49] Indeed, Levinas says that "what is most important is the idea that not only does the essence of the State not contradict the absolute order, but it is called by it."[50] A midrash he cites illustrates this point:

R. Simeon b. Lakish said: "And God saw everything that he had made, and behold it was very good" (Gen. 1:31). "It was very good" alludes to the kingdom of God, "*and* it was very good" alludes to the kingdom of the Romans. Is then the kingdom of the Romans very good? How strange! Indeed it is so, since it exacts law and justice for creatures, as it says, "It was I who made the earth and created humans on it" (Isa. 45:12).[51]

Levinas's way of binding ethics and politics, then, is to justify the state for the sake of ethical fraternity and, more problematically, to regard ethical fraternity as necessarily requiring a state. Critics have taken issue with this. If ethics lays the moral foundations for the French Republic, then, according to Critchley, Levinas becomes "some sort of apologist for a conservative republicanism." If it leads to Zionism, then, in Critchley's words, "the non-place of the ethical relation to the other becomes the place of Israel's borders. Israel risks functioning as the name par excellence for a just polity, a polity based on the pre-political priority of ethical obligation to the other."[52] Occasional remarks by Levinas seem to corroborate this view: "It should not be forgotten that *my* family and *my* people, despite the possessive pronouns, are my 'others,' like strangers, and demand justice and protection. The love of the other—the love of one's neighbour. Those near to me are also my neighbours."[53] Here, what seems decisive in the passage from ethical to political fraternity is neither ethics nor politics but fraternity, a form of statist republicanism that has led Zionism to be denounced as racism and that is on the rise in today's Europe as it negotiates the conflict between heritage and hospitality. After so much interpretative expropriation of Judaism under the name of ethics, some will no doubt see Levinas's account of the passage between ethical and political fraternity as an example of what Gilles Deleuze and Félix Guattari call an "abject reterritorialization."[54] At a certain point it even becomes unclear whether Levinas himself was among those who sought a Jewish state to have justice or sought justice to ensure the survival of the state of the Jews.

An ambivalence of fraternity thus runs throughout Levinas's work, dividing it against itself even as it divided Levinas against himself. For example, within the one concluding paragraph of "The State of Caesar and the State of David," we find him decrying the "facile eloquence of a careless moralism" and at the same time indulging the "painful necessities of the occupation."[55] Scandalous as this is, this position is not inconsistent with Levinas's view of the relationship between ethical and political fraternity. Without political fraternity, the universal anarchic individualism of a purely ethical fraternity is ineffable and ineffectual. Certain "concessions" and even a "provisional abdication" of responsibility for the other might therefore be justified since "the temporal order in which it arises [that is, the State] itself receives some justification in the absolute [that is, ethics]."[56] Levinas seems to have thought the occupation was necessary for the security of the State of Israel; his view of the role of political fraternity in cohistoricizing ethics in the form of a state therefore led him to indulge the occupation. But Caygill is right in suggesting that here ethics is sacrificed on the altar of the State. At the very least, in becoming political, ethics goes to war against itself. Levinas's discussions of Zionism and the Palestinians reflect this ambivalence of fraternity.

But ambivalence has two sides. The ethical fraternity that legitimizes the state also exceeds the territorialization of political fraternity in the guise of statist ethnic nationalism. Indeed, Levinas's whole point is that only ethics provides the moral resources for judging the state. Far from being immune to critique from Levinas's philosophy of Judaism, the State of Israel, like every state, is subject to it.[57] His philosophy of Judaism-as-ethics enables a critique of the state, of any state, as "the ultimate refuge of idolatry . . . the State in search of hegemony, the conquering, imperialist, totalitarian, oppressive state, attached to realist egoism. Incapable of being without self-adoration, it is idolatry itself."[58] As Caygill pointedly concludes, "This means that through a brutal irony of history the prophetic mission of Israel becomes endangered by its own adoption of the form of the state."[59] Thus the other side of Levinas's ambivalence: "A person is more holy than a land, even a holy land, since, faced with an affront made to a person, this holy land appears in its nakedness to be but stone and wood."[60]

Levinas's personal ambivalence, which denounced the idolatry of the state and yet indulged the Occupation, suggests that he too, at times, was not immune to the risks of the idolatrous territorializations of political fraternity. Yet, in "The State of Israel and the Religion of Israel," he develops the argument that "the true sovereignty of [the state of] Israel . . . stems from the religion which modern political life supplants," and this new "religion" is, of course, the Judaism he has secularized as ethics. Accordingly, if naively (this is 1951), "an Israeli experiences the famous touch of God in his social dealings."[61] The "religion" of everyday political life—that is, ethics—is iconoclastic with respect to the idolatries of stone and wood, especially when the state itself enshrines these idolatries. Only through political fraternity can "ethics" amount to more than an abstract humanism that paradoxically serves the very individualism it sets out to contest. Yet political fraternity is precisely what risks compromising the ethicality of ethics by denying the other for the sake of "my 'others.'"

But nothing I have said by way of explicating the politics of Levinas's philosophy of Judaism implies a notion of Zionism as the political embodiment of the fraternity of the Jews. The political theology correlative to Levinas's philosophy of Judaism has purchase over the secular character of the state, not over the identities of its citizens. Levinas's secularized political theology makes no assumptions about the identity of the members of the body politic. If Levinas thinks of ethics as implying a model of political fraternity realized, for example, in the State of Israel, that is not because of Jews but because of Judaism. For the very same reason he regards the French Republic as an example of the necessary political supplement to ethics, not because of the identity of its citizens but because of the Judeo-Christian character of the fraternity it institutionalizes for the sake of the other. Ethical fraternity implies a weak, secularized political fraternity correlative to the cohistoricizing of a heritage of thinking in the service of the other. Critchley was right in noting that Levinas's account of ethics implies an affirmation of some sort of civic republicanism, but his labeling of this republicanism as "conservative" and his suggestion that Zionism is at greater risk of degrading into political ontology than are other republicanisms is tendentious.

This leads to a final but fundamental problem associated with Levinas's philosophy of Judaism, indeed, with any political theology that derives from Judaism or Judeo-Christianity. Even if a political attestation of the philosophy of Judaism runs merely the same tremendous risks as every other civic republicanism that cohistoricizes the heritage of its thinking for the sake of the other, how are we respond to the proposition, asserted by Levinas himself, that "those near to me are also my neighbors"?[62] Is there not a contradiction, evidently borne out by the majoritarian self-interest of all republics, that the other who will be served in the name of the republic's ethical heritage will invariably be someone near and not someone far? It is not enough to point to the fact that "the Other" does not really have any properties and that "every other is wholly other," as Derrida said, because cohistoricization demands not only that we communicate and struggle with our heritage but also that we affirm the institutional implications of political fraternity. Although the ethical self lacks all proper identity, and although the other can be truly approached only as the singularity of a name that cannot be identified with any set of descriptions, the necessity of cohistoricizing ethics as political fraternity means that we cannot avoid problems of inclusion, exclusion, and intrusion. Surely Levinas did not simply slip from an allegorical account of Judaism to an assertion about authentic Jewishness or to a view of Zionism, all proportions aside, as the authentic destiny of the *Volk* of Judaism. Accordingly, the unavoidable question for Levinas's philosophy of Judaism is one posed long ago by one Jew to another, before the invention of "universal religion" and the "metaphysics of morals," posed, moreover, within this heritage of thinking and communicated to us by another evangelist to the Gentiles: Who is my neighbor?

"Nothing is more burdensome than a neighbor"

According to Luke, who is the only evangelist to record the incident, Jesus relates the story of the Good Samaritan in response to a question from a Jewish lawyer. Because of the priest and the Levite who ignore the man lying beaten on the road, the parable has often been misinterpreted as a critique of Jewish purity laws or temple cult (or both).[63] But the priest and the Levite, together with the anonymous wretch left half-dead on the road, are in fact a synecdoche for the people of Israel as a whole, since the ecclesia of Israel is composed of strata of priests, Levites, and ordinary Israelite folk. In short, the parable has nothing to do with a critique of purity or cult. Its provocation lies in the interplay between the fraternity of the people of Israel, the great commandment to love the neighbor, who is presumed to be an Israelite, and the distorting effects of the Samaritan on this established nexus between fraternity and obligation. The parable is therefore a commentary on the identity politics of first-century Palestine, which apparently have not changed that much.

Another common reading proposes that Luke's point is to make known that the Samaritan is the real neighbor and therefore that Jesus came to break the narrow bonds of Judaic fraternity. According to this view, the Good Samaritan effects a transformation of Jewish ethnocentricism into an open community in which one's genealogical identity as a member of the people of Israel, that is, in which being Jewish, does not matter. By illustrating the commandment to love your neighbor as yourself by way of the Samaritan, the parable, in this reading, is said to teach that there is no longer insider or outsider, friend or enemy, Jew or Samaritan, for all are one. The evangelist would therefore be suggesting that true love of the neighbor involves the renunciation of the fraternity of Israel, the abrogation of political ontology, and even the abolishment of Jewish identity as such. This is exactly the opposite of the account of neighborly love to which Levinas's philosophy of Judaism leads. As we have seen, ethics depends on political fraternity in order to cohistoricize the heritage from which it is drawn. Such an interpretation would lead to the conclusion that since Levinas's philosophy of Judaism relies on a restrictive "communitarian" account of political fraternity it falls short of the Christian radicalization of the commandment to love the neighbor.

Despite its prominence, however, this is neither the best interpretation of the story of the Good Samaritan nor a good way of interpreting Levinas's view of love of neighbor. The Jewish lawyer indeed holds a restrictive definition of "neighbor"; his very question presupposes that some people are not neighbors. But the parable does not redefine the term "neighbor" or abolish the distinction between Jew and Gentile. Crucially, Samaritans were not regarded as Gentiles in ancient Israel. There was indeed long-standing historical enmity between Samaritans and Jews. Jews dismissed Samaritan claims for a different location of the temple, a modified text of the Torah, and an alternative line of priests. And the antipathy seems to have been mutual, as both Josephus and the Gospels attest. Despite this enmity, by the time of Jesus, the Samaritans had lived alongside other Israelites for several hundred years. The earliest rabbinic (*tannaitic*) views consider Samaritans to be Israelites, and it is only later *amoraic* rabbis who regard them as Gentiles.[64]

Although a proper historical interpretation would require more complex and more cautious considerations, there is sufficient evidence to determine that the Good Samaritan was not regarded as an outside alien whose intrusion breaks down the very idea of Jewish political fraternity but as an internal alien with entrenched opposition to Pharisaic Judaism. The point of the story, then, is not to redefine the category of "neighbor" so that it includes everyone but to emphasize that the commandment to love the neighbor refers especially to a deposed neighbor such as the Samaritan. The story does not abrogate the political fraternity of Israel by redefining the category of "neighbor" so as to include Gentiles; there is no reference to Gentiles in the parable and there is reason to think that Samaritans were regarded as Israelites, despite the enmity between them and the Pharisees. As biblical scholars have noted: "The effect of this for a Jew in Jesus' day would have been roughly analogous to the effect of a modern Jew, were a similar story told about an Israeli citizen ignored by passing Israeli officials but aided by a passing Arab."[65] This analogy holds, however, only if the "passing Arab" is an Israeli Arab, in other words, a person with a formally legitimate place in the political fraternity of (ancient) Israel whose concrete identity is nevertheless inimical the juridical authorities. But the analogy does not hold if it is meant to indicate a critique of the very idea of political identity and political fraternity, such as this Christian scholar implies when he proceeds to insist that "the command to love the neighbor breaks down all barriers which divide men."[66] What is exposed by the Samaritan is not the breaking down of identities but the excess of the law of love over political sectarianism, and the decisive factor here is that the surplus of love is immanent to the Law. The commandment in Leviticus 19:18 to love the neighbor and the story of the Good Samaritan that interprets it point to a model of political fraternity as founded on the commandment to accommodate the disturbing and distorting presence of the repulsive other, the other who gets under one's skin and violates the fantasy of a harmonious political ontology. The problem of love of the neighbor is a problem of sectarianism, of obligations to others who simultaneously undermine and confirm political fraternity, or of obligations that impose political fraternity in the absence of political ontology. Accordingly it is not a matter of overthrowing the Law or its implied political fraternity but of affirming a fraternity of Law that is absolutely indifferent to the face of the other and thereby, as in ethics, "commands me to the undesirable par excellence: *the other person.* . . . Here we find a love without eros."[67] The Good Samaritan shows how to love the enemy, but he does not announce the good news that all mankind is one. On the contrary, the story presumes the validity of the Law as precisely that which bears the immanent excess of the commandment to love the neighbor within the political fraternity it confirms. Žižek has caught sight of this dimension of neighborly love: "When the Old Testament enjoins you to love and respect your neighbour, this does not refer to your imaginary *semblable*/double, but to the neighbor qua traumatic Thing."[68]

Moreover, Luke is not alone in making this point. The commandment to "love your neighbor as yourself" first appears in Leviticus 19:18 in the context of a system of national law that explicitly denies that Jews are legally obliged only to love one another. That view of the restrictive nature of the legal fraternity of Judaism ironically restricts Jewish ethics to one verse without understanding the full charter of Leviticus 19. Leviticus 19:34 (cf. Deuteronomy 10:19) mandates: "The stranger who resides with you shall be to you as one of your citizens; you shall love him as yourself, for you were strangers in the land of Egypt: I the LORD am your God." By using the same language as Leviticus 19:18, verse 34 equates the love prescribed to one's fellow Israelite with love for the stranger.[69] And it establishes that the political fraternity constituted through law is traversed by a moral narrative of compassion for the enslaved and displaced that draws on its heritage of memory ("for you were strangers in the land of Egypt") while including "the stranger who resides with you" within the demands of love. The political fraternity of this heritage of thinking does not exclude the stranger but, on the contrary, acknowledges that the intrusion of the other marks the very opening of its own immanent ethical excess.[70]

I am suggesting, then, that Levinas's recourse to political fraternity, with its civic, even statist, republican implications, does not undermine ethics but provides for the cohistoricization of the excess of ethics immanent to a legal fraternity. Law is a principle of particularity and fraternity, but this does not mean that it excludes others on the basis of an authentic conception of the *Volk*. Levinas was indeed concerned with communicating and struggling over the "ethical destiny" of his heritage and therefore endorsed the concrete cohistoricizing of this heritage in the form of juridico-political fraternity. And although he himself waivered in the face of the ambivalence of fraternity, his philosophy and the heritage that it secularizes provide a consistent way of retaining the concrete political conditions for its realization without reducing ethics to ontology, that is, without limiting the obligations that constitute the covenant to the identity of the majority of its members. Almost everything Levinas said makes this point: the irreducibility of Torah to *nomos*; the risk of idolatry inherent in the establishment of a state on the basis of this heritage of Torah; the first figure, that of the stranger, who provides the raison d'être for the political order; and the second figure, that of the neighbor, who indicates the immanent excess of the ethical covenant with the undesirable other within the theologico-political fraternity.

"What if," asks Žižek, "we restore to the Levinasian 'face' all its monstrosity: face is not a harmonious Whole of the dazzling epiphany of a 'human face,' a face is something the glimpse of which we get when we stumble upon a grotesquely distorted face, a face in the grip of a disgusting tic or grimace, a face which, precisely, confronts us when the neighbour 'loses his face'?"[71] The interpretation of the parable of the Good Samaritan offered here leads us to this very conclusion, which corresponds to the philosophy of Judaism outlined by Levinas 2. For the author of *Otherwise than Being*, ethics is a "passion . . . touched by the *nondesirable* (the other is undesirable, and this includes here the meaning that some give to this term when speaking of foreigners!)," in which the other appears "diabolically."[72] Žižek's attempt to distance himself from Levinas thus in fact leads from Levinas 1 to Levinas 2:

The problem with this solution, acceptable in itself, is that it undermines the ethical edifice Levinas is trying to build upon it: far from standing for absolute authenticity, such a monstrous face is, rather, the ambiguity of the Real embod-

ied, the extreme/impossible point at which opposites coincide, at which the innocence of the Other's vulnerable nakedness overlaps with pure evil. . . . What if the
Levinasian face is yet another defense against this monstrous dimension of subjectivity? And what if the Jewish Law is to be conceived as strictly correlative to this
inhuman neighbor? . . . In short, *the* temptation to be resisted here is the ethical
"gentrification" of the neighbour, the reduction of the radically ambiguous monstrosity of the Neighbor-Thing into an Other as the abyssal point from which the
call of ethical responsibility emanates.[73]

I have argued that the ethical self of *Otherwise than Being* is precisely
an exposure to the traumatizing monstrosity of the other. It is for this very
reason that the "ethical language" of Levinas 2 is so severely deformed,
even defaced. As if anticipating Žižek's misplaced critique, Levinas already
acknowledged that "in a sense nothing is more burdensome than a neighbor. Is not this desired one the undesirable itself? The neighbor who could
not leave me indifferent, the undesirable desired one, has not revealed to
desire the ways of access to him. . . . Here the blow of the affection makes
an impact, traumatically, in a past more profound than all I can reassem-
ble by memory, by historiography, all that I can dominate by the a priori"
(OB, 88/AE, 111). Accordingly, in place of *exclusion* (or "Jewish particularism") and *inclusion* (or "Christian universalism"), Levinas's philosophy of
Judaism calls for an ethics of *intrusion* borne by its own heritage of thinking. It is in this gaping exposure of the self to the other, the "trauma" or
"passion" of the ethical creature, that I find what Santner calls "*a way out*,
a way of intervening into this dimension that otherwise seems to foreclose
the possibility for new forms of collective life . . . in a word, for *soothing* the
agitations of creaturely life."[74]

Only political fraternity makes ethics concrete, but only by loving
the undesirable neighbor can this concretion avoid becoming but another altar of stone and wood. Only the intrusion of the burdensome
neighbor separates political fraternity from political ontology. In this way
Levinas's civic republicanism, whether in French, Israeli, or any other
form, cohistoricizes the "ethical destiny" of his secularized philosophy of
Judaism. The ethical self is the "coring out" (*dénucléation*) of identity in
response to the other, a position whose radicality risks abandoning ethics to the self alone in relation to "all" others. Insofar as this ethical self
puts *politique après*, all it can do is gesture *après vous*. Political fraternity,
which cohistoricizes ethics, is thus a *necessary risk* for Levinas's philoso-

phy of Judaism. Ethical solidarity with "all" requires the heritage of this thinking to be shared, through communication and struggle, in concrete political fraternity with some. But fraternity is not a relation between subjects with properties, or even a relation of identities. It is the sharing of an exposure to a heritage in which identity comes to pass as co-responsiveness. If Levinas's philosophy of Judaism (ethics) has a part to play in modern political (or biopolitical) life, it will be only insofar as it remains exposed and responsive to the unpresentable neighbor. Political fraternity is the *sharing* of a creaturely exposure to the name of the other. But since the name designates without describing and glorifies without knowing, the political creature is absolutely indifferent to the identity of the other.

Conclusion

> Even Jesus of Nazareth, who imagined he will be the messiah but was put to death by the court, has been prophesied by Daniel, for it says "and the lawless children of your people shall rise to fulfill the vision, but they will fail" (Dan. 11:14). For is there a greater failure than this! All the prophets maintained that the messiah redeems Israel, saves them, gathers their oppressed and strengthens their commandments, but he caused Israel to be destroyed by the sword, their remnant to be dispersed and humiliated, the Torah to be modified and most of the world to stray by worshiping a god besides the Name. But it is beyond human limits to apprehend the designs of the Creator; for our ways are not his ways, neither are our thoughts his thoughts: all these matters concerning Jesus of Nazareth and the Ishmaelite [Mohammed] who came after him, only served to clear the way for the messiah king, to prepare the whole world to worship the Name together, as it is written, "for then I will make the peoples pure of speech, so that they all invoke the name YHWH, and serve Him, shouldering as one" (Zeph. 3:9). How so? For the entire world is full of messianic matters, words of Torah and talk of the commandments, and these words have spread to distant isles and among many people of uncircumcised heart. They discuss and debate these words, including the commandments of the Torah.
>
> —Maimonides, *Laws of Kings* 11.4 (in *Mishneh Torah*)

Kant taught that concepts without intuitions are empty and that intuitions without concepts are blind. But what happens when the concept of ethics is theological and its intuition secular? Is the theological concept empty and the secular intuition blind? That would make Levinas an atheist in theology and a dogmatist in ethics. At least this would explain the hostility his work has received from orthodox theological and secular quarters, from theologians who reject the experience of atheism and secularists who cannot suffer theology. Can one call on the name of the ethical other in prayer? Can one rationally critique the revelation of "the face" from a position that is neither Judaic nor Judeo-Christian? Neither the theologian nor the secularist will be satisfied.

But Levinas is a Heideggerian, not a Kantian, thinker. There are no formal ethical concepts and no pure ethical intuitions. Our moral concepts are historical, our ethical intuitions are hermeneutical. What some see as a choice between a theology emptied of God and an ethics blinded by the Other is, rather, a question of the historical conditioning of our moral concepts and the hermeneutical character of our ethical intuitions. Insofar as this is our phenomenological situation, Levinas not only makes good sense of our experience of ethics but provides a way of understanding the fundamentally ethical basis of our historical coexistence. It is not a formal argument about God or an empirical argument about ethics but a descriptive argument about who we are, we who experience each other and the world through a shared and contested heritage of thinking.

This is also to say that all significant concepts in ethics are secularized theological concepts. The power of these secularized theological concepts today is dispersed in ways of thinking, acting, and judging that are only tenuously connected to the historical forms of life that gave rise to them. Ethics itself is the dispersal of the Judeo-Christian God in modern social life. The God who created a good world amid the chaos of mere existence, the one who confronted evil by speaking rather than killing, the one whose desire extends to the singular over the general and whose freedom transcends the grasp we once had of Him—all these are secularized by Levinas 1. Ethics is life in the image of God, an image that both indicates and blocks the way to Him.

To say that "ethics is first philosophy" (TI, 304/TeI, 340) is to recall that the world is created as an ethical covenant, that its intelligibility is radically contingent, all the way down to our covenantal faithfulness to one another. For Levinas, thinking is thanking. But the covenant of creation does not simply give rise to the idea of an intelligible world; it gives rise to the idea of a world whose goodness, or lack thereof, is a matter of ethical faith. The covenant of ethical faith determines when the misfortunes of brute existence become injustices for which we are responsible. Since the evil of superfluous suffering can never be eliminated, the goodness of the world must be continuously re-created. This is a messianic task, since it desires good-ness for particular others beyond one's reach, whether because of structural asymmetry, like the orphan and the stranger, or whether because of the fe-cundity of desire for the good, which reaches beyond oneself, to a child, or a generation, or a world to come.

Levinas 2 modifies his position in an essential way that nevertheless retains the fundamentally covenantal character of creation. To live other-wise than being is to live as an ethical creature, caught in the grip of names that indicate singular obligations to the elusive presence of the other, to the one whose uniqueness can neither be described nor negated but only ap-proached and honored, or ignored, or murdered. The ethical creature does not create a moral world; it does not act freely from a position of separa-tion, like a God who stands outside the order he produces. To be an ethi-cal creature is to bear witness, in one's flesh, to the undeclinable goodness of an exposure to the other that precedes self-identity and thus testifies, de-spite oneself, to the glory of the Good: "Before the bipolarity of good and evil presented to choice, the subject finds himself committed to the Good in the very passivity of supporting" (OB, 122/AE, 157). The ethical crea-ture is exposed to this glory in the extimacy of its soul, a passive bondage to the undesirable other that attests to "the original goodness of creation" (OB, 121/AE, 155). "It is perhaps here," Levinas writes, "in this reference to a depth of anarchical passivity, that the thought that names creation dif-fers from ontological thought" (OB, 113/AE, 144). This anarchical passiv-ity is our covenant as ethical creatures: the responsive expropriations of our shared heritage of thinking and the co-responsiveness to the world through which we are exposed to and responsible for one another. We are this cov-enant of ethical creatures.

Notes

PREFACE

1. Carl Schmitt, *Political Theology*, 36.

2. *Otherwise than Being or Beyond Essence*, xlii/*Autrement qu'être ou au-delà de l'essence*, x.

3. Interview with Raoul Mortley, "Emmanuel Levinas," in Mortley, *French Philosophers in Conversation*, 13.

4. Howard Caygill, *Levinas and the Political*, offers a compelling explanation for the haunting presence of the Holocaust in Levinas's thought. In Caygill's view, the Holocaust, for Levinas, is the ever-present specter of political evil, not unlike the Hobbesian state of nature. Levinas's account of ethics therefore is established on the basis of radical political evil but is also always haunted by it. In Caygill's words, "The political present is largely absent in Levinas's texts, leaving marks as the memory of horror or the prophetic intimation of peace (3)."

5. Levinas, *The Theory of Intuition in Husserl's Phenomenology*.

6. Levinas, "Some Thoughts on the Philosophy of Hitlerism," in *Unforeseen History*; and "L'actualité de Maimonide," trans. Michael Fagenblat as "The Contemporary Relevance of Maimonides" (1935).

7. Levinas, "Il y a."

8. Salomon Malka, quoting Levinas on the occasion of his eightieth birthday, in his *Emmanuel Levinas*, 84. The summary I offer of Levinas's Jewish life is largely taken from Malka's congenial biography.

9. Malka, *Emmanuel Levinas*, 132. One of Levinas's final publications was a preface to a new French translation of Maimonides' *Book of Commandments*, *Le livre des commandments*, 9–11.

10. These include the weekly reading of the Torah (the Pentateuch), repeated every year from beginning to end, the extensive selection of prophetic writings that accompany the weekly lection (the *haftorah*), the additional exegesis and anthologization of the Bible that constitute a great part of the Jewish prayer book, and the further biblical texts (especially from the Hagiographa) and rabbinic glosses recited on Jewish festivals.

11. His first appointment was at Poitiers; his next was at the prestigious Nanterre (Paris X) from 1967–1973, when it was headquarters to the May 1968 uprising; and his last was at the Sorbonne (Paris IV). For more detail, see Marie-Anne Lescourret, *Emmanuel Levinas*, 221–54, and Levinas's brief but potent autobiographical sketch, "Signature," in *Difficult Freedom*, 291–95.

12. For a particularly lucid and succinct introduction, see Simon Critchley, "Introduction," in Simon Critchley and Robert Bernasconi, eds., *The Cambridge Companion to Levinas*, 1–32.

13. Martin Heidegger, *Being and Time*, 323/SZ, 278. All references to *Being and Time* will appear in the text, followed by the page numbers in the German original of *Sein und Zeit* (Frankfurt am Main: Vittoria Klostermann, 1976) as SZ. One could say that Heidegger criticizes prevalent moral philosophies solely to expose *the ethics of being*, since the analysis of conscience (§§55–60) is deployed entirely in order to explore the possibility of Dasein's authentic attestation. In this respect Levinas, for whom the ethical response to the voice of the other provides the ultimate attestation of self, would be extremely close to Heidegger. These themes are explored in François Raffoul and David Pettigrew, eds., *Heidegger and Practical Philosophy*, especially in Jean-Luc Nancy, "Heidegger's 'Originary Ethics,'" 65–86, Françoise Dastur, "The Call of Conscience," 87–98, and Raffoul, "Heidegger and the Origins of Responsibility," 205–18.

14. Heidegger, *Being and Time*, §59.

15. Even so, Levinas's work has important affinities with several established positions in moral philosophy. I have mentioned its proximity to a Kantian sense of ethics as unconditioned obligation. It can also be noted that *Totality and Infinity* is a teleological, or at least an eschatological, work that could favorably compare to a certain Aristotelianism. I take it that Levinas generally distinguished between "ethics" and "morality" to differentiate what he was doing from Kantian *Moralität*, or what is nowadays called "value theory." A similar distinction between ethics and morality was introduced into analytical moral philosophy by Bernard Williams in *Ethics and the Limits of Philosophy*, 6. Williams's distinction between ethics and morality belongs to a shift among many analytic philosophers from Kantian and utilitarian theories of moral objectivity to Aristotelian-inspired accounts of ethical contextualism. The relationship between Levinas's post-Heideggerian ethics and certain neo-Aristotelian analytic moral philosophers has not yet been sufficiently explored. For a helpful beginning, see Dwight Furrow, *Against Theory*, and Michael Morgan, *Discovering Levinas*, chap. 9, although I discovered Morgan's book too late to incorporate it into this study.

16. All references to *Totality and Infinity* will be given in the body of this work as TI, followed by the pagination in the French original, *Totalité et infini: Essai sur l'extériorité*, as TeI.

17. Jacques Derrida, "Violence and Metaphysics," in *Writing and Difference*, 111. Throughout the book, all emphasis in quotations is from the original unless stated otherwise.

18. All references to *Otherwise than Being or Beyond Essence* will be given in the body of this work as OB, followed by the pagination in the French original, *Autrement qu'être ou au-delà de l'essence*, as AE.

19. James L. Kugel applies the notion of "reverse-engineering" to the study of midrash in the precise sense of discerning the particular texts from early tradents that constitute later midrashim; see his *In Potiphar's House*. Although this process can to some extent be replicated with Levinas's philosophical works, my argument is that his work is midrashic in the looser sense, that it is constituted by conceptual and textual borrowing from the Judaic tradition rather than by direct citation and combination.

20. The most notable exception to this is Hermann Cohen, whose *Religion of Reason from Out of the Sources of Judaism* was an even more explicit—perhaps too explicit—argument for the value of Judaism for contemporary moral philosophy. For a discussion of this, see Kenneth Seeskin, *Jewish Philosophy in a Secular Age*, chap. 1; and for a comparison of Cohen and Levinas, see Leora Batnitzky, *Leo Strauss and Emmanuel Levinas*, chap. 4.

21. The comparison with Ibn Gabirol is also made by Malka, *Emmanuel Levinas*, 281.

22. Samuel Moyn, *Origins of the Other*; see also his "Emmanuel Levinas's Talmudic Readings."

CHAPTER 1

1. See "Interview with François Poirié," in Jill Robbins, ed., *Is It Righteous to Be?*, 61–62.

2. Salomon Malka, *Emmanuel Levinas*, 268, in which Marcel's comment is relayed by Levinas's son Michael.

3. Malka, *Emmanuel Levinas*, 196. Compare Ricoeur's similar comments to Heidegger at the Colloque de Cerisy in 1955, following Heidegger's lecture "What is Philosophy?," noted and published by Jean Beaufrey, "Heidegger et la théologie," in Richard Kearney and Joseph O'Leary, eds., *Heidegger et la question de Dieu*, 22; see also Ricoeur's "Introductory Note" to that volume. For an illuminating discussion, see Marlène Zarader, *The Unthought Debt*, 186–95.

4. Two recent monographs devoted to the topic are Oona Ajzenstat's *Driven Back to the Text* and Catherine Chalier's *La trace de l'infini*. The differences between my Judaic reading of Levinas and theirs are significant. Ajzenstat takes Levinas to be a postmodern Kabbalist, whereas Chalier thinks of him more as a Hasid. Others also take Levinas to have incorporated important Kabbalistic themes, for example, Charles Mopsik, "La pensée d'Emmanuel Levinas et la Cabale," and

Richard A. Cohen, *Elevations*, 241–73. I am most persuaded by Elliot R. Wolfson, "Secrecy, Modesty, and the Feminine," and Jacob Meskin, "The Role of Lurianic Kabbalah in the Early Philosophy of Emmanuel Levinas." Even so, at the very least the emphasis of these studies seems to me in need of correction. Levinas openly distanced himself from the Kabbalah, seems only to have read one Kabbalistic work (the eighteenth-century digest of Hayim Volozhin, *Nefesh ha-Hayyim*), and derided the Hasidic popularization of the Kabbalah. Other studies on the Jewish elements of Levinas's thought include: Tamra Wright, *Twilight of Jewish Philosophy*; Chalier, "The Philosophy of Emmanuel Levinas and the Hebraic Tradition"; Robert Gibbs, "Height and Nearness"; Shmuel Trigano, "Levinas and the Project of Jewish Philosophy"; James Hatley, "Levinas in the Jewish Context"; Susan Handelman, *Fragments of Redemption*; Hilary Putnam, "Levinas and Judaism"; and Edith Wyschogrod, *Emmanuel Levinas*.

5. Gillian Rose takes Hegel's *Entzweiung*, "diremption," as a trope for critiquing the postmodern (Jewish) philosophy of Levinas and many others in *The Broken Middle* and *Judaism and Modernity*. Rose's critique of "Judaism as the sublime Other of modernity" is stimulating, although I do not agree with her conclusion, which seems to be that the only way of reviving Judaism from the lifeless posture of "philosophy's Other," from whence it can merely gesture mutely like an irate angel, is to develop a Jewish Hegelianism. I am proposing that there is more to be gained by a hermeneutical integration of Judaism and philosophy.

6. Judith Butler, "Ethical Ambivalence," 48.

7. Dominique Janicaud et al., *Phenomenology and the "Theological Turn,"* 45.

8. Alain Badiou, *Ethics*, 22–23.

9. Immanuel Kant, *Religion Within the Limits of Reason Alone*, 116ff. For valuable discussions, see Stephen B. Smith, *Spinoza, Liberalism, and the Question of Jewish Identity*, 170–79 (and 255n88 for references to earlier discussions), and Yirmiyahu Yovel, *Dark Riddle*, 3–20. Yovel (11) and Smith (170) agree that Mendelssohn is here indebted to Spinoza. Kant does not say so, but in *Religion* he clearly seems to be paraphrasing Spinoza's depiction of Judaism in the *Theologico-Political Treatise*, probably via Mendelssohn's mediation; see esp. Mendelssohn, *Jerusalem*, 97.

10. Benedict de Spinoza, *A Theologico-Political Treatise and A Political Treatise*, chap. 5.

11. Maimonides, *Mishneh Torah, Laws of Kings*, 8:11.

12. Most contemporary scholars regard the latter as the correct version. This is how it is rendered in *The Code of Maimonides. Book XIV: The Book of Judges*, trans. Abraham M. Hershman, 230; see also 308. The bibliography surrounding the different versions of this text of Maimonides' is extensive, drawing into its orbit a cluster of associated questions concerning Maimonides' regard for the independence of truth and morality from revelation and tradition. Mendelssohn, who did not know of an alternative manuscript to the printed edition cited by Spinoza, was

greatly perplexed by what he (rightly) took as an anomaly; see Alexander Altmann, *Moses Mendelssohn*, 294–95. Two thorough discussions of the mountains of Jewish thought hanging from the threads of this one word can be found in David Novak, *The Image of the Non-Jew in Judaism*, chap. 10, esp. 288–90, 300–04; and Steven Schwarzschild, "Do Noahides Have to Believe in Revelation?" I was first alerted to the issue by Moshe Halbertal, *Interpretative Revolutions in the Making*, 29n38.

13. For example, Novak and Halbertal (cited in the preceding note), and David Hartman, *Maimonides*, 52–56 and 222n62.

14. For a critique of this view, see Avi Sagi and Daniel Statman, *Religion and Morality*. I explore this further in "Ethics and Halakhah in Levinas."

15. Ajzenstat makes the astute observation that Levinas's oppositional characterization of the relation between Judaism and philosophy belongs to his philosophical works, whereas, interestingly, in his Jewish writings he seeks to synthesize them; see her "Levinas Versus Levinas."

16. Levinas's most sustained attempt to offer an account of revelation that is neither dogmatic nor based on reason alone appears in "God and Philosophy," in his *Of God Who Comes to the Mind*, 55–78; see also Jeffrey L. Kosky's illuminating discussion, *Levinas and the Philosophy of Religion*, chap. 8.

17. Robert Gibbs offers a subtle exploration of this issue in *Correlations in Rosenzweig and Levinas*. Cf. Daniel Boyarin's discussion of "essentialism as resistance," in *A Radical Jew*, 241.

18. Shortly after the publication of *Totality and Infinity* (1961) we find Levinas already protesting at the dichotomous reception of this work, which from the outset understood him to be asserting that ethics was outside the realm of theory and philosophy; see the discussion following "Transcendence and Height" in Levinas, *Basic Philosophical Writings*, 24. Robert Bernasconi provides a valuable corrective to this widespread misunderstanding of Levinas in "Rereading *Totality and Infinity*."

19. Moyn, *Origins of the Other*, 12.

20. Moyn, *Origins of the Other*, 12, 201, 230.

21. Moyn, *Origins of the Other*, 16–17.

22. Gibbs, *Correlations*, 173.

23. Leora F. Batnitzky, "On Reaffirming a Distinction Between Athens and Jerusalem," 228.

24. Moyn, *Origins of the Other*, 230.

25. Kosky provides another interpretation that adopts similar presuppositions. In his view Levinas should not be understood as a Jewish thinker, as Moyn's historical and Batnitzky's conceptual arguments also maintain, but as offering a "philosophy of religion." Precisely because it *is* philosophical, Levinas's thought is not dependent on Judaism at all. Rather, Levinas's work "produces the pure possibility, the nonnoematic meaning or even 'essence,' of religion—the possibility of religion

before any recourse to religious experience and before any recourse to the revelation kept by historical traditions" (Kosky, *Levinas and the Philosophy of Religion*, 161). The problem here is that this application of Derrida's idea of "religion without religion" makes Levinas's work sound like a kind of natural theology, arguably *the* metaphysical discourse par excellence: "the religiosity met in Levinas's phenomenology of responsibility is not an actual religion but the possibility or nonnoematic meaning of religion" (Kosky, xxi). To subtract "historical traditions" and "actual religion" from "religiosity" is precisely the fantasy of metaphysical theology. If that is what is meant by "religion without religion"—although it is not how I read Derrida or John Caputo—then I would argue that there is no such thing. This version of "religion without religion" would be but the last hurrah of a very metaphysical natural theology that inevitably correlates with the doctrines of a "universal" religion such as Christianity. It is hardly surprising, then, that Kosky is followed by Michael Purcell, in whose work the neutralization, effectively the de-Judaization of Levinas's "philosophy of religion," becomes a "propaedeutic" for Catholic theology; see Purcell, *Levinas and Theology*, 158. For a critical discussion of Christian appropriations of Levinas see Robyn Horner, "On Lévinas' Gifts to Christian Theology." From the Jewish side, Wright's fine study, *Twilight of Jewish Philosophy*, strikes me as flawed on this point: "Neither *Totality and Infinity* nor *Otherwise than Being* should be interpreted as theological texts. . . . The apparently theological claims in *Totality and Infinity* can be understood phenomenologically as belonging to the description of the relationship between the self and a transcendent other" (93). The worry seems to be that if Levinas's philosophy is read too Jewishly then it loses its philosophical force. The Judaic-hermeneutical approach I develop in the remainder of this chapter is intended to alleviate that concern. For a position close to mine, see Theodore de Boer, "Theology and the Philosophy of Religion," in *The Rationality of Transcendence*, 182–83.

26. In *Leo Strauss and Emmanuel Levinas*, Batnitzky astutely observes that "Levinas saw himself as continuing what he regarded as Maimonides' 'medieval synthesis'" (10).

27. This interpretation is confirmed by Maimonides' *Commentary to Mishnah Hagigah* 2:1, the classical rabbinic text prohibiting the disclosure of the Account of the Chariot. On this, see Halbertal, *Concealment and Revelation*, esp. 8–13, and, on Maimonides' disclosure of the esoteric, 60–68.

28. Gershom Scholem, *Major Trends in Jewish Mysticism*, 26.

29. Levinas, *Autrement que savoir*, cited by Kosky, *Levinas and the Philosophy of Religion*, 157.

30. Gibbs, *Correlations*, 173.

31. Batnitzky, "On Reaffirming a Distinction Between Athens and Jerusalem," respectively 228, 227, and 214. Why Batnitzky accuses Levinas of *uncritical* reflection on this question escapes me, since *Totality and Infinity* is explicitly based

on the avowed "hypocrisy" of being "attached both to the philosophers and the prophets" (TI, 24). Right or wrong, the conflation of Athens and Jerusalem is therefore effected with the full critical force of reason.

32. Derrida, "Violence and Metaphysics," in *Writing and Difference*, 84.

33. Donald Davidson, "On the Very Idea of a Conceptual Scheme," in *Inquiries*, 183–98.

34. Cf. Davidson, "Radical Interpretation," in *Inquiries*, 125. The usefulness of Davidson's philosophy for religious studies has begun to be explored in Nancy K. Frankenberry, ed., *Radical Interpretation in Religion*.

35. If allegory didn't have such a bad reputation, one could say that Levinas provides an allegorical interpretation of Judaism, as I will indeed argue later. For a sympathetic view of allegory that also draws on Davidson, see Gerald L. Bruns, "Allegory as Radical Interpretation," in *Hermeneutics Ancient and Modern*, chap. 4, esp. 83–86. The major problem with the modern view of allegory is that it imagines the interpreter transposing the meaning of the text from its original context to an abstract realm of ideas, that is to say, to a plane of pure signifieds. In practice, however, the best allegorists, such as Origen and Maimonides, work intertextually. They do not simply correlate their sacred texts with an abstract realm of pure ideas but produce allegorical interpretations by interposing texts in new, creative ways. See, for example, James Arthur Diamond's discussion of the intertextual character of Maimonidean allegory in his *Maimonides and the Hermeneutics of Concealment*; Arthur Green's critical remarks on Scholem's position in "Shekhinah, the Virgin Mary, and the Song of Songs," esp. 44; Patricia Cox Miller's view of Origen's method in "Poetic Words, Abysmal Words"; Mark J. Edwards, *Origen Against Plato*; and Boyarin, "By Way of Apology: Dawson, Edwards, Origen."

36. Batnitzky, "On Reaffirming a Distinction Between Athens and Jerusalem," 215.

37. Diamond, *Maimonides and the Hermeneutics of Concealment*, 151.

38. Gibbs's more recent view in *Why Ethics?* is more nuanced and avoids the false problem of an "untranslatable core." There he writes: "In Levinas's philosophical work, the Jewish saying clearly challenges and judges the modern Western philosophical tradition. But in order to make even that judgement intelligible, it is necessary to translate into that Western language" (301). The last sentence undermines the very idea of untranslatability that Gibbs's *Correlations* cherished. I return briefly to Davidson and the role of charity in Chapter 5. As Hubert Dreyfus, Jeff Malpas, and others have shown, Davidson's views are close to a certain reading of Heidegger, and my Heideggerian reading of Levinas's philosophy of Judaism thus has Davidson in mind at several points—usually when it is a matter of suggesting that Levinas's profoundly interpretative philosophy does not abandon plausible philosophical positions about the nature of "objective" knowledge. For references, see note 72 in Chapter 5.

39. Boyarin, *Border Lines*, 29, 32, 89.
40. G. W. F. Hegel, *History of Philosophy*, vol. 3, 258.
41. Batnitzky, "On Reaffirming a Distinction Between Athens and Jerusalem," 228–29.
42. Heidegger, "Comments on Karl Jaspers's *Psychology of Worldviews*," in *Pathmarks*, 4.
43. Heidegger, *Being and Time*, 61/SZ, 37 (Heidegger's emphasis).
44. Levinas was the first to appreciate this. His first book, which was among the earliest works on phenomenology in France and influenced a generation of phenomenologists, from Jean-Paul Sartre and Ricoeur to Derrida and Jean-François Lyotard, was *ironically* titled *The Theory of Intuition in Husserl's Phenomenology*. Its conclusion calls for a Heideggerian critique of the merely theoretical nature of Husserl's account of intuition.
45. Heidegger, *Pathmarks*, 4–5.
46. Obviously one cannot in advance specify who counts for "we." Hermeneutics invariably involves an exploration and disruption of the contours that constitute who "we" are, above all those constituting the "we" of each "I."
47. It is notable that those arguing for Levinas's proximity to Heidegger, even at points at which he seeks to distance himself, almost all hail from France, whereas American commentators of Levinas have a far greater tendency to accept his critique of Heidegger and his characterization of the gulf between them. This false loyalty has unfortunately left Levinas's work stranded. Whereas Heidegger's work has been drawn into fruitful conversation with philosophers such as Davidson and Rorty, Levinas's work has largely fallen on deaf ears among postfoundational American philosophers. Morgan, *Discovering Levinas*, is a welcome correction. The profound proximity between Levinas and Heidegger is a natural way for those conversations to develop, as one sees, for example, with Cavell.
48. Zarader, *The Unthought Debt*, 148–49; cf. Levinas, OB, 189n28, 49n28.
49. Zarader, *The Unthought Debt*, 185.
50. Zarader, *The Unthought Debt*, 199.
51. Derrida, "At This Very Moment in This Work Here I Am," 16.
52. Derrida, "At This Very Moment in This Work Here I Am," 18.
53. On the instability of *Écriture* as writing/Scripture, see Kevin Hart, *Trespass of the Sign*, 49–51, 60–61.
54. In *Intertextuality and the Reading of Midrash*, Boyarin argued for a firm distinction between midrash and allegory, consigning philosophical (and Christian) exegesis to the latter. In more recent work Boyarin seems to have come around to the view that certain philosophers writing in the post-metaphysical (post-Heideggerian) epoch, especially Derrida, are effectively practicing philosophy as midrash; see "Midrash and the 'Magic Language.'" Likewise, in *Border Lines* he embraces early Christian literature as midrash.

55. Handelman, *Fragments of Redemption*, 264.

56. "Emmanuel Levinas," in Mortley, *French Philosophers in Conversation*, 13.

57. Perhaps Marlène Zarader is correct to refer, for philosophical purposes, to an interpretation of the "Hebraic heritage" rather than "Judaism" (*The Unthought Debt*, 9–13). Throughout this book I retain the incautious appellation of a "philosophy of Judaism," even though occasionally, and still more recklessly, I could have said "a philosophy of Judeo-Christianity." This is partly on account of convention, partly because of my own immemorial "identity," and partly in the hope that by assuming a name that is still in use—"Jewish," and not simply "Hebraic"— an internal, concrete critique might transpire. More to the point, Levinas manifestly draws his philosophy of Judaism not simply out of the "Hebraic" tradition but also from the rabbinic (often Aramaic), medieval (often Arabic), and modern (often German) Jewish traditions of thinking. His philosophy is clearly nurtured by the sense of a fractured and disrupted but living heritage of Judaism that is not simply a repository of Hebraic texts. We might as well then call it Jewish or Judaic and thereby also interrogate Judaism as it is lived today by a philosophy of Judaism as presented by Levinas.

58. Levinas, "Being Jewish," 206. For an incisive commentary, see Annabel Herzog, "Benny Levy Versus Emmanuel Levinas on 'Being Jewish.'"

59. Stanley K. Stowers makes the case in *A Rereading of Romans* that many of Paul's harshest words in Romans against the law should be understood as part of his rhetorical use of *prosopopeia*, whereby a rival Jewish teacher is fictively conjured in order to be refuted.

60. The bibliography is immense; see David Bolton and Emmanuel Nathan, "New Understandings of Paul and His Jewish Heritage," and Michael F. Bird, "The New Perspective on Paul." I am particularly indebted to the work of two leading figures, Lloyd Gaston, *Paul and the Torah*, and John G. Gager, *Reinventing Paul*. Admittedly, they represent the radical side of the "New Perspective," according to which Paul affirms the Law for the Jews. Others, such as James D. G. Dunn, contend that Paul was not opposed to the Law as such but that he nonetheless sought to break down barriers between Jew and Gentile and to that extent derogated the Law even if he did not quite abrogate it for the Jews; see Dunn's *The New Perspective on Paul*. I learned too late of David G. Horrell's important study, *Solidarity and Difference: A Contemporary Reading of Paul's Ethics*, to engage with it here, although I hope to return to it.

61. More radically, some think Paul was not preaching salvation through faith *in* Christ but salvation through Christ's faithfulness. On this, see Gager, *Reinventing Paul*, 109–11, 120–21, 125–26, and 146.

62. Alan F. Segal, "Universalism in Judaism and Christianity," 25.

63. Levinas, *Nine Talmudic Readings*, 99.

64. Levinas, *Difficult Freedom*, 22.

65. Levinas, *In the Time of the Nations*, 84.
66. Putnam, "Levinas and Judaism," 33–34.
67. Putnam, "Levinas and Judaism," 47.
68. Putnam, "Levinas and Judaism," 47.
69. Jacob Taubes, *The Political Theology of Paul*, 52–53.
70. Levinas, *Difficult Freedom*, 17.
71. Levinas, *Beyond the Verse*, 107. Cf. TI, 78–79.
72. Badiou, *Saint Paul*, 103 (emphasis in the original).
73. Gager, *Reinventing Paul*, 104–5.
74. Badiou, *Saint Paul*, 100.

75. Derrida was referring to Jan Patočka, but also mentioned Levinas, along with Kant, Hegel, Heidegger, Marion, and Ricoeur; see Derrida's *The Gift of Death*, 49.

76. Menachem Kellner, *Maimonides' Confrontation with Mysticism*, 238. Maimonides does not explicitly identify the Israelites in the Mishnah with those non-Jews who have actualized their intellects and thus "attain the world to come." What Maimonides says, however, is that *not all* of the descendants of Abraham, Isaac, and Jacob attain the world to come, despite the explicit wording of Mishnah Sanhedrin 10:1, "All Israelites have a share in the world to come," and that some non-Jews do attain the world to come by actualizing their intellects. It therefore follows that "Israelites" who attain the world to come is a term that is not coextensive with "descendants of Abraham, Isaac, and Jacob." For more, see Kellner's discussion and references. Note that Paul also insists that "all Israel will be saved" (Rom. 11:26); see Gager, *Reinventing Paul*, 128–42 for a discussion of the new perspective on this.

77. Badiou is quite right to say that "the Law always designates a particularity, hence a difference. It is not possible for it to be an operation of the One, because it addresses its fallacious 'One' only to those who acknowledge and practice the injunctions it specifies" (*Saint Paul*, 76). This is precisely why it is crucial to see that Torah does not simply mean "law," as Gaston elaborates in *Paul and the Torah*, esp. 15–34. Alan F. Segal, in "Torah and *Nomos* in Recent Scholarly Discussion," comes to the same view from a different angle. He shows how *nomos* became, for Hellenistic Judaism, a term designating not simply the law that regulates human activity but also the transcendent law of the cosmos.

78. Jon D. Levenson, "The Universal Horizon of Biblical Particularism," 151.
79. Paul Ricoeur, "Experience and Language in Religious Discourse," 145.
80. Badiou, respectively, *Saint Paul*, 101, and *Polemics*, 162; see also *Polemics*, 185. It was, of course, Isaac Deutscher who coined the term "non-Jewish Jew" for purposes similar to Badiou's. Inverting this concept, Steven Schwarzschild devises a category of "Jewish non-Jews" that perhaps expresses Levinas's intentions; see Schwarzschild, "An Agenda for Jewish Philosophy in the 1980s," 101–25, esp. 116.

81. Kosky, *Levinas and the Philosophy of Religion*, 161 (my emphasis). Interestingly, both Paul and Levinas are strangely reticent about the nature of the Event that has brought about their respective expropriations of Judaism. What is important for both is not the biography or character of the Other but the fable this Event engenders, leading to a radical reinterpretation of the *logia* entrusted to the Jews so as to proclaim a message for the whole of humanity.

82. Gaston, *Paul and the Torah*, 78–79.

83. It is no doubt for this reason that Franz Rosenzweig, who regarded his *Star of Redemption* as a philosophical work and not a work of Jewish thought, equated Heidegger's "philosophical position" with "precisely our own"; see Rosenzweig, "Transposed Fronts," in *Philosophical and Theological Writings*, 148. See also Peter Eli Gordon's important work, *Rosenzweig and Heidegger*, esp. chap. 6.

84. For useful analyses that take this approach, see Trigano, "Levinas and the Project of Jewish Philosophy," and Kosky, *Levinas and the Philosophy of Religion*, 149–54.

85. Critchley, "Introduction," in *Cambridge Companion to Levinas*, 18.

86. Idan Dershowitz informs me that *lemor* ("saying") appears 305 times in the Five Books of Moses (the Pentateuch) alone.

87. Levinas, "The Pact," in *Beyond the Verse*, 80. Although this lecture was delivered in 1980, several years after *Otherwise than Being* (1974), there is no reason not to accept Levinas's claim that he is conveying a teaching from Chouchani from the years after World War II. Levinas studied with Chouchani from 1947 to 1952, when the latter left Paris. Chouchani died in 1968.

88. BT Sanhedrin 68a, which Levinas comments on in "Desacralization and Disenchantment" [1971], in *Nine Talmudic Readings*, 136–60.

89. Levinas, *Beyond the Verse*, 80.

90. Levinas, *Beyond the Verse*, 80 (my emphasis).

91. As far as I know, Levinas refers to this well-known Mishnah only once, in a 1985 publication; see "The Rights of Man and the Rights of the Other," in *Outside the Subject*, 118.

92. On the significance of fraternity in Levinas's thinking, see Howard Caygill, *Levinas and the Political*, to which I return in Chapter 6.

93. Levinas, TI, 214/TeI, 189; cf. 198–201, 278–80, 304–6.

94. He may also have another well-known midrash in mind, from the commentary in Genesis Rabbah on Genesis 4, which is itself indebted to our Mishnah. There Rabbi Shimon bar Yochai accuses God of allowing Cain to murder Abel. Rabbi Shimon's daring *j'accuse* to God—which reads in Genesis 4:10 as saying "the voice of your brother's blood cries out *at* me," as if God were under accusation—has the human face of justice in mind, as if everything Rabbi Shimon knows of God's justice is expressed on the bloodied face of Abel. Compare this with Tertullian (*Ad Martyras*, chap. 3, and *Scorpiace*, chap. 6), who uses the same imagery to

justify martyrdom in the name of God's love of the faithful blood of the martyrs.
Rabbi Shimon, by contrast, refuses to justify God in the name of human justice.
For the Tertullian references I am indebted to Joshua Levinson.

95. For a comprehensive treatment consistent with this view, see Yair Lorberbaum, *Image of God*, esp. 376–77 and 390–91.

96. E. E. Urbach, "Whoever Saves One Soul . . . ," in *The World of the Sages*; see also Maimonides, *Commentary to the Mishnah Sanhedrin* 4:5, and *Hilchot Sanhedrin* 12:3.

CHAPTER 2

1. For the biographical details, see Marie-Anne Lescourret, *Emmanuel Levinas*, 118–28, and Salomon Malka, *Emmanuel Levinas*, 64–82. On their escape route to the monastery in Orléans, Levinas's wife, Raissa, his daughter, Simone, and his mother-in-law, Frieda Lévi, hid for several weeks in the apartment of his friend Maurice Blanchot.

2. "Interview with François Poiré," in Jill Robbins, ed., *Is It Righteous to Be?*, 46.

3. Levinas, TI, 26/TeI, xiv, and TI, 110–14/TeI, 82–86, respectively. Levinas makes use of two senses of the verb "produce," to manufacture something and to stage it or bring it to light (TI, 26/TeI, xiv). See also *Time and the Other*, 53, and the translator's note ad loc. Paul Ricoeur, in *The Symbolism of Evil*, notes that the ancient Near Eastern mythic accounts of creation from chaos anticipate "typologically the most subtle ontogeneses of modern philosophy, especially those of German idealism" (177). Ricoeur's observation applies to Levinas's work, whose transcendental phenomenology extends the ontogenetic idealist approach.

4. Levinas's *De l'existence à l'existent* was translated by Alphonso Lingis as *Existence and Existents*. Lingis is Levinas's principal and generally excellent translator, but in this case the title elides the crucial sense of a movement *from* the indifference of existence in general *to* the particular existent.

5. "Interview with François Poiré," in Robbins, ed., *Is It Righteous to Be?*, 45.

6. Paul Davies, "A Linear Narrative?"

7. Levinas divides the process of creation into two stages. The first he calls "hypostasis," which refers to the way existence is riveted to itself in the reflexive mode of a self, and the second he calls "production," which describes how the self relates to the other and thus stabilizes its temporal and semantic field.

8. I am referring to *Time and the Other*, *Existence and Existents*, and *Totality and Infinity*. In this chapter I am proposing a conceptual and phenomenological parallel, not a terminological one. Levinas may have even been prompted to make the terminological distinctions between "creation," "accomplishment," and "production" on the basis of the well-known "four worlds" vocabulary of Lurianic Kabbalah that distinguishes four registers of emanation (*assiyah*), creation (*briyah*), production (*yetzirah*), and action (*'asiyah*).

9. Jon D. Levenson, *Creation and the Persistence of Evil*, 12 (my emphasis). Levenson's superb book provides the hermeneutical inspiration for the reading of Levinas undertaken in this chapter. See also Richard J. Clifford, "The Hebrew Scriptures and the Theology of Creation," 510.

10. Levenson, *Creation and the Persistence of Evil*, 12, and Levinas, *Existence and Existents*, Part IV.

11. I am not the first to have noticed that the *il y a* recalls the *tohu wa'bohu* of Genesis 1:2; see also Catherine Chalier, *Lévinas*, 42; Chalier, *La trace de l'infini*, chap. 1; and Scott Hennessy, "Creation, Chaos, and the Shoah." Chalier suggests that the *il y a* was a "retour du premier moment du monde . . . qui, dans la Bible, précède la parole et la lumière" (*Lévinas*, 42). She also suggests that this reversion "ne constituent pas un état dépassé du monde mais l'une de ses possibilités constantes, l'une de ses plus dramatiques tentations même" (42). But Chalier did not see that the resemblance between the *il y a* and the *tohu wa'bohu* implies a Levinasian account of creation *ex hylus* that is crucial for understanding his idea of the evil of mere existence. The recovery of the *tohu wa'bohu* under the name *il y a* was also briefly noted by Shmuel Trigano, "Levinas and the Project of Jewish Philosophy," although he says, mistakenly in my view, that this is the "notion with which rabbinic thought expresses the idea of creation *ex nihilo*" (289), and by John D. Caputo, *The Weakness of God*, 315n2. My interpretation is close to Hennessy's, although I arrived at it independently in earlier publications ("Back to the Other Levinas" and "*Il y a du quotidien*," 584) and am extending that argument here.

12. Levinas, *Existence and Existents*, 57–58. The description of the *il y a* was initially composed in the Stalag, then printed independently in *Deucalion* 1 (1946), 141–54. This was Levinas's first publication following World War II, the Destruction, and the murder of his family.

13. Respectively, *JPS Hebrew-English TANAKH*; E. A. Speiser, *Genesis: Introduction, Translation, and Notes*; and Robert Alter, *The Five Books of Moses*. The *King James Version* and the *New Revised Standard Version* both have "without form and void." My interpretation of Levinas on creation *ex hylus* is close to Karl Barth's exposition in *Church Dogmatics: Vol. III*, 102–10.

14. Levenson, *Creation and the Persistence of Evil*, 121.

15. Levinas, *Existence and Existents*, 64.

16. Levinas, *Ethics and Infinity*, 48 (my emphasis). I have profited from George Hansel, first in correspondence and then by way of Cristian Ciocan and George Hansel, *Levinas Concordance*, which reminded me of several important references to "creation" in Levinas works that I had forgotten, such as this one.

17. Levinas, *Time and the Other*, 51.

18. Israel Knohl, *The Divine Symphony*, 13. See also Gerhard May, *Creatio ex Nihilo*, who likewise says of early rabbinic views of creation that "it is not . . . a

matter of a cosmological theory but of a theological affirmation that is forced to use cosmological categories" (24); cf. 39–41.

19. Levenson, *Creation and the Persistence of Evil*, xx.

20. On the entanglement of facts and values, see Hilary Putnam, *The Collapse of the Fact/Value Dichotomy*, chaps. 1 and 2, and "Richard Rorty on Reality and Justification." Although I think that Putnam and Levinas are quite close on this point, I am here suggesting only that Levinas's point can be argued in a more conventional philosophical idiom.

21. Levinas, "Signature," in *Difficult Freedom*, 292.

22. Levinas, "Nameless," in *Proper Names*, 119–23. Levinas does not consistently distinguish terminologically between being and existence. My interpretation posits a distinction between "existence," which is "without a world," and "being," which, following Heidegger, is "in the world." On this, see Fagenblat, "*Il y a du quotidian.*"

23. Levinas, "Nameless," in *Proper Names*, 119, which also describes this "world put in question" as "Evil."

24. John Bright, *Jeremiah*, 30. For a useful examination of the many interpretations of *tohu wa'bohu* that modern scholars have proposed, see David Toshio Tsumura, "The Earth in Genesis 1." These interpretations fall primarily into two camps, those that view the *tohu wa'bohu* as chaos and those that see it as emptiness, an uninhabited and unproductive place that has not yet been subject to God's creative work. Although Tsumura argues that the *tohu wa'bohu* "has nothing to do with 'chaos'" (327), I follow Albright, Bright, Cassuto, Levenson, and Westermann, who argue for the former. The point does not bear greatly on my argument, however, since my claim hinges less on whether the primordial elements are chaotic or simply barren and more on the fact that they (1) are primordial and uncreated, (2) stand in opposition to creation, (3) are valued inversely to the goodness of creation, therefore as evil, and (4) belong to the sphere of myth.

25. Richard Bernstein, *Radical Evil*, 167. Bernstein observes that "in the extensive secondary literature dealing with Levinas, evil (*mal*) is barely even mentioned" (167). By my reckoning, Levinas's account of evil, which expresses his perception of the significance of the Holocaust, is his most important philosophical motivation. Two scholars who appreciate this are Hennessy, "Creation, Chaos, and the Shoah," and Howard Caygill, *Levinas and the Political*.

26. Levinas, *Existence and Existents*, 20.

27. This is what I take Levinas to mean when he says that "existence is not synonymous with the relationship with a world; it is antecedent to the world." Levinas, *Existence and Existents*, 21.

28. Levinas, *Existence and Existents*, 21.

29. Levinas, *Time and the Other*, 54; see also *Totality and Infinity*, 132.

30. Levinas, *Time and the Other*, 46.

31. Levinas, *Existence and Existents*, 21. For Levinas's cautious attitude toward myth, which he associates with art, see his "Reality and Its Shadow," in *Collected Philosophical Papers*, 1–13, and for a valuable discussion, see Alain P. Toumayan, *Encountering the Other*.

32. Ricoeur, *The Symbolism of Evil*, 162–63, 170.

33. *Mythology der Vernunft*, 13, quoted in Eric L. Santner, *On the Psychotheology of Everyday Life*, 131. As Santner explains, this text was published by Rosenzweig, who attributed it to Schelling, although scholars today believe it was penned by the young Hegel.

34. Norbert M. Samuelson, in *Judaism and the Doctrine of Creation*, defends the compatibility of the Jewish view of creation with that of the *Timaeus*. I am not convinced by Samuelson that the author of Genesis 1 has an implicit philosophical-scientific view he wishes to convey. From my reading, following Knohl and Levenson, the significance of Genesis 1 lies primarily in its moral and theosophical innovations—accounting for the ontology of evil without ascribing it active potency and erasing theogony from the account of creation. The relevant discipline is not science or cosmogony but ethics, thus its pertinence in interpreting Levinas.

35. Levinas, "Nameless," in *Proper Names*, 121.

36. Most translations, including this JPS one that I have slightly modified, translate *Yāmm* as "the sea." But scholars generally agree that *Yāmm* in this case, rather than being a common noun, is a proper name referring to a personified god.

37. Knohl, *The Divine Symphony*, 13.

38. Levenson, *Creation and the Persistence of Evil*, 19.

39. See Levinas, "Useless Suffering," in *Entre Nous*, 91–102.

40. Martin Heidegger, *Identity and Difference*, 70–72.

41. Jean-Luc Marion, "Metaphysics and Phenomenology," esp. 579.

42. Marion, *God Without Being*, 35.

43. Levenson, *Creation and the Persistence of Evil*, 7.

44. See esp. Marion, *God Without Being*, chaps. 1 and 2.

45. On this, see Yehoyada Amir's useful survey, "From Negation to Rehabilitation." Levinas is not mentioned in this study.

46. Michael Fishbane, *Biblical Myth and Rabbinic Mythmaking*, 208; cf. 206–13.

47. Cf. Adi Ophir, *The Order of Evils*, 13, 267.

48. Levinas, "The Paradox of Morality," 175.

49. Phillip Blond, "Emmanuel Levinas: God and Phenomenology," 215–16.

50. Blond, "Emmanuel Levinas: God and Phenomenology," 216.

51. Michel Haar, in "The Obsession of the Other," also asserts that "Levinas's polemic against Being actually falls into Manicheism" (98). Similarly, Didier Franck remarked to Salomon Malka: "To equate being with evil . . . that's colossal.

It isn't even biblical, besides, since Creation is good" (Malka, *Emmanuel Levinas*, 278). But the point is that creation is not a synonym for being but a way of acknowledging the originary and unsurpassable implication of being and ethics.

52. Hans Jonas, "Gnosticism, Nihilism and Existentialism," in *The Gnostic Religion*, 320–40.

53. See note 20 to this chapter, as well as Putnam, *Ethics Without Ontology*.

54. Caputo, *The Weakness of God*, 332n7.

55. Ophir, *The Order of Evils*, 13. Although Ophir was avowedly indebted to Levinas, on the same page he associates Levinas with a theological project that cannot be reconciled with a secular account of the problem of evil. In my view the distinction between the theological and the secular is extremely unstable throughout Levinas's thought and, with respect to the problem of evil, his account succeeds in secularizing theology.

56. Ophir, "Evil, Evils, and the Question of Ethics," 182.

57. Ophir, "Evil, Evils, and the Question of Ethics," 182. Ophir posits a useful analogy between Heidegger's critique of moral values and his critique of technology. Just as technologies enframe being, so values enframe ethics (179). But when Heidegger said that "thinking in values is the greatest blasphemy imaginable against Being" ("Letter on Humanism," in *Pathmarks*, 228), he threw out the ethical baby with the bathwater of "values." For although values do enframe being in a way that belies the ever-changing and contingent disclosure of phenomena, it is only ethics—ethics without values—that enables us to enframe the evil of being itself.

58. Ophir, "Evil, Evils, and the Question of Ethics," 182.

59. Ricoeur, *The Symbolism of Evil*, 172.

60. Silvano Petrosino, "L'idée de creation dans l'oeuvre de Lévinas."

61. Putnam, "Levinas and Judaism," 36–38.

62. As was done by Stanley Cavell in his extraordinary reading of *Endgame* as a modernist reproduction of the Deluge; see his *Must We Mean What We Say?*, chap. 5.

63. Ophir, "Evil, Evils, and the Question of Ethics," 182–83.

64. Fishbane, *Biblical Myth and Rabbinic Mythmaking*, 34–36.

65. Richard J. Clifford, "The Hebrew Scriptures and the Theology of Creation," 513, and Levenson, *Creation and the Persistence of Evil*, 7–9.

66. Ricoeur, *The Symbolism of Evil*, 196–98.

67. Levenson, *Creation and the Persistence of Evil*, chap. 5, in which this idea is traced back to Psalm 104.

68. Knohl, *The Divine Symphony*, 14.

69. Levinas is quite different from Habermas, although he can be regarded as providing Habermas with meta-ethical phenomenological justification. For Levinas, ethics is an approach to the singularity of the other, and thus to the face, rather

than an approach to the rationality of agents bound by impartial rules of communication. For a lucid discussion, see Steve Hendley, *From Communicative Action to the Face of the Other*. Needless to say, I do not for a moment think that the biblical priests, defenders of the logos model, were envisaging communicative action or were averse to waging war on their enemies or even to imagining such enemies as historical embodiments of ontological evil (e.g., Exod. 15:5, and see Levenson, *Creation and the Persistence of Evil*, 76; cf. Ricoeur, *The Symbolism of Evil*, 204).

70. Kant's ambivalence is encapsulated in the anti-Pauline phrase "works of grace," which is the only antidote to evil he can contemplate (*Religion*, 48–49). For an incisive analysis of Kant's view, see Richard Bernstein, "Radical Evil: Kant at War with Himself," chap. 1 of his *Radical Evil*. Kant is without doubt Levinas's most cherished moral philosopher and the "war" that Kant has with himself, in which the will is perennially struggling to realize its rational disposition, is congruent with the moral dualism that we find in the Priestly and Levinasian ontogenetic myths and with rabbinic anthropology, in which the combat against evil is waged through obedience to the Law. This is also true in the Letter of James 2:14–26.

71. Immanuel Kant, *Religion Within the Limits of Reason Alone*, 40.

72. For an analysis of Habermas's view of radical evil, see Peter Dews, "Disenchantment and the Persistence of Evil," esp. 54. Freud also provides a psychological myth of the persistence of evil and thereby explains what Kant takes for granted. On this, see Bernstein, "Freud: Ineradicable Evil and Ambivalence," in *Radical Evil*, chap. 5. Bernstein proposes that Freud's "psychological realism" is based on an account of evil as a "permanent feature of the psychic life of humans." Of course, for Freud, whose realism is perhaps more pessimistic than others, neither the *logos* of reason (Kant), nor the *logos* addressed to the other (Levinas), nor the *logos* of the Torah (the rabbis) has sufficient power to overcome evil.

73. See Levenson, *Creation and the Persistence of Evil*, 33–46, and Fishbane, *Biblical Myth and Rabbinic Mythmaking*, 112–31.

74. *Tanhuma*, Genesis 1.

75. Fishbane, *Biblical Myth and Rabbinic Mythmaking*, 129; and see the similar, equally remarkable myth from *Zohar* II, 113b, cited by Fishbane at 130.

76. "A tradition of myth thus serves the author with highly charged resonances, even as the divine powers remain subtly concealed within their stylistic tropes and never quite emerge as independent personifications" (Fishbane, *Biblical Myth and Rabbinic Mythmaking*, 92). If for Canticles, *mutatis mutandis* for Levinas. Incidentally, according to Malka (*Emmanuel Levinas*, 284), Levinas left behind a "handwritten reading and translation of the Song of Songs." The release and analysis of this text, along with unpublished course notes on Halevi, Maimonides, and Heidegger, is eagerly awaited.

77. For examples of the agon model extending into modern political discourse, see Alan D. Schrift, "Introduction," in *Modernity and the Problem of Evil*, esp. 3.

78. The latter is cited by Menachem Kister in an article of great erudition and relevance to my theme, "*Tohu wa-Bohu*, Primordial Elements and *Creatio ex Nihilo*," 236.

79. It is not logos as reason that interrupts existence in order to create but the speech that words creation into form; cf. Fishbane, *Biblical Text and Texture*. For an exquisite account of hermeneutics *as* the sharing of multiple voices, see Jean-Luc Nancy, "Sharing Voices."

80. Levenson, *Creation and the Persistence of Evil*, 47.

81. Ricoeur, *The Symbolism of Evil*, 355; see also 161–63, 351–57.

82. Levenson, *Creation and the Persistence of Evil*, 47.

83. See Caputo, *The Weakness of God*, chap. 1, "God Without Sovereignty."

84. May, *Creatio ex Nihilo*; Maren Niehoff, "*Creatio ex Nihilo* Theology in *Genesis Rabbah*"; and David Winston, "The Book of Wisdom's Theory of Cosmogony."

85. May, *Creatio ex Nihilo*, 148–78. Among Jews, 2 Macc. 7:28 is often regarded as earlier evidence for *creatio ex nihilo*, but most scholars regard such an interpretation as anachronistic; see Niehoff, 44, and, for further references, see the following note.

86. Genesis Rabbah 1:9; see Niehoff, 45–55. Warren Zev Harvey provides a different view, which I do not accept. He argues that in Genesis Rabbah 1:9, Rabban Gamaliel II does not decide between creation *ex nihilo* and the eternity of matter but offers a "strictly non-philosophical" interpretation of Genesis 1; see his "Rabbinic Attitudes Toward Philosophy," 93. Niehoff's view is challenged by Kister ("*Tohu wa-Bohu*, Primordial Elements and *Creatio ex Nihilo*"), who argues for the antiquity of the doctrine of creation *ex nihilo* in the Jewish tradition, based especially on Jubilees 2:2–3, in which God is said to have created *all* the elements and which elides all mention of the *tohu wa'bohu*. That Kister might be correct in regarding the doctrine of creation *ex nihilo* as much older than Niehoff supposes would not affect the substance of my argument, since I rely more on a reading of Genesis 1 than on its rabbinic reception (although Kister also contests that interpretation in his note 33). In any case, it is sufficient for my argument that an alternative to creation *ex nihilo* is perceived as plausible by interpreters of Genesis 1 and that this interpretation either derives from or implies moral dualism. That claim has not been shaken by Kister's illuminating study. Tsumura has written extensively against the idea that the primeval elements in Genesis should be understood as evilly compounded; see, for example, "The Earth in Genesis 1," in the marvelously titled *"I Studied Inscriptions from Before the Flood."*

87. Genesis Rabbah 1:5; see Niehoff, 55–60, and Levenson, *Creation and the Persistence of Evil*, xx.

88. May, *Creatio ex Nihilo*, 23. He also says, "To rabbinic Judaism the questions raised by Greek ontology were relatively remote. But the chief reason why it

did not come to the formation of a specific doctrine of *creatio ex nihilo* is to be seen in the fact that it was not demanded by the text of the Bible" (24).

89. See Rashi's commentary to Genesis 1:2, and Gersonides, *The Wars of the Lord*, 6.2.8, p. 449. For a brief but useful discussion of Rashi's view, see Knohl, *The Divine Symphony*, 11–12, 164nn17–18, for references to modern authorities who follow this view; see also Catherine Keller, *Face of the Deep*, 114–15. On Gersonides, see Samuelson, *Judaism and the Doctrine of Creation*. Kenneth Seeskin provides a useful overview in his *Maimonides on the Origin of the World*, 14–22, although he decides that "creation *ex nihilo* is implied" (22) in the text of Genesis, which is not the conclusion I derive from the evidence he adduces.

90. This question has been the subject of much controversy in medieval and modern Maimonidean studies, with leading scholars variously arguing that Maimonides believed in a Platonic view of creation *ex hylus*, an Aristotelian view of the eternity of the world, or the apparently conventional Jewish view of creation ex nihilo. For recent work that references the major medieval and modern studies on this topic, see Marc B. Shapiro, *The Limits of Orthodox Theology*, 71–77, and Samuelson, "Maimonides' Doctrine of Creation." A convincing case for *creatio ex nihilo* is made by Seeskin, *Maimonides on the Origin of the World*.

91. Menachem Kellner, *Dogma in Medieval Jewish Thought*.

92. The Neoplatonic notion of emanation is of course ubiquitous among philosophers no less than among Kabbalists. Levinas differs from *philosophical* Neoplatonists because he thinks that evil is not a lack of being but a very real presence within creation. Kabbalistic Neoplatonists tend to think likewise, so Levinas often seems closer to them, but unlike them he refuses to see the reality of evil as emanating from God. For the kabbalistic view, see Gershom Scholem, "Sitra Ahra," and for the anthropological implications, see Elliot R. Wolfson, "Light Through Darkness."

93. Elliot R. Wolfson, *Venturing Beyond*, 7–9.

94. The true "separation" that takes place in Levinas's early thought is not between the self and the other but between a world created on the basis of ethics (our world) and the idea of an inhuman world (the *il y a*, "existence without a world") that pretends to neutrality but is really, or therefore, evil. Hennessy sees this when he takes the bold step of identifying later Levinas's view with the suffering servant who bears rather than causes all evil; see his "Creation, Chaos, and the Shoah."

95. It is not a matter of reverting to an "anthropocentric" ontology but of conceding that what Putnam calls "the collapse of the fact/value dichotomy" (2002) means that ontology *is* ethical. "Human" in this sense just means "creators of norms" (as Robert Brandom might say), in other words, precisely the opposite of an essentialist definition of the human.

96. Keller, *Face of the Deep*, 117, 123.

97. Keller, *Face of the Deep*, 28.

98. Keller, *Face of the Deep*, 28. Keller explains that "the face of the deep was first—as far as we can remember—a woman's. . . . Behind Genesis 1.2 . . . lies not the Leviathan but the oceanic all-mother Tiamat" (28).

99. On this, see Steven G. Smith, *Argument to the Other*, and Graham Ward, *Barth, Derrida, and the Language of Theology*, chap. 9.

100. Keller, *Face of the Deep*, 91.

101. The Priestly view of chaos as evil is ritualized on Yom Kippur, when it is precisely a matter of ritualizing the separation from evil that took place "when God created the world"; see Knohl, *The Divine Symphony*, 16–19, and Levenson, *Creation and the Persistence of Evil*, 121–27.

102. Genesis Rabbah X.2. The midrash is also playing on the relationship between *keli* (vessel or utensil), in Proverbs 25:4, and the finishing of the work of creation (*wayye-kullu*).

103. Other midrashim reflect in more agonistic terms on the act of creation, which Fishbane describes as "the suppression of the sea" that becomes, in history, "a cycle of strife and suppression." This again demonstrates the remarkable continuity between rabbinic exegetical reformulations and the biblical myths themselves; see *Biblical Myth and Rabbinic Mythmaking*, chap. 6, esp. the analysis of Genesis Rabbah V:2–4, which contrasts with the passive model of the *tĕhôm* in the midrash I have cited.

104. *Nine Talmudic Readings*, 30. Levinas skips the conspicuous allusion to Genesis 1:2 when he comes to the passage on p. 41.

105. It is here that I would relate Levinas to the Kabbalah, since the Kabbalists and Levinas agree that our action supports, rectifies, and is responsible for the divine constitution. On kabbalistic theurgy, the first point of call is Moshe Idel, *Kabbalah: New Perspectives*.

106. R. J. Zvi Werblowsky, "Faith, Hope and Trust," 100.

107. Levenson, *Creation and the Persistence of Evil*, 14. I have substituted "our" and "we" for "God and "he" throughout this passage.

108. Judith Shklar, *The Faces of Injustice*, esp. chap. 2, "Misfortune and Injustice."

109. In Robert B. Brandom's words, "Pragmatism about norms implicit in cognitive activity came down to us in the first half of the twentieth century from three independent directions: from the classical American pragmatists, culminating in Dewey; from the Heidegger of *Being and Time*; and the Wittgenstein of the *Philosophical Investigations*" (*Articulating Reasons*, 34).

CHAPTER 3

1. Levinas remarked that his own view "seems suggested by the practical philosophy of Kant, to which we feel particularly close" ("Is Ontology Fundamental?," in *Basic Philosophical Writings*, 10). For a lesser-known but illuminating discussion

of Kant by Levinas, see "The Contemporary Criticism of the Idea of Value and the Prospects for Humanism." For discussion of Levinas and Kant, see Jean-François Lyotard, "Levinas' Logic," and Catherine Chalier, *What Ought I to Do?*

2. On the religious character of Kant's philosophy, see Ian Hunter, *Rival Enlightenments.*

3. Immanuel Kant, *Critique of Practical Reason*, 44.

4. Levinas, *On Escape*, 49.

5. Levinas, *On Escape*, 71. These two essays are strictly correlative. The last sentence of the philosophical essay could easily be a "translation into Greek" of the exhortation to uphold "the folly or the faith of Israel," which concludes the brief article on Maimonides. Levinas comments that "it is a matter of getting out of being by a new path, at the risk of overturning certain notions that to common sense and the wisdom of the nations seemed the most evident" (*On Escape*, 73). On this formative period in Levinas's work, see Samuel Moyn, "Judaism Against Paganism," and, more generally, his *Origins of the Other*. Maimonides, however, features only incidentally in Moyn's account.

6. Levinas, "Some Thoughts on the Philosophy of Hitlerism," in *Unforeseen History*, 13–14. For other commentaries, see Franscesca Albertini, "Emmanuel Levinas' Theological-Political Interpretation of Moses Maimonides," and Chalier, *La trace de l'infini*, 29ff., 59–60, 97ff., 145–46.

7. Despite the flourishing of scholarship devoted to Levinas and to Maimonides—probably the two most-studied Jewish philosophers in the academy today—the relation between them, which goes back to Levinas's formative period, has not received much attention. The exceptions are Albertini and Chalier, cited in the preceding note; Henri Bacry, *Emmanuel Levinas*, 13–19; Shmuel Trigano, "Levinas and the Project of Jewish Philosophy"; and Edith Wyschogrod, *Crossover Queries*, 30–33, 41–42. On the other hand, Salomon Malka (*Emmanuel Levinas*, 132, 284) provides anecdotal evidence suggesting that Levinas was keenly interested in Maimonides throughout his life, frequently relying on the *Mishneh Torah* in order to select his Talmudic commentary, and, most significantly, that "a good number" (284) of his unpublished texts are devoted to Maimonides.

8. See, for example, Maimonides' discussion at the end of the *Guide* II.6, 264–65. For a perspective from a classicist that accords with this interpretation, see Friedrich Solmsen, *Aristotle's System of the Physical World*, 222ff., 288–89, 310, 385ff., and 451, in which the author discusses Aristotle's *Physics* VIII and the important passages from *On Generation and Corruption*, *On the Heavens*, and *On Meteorology*.

9. Levinas, "The Contemporary Relevance of Maimonides," 93.

10. Herbert Davidson provides a third plausible interpretation of Maimonides as believing neither in eternity nor in *creatio ex nihilo* but in a Platonic cosmogony; see Davidson, "Maimonides' Secret Position on Creation." This

view is close to the creation *ex hylus* account we considered in Chapter 2. Here, however, we are concerned with the reception of Maimonides more than with Maimonides' own view about creation. For a recent and cogent argument that Maimonides himself believed in creation ex nihilo and *ab novo* (after not having been), see Kenneth Seeskin, *Maimonides on the Origin of the World*. On the history of the radical, esoteric interpretation of the *Guide*, see Aviezer Ravitzky, "Samuel Ibn Tibbon and the Esoteric Character of the *Guide of the Perplexed*." Debates about the allegedly esoteric nature of the *Guide* in fact concentrated more on questions of providence, intellectual union with the Active Intellect, the immortality of the soul, and allegory more than on the question of creation or eternity. But belief in the eternity of the world is the conceptual cornerstone of the other esoteric positions. On this, see Ravitzky, "Samuel Ibn Tibbon," 119, and his "The Secrets of the *Guide to the Perplexed*," 184–86, including notes 86 and 88, for additional references; and Moshe Halbertal, *Between Torah and Wisdom*, chaps. 2 and 4, esp. 20 and 63. Herbert A. Davidson denies that Ibn Tibbon believed in the eternity of the world in his "Maimonides on Metaphysical Knowledge," 50n3. The debate continues in a recent journal, *Aleph: Historical Studies in Science & Judaism* (2008).

11. Levinas, "The Contemporary Relevance of Maimonides," 93.

12. Richard C. Dales, *Medieval Discussions of the Eternity of the World*, 45, 97–102, 116, 132–40, 153.

13. On this, see Halbertal, *Between Torah and Wisdom*, 75–79.

14. See esp. the *Guide* I.71, II.16, II.17, and II.24. For an argument for indirect Maimonidean influence on Kant in the crucial strategy of formulating antinomies of pure reason, see Shlomo Pines, "Maïmonide et la philosophie latine," and "St. Thomas et la pensée juive," 123–24, both reproduced in his *Studies in the History of Jewish Thought*, esp. 402–3, 482–83, and 476n14. I will return to Pines and these proto-Kantian considerations in Chapter 4. Dales's analysis of the so-called "Doctrine of the Double Truth," truths of faith and truths of reason, supports this proto-Kantian interpretation; see his "The Origin of the Doctrine of the Double Truth" and "Maimonides and Boethius of Dacia on the Eternity of the World." My assertion is not that Maimonides *in fact* completely eschewed proofs for creation but that his construction of the antinomy of creation and eternity allowed it to be thought through coherently, as its reception history attests.

15. Levinas, "The Contemporary Relevance of Maimonides," 94. In 1966 Levinas briefly extended his moderate reading of the *Guide*, according to which philosophy is neither handmaid nor master to revelation. Dismissing as "detective fiction" Leo Strauss's interpretation of Maimonides as perceiving a deep conflict between reason and religion, Levinas reiterated his moderate and quite classical interpretation of Maimonides as harmonizing revelation with reason; see *Difficult Freedom*, 111.

16. Despite widespread reporting of it by Gadamer, it was only in the 1980s that scholars discovered the crucial influence of Aristotle on early Heidegger. There is now a large body of literature spawned by the publication in 1992 of the most important of these lectures, Heidegger's *Plato's Sophist*. Here I follow Franco Volpi, "*Being and Time*: A 'Translation' of the *Nichomachean Ethics*?"; Volpi, "Dasein as *Praxis*"; Jacques Taminiaux, "The Reappropriation of the Nicomachean Ethics," in *Heidegger and the Project of Fundamental Ontology*, 111–37; John van Buren, *The Young Heidegger*, 220–34; and especially Kisiel, *The Genesis of Heidegger's "Being and Time,"* Part II. Ted Sadler offers a deflationary account in *Heidegger and Aristotle*.

17. Stanley Rosen, *The Elusiveness of the Ordinary*, 120–21. A more charitable and productive reading of the relationship between authentic resoluteness and *phronesis* is suggested by Hubert L. Dreyfus throughout his various pragmatic readings of Heidegger; see, for example, *Heidegger, Authenticity, and Modernity*, 318, and *Being-in-the-World*.

18. Rosen and Volpi argue that *phronesis* has become conscience (*Gewissen*) in *Being and Time*, whereas Taminiaux suggests a slightly different transposition of *phronesis* into resoluteness (*Entschlossenheit*). Robert Bernasconi, in "Heidegger's Destruction of Phronesis," argues that for Heidegger *phronesis* remains the general ontological praxis of circumspection (*Umsicht*) rather than a specifically ethical one. I tend to agree with Bernasconi, although I do not think the various interpretations are as incompatible as he suggests. For a dissenting view, see Sadler, *Heidegger and Aristotle*, 141–58. Rosen's conclusion is that "Heidegger replaces the Aristotelian variability of practical affairs with their uncertainty, and he replaces the correctness of judgment, that is, its accord with *orthos logos*, with resoluteness. One is tempted to say that stubbornness replaces reasonableness" (*The Elusiveness of the Ordinary*, 134). This interpretation is insupportable, for *Entschlossenheit* "simply cannot *become rigid* as regards the Situation, but must understand that the resolution, in accordance with its own meaning as a disclosure, must be *held open* and free for the current factical possibility. The certainty of the resolution signifies that one *holds oneself free for* the possibility of *taking it back*" (*Being and Time*, 354/ *SZ*, 307–8; all emphases in original). Resoluteness is a responsiveness to the situation, not a stubbornness that rides roughshod over it. Such misinterpretations of Heidegger are almost always collateral damage accrued from his Nazism. Even if they make us feel better, they get us nowhere philosophically.

19. For a view of a classicist that accords with Maimonides' interpretation of Aristotle, see Solmsen, *Aristotle's System of the Physical World*, 222ff., 288–89, 310, 385ff., 451. On these pages Solmsen discusses *Physics* VIII and other passages from *On Generation and Corruption*, *On the Heavens*, and *On Meteorology*. Aristotle is contesting Plato's view in the *Timaeus*. Cf. Maimonides' discussion at the end of the *Guide* II.6, 264–65.

20. Seeskin, *Maimonides on the Origin of the World*, 71.

21. Jürgen Habermas, "Work and Weltanschauung," 438–39 (my emphasis). He also comments that "Heidegger rigidly maintained the abstraction of historicity (as the condition of historical existence itself) from actual historical processes" (437). I do not agree with the general thrust of Habermas's interpretation, although here I think he points to an important feature of the transcendental logic of *Being and Time*.

22. Levinas, *Time and the Other*, 45.

23. In addition to the argument just stated, Aristotle derived his belief in eternity from the idea that (1) every moment or now by definition refers to a prior and subsequent moment, (2) primary matter is ungenerated, and (3) everything that is possible must have a substratum. For a lucid summary of these views, see Seeskin, *Maimonides on the Origin of the World*, 63–70, and Dales, *Medieval Discussions of the Eternity of the World*, 39–42. See also Aristotle, *On Generation and Corruption*, 336a–338a4; *On the Heavens*, 283b–284a; *Physics*, 203b29 and 250b–252b; and *Metaphysics*, 1050b8–15.

24. Solmsen, *Aristotle's System of the Physical World*, 225.

25. This was the dominant interpretation of Aristotle promoted by Alfarabi and Avicenna; see Herbert A. Davidson, *Alfarabi, Avicenna, and Averroes, on Intellect*, 206; cf. Maimonides, *Guide* II.12.

26. Seeskin, *Searching for a Distant God*, 70. Seeskin cites from *Guide* II.17, 298, to prove his point. This is the very chapter Levinas cites in his 1935 article on the "Contemporary Relevance of Maimonides," in which Maimonides is said to have "glimpsed what one calls, six centuries later, the critique of pure reason" (94).

27. Maurice Blanchot, *The Infinite Conversation*, 245.

28. Hannah Arendt, *The Human Condition*, 9.

29. Seeskin, *Maimonides on the Origin of the World*, chap. 5.

30. David Burrell, *Knowing the Unknowable God*, 81.

31. For insightful analyses of this feature of Heidegger's work, see Robert J. Dostal, "The Problem of '*Indifferenz*' in *Sein und Zeit*," and Michel Haar, "The Enigma of Everydayness."

32. Jean-Luc Nancy, *Being Singular Plural*, 9.

33. Nancy, *Being Singular Plural*, 15–21. There are significant differences between Levinas and Nancy, as the latter sometimes highlights. The point of my comparison, however, is that Nancy and Levinas agree that Heidegger's social ontology needs to be modified by accounting for the singularity within everydayness and that *creatio ex nihilo* provides a useful way of doing that.

34. That these thoughts go back to 1935 is clear from the conclusion of *On Escape*, 71.

35. Moyn, *Origins of the Other*, 188. Moyn overstates matters when he asserts that "there is no hint, none at all, that Levinas had broken through to a secu-

lar ethic in this period" of the mid-1930s (187). The article on Maimonides, after all, is entirely concerned with the *political* implications of Maimonidean faith, which is contrasted not merely with pagan theology but with "pagan morality" (Levinas, "The Contemporary Relevance of Maimonides," 94). Moyn is right in saying that "it is in these articles that Levinas first unveiled and elaborated the positive alternative to Heidegger that he would later integrate and secularize into philosophy" (189). But the point of Levinas's comparison between Maimonidean creation theology and Kantianism is to draw out the ethico-political, that is, "secular," implications of the antinomies of pure reason.

36. David Hartman, *A Living Covenant,* 22–23. Further correspondences between Levinas and Hartman could readily be established. Compare, for example, Levinas's oft-cited remark that "it is certainly a great glory for the creator to have set up a being capable of atheism, a being which, without having been *causa sui,* has an independent view and word and is at home with itself" (TI, 58–59/TeI, 30) with Hartman's strikingly similar view: "The creation of a being capable of saying no to divine commands is the supreme expression of divine love, insofar as God makes room for humans as independent, free creatures" (*A Living Covenant,* 24). Hartman and Levinas also share a philosophical approach to the Talmud, even if their intellectual temperaments lead them to quite different exegeses. On this, see Jonathan Cohen, "Educating for Spiritual Maturity," 123–26.

37. Maimonides is referring to *Guide* I.1, in which he interprets the notion of the image of God as "that from which human apprehension derives" (22).

38. For an illuminating discussion, see Yair Lorberbaum, "Maimonides on Imago Dei," and for a comprehensive treatment, see his *Image of God: Halakhah and Aggadah.*

39. I am indebted to Alon Goshen-Gottstein, "The Body as Image of God in Rabbinic Literature," for some of the following remarks on the image of God, to related work by Lorberbaum cited in the preceding note, and to Halbertal, *Interpretative Revolutions in the Making,* chap. 7.

40. At least this is the conventional reading of Maimonides, which will be complicated in Chapter 4.

41. Levinas, *In the Time of the Nations,* 172.

42. Levinas, *In the Time of the Nations,* 169.

43. Chalier nicely emphasizes this point in *La trace de l'infini,* 59–60.

44. Levinas, *In the Time of the Nations,* 170. Levinas even censures Maimonides for subordinating the ethical purpose of revelation to the goal of acquiring rational knowledge: "In Maimonides, spirituality is essentially knowledge: knowledge in which being is present to the mind, in which that *presence* of being to the mind is the truth of being, . . . assimilation by thought and immanence, in which the transcendence of God can signify only negatively" (*In the Time of the Nations,* 169–70). Cf. *Beyond the Verse,* 138, 145, and Jill Robbins, ed., *Is It Righteous to Be?* 283.

45. According to Moshe Greenberg's thesis, this is the paradoxical rationale behind the *lex talionis*: the idea of humanity in the image of God gave rise to the postulate of the incommensurability of human life and economic value and therefore, paradoxically, to the view that the offender must pay for the sin of murder with nothing but his own life. See Greenberg, "Some Postulates of Biblical Criminal Law," in *Studies in the Bible and Jewish Thought*, 25–42.

46. Fishbane, *Biblical Text and Texture*, 11.

47. See also TI, 216/TeI, 191; TI, 303/TeI, 278; and *Alterity and Transcendence*, 127.

48. Genesis Rabbah 34:14. Cf. Mishnah Sanhedrin 4:5 and the end of Chapter 1 of this book.

49. Tosefta Yevamot 8:7 (trans. by Alon Goshen-Gottstein, "The Body as Image of God," 191, slightly modified).

50. Such an application of the literal interpretation of the *imago dei* in fact exists in the polygamous customs of contemporary Mormons, who, according to Ernst Benz, derive their view concerning the sanctity of procreation directly from this theologoumenon; see Ernst W. Benz, "*Imago Dei*," 250.

51. Goshen-Gottstein, "The Body as Image of God in Rabbinic Literature," 171.

52. The reference to Isaiah is one of the few places in which Levinas cites the Bible in *Totality and Infinity*. As is almost always the case, Levinas's biblical citations and allusions come from scriptural passages embedded in the Jewish liturgy, suggesting that much of what he derived from the Bible resulted from meditations in the synagogue. The Isaiah passage is read as the *haftorah* on Shabbat Eikev (Deut. 7–11) in the weeks leading up to Rosh Hashanah.

53. For a useful collection of essays addressing these and related issues, see Tina Chanter, ed., *Feminist Interpretations of Emmanuel Levinas*.

54. As Gibbs first argued in *Correlations*, 237–40; see also 28–29. Gibbs notes that fecundity also attests to Levinas's view of the asymmetrical nature of responsibility because one is responsible for one's child, and even for the child's responsibilities, but the converse is not the case. Fecundity thereby "produces a true experience of the future as not merely an extension of the present. The ability to respond for others is then reproduced, not for my sake but for other others, and so Levinas claims that the discontinuity of the generations creates a true time, an infinite future" (238).

55. Levinas, "Meaning and Sense" (1964), in *Basic Philosophical Writings*, 50.

56. Rabbinic Judaism articulates this ideal hermeneutically, with its notion of the fecundity of the Oral Torah: there is no Torah without innovation, *ein torah bli hidush*.

57. See also "Dialogue with Emmanuel Levinas," in Richard A. Cohen, ed., *Face to Face with Levinas*, 30–31.

58. Maimonides, *Mishneh Torah, Book of Judges, Laws of Kings* 11.3.

59. Maimonides, *Mishneh Torah, Book of Judges, Laws of Kings* 12.1. See Maimonides, *Laws of Kings,* in *Mishneh Torah,* chaps. 11 and 12, and *Guide* III.11. For valuable analyses, see Ravitzky, "To the Utmost of Human Capacity," and Menachem Lorberbaum, *Politics and the Limits of Law,* 17–89.

60. Levinas, *Beyond the Verse,* 181, and Maimonides, *Mishneh Torah, Book of Judges, Laws of Kings* 12.1. In a similar vein, in his messianic commentaries in *Difficult Freedom,* Levinas credits Maimonides with "only the negation of the miraculous" (296) even as he praises him for offering an alternative to the mystical and apocalyptic views he had recently read in Scholem's essay, "Toward an Understanding of the Messianic Idea in Judaism" (1959). See also Franscesca Albertini, "Emmanuel Levinas' Theological-Political Interpretation of Moses Maimonides."

Note also that for Levinas the naturalistic messianism expounded by Maimonides provided a valuable model for thinking about the historical relation between the people of Israel and the nations of the world. In chapter 11 of the *Laws of Kings* (in *Mishneh Torah*), Maimonides considers the possibility that the truth of Judaism might be disseminated historically by a wily divine plan that deploys Christianity and Islam to propagate the metaphysical knowledge of God revealed to Moses. The passage is cited as the epigraph to the conclusion of this book. Overcoming Maimonides' hesitation, Levinas endorses the "missionary role of Christianity in the service of monotheism" even as he is "less optimistic but more direct" about such an alliance after the Holocaust (*Difficult Freedom,* 163; cf. *In the Time of the Nations,* 182). The omission of Islam in this context attested to Levinas's distinctly Judeo-Christian interpretation of the moral and political culture of the French Republic.

61. Isaiah 11:8, interpreted in this intellectualist way by Maimonides in *Guide* III.11, 441, and as the final word and ultimate purpose of the *Mishneh Torah* (*Book of Judges, Laws of Kings* 12.8).

62. Levinas, *Beyond the Verse,* 181.

63. This does not mean that Levinas's eschatology is not simultaneously a reworking of Kant's notion of the "kingdom of ends" and a type of Aristotelian teleology according to which the happiness I ultimately desire refers me to the happiness of others still to come. But the fact that a modified Maimonidean picture should resemble a Kantian or Aristotelian picture is hardly surprising. Jewish thought has always been a happy and fruitful intermarriage, and usually to one of those two grooms. Maimonides' view is of course heavily indebted to the tension in Aristotelian ethics between the moral and the contemplative purposes of life, as is pointedly evident at the end of the *Nichomachean Ethics.* On Aristotle's teleological conception of eudaimonia, see the illuminating analysis of Jonathan Lear in *Happiness, Death, and the Remainder of Life,* which could usefully be applied to Maimonides' notion of "the world to come" and to Levinas's account of

the infinity of time. For a recent elaboration of modern Jewish messianism, including its Maimonidean background, see Martin Kavka, *Jewish Messianism and the History of Philosophy*.

INTERLUDE

1. The turn can be dated with some precision to the important essays and lectures given after *Totality and Infinity*, such as "The Trace of the Other" (1963) and "Phenomena and Enigma" (1964), most of which respond to Maurice Merleau-Ponty's *Signs* (1960), and not, as is often thought, to Jacques Derrida's "Violence and Metaphysics" (1964). The Jewish writings confirm this periodization since it is in "The Temptation of Temptation" (October 1964, in *Nine Talmudic Readings*) that Levinas first explores his new position, in which the desire for the other who is "separate" gives way to the condition of the witness or hostage passively exposed to the prereflective immanence of the other.

2. Jean-Luc Marion is also of the view that there is "a strict periodization between 1961 (*Totality and Infinity*) and 1974 (*Otherwise than Being*)" ("A Note Concerning the Ontological Indifference," 26).

3. Levinas, TI, Section II, "Interiority and Economy."

4. A similar point is made by Hilary Putnam in "Levinas and Judaism" (35), although I think the point applies only to later Levinas. In "Levinas' Logic," Jean-François Lyotard makes a similar argument specifically with respect to *Otherwise than Being*, in which the prescriptive does not depend on a descriptive or "denotative" logic.

5. The "Stranger," who dominates *Totality and Infinity*, appears only four times in *Otherwise than Being* (OB, 91, 92, 123, and 143/AE, 116, 117, 157, and 182), and even then as "a stranger in the neighbor" (OB, 123/AE, 157).

6. *Time and the Other*, 40. For further analysis, see Marion, "A Note Concerning the Ontological Indifference," and Leora Batnitzky, "Encountering the Modern Subject in Levinas," although Batnitzky thinks Levinas remains essentially Cartesian to the end.

7. Martin Heidegger, *The Basic Problems of Phenomenology*, 299–300.

8. Levinas, OB, 200/AE, 230n. Levinas is most likely alluding to Deuteronomy Rabbah II.X. In BT Baba Bathra 17a, six persons are mentioned who died by the kiss of God. For discussion of these sources, see Michael Fishbane, *The Kiss of God*, 17–19. Fishbane's book makes it clear that death by the kiss of God belongs primarily to the registers of mystical experience and martyrology. These two registers are conjoined in *Otherwise than Being*. More should be said about this, beginning with the seminal discussion in Maimonides, *Guide* III.51, 627–28.

9. On this, see Kosky, "Contemporary Encounters with Apophatic Theology," and Oliver Davies, "Beyond the Language of Being," 32–40. For extensive discussion, see Hent de Vries, *Minimal Theologies*, esp. 508–18.

10. Eric Santner, *On Creaturely Life*, 28. Having arrived at the notion of ethical creatureliness in Levinas independently, I have since found Santner's account of creaturely life, which emphasizes the political more than the ethical, to elucidate beautifully what I regard as one of later Levinas's most important ideas.

11. Levinas, "The Trace of the Other" (1963). Levinas excerpted the most important parts of this text, including the reference to the *Parmenides* and the *Enneads*, in the final section of "Meaning and Sense" (1972), in *Basic Philosophical Writings*.

12. Moses de Leon, *Sefer Shekel ha-Kodesh*, 19–20.

13. Santner, *On Creaturely Life*, 26.

14. As far as I know, he did not study other kabbalistic or Hasidic works, with the important exception of *Nefesh Hayim*, a lucid and wonderfully narrated digest of late medieval Kabbalah by a Lithuanian Talmudist.

15. Solomon Ibn Gabirol, *Crown of Kingship ("Keter Malkhuth")*, canto II.

16. Paul Celan, "The Meridian," respectively, 39, 36, 37.

17. Levinas, "Paul Celan: From Being to the Other," in his *Proper Names*, 43. In a note to these remarks Levinas cites Simone Weil, who writes: "Father, tear this body and this soul away from me, to make of them your things, and let nothing remain of me eternally but that tearing-away itself" (*Proper Names*, 176n16). The sentiment resonates closely with the passage from de Leon's *Shekel ha-Kodesh*, cited earlier. See also Shira Wolosky's illuminating study, *Language Mysticism: The Negative Way of Language in Eliot, Beckett, and Celan*, which includes discussion of Levinas and the Kabbalah.

18. *Duties of the Heart* 1.10, 84, translated by Lobel, in *A Sufi-Jewish Dialogue*, 79. The term "intuitive mind" translates Ibn Pakuda's *wahm*, an Arabic term that Lobel says is "a general term for the mind; it is also a realm in which images and likeness can be conceived. . . . [W]ahm is thus the medium in which one receives images of God and ascends step-by-step to a more refined understanding of these images" (78–79). Chapter 4, "The One," of Lobel's book provides a valuable account of the Sufi context in which Ibn Pakuda developed his refined Neoplatonism.

CHAPTER 4

1. Levinas, "The Contemporary Relevance of Maimonides," 94.

2. Levinas, "Toward the Other" (1963), in *Nine Talmudic Readings*, 14.

3. Levinas, *In the Time of the Nations*, 172. The allusion at the end is to Leo Strauss, and perhaps to Shlomo Pines too.

4. Shlomo Pines, "The Limitations of Human Knowledge," in *Studies in the History of Jewish Thought*, 100.

5. Pines diffidently admits that "there are passages in the *Guide* which appear to disprove" his view (100). He was roundly taken to task by Herbert A. Davidson, "Maimonides on Metaphysical Knowledge," and R. Z. Friedman, "Maimonides and Kant on Metaphysics and Piety."

6. For example, Levinas, *Beyond the Verse*, 138, 145, and in Jill Robbins, ed., *Is It Righteous to Be?* 283.

7. Levinas, "The Contemporary Relevance of Maimonides," 91. The idea of a philosophical interpretation of the history of philosophy, in contrast to a historical interpretation, was first articulated by Heidegger; for a lucid presentation of the main ideas, see John D. Caputo, *Heidegger and Aquinas*.

8. Levinas, "A Religion for Adults" (1957), in *Difficult Freedom*, 17.

9. This interpretation draws on the important role that Islamic Neoplatonism in general and Sufism in particular played in Maimonides' intellectual and familial life. For an excellent defense of this view see Diana Lobel, "'Silence Is Praise to You': Maimonides on Negative Theology."

10. Yair Lorberbaum, "On Contradictions, Rationality, Dialectics, and Esotericism in Maimonides's *Guide of the Perplexed*."

11. Ehud Z. Benor, "Meaning and Reference in Maimonides' Negative Theology."

12. Joseph Stern, "Maimonides' Demonstrations: Principles and Practice." For further general discussion of the implications of Maimonides' negative theology, see also Stern, "Maimonides' Epistemology." Kenneth Seeskin, *Searching for a Distant God* (91–123), provides a lucid account of the relation between negative theology and normative life.

13. A more comprehensive treatment of this proposal would also include discussion of Hermann Cohen, who likewise found Maimonides' negative theology and Kant's practical philosophy to confirm each other. Kenneth Seeskin has consistently emphasized this; see his valuable discussions, including analysis of additional contemporary Maimonidean scholarship, in "The Positive Contribution of Negative Theology," chap. 2 of *Jewish Philosophy in a Secular Age*, and "*Imitatio Dei*," chap. 5 of *Searching for a Distant God*.

14. For example, see Joseph A. Bujis, "The Negative Theology of Maimonides and Aquinas." For an alternative view of Aquinas, see Jean-Luc Marion, "Thomas Aquinas and Onto-theo-logy."

15. Levinas, *God, Death, and Time*, and "God and Philosophy," in *Of God Who Comes to Mind*, 69; cf. Levinas, OB, 149/AE, 190. The same logic lies behind Yeshayahu Leibowitz's Maimonidean negative theology, except that for Leibowitz it is the practice of halakhah, rather than ethics, that ensures that divine transcendence and negativity are not encroached; see especially his *The Faith of Maimonides*. This structural homology lies behind the surprising convergence between Leibowitz's anti-ethical interpretation of Judaism and Levinas's ethical one. I have discussed this in Michael Fagenblat, "Lacking All Interest."

16. Levinas, *God, Death, and Time*, 223–24; the whole passage should be studied in more detail.

17. Levinas, "Meaning and Sense," in *Basic Philosophical Writings*, 64. Levinas is emphasizing the twofold meaning of the French *sens* as "meaning" and "direction."

18. The distinction between meaning (*signification*), which is cognitive, and sense (*sens*), which is normative, is fundamental to Levinas's turn from positive secular theology to negative secular theology. See esp. "Meaning and Sense" (1964), in *Basic Philosophical Writings*, whose conclusion incorporates Levinas's essay "The Trace of the Other" (1963), discussed in the Interlude.

19. *Nicomachean Ethics* IV, 3 (1123b13–15).

20. Cf. Maimonides, *Commentary to Avot* IV:4, and *Shemonah Perakim*, chap. 4, which the *Commentary to Avot* radicalizes.

21. *Shemonah Perakim*, chap. 4; see the discussion by Daniel Frank, "Humility as a Virtue," 97.

22. Frank, "Humility as a Virtue," 98.

23. Humility and anger are the exceptions to the Aristotelian view that Maimonides adopts in his legal writings.

24. Sifre, 'Ekev 49, BT Shabbat 133b. This is the source of the rabbinic notion of *imitatio dei*, which becomes crucial for Maimonides. There is extensive literature on this topic. I have taken Herbert A. Davidson's bold article as my point of departure since it relates *imitatio dei* to the issue of apophatic anthropology, albeit not quite in these terms. For a more moderate reading see Howard Kreisel, "Imitatio Dei in Maimonides' 'Guide of the Perplexed,'" who also cites several other valuable studies at 169n1.

25. Herbert A. Davidson, "The Middle Way in Maimonides' Ethics," 65.

26. Davidson, "The Middle Way in Maimonides' Ethics," 66–67.

27. Davidson, "The Middle Way in Maimonides' Ethics," 65.

28. My interpretation of *imitatio dei* as apophatic anthropology suggests that there is more common ground between Davidson's intellectualist interpretation and Pines's skeptical view. Here again I would emphasize the Neoplatonism at work in Maimonides' most radical thinking. Davidson almost concedes this. He admits that the issue can be framed in terms of a shift from an Aristotelian ethic to a Neoplatonic one (p. 61) but then rejects this interpretation for reasons I find far less persuasive than the admittedly "vague and illusive" explanation he postulates, namely, "a change in Maimonides' personality" (p. 62). For an account that emphasizes the Neoplatonism of Maimonidean negative theology, see Diana Lobel, "'Silence Is Praise to You.'" Among the medievals, Meister Eckhart's application of Maimonidean negative theology stands out, as Yossef Schwartz has shown in "*To Thee Is Silence Praise*." Among moderns, Marion has formulated a phenomenology of the *via eminentia* that is thoroughly inspired by Christian Neoplatonism. I am indebted to Marion's work in my attempt to expose a non-metaphysical *via eminentia* within Maimonidean "metaphysics." Marion is, in turn, fundamentally indebted to Levinas for his account of the saturated phenomenon and *l'interloqué* who responds to it.

29. As Marion quips: "Where man is made in the image of God, if God is

unknowable then man is unknowable too" (in Caputo and Scanlon, eds., *God, the Gift, and Postmodernism*, 47).

30. OB, 142/AE, 181; Maimonides, *Mishneh Torah, Laws of Teshuva* 10:3, and *Guide* III.51, 627–28.

31. It is not a matter of collapsing these two articulations of negative theology into each other but of seeing that both thinkers regard Jewish negative theology as a practice that implicates the subject of desire in its own abnegation.

32. My emphasis. This concern was first raised by Maurice Blanchot in *The Infinite Conversation* (63), and then again, with remarkable apophatic poignancy, with respect to Levinas's later work in *The Writing of the Disaster*, 18–25. Recall Jacques Derrida's remark that Levinas once confessed to him that it was "holiness" and "not really ethics" that interested him. For a fine discussion, see Paul Davies, "On Resorting to an Ethical Language." Although Levinas distanced himself from the language of positive theology, his reliance on apophatic techniques throughout *Otherwise than Being* suggests that the language of negative theology is indispensable for his project, perhaps even more so than the "ethical language" to which he resorted.

33. This is the well-known Millian account of proper names that Saul Kripke applied to natural kinds in general in *Naming and Necessity*.

34. Kripke, *Naming and Necessity*, 95.

35. Moshe Halbertal and Avishai Margalit, *Idolatry*, 157–58, and see pp. 152–59 for a more detailed analysis also indebted to Kripke. I do not see why Hilary Putnam, in "On Negative Theology," objects to the application of the theory of direct reference when he says, "However, in the case of the word 'God,' or of any of the Names of God that Maimonides discusses (e.g., YHWH), there was *never* a point at which some human speaker was able to indicate to Whom he or she was referring by using a literally correct definite description" (17). Putnam mentions Moses in the footnote to this sentence, but refuses to allow that he or anyone else could be the anchor for the name of God because "it is not the *semantic of their words* that enables us to do this, but something else, something that is beyond language altogether" (note 31). According to my reading of Maimonides, however, Moses has a direct, *nonsemantic* referential acquaintance with YHWH; this is precisely Halbertal and Margalit's point.

36. See *Hilchot Yesodei Hatorah* VIII–X. For a more comprehensive discussion and further references, see Halbertal, "Maimonides' Book of Commandments," 462–64.

37. Marion, "In the Name: How to Avoid Speaking of It," in *In Excess*, 144–45.

38. Levinas, "The Name of God According to a Few Talmudic Texts," in *Beyond the Verse*, 119.

39. Levinas, *Proper Names*, 4–5 (trans. slightly modified). Note, of course, the title of this work, published in 1976 and thus within the strict periodization demarcating Levinas 1 and 2.

40. The English translation renders the final *nom* as "noun," but I think it should be "name." The homonymy of *nom*, with the quite different philosophical and ethical implications of proper names and common nouns, should be accounted for every time Levinas used the word *nom*.

41. Cf. Marion, "In the Name: How to Avoid Speaking of It," in *In Excess*, 140, who writes of "the strictly pragmatic function of language—namely, to refer names and their speaker to the unattainable yet inescapable interlocutor beyond every name and every denegation of names." In referring to an "unattainable yet inescapable interlocutor beyond every name" Marion seems to have in mind some ineffable divinity beyond the Name. The Maimonidean/Levinasian view I am proposing does not, either in ethics or in theology. In my view, the proper name precedes and enables interlocutors and there is no way to think about a pragmatic approach to an interlocutor beyond the name. The name designates only itself. It is the name that is beyond being; there is no being of the interlocutor beyond the name. (But this is its glory, as we shall presently see.) This may well be Marion's view too, made more difficult to interpret on account of the homonym, which might be better understood as referring to an "interlocutor beyond every noun," that is, to an interlocutor only in name.

42. Eric Santner, *On Creaturely Life*, xix.

43. Santner, *On Creaturely Life*, 39.

44. Santner, *On Creaturely Life*, 21–22.

45. Surprisingly, none of the modern authors who argue for the decisive significance of the proper name of God within the logic of Maimonides' negative theology even mention this chapter, which immediately follows the one devoted to the uniqueness of the Tetragrammaton (*Guide* I.63). These commentators move from the uniqueness of the Name *back* to the metaphysical God of moral and intellectual perfection, whereas Maimonides moves forward to a profound equivocation between YHWH and glory.

46. Cf. Maimonides, *Guide* I.5, I.18, I.25. This is the position defended by Menachem Kellner, *Maimonides' Confrontation with Mysticism*, 179–215.

47. Glory thus functions much like love in the Christian tradition of negative theology, as another proper name and non-metaphysical referent for God, as Caputo has beautifully argued, for example, in *On Religion*. See also Derrida, "*Sauf le nom* (Post-scriptum)," in *On the Name*, 68–79. It is this that allows Augustine to ask, What do I love when I love God? And what allows Levinas to ask, What do I glorify (honor) when I glorify (honor) the name of the other?

48. Jewish mysticism attributes the glory to YHWH, and sometimes even identifies YHWH with the glory. For a seminal treatment, see Elliot R. Wolfson, *Through a Speculum That Shines*, esp. 125–88. My view does not deny this identification but highlights that, phenomenologically speaking, one can access each independently.

49. Marion, *Being Given*, 203–4; see also 363n47, in which Marion explains that his emphasis is on the sense of weightiness in the Hebrew *kavod*, which he explains as an excess of phenomenality that cannot be borne by the gaze. See also Marion, *God Without Being*, 84–95.

50. Benedict de Spinoza, *Ethics*, Part V, Prof. XXXVI, 265. The relation between *kavod* as weightiness and *kavod* as reverence deserves further attention. There is no beholding the glory (*kavod*) without honor, awe, or reverence (*kavod*).

51. Wolfson has argued extensively that the Jewish mystical tradition has always sought to *say* in poetic and imaginative language what could only be poorly *said* by reason; see his *Language, Eros, Being*, for example, p. xiii.

My interpretation of Maimonides is plainly at odds with the prevalent and incontestable view of him as a rationalist for whom God can be known only through the intellectual faculty. I do not mean to question the privilege Maimonides almost always accords the intellect. My claim instead is that Maimonides' *via negativa* takes us beyond the capacity of the human intellect to apprehend God and beyond the idea of God as intellect, as others who have advocated for a "skeptical interpretation" of Maimonidean negative theology have proposed (see note 12 to this chapter). But rather than concentrate on the fragmentary, intuitive, or pedagogical effects of negative theology, I wish to draw attention to the argument in *Guide* I.63 that the Name succeeds in referring to the reality of God independently of knowledge and without descriptive, metaphysical theology, as Benor too argued (see note 11 to this chapter). Where I differ from Benor is in emphasizing the passage from *Guide* I.63 to I.64, in which Maimonides changes track, or, rather, goes over the same ground from an altogether different perspective. In I.64, *kavod* is singled out as another way of saying "the essence and true reality" of God beyond the limits of the intellect and without relying on the Name. Glory is a negativized or, as I would prefer, a saturated phenomenon. Like the Name, it is not a metaphysical concept and the intellect is not a privileged way of honoring it. In this respect I disagree with Kellner's view that glory is simply another way of speaking of the wisdom of nature.

According to Kellner, *kavod* functions like the Attributes of Action; it is the "divine wisdom as expressed in nature" that can be understood by the intellect but not by the senses (*Maimonides' Confrontation with Mysticism*, 215; cf. 196, 198). Some of the evidence Kellner adduces supports this interpretation, especially Maimonides' *Commentary to Mishnah Hagigah* 2:1, although it is relevant to my alternative interpretation that this text was written long before the radical negative theology of the *Guide*. In any case, most of the evidence equivocates. Kellner himself admits that in *Guide* I.54 "*kavod* is made to mean God's essence," as is the case in I.64 and III.13, in which "*kavod* can mean God's essence" (195, 198). Kellner does not think much of this. His argument is wholly oriented toward defending the intellectualist interpretation of glory as what is known "to intellectual apprehension, not to sensual apprehension" and as what yields a "high understanding of the truth about God" (193, 197). Yet at the same time he acknowledges that "*kavod* as understood here [in I.54] is in principle beyond human understanding" (195). Kellner simply affirms the first possibility without exploring the implications of the second. The reason for this is that Kellner, like many scholars, concentrates on the disjunction Maimonides establishes between the perceptual encounters with "God," which he regards as idolatrous, and truths about God apprehended by the intellect. Everything hinges on the superiority of the intellect over sense-perception. But my reading emphasizes the fact that when Maimonides turns to the *via negativa* he argues that the intellect is just as limited as the senses in apprehending the truth of God. From the perspective of negative theology, the idol of metaphysics must be destroyed along with the perceptual idol and anthropomorphic idol. Kellner assumes that the governing disjunction in Maimonides is between the intellect and the senses, but the important contrast in negative theology is between the intellect and the senses on the one hand and, on the other hand, the reality of God attested by the Name and the glory. Glory manifests the excess of divine reality; the intellect is dazzled by it even as the earth is saturated with it.

52. Cf. Marion, "L'interloqué."

CHAPTER 5

1. For a sustained argument that Levinas's contribution reaches further into religious studies than into moral philosophy, see Jeffrey Kosky, *Levinas and the Philosophy of Religion.*

2. Levinas, "Is Ontology Fundamental," in *Collected Philosophical Papers*, 7.

3. Respectively, OB, 197n25, 168/AE, 155n1, 214. Or again: "One is tempted to call this plot religious; it is not stated in terms of certainty or uncertainty, and does not rest on any positive theology" (OB, 147/AE, 188).

4. Levinas, "Judaism and Christianity," in *In the Time of the Nations*, 164.

5. Levinas, *Beyond the Verse*, xiv, referring to the section called "Theologies" in that book.

6. Levinas, *Beyond the Verse*, 138–39.

7. For support of this view, see Menachem Kellner, *Dogma in Medieval Jewish Thought*, and Marc B. Shapiro, *The Limits of Orthodox Theology*; for a defense of theological dogma in Judaism, see Yitzhak Blau, "Flexibility with a Firm Foundation."

8. Abraham Isaac Kook, *Abraham Isaac Kook*, 42.

9. Kook, *Orot*, 126ff.

10. Levinas and Leibowitz briefly corresponded, and although they appear to hold opposite views about the relationship between morality and Jewish religious practice, I have argued that in fact they converge on most of the essentials; see Michael Fagenblat, "Lacking All Interest."

11. Jean-Luc Marion, *God Without Being.* John D. Caputo, in *On Religion,* provides a spirited Derridean defense of "religion without religion," religion in which true belief becomes entirely a matter of doing or, rather, loving.

12. Levinas, *Of God Who Comes to the Mind,* ix.

13. Wilfred Cantwell Smith, *Faith and Belief.*

14. But Cartesian skepticism plays an important role in Levinas's thought, for which it has rightly been compared to Stanley Cavell's work, and, indeed, recently by Cavell himself in "What Is the Scandal of Skepticism?," in *Philosophy the Day After Tomorrow,* 132–54.

15. On this, see Wilfred Cantwell Smith, *Believing: An Historical Perspective.*

16. The link between a Christian and a metaphysical picture of religion as centered on belief has been forged by many modern scholars. For example, "Belief appears as a universal category [for describing religion] because of the universalist claims of the tradition in which it has become most central, Christianity" (Donald S. Lopez Jr., "Belief," 33). Other notable scholars who make this case include Talal Asad, *Genealogies of Religion,* 30–45, who claims it is a post-Reformation development bound up with the Enlightenment, and Daniel Boyarin, who thinks its origins belong in the fourth century with the formation of imperial Christian identity (*Border Lines,* chap. 8). As will become clear later in this chapter, I think Asad is closer to the mark than is Boyarin.

17. Levinas, "God and Philosophy," in *Collected Philosophical Papers,* 170; cf. OB, 149/AE, 190.

18. W. K. Clifford, *The Ethics of Belief and Other Essays.* Clifford's essay was, of course, the stimulant for William James's famous response, "The Will to Believe."

19. "Dialogue with Emmanuel Levinas," in Richard A. Cohen, ed., *Face to Face with Levinas,* 18. Jon D. Levenson provides a characteristically lucid and compelling interpretation of the ancient Israelite covenant in *Sinai and Zion,* which, in this respect as in many others, echoes Levinas's Judaic phenomenology. As Levenson says, covenantal faith "is not derived from introspection, but from a consideration of the public testimony of God. The present generation makes history their story, but it is first history. They do not determine who they are by looking within, by plumbing the depths of the individual soul, by seeking a mystical light in the innermost reaches of the self. Rather, the direction is opposite. What is public is made private. . . . One does not *discover* one's identity, and one certainly does not forge it oneself. He *appropriates* an identity that is a matter of public knowledge" (38–39). Cf. Levinas, "Being Jewish" (cited in note 60 to Chapter 1 of this book).

20. See, for example, Ludwig Wittgenstein, *Culture and Value,* 64, 81, and the illuminating analyses of those passages in, respectively, Putnam, "Introduction," in Franz Rosenzweig, *Understanding the Sick and the Healthy,* esp. 10; and Moshe

Halbertal, "On Believers and Belief."

21. Kenneth Seeskin, "Judaism and the Linguistic Interpretation of Faith," 226–27. Seeskin bases his argument on the difference, commonly asserted, between belief *in* God and belief *that* God exists. Halbertal points out ("On Believers and Belief," 13) that this distinction is difficult to sustain, since belief *in* God can readily be reformulated as a belief *that* God is faithful or loyal. This does not concern my point, which is that faith involves *actions* that confirm fidelity to *persons* (or *Personhood* in the case of God).

22. For example, Deuteronomy 32:4. Cf. Habbakuk 2:4, cited by Paul in Romans 1:17 and misinterpreted by post-Reformation exegetes as referring to righteousness through faith when Paul seems to be referring to the faith of the righteous; see Lloyd Gaston, *Paul and the Torah*, 118–19.

23. Halbertal, "On Believers and Belief," 12. For two valuable essays exploring traditional concepts associated with *emunah*, see R. J. Zvi Werblowsky, "Faith, Hope and Trust," and Moshe Greenberg, "Aspects of *Bittahon* in Hebrew Thought," in his *Studies in the Bible and Jewish Thought*, 63–74.

24. Richard Firth Green, *A Crisis of Truth*; see also Nigel Saul's review, "From Trothe to Truth." Andrea Frisch, in "The Ethics of Testimony," provides an effective hermeneutical clarification of the value and errors of modern theories of testimony such as those provided by Agamben, Derrida, Felman, Levinas, and Lyotard in relation to medieval accounts of testimony. In her view, "it is in Lévinas's work that one can perceive the most persistent echoes of the ethics of medieval folklaw, particularly with respect to the witness" (51). Following J. L. Austin and the later Wittgenstein, analytic philosophers have also taken a keen interest in the role of testimony in epistemology; see C. A. J. Coady, *Testimony*.

25. Maimonides, *Guide* I.50, III. There is a sizable literature surrounding Maimonides' notion of belief. In addition to the works cited earlier in note 7 to this chapter, see the useful comments and references in Michael Schwartz's recent translation of the *Guide*, "Preface," 10n15, and I.50, 112–13. See also the illuminating essay by Kellner, "The Virtue of Faith."

26. Cited by Shalom Rosenberg, "The Concept of *'Emunah* in Post-Maimonidean Philosophy," 261.

27. BT Shabbat 31a. For a closer reading, see David Kraemer, "Formation of the Rabbinic Canon."

28. Jacques Derrida, *Edmund Husserl's Origin of Geometry*.

29. Samuel C. Wheeler, *Deconstruction as Analytic Philosophy*, 146. To Wheeler's list one could add Robert B. Brandom, whose work promises to be of much use for understanding religious beliefs in particular. For a different Davidsonian defense of religious belief, see Terry F. Godlove Jr., "Saving Belief: On the New Materialism in Religious Studies," in Nancy K. Frankenberry, ed., *Radical Interpretation in Religion*, 10–24.

30. Wittgenstein, *Philosophical Occasions*, 377; cited by Donald Davidson in "Externalisms," 14.

31. Wittgenstein, *On Certainty*, 509.

32. Levinas, "Being Jewish," 209.

33. Cf. Martin Buber, "Job," in *On the Bible*, 192, and *Two Types of Faith*, 40.

34. Jon D. Levenson, *Creation and the Persistence of Evil*, 141.

35. Levinas, "The Temptation of Temptation," in *Nine Talmudic Readings*, 42.

36. For example, by Michel Haar, "The Obsession of the Other."

37. Putnam, "Levinas and Judaism," 55.

38. Maurice Blanchot, *The Writing of the Disaster*, 25–26.

39. Blanchot, *The Writing of the Disaster*, respectively, 21, 19.

40. Slavoj Žižek, "A Plea for Ethical Violence."

41. Cf. Levenson's description of the "enormous risk" of "covenantal theonomy" in *Creation and the Persistence of Evil*, 141–56; for Levinas on the risk of ethics, see Paul Davies, "A Fine Risk."

42. Heidegger, *Being and Time*, §44; Donald Davidson, for example, *Subjective, Intersubjective, Objective*, 149–50, 194–97, 209–14; *Inquiries*, 196–201.

43. Gianni Vattimo, *Belief*, esp. 64, and *Beyond Interpretation*, esp. 40.

44. Heidegger, *Being and Time*, 492 note v/SZ, 139 note v, quoted from Augustine's *Contra Faustum* 32:18.

45. "Truth I love, but I love Plato more," which reverses the famous words imputed to Aristotle, "*Amica Plato, sed magis amicus veritas*"; Vattimo, *Beyond Interpretation*, 40. See also Vattimo's remarks on trust as the root of truth in *After Christianity*, 8.

46. Augustine, *On Christian Doctrine*, 1.36.40 (cf. I Cor. 13). The significance of Augustinian *caritas* for modern hermeneutics does not seem to have been sufficiently appreciated, doubtless because Augustine is often regarded as the arch Platonizer of meaning (most famously by Wittgenstein at the beginning of *Philosophical Investigations*). But this obscures the tremendous significance of Augustine's account of scriptural hermeneutics for modern theories of interpretation. This divided view of Augustine is manifest in Hans-Georg Gadamer's *Truth and Method*, for example, which associates Augustine with a Platonic view that values the abstract meaning over the word (419–22), but later, when it comes to remarking on Augustine's exegetical regard for language, reverses the judgment: "In Augustine's ingenious interpretation of Genesis we can discern the first hint of the speculative interpretation of language that we have elaborated in the structural analysis of the hermeneutical experience of the world, according to which the multiplicity of what is thought proceeds only from the unity of the word" (484). The ambivalence hinges on the difference between Augustine's view of language in general, which is Platonic, and his view of biblical language in particular, which emphasizes interpretative charity and plurality. For an introduction to the lat-

ter, see William Thomas, "Biblical Interpretation." Joel Weinsheimer, in "Charity Militant," provides a fine rapprochement of Augustinian exegetical *caritas* and the hermeneutical charity proposed by Gadamer, Heidegger, and Davidson. Augustine's major debt to Origen for his account of biblical exegesis should be noted, not merely because of its factuality but also because it keeps in view the relation between charity, allegory, and heresy.

47. See Levinas, "Philosophy and Awakening."

48. For example, Jean-Luc Nancy, *Being Singular Plural,* esp. 1–46, 93–99; and "Heidegger's 'Originary Ethics,'" in "Sharing Voices."

49. The antithetical characterization of the Levinas-Heidegger relation and the Heidegger-Judaism relation is wide-ranging but counterproductive. For the beginning of a corrective, see Allen Scult, *Being Jewish/Reading Heidegger,* esp. 106, 122, 139, and his occasional references to Levinas, for example, 143n28. A similar conclusion is implied by Wheeler, "A Rabbinic Philosophy of Language," chap. 7 of *Deconstruction as Analytic Philosophy.* But the best proof comes from pioneering scholars of Jewish thought and literature such as Elliot R. Wolfson, whose recent work *Language, Eros, Being* is explicitly indebted to Heidegger; or Boyarin, who regards midrash as protodeconstruction, for example, in "Midrash and the 'Magic Language.'" Above all, two studies that have shifted the very terms of debate (it seems to me in favor of the interpretation I am proposing) are Peter Eli Gordon, *Rosenzweig and Heidegger,* and Marlène Zarader, *The Unthought Debt.*

50. I return to this in Chapter 6.

51. "Dying for . . ." (1987), in *Entre Nous,* 212. In the remaining pages Levinas makes the argument for the inadequacy of the position he has just described, suggesting that although an ontological ethic certainly assures an approach to the other, it does so only "in terms of occupations and works in the world, without encountering faces" (214–15). But Heidegger explicitly says that authentic solicitude or care for the other does *not* relate to the other as a mode of ready-to-hand: "This kind of solicitude pertains essentially to authentic care—that is, to the existence of the Other, not to a '*what*' with which he is concerned" (*Being and Time,* 159/SZ, 122). These are admittedly sparse indications.

52. In particular, the conclusion to *The Theology of Intuition in Husserl's Phenomenology,* which roundly criticized Husserl's account of phenomenological intuition for still being too theoretical (hence the ironic title of Levinas's book) and favored Heidegger's attention to the concrete historical situation. See also "Martin Heidegger et l'ontologie" [1932], in *En découvrant l'existence avec Husserl et Heidegger,* 74. Levinas's early articles on Heidegger generally reflect a more appreciative view of the German philosopher but, in what appears to be an act of censorship, were unfortunately excised from the English translation, which became *Discovering Existence with Husserl.*

53. Levinas, "Martin Buber and Contemporary Judaism," in *Outside the Subject*, 18–19. For more on the Levinas-Buber relation, see Peter Atterton, Matthew Calarco, and Maurice Friedman, eds., *Levinas and Buber*.

54. See Edmund Husserl, *Cartesian Meditations*, §§50–54. Levinas translated the most important of Husserl's meditations, the fourth and the fifth, into French. Samuel Moyn correctly calls Levinas's resort to ethics in place of analogical apprehensions an "attempt to reinvent the theory of intersubjectivity" (*Origins of the Other*, 12). But *Otherwise than Being* rejects the theory of intersubjectivity and the account of "solitude" on which it is based. This is the main reason why it is a much more Heideggerian work than *Totality and Infinity* and why its main philosophical target is Husserlian egology, as I have suggested in the Interlude.

55. Levinas, *Time and the Other*, 40.

56. Heidegger, *The Basic Problems of Phenomenology*, 28; cf. 297–98. Heidegger may be alluding directly to Buber's *Ich und Du* (published in 1923) or else has phenomenological theories such as Husserl's and Scheler's in mind, theories which still set out to answer the so-called problem of the alter ego by "constituting" the intersubjective field of values on the basis of a primordial "sympathy" among isolated transcendental subjects. The lectures by Heidegger come from a seminar held in the summer of 1927, while *Being and Time* was in press. Levinas studied with Heidegger and Husserl in 1928 and 1929.

57. Heidegger, *Being and Time*, 120/SZ, 156–57.

58. *Totality and Infinity*, Section II, "Interiority and Economy."

59. "A Note Concerning the Ontological Indifference." But Marion thinks that both Heidegger and Levinas leave unexplained the reason for the *name* they give to the call (as coming either from Being or the Other), which leads him to emphasize the role of the one who is called as the only one able to decide on the name; see also his "L'Interloqué" and its rigorous elaboration in *Being Given*, 248–319. Having noted this, I should not fail to mention that Marion's own position is already outlined *in nuce* in *Otherwise than Being*, in which the "ethical self" is effectively "l'interloqué," the one called to name the call to which it responds. See especially OB, 150–56/AE, 192–96, in which Levinas emphasizes that "revelation is made by him that receives it" since "I hear my own saying" in the response I give to the question posed to me by the other.

60. Zarader, *The Unthought Debt*, 147–48. Levinas's deneutralization of Heidegger's discovery of our prereflective phenomenological origins is all the more important in light of the latter's silent, pervasive, and, indeed, "unthought debt" to the Hebraic tradition. As Caputo, in "People of God, People of Being," writes: "What is perhaps most ominous about Heidegger's repression of the biblical provenance of his thought, is that he has stripped this call of its character as a call for *hospitality* and *justice*" (99; cf. 92). Whereas philosophy enters Christianity through Origen's and then Augustine's exegesis of the despoiling of the Egyptians in Exodus 11–12, which

they interpret as God's sanctioning of the risky use of philosophy (the spoils taken from Alexandria) for the sake of Christian truth, with Heidegger the movement is reversed. The heritage of Israel is here plundered in the name of a post-Christian thinking constructed out of Hebraic loot: thinking as interpretation, thanking, and memory; the word not only as sign but as the presence of the thing (*davar*); the temporality of truth as a revelation that withdraws its own presence. Caputo comments that "the structure of a history of salvation borrowed from the Hebrew and Christian scriptures, and utterly unknown to the Greeks, became the overarching framework for his reading of Greek texts. The meditation on thinking and language in terms of welcoming a call and keeping it in our hearts, that Heidegger told us he found by ruminating upon Parmenides and Heraclitus, clearly reproduces the 'essential dimensions' of the Hebrew word" (Caputo, 96, reiterating Zarader).

61. Levinas, "Jean Wahl's *Petite histoire*," in *Unforeseen History*, 69. Levinas much more commonly misconstrues Dasein as but an inflection of the *cogito*, as if *Jemeinigkeit* has ontological priority to *Mitsein*. For a moral corrective to the social ontology of *Being and Time* that avoids this mistake, see Nancy, *Being Singular Plural*, esp. 26–36. In general, one should never accept the contrast Levinas makes between his own thought and Heidegger's at face value.

62. Theodore Kisiel, *The Genesis of Heidegger's "Being and Time,"* 537n17.

63. Derrida, "Faith and Knowledge," in *Acts of Religion*, 96; see also his interesting discussion of belief, including Heidegger's ambivalence regarding it, in the ensuing pages, which include mention of "the faithful belief in what . . . would constitute the condition of *Mitsein*, of the relation or address of the other in general" (98–99). Generally speaking, the distinction between faith and belief that I am developing in this chapter correlates with Derrida's "two sources" of religion.

64. Kisiel, *The Genesis of Heidegger's "Being and Time,"* 87.

65. Seeskin, "Judaism and the Linguistic Interpretation of Faith," 219; Seeskin is arguing along the lines developed by Buber, *Two Types of Faith*.

66. Kisiel, *The Genesis of Heidegger's "Being and Time,"* 82. Heidegger's influences during this period include Paul, Augustine, Meister Eckhart, Bernard of Clairvaux, Teresa of Avila, Martin Luther, Friedrich Schleiermacher, Søren Kierkegaard, Wilhelm Dilthey, and Rudolf Otto; that is, his influence is "as much Lutheran as it is Catholic, or simply Christian in the most 'primitive' sense of that heritage" (Kisiel, 115).

67. Heidegger's remark, from 1919, is cited by Kisiel, *The Genesis of Heidegger's "Being and Time,"* 107.

68. See earlier, Chapter 1, "Neither Philosophy" section, pp. 2–7 of this book.

69. The latter terms are used extensively by Bernard Williams in *Truth and Truthfulness*. Williams argued that truth and truthfulness, or "accuracy" and "sincerity," are equally basic. I think Richard Rorty answered Williams properly in his review, "To the Sunlit Uplands."

70. Cf. Nancy, *Being Singular Plural*, 99.

71. This is what Davidson's notion of "triangulation" emphasizes, for example, in *Subjective, Intersubjective, Objective*, xv, 105, 117–20, 128–30, 202–3, 212–13, or "Externalisms." Where Levinas follows Heidegger and Hegel in this direction, Davidson has "embraced the Wittgensteinian intuition that the only legitimate source of objectivity is intersubjectivity" ("Externalisms," 12–13; see also "The Second Person" (essay 8), in *Subjective, Intersubjective, Objective*, 107–22).

72. Here again I am following Nancy. A philosophical encounter between Nancy and Donald Davidson would be worth staging. Davidson has been compared to Heidegger and Hans-Georg Gadamer, but Nancy is probably the thinker who has extended their work in the most compelling, post-metaphysical sense, so the comparison demands some attention. On Davidson and Heidegger, see Jeff Malpas, *Donald Davidson and the Mirror of Meaning*, and Timothy J. Nulty, "Davidsonian Triangulation and Heideggerian Comportment." On Davidson and Gadamer, see Malpas, *Donald Davidson and the Mirror of Meaning*, 98–99, 177–80; Bjørn T. Ramberg, *Donald Davidson's Philosophy of Language*, 138–41; and David Hoy, "Post-Cartesian Interpretation." Ramberg modified his view considerably, toward a deflationary comparison, in "Illuminating Language." See also Gerald L. Bruns, *Hermeneutics Ancient and Modern*, 83–86, and Joel Weinsheimer, "Charity Militant."

73. See also an important passage in OB, 48/AE, 61–62. This Heideggerianism suggests that Levinas's project is much closer to philosophers who defend semantic "externalism." The scarcity of an explicitly moral interpretation of externalism among American philosophers is striking, whereas Levinas aims to draw attention to the ethical implications of externalist accounts of mind. He therefore thinks of "ethics" not in terms of values and rules but in terms of the constitution of the semantic field as such and of the ethical effects of its influx into the "subjective" realm of the mind.

74. Malpas, *Donald Davidson and the Mirror of Meaning*, 139–40.

75. Maimonides, *The Eight Chapters*. For a discussion, see Kellner, *Maimonides on Judaism*, 18–19, and the notes on those pages. Maimonides is often regarded as prioritizing belief in metaphysical truths at the expense of faithfulness to tradition or community; the matter is far from straightforward, however. For a discussion, see Kellner, "The Virtue of Faith," as well as the essays by Nuriel, Rosenberg, and Herbert Davidson to which he refers.

76. Lewis Edwin Hahn, ed., *The Philosophy of Donald Davidson*, 360. This comment follows Davidson's objection to Bill Martin's attempt at "excavating Davidson's ethical theory," which Martin takes to be a type of Kantian moral realism. In Davidson's rejection of Martin's Kantian/realist interpretation, however, I find an affirmation of a more minimal morality regarding the inextricability of rationality, truth, discourse, sociality, and trust. This is closer to Levinas's view, although Levinas clearly thought it was far more significant than did Davidson.

77. Isadore Twersky, *Introduction to the Code of Maimonides*, 386, 385, respectively. See also 380–87, 498 (including note 365), and Hartman, *Maimonides*, 33. For Maimonides' interpretation of Deuteronomy 4:6, see esp. *Guide* II.11, 276, III.31, 524, and *Perek Helek*, in *Commentary to the Mishnah Sanhedrin*.

78. BT Sotah, 32a.

79. Levinas, *Beyond the Verse*, 75. I avoid the term "universalization" to describe the position I am defending, for reasons that Davidson and Nancy make clear in quite different ways. It is less a matter of working toward a universal truth applicable to everyone than of sharing truth with anyone for whom it can make sense.

80. Cf. Nancy, *Being Singular Plural*, 33. See also Lawrence Vogel, *The Fragile "We."*

81. Compare Simon Blackburn's worry in *Truth: A Guide for the Perplexed* about the sort of argument I am running, which he calls "Wittgensteinian theology." It "sounds shifty, as if it is trying to maintain all the benefits of belief without any of the costs. . . . [A]n abyss of 'anything goes' relativism opens up. For these interpretations offer the sayings of religious storytellers a general-purpose immunity to any kind of criticism or evaluation. And then the all-important barrier between fantasy and fact is being dismantled on their behalf" (17). Needless to say, I do not agree with Blackburn that the only genuine candidate for objectivity is an interpretation-free truth or that the barriers between fantasy and fact break down when truth is saturated by interpretation. The point is to understand interpretation as dialogical, triangulated, and regulated by external causes (objects, texts, events—in short, phenomena whose senses are not predetermined or simply given) rather than as the expression of a subjective cog turning on itself, as Blackburn seems to think.

82. Halbertal concludes his essay "On Believers and Belief," which has stimulated me generally throughout this chapter, with an argument for this position. See also the thought-provoking work of Peter Winch, *Trying to Make Sense*, and Norman Malcolm, "The Groundlessness of Belief," in *Thought and Knowledge*, 199–216. Both point in a similar direction.

83. Moshe Idel provides wonderful illustrations of this endless hermeneutic in *Kabbalah*, chap. 9, esp. 248, extensively expanded in *Absorbing Perfections*, esp. the first chapters. Both Idel and Elliot R. Wolfson frequently point to common hermeneutical assumptions and methods at work in kabbalistic and postfoundational modern interpretative practices.

84. Umberto Eco and Cardinal Martini, *Belief or Unbelief?* 80.

85. Eco and Martini, *Belief or Unbelief?* 90.

86. Halbertal, "On Believers and Belief," 32–36.

87. As the Talmud puts it: "An Israelite remains an Israelite even if he sins" (BT Sanhedrin 44a). Kellner, in *Dogma in Medieval Jewish Thought*, has shown that efforts to construct a definitive Jewish theology were quite restricted. Boyarin

has recently offered a fascinating account of how rabbinic Judaism came to reject the category of theological heresy by rejecting the very idea of religion as conceived by fourth-century Christians in terms of a system of propositional beliefs (*Border Lines*, chap. 8). Although Boyarin's construction of rabbinic heresiology is compelling, I am not convinced that the Christian account of religion as a belief system is a fourth-century invention. It does not adequately account for the noncognitive and nonpropositional dimensions of premodern Christian faith (see note 16 to this chapter). For strong indications and interesting philosophical explanations that accord with this view, see William Alston, "Christian Experience and Christian Belief," and Derrida, "Faith and Knowledge," in *Acts of Religion*.

88. Shmuel Trigano, "Levinas and the Project of Jewish Philosophy," 304.

CHAPTER 6

1. In the end, I do not deny Samuel Moyn's perspicacious analysis of the philosophical and Protestant sources of Levinas's philosophy but have supplemented them with an analysis of the Judaic sources that form the other arc of the hermeneutical circle of his work. To the extent that Levinas's phenomenology is hermeneutical the Judaic cannot be excised from an analysis of its origins. My concern is that Moyn makes the very assumption he rightly insists the historian should not make, namely, determining "the proper line between new interpretation and subversive demolition" of Judaism (*Origins of the Other*, 18).

2. Jeffrey Kosky, *Levinas and the Philosophy of Religion*, 161 (my emphasis).

3. For an analysis of this Mishnah, see Moshe Halbertal, *Concealment and Revelation*, 8–12; for a discussion of the voluminous rabbinic exegesis that flourished despite or because of the Mishnah's prohibition, see Philip S. Alexander, "Preemptive Exegesis: Genesis Rabbah's Reading of the Story of Creation."

4. On this see Leo Strauss, "The Literary Character of the *Guide for the Perplexed* [1941]," in his *Persecution and the Arts of Writing*, and critiques of Strauss from different angles by Yair Lorberbaum, "On Contradictions, Rationality, Dialectics, and Esotericism in Maimonides's *Guide of the Perplexed*," and Halbertal, *Concealment and Revelation*, 49–68.

5. This is not to say that Maimonides wrote the *Guide* for Jews and non-Jews; he didn't. The *Guide* is explicitly addressed to Jewish readers perplexed by the apparent contradictions between scripture and philosophy. Nevertheless, in transgressing the prohibition on disseminating the secrets of creation and of the Chariot, Maimonides makes them available to anyone, a point that Gil Anidjar has emphasized in his study, "*Our Place in al-Andalus*," 10–56.

6. BT Berakhot 54a and 63a, cited by Maimonides in the introduction to the *Guide*, 16.

7. Daniel Boyarin, *A Radical Jew*, 15.

8. Walter Benjamin, *The Origin of German Tragic Drama*, trans. John Osborne (London: NLB, 1977), p. 178, cited by Eric Santner, *On Creaturely Life*, 19. See Santner's subtle discussion, 16–21.

9. On this see Levinas, "Being Jewish," and Annabel Herzog's insightful essay, "Benny Levy Versus Emmanuel Levinas on 'Being Jewish.'"

10. *Sifra Behukotai* 2:7; BT Sanhedrin 27a. Later traditions understood the first-person plural form of confessional and atonement liturgies, as used especially on Yom Kippur, as deriving from this ethico-juridical imbrication of one for the other (*Sefer Hasidism* 421; although the earlier reason is also retained, namely, that the sinner not be shamed by confessing in public).

11. For an important particularistic defense of Jewish corporeal election, see Michael Wyschogrod, *The Body of Faith*.

12. Boyarin, in his discussion of Paul's allegoresis of Jewish identity, argues against the sort of poststructuralist allegorization of being Jewish that I discern in Levinas's account of the ethical creature and that he correctly sees at work in essays by Jean-Luc Nancy, Jean-François Lyotard, and Maurice Blanchot. Boyarin is well aware that rejecting allegory amounts to embracing authenticity, a literal and even essentialist notion of identity, and yet he rejects the allegorization of "the true Jew" in these contemporary writers. His concern is that such allegorization abstracts from and thereby denies the value and significance of the Jewishness of real concrete and historical Jews. Boyarin's claim is that these poststructuralist authors, and I suppose Levinas, too, in my reading, philosophically exclude the body of the Jew from European discourse in a way that has a troubling resemblance to the political exclusion of concrete Jews in the Christian allegorization of "the true Israel" and to the extension of this exclusion of Jewish difference in Enlightenment political discourse. Boyarin therefore rejects the allegorization of Jewishness and is left to defend a nonallegorical account of being Jewish as it is embodied in the flesh and material practices of actual Jews. In the wake of the failure of Christian and philosophical enlightenments to allegorize the Jews without excluding or even exterminating their bodies it becomes a matter of deploying "essentialism as resistance," that is, of affirming the essential difference, the nonallegorical remainder of Jewishness (and other corporeal differences), in order to contest the violence perpetrated on such bodies in the name of a spiritual, conceptual, or even metaphysical identity, in short, to contest the violence of allegory. "For subaltern groups," he writes, "essentialism is resistance, the insistence on the 'right' of the group to actually exist" (*A Radical Jew*, 241, and see his stimulating discussion in chapter 10 of that book generally). Although I do not agree with Boyarin's exegesis of Paul's "essentially dualist anthropology" (61), the first and last chapters of that book raise fundamental issues regarding the political implications of what Boyarin calls the "direct connection between anthropology and hermeneutics" (13) and what I have been discussing in terms of the relationship between allegory and

authenticity. These issues have taken an interesting turn in light of Alain Badiou's explicit affirmation of Paul's indifference to identity in his *Saint Paul*. (Badiou's avowal of Paul's anti-identitarianism and Boyarin's objections, as well as other relevant perspectives, are brought together in John D. Caputo and Linda Martin Alcoff, eds., *St Paul Among the Philosophers*). I do not accept Boyarin's recourse to essentialism or Badiou's recourse to universalism but favor an anarchical expropriation of the nonuniversality of Judaism for anyone susceptible to responding to such an appeal. Badiou subtracts too much of Paul's narrative and hermeneutical context, whereas Boyarin holds too firmly to it.

13. For example, *Entre Nous*, 110, and *God, Death, and Time*, 199.

14. The injunction to love the enemy is certainly one of the defining features of early Christian ethics. This does not mean, however, that it was incompatible with earlier biblical or contemporaneous Pharisaic ethics (e.g., Exod. 23:4–5; my thanks to Noam Zion for reminding me of this). In my view it is more accurate to view the Christian appropriation and the rabbinic disavowal of the injunction to love one's enemies as a product of "the partitioning of Judeo-Christianity," a partitioning that is today less stable than it has been since the congealment of Christian and Jewish identity in late antiquity. On the rabbinic rejection of the injunction to love the enemy, see Ernst Simon, "The Neighbor (*Re'a*) Whom We Shall Love," whose self-critical zeal did not take into account the more subtle developmental issues. A quite different and valuable perspective is provided by Marc Hirshman, "Love Thy Companion as Thyself." For an exegetical reconstruction of how the Rabbis came to insist that "love the neighbor" applies only to someone who is one's compatriot in the Law, see Herbert W. Basser, *Studies in Exegesis*. On the partitioning of Judeo-Christianity, see Boyarin, *Border Lines*, and Adam H. Becker and Annette Yoshiko Reed, eds., *The Ways That Never Parted*.

15. Victor Paul Furnish, *The Love Command in the New Testament*, 81, and see the note ad loc. for references to Luther. Furnish also cites the passage from BT Sotah 14a. Other midrashim could also be adduced, for example, Midrash Tannaim 15.9: "My children, when you gave food to the poor I counted it as though you had given it to Me." See also Furnish's remark on Karl Barth's view that Paul "thought that Christ himself was met in the needy neighbor" (p. 104).

16. "A Man-God?" in *Entre Nous*, 53–54. Cf. "Being Jewish," 208.

17. Slavoj Žižek, "A Plea for Ethical Violence," 149; Žižek also cites I John 4:12 on p. 141. I return later to Žižek's reading of Levinas.

18. "Judaism and Kenosis," in *In the Time of the Nations*, 114; see also *Alterity and Transcendence*, 182, in which Ps. 91:15—"I am with him in distress"—is interpreted in terms of kenosis, and similar remarks in Jill Robbins, ed., *Is It Righteous to Be?* 282. For relevant analysis of this theme in Judaism, see the independent essays by Robert Gibbs and Elliot R. Wolfson in the book they edited, *Suffering Religion*.

19. Midrash Tannaim to Deuteronomy 21:23, cited and translated by Alon

Goshen-Gottstein, "The Body as Image of God," 176. For a fascinating analysis of rabbinic legal exegeses of biblical death penalties that sheds further light on the rabbinic notion of the bodily image of God, see Halbertal, *Interpretative Revolutions in the Making*, chap. 7. Writing about one hundred years before Rabbi Meir, Paul cites the same verse from Deuteronomy to describe Christ on the cross: "Christ redeemed us from the curse of the law, having become a curse for us—for it is written [Deut. 21:23], 'Cursed be every one who hangs on a tree'" (Gal. 3:13). It is interesting that Paul makes no mention of the iconic likeness between Jesus, the accursed one on the wood, and God, but uses the verse to make a quite different point, "that in Christ Jesus the blessing of Abraham might come upon the Gentiles, that we might receive the promise of the Spirit through faith" (3:14).

20. A more tentative but more traditional view of Jewish incarnational theology is proposed by Michael Wyschogrod, "A Jewish Perspective on Incarnation," esp. 207–8. A much less tentative view is proposed by Wolfson, who has argued in several recent publications for a kabbalistic account of the Torah as incarnation of God. See, for example, his "The Body in the Text." Either way, we are moving in Levinas's direction, especially when one takes into account his view of scripture (iconic or incarnational?), which we cannot do here.

21. This point is made by Goshen-Gottstein, "Judaisms and Incarnational Theologies," who also provides an insightful survey of major developments in what is still very much an emerging and controversial revisioning of rabbinic anthropology. For a comprehensive treatment of rabbinic accounts of the image as icon of God, see Lorberbaum, *Image of God*. Another Levinasian reading of this midrash, which I cannot take up here, would view the two twins in the midrash as Judaism and Christianity in order to explore what Levinas calls "the Passion of Israel at Auschwitz" (*Alterity and Transcendence*, 181). The Christian cross, symbol of the passion, is double crossed by the Jewish *Muselmann*, a figure whose allegorical name itself demands a complicated response.

22. See also OB, 191n4/AE, 87n4; OB, 109/AE, 140; OB, 111/AE, 142; OB, 137/AE, 174–75; OB, 161/AE, 206.

23. "Secularism and the Thought of Israel," in *Unforeseen History*, 117.

24. In Gianni Vattimo's words, "Ontological hermeneutics is nothing but the theory of Christian modernity" (*After Christianity*, 65). Or again: "The only great paradox and scandal of Christian revelation is the incarnation of God, the kenosis—that is, the removal of all the transcendent, incomprehensible, mysterious and even bizarre features that seem to move so many theorists of the leap of faith. In the name of such a transcendence, it is easy to smuggle in a defence of the authoritarianism of the Church and of its many dogmatic and moral positions, bound up as they are with the absolutization of doctrines and contingent historical events, which have been more or less overcome" (*Belief*, 55). Vattimo reads Levinas in exactly the opposite way that I do; he laments the "predominance

of Judaic religiosity in the return of religion into contemporary thought (let me make clear that this observation has no anti-semitic intention whatsoever). It is a fact that the total otherness of God with respect to the world appears to be affirmed at the expense of any recognition of novelty in the Christian event. For example, for Emmanuel Levinas—and for Derrida, to a certain extent . . . particular [contextual] traits are given little consideration, compared to the purely 'vertical' relation to the Eternal, to the Other" (*Belief*, 85; cf. *After Christianity*, 37, 43). But this postmodern supersessionism is untenable given all we know of the saturation of the "purely vertical" in Judaic spirituality by interpretation. If hermeneutics is at odds with a "purely 'vertical' relation to the Eternal," then Judaism is a completely nonvertical religion. Is this not the plain meaning of the celebrated rabbinic affirmation that the Torah "is not in Heaven" (BT Baba Metzia 59b)—precisely a transfer of truth from the verticality of the Father to the historical life of the children and therefore a denial of metaphysical theology and a weakening of the brute givenness of law and revelation? In response to the rabbinic appropriation of Heaven we are told that God "laughed and said: My children have defeated me, My children have defeated Me."

25. On prophecy in the medieval period see Abraham Joshua Heschel, *Prophetic Inspiration After the Prophets*, and Howard Kreisel, *Prophecy: The History of an Idea in Medieval Jewish Philosophy*. Eliezer Schweid has shown how modern Jewish thinkers continue to employ the trope of prophecy to describe their activities and objectivities; see his "'Prophetic Mysticism' in the Twentieth Century," although it does not mention Levinas.

26. Levinas, "Secularization and Hunger."

27. For an illuminating discussion of Derrida's confession that he "rightly pass[es] as an atheist," see Kevin Hart, "Jacques Derrida: The God Effect."

28. This point has been developed by Jean-Luc Marion into his concept of "L'interloqué."

29. The most trenchant criticism was articulated by Gillian Rose and Alain Badiou, but it was voiced by numerous other critics also.

30. Critchley, "Five Problems in Levinas's View of Politics," 97.

31. *Being and Time*, 436/SZ, 384.

32. As is well known, Heidegger rejected both individualism and humanism, since both treat Dasein as an ahistorical object with essential universal properties and thereby obscure its fundamental worldliness and temporality. His own interpretation of *Being and Time* states this plainly: "The highest determinations of the essence of the human being in humanism still do not realize the proper dignity of the human being. To that extent the thinking in *Being and Time* is against humanism" ("Letter on Humanism" [1946], in *Pathmarks*, 251). Just as Heidegger concluded that "humanism is opposed because it does not set the *humanitas* of the human being high enough," Levinas too thinks

that "humanism has to be denounced only because it is not sufficiently human" (OB, 128/AE, 164).

33. Marlène Zarader, *The Unthought Debt*, 144. Zarader concentrates on the proximity between later Levinas and *later* Heidegger, a view that might seem to contradict my claim for a proximity between the ontological problem of cohistoricizing as it emerges in *Being and Time* and the problem of the relation between ethics and politics. But later Heidegger presumes all that *Being and Time* made explicit and so the distance between early and late Heidegger makes no difference to the way I perceive the problem.

34. James Phillips, *Heidegger's Volk*, 26.

35. Phillips, *Heidegger's Volk*, 49.

36. This is the point of Derrida's stunning reading of *Otherwise than Being*, "At This Very Moment in This Work Here I Am." See also Paul Ricoeur's convergent, although more tentative, remarks in the final pages of *Oneself as Another*.

37. Levinas comes closest to such an ontological account of the people in his provocative notion of "the Passion of Israel." For a useful start at analyzing this complex and important notion in Levinas's work, see Howard Caygill, *Levinas and the Political*, 162–66.

38. Gilles Deleuze and Felix Guattari, *What Is Philosophy?* 108, cited by Phillips, *Heidegger's Volk*, 46.

39. "Politics After!" in *Beyond the Verse*, 190.

40. Caygill, *Levinas and the Political*, 8. I have been sent back to Levinas's texts on Zionism after reading Caygill's perspicacious study and have benefited considerably from his analysis.

41. Caygill, *Levinas and the Political*, 102. The notion of political fraternity implicates ethics in the problem of political ontology and in the gender politics of ethics, as others have shown. See Critchley, "Five Problems," and Chanter, *Feminist Interpretations of Emmanuel Levinas*.

42. Žižek, "A Plea for Ethical Violence," 149. Žižek takes himself to be providing an alternative to Levinas here, but I take him to be describing a Levinasian view of the political, as did Derrida in "A Word of Welcome," in *Adieu to Emmanuel Levinas*, esp. 99.

43. Caygill, *Levinas and the Political*, 152

44. *Beyond the Verse*, 187.

45. *Beyond the Verse*, 187.

46. Robert Bernasconi has written a series of articles that greatly illuminate Levinas's Eurocentricism without denying "the resources his thought offers for breaking through the dominant schema of Western dogmatism" ("Who Is My Neighbour?" 26; see also his "One-Way Traffic").

47. Levinas, "The State of Israel and the Religion of Israel" [1951], in *Difficult Freedom*, 218.

48. *Difficult Freedom*, 218.

49. Levinas, "The State of Caesar and the State of David" [1971], in *Beyond the Verse*, 187.

50. *Beyond the Verse*, 177, 179, 180, respectively. As Derrida puts it, "It is necessary to deduce a politics and a law from ethics. This deduction is necessary in order to determine the 'better' or the 'less bad,' with all the requisite quotation marks: democracy is 'better' than tyranny. Even in its 'hypocritical' nature, 'political civilisation' remains 'better' than barbarism" (*Adieu to Emmanuel Levinas*, 115). One should emphasize, however, that the cohistoricizing of ethics "always already" has political implications. It is therefore not a matter of deducing the particular political form of modern liberal states from ethics (hence Derrida's "*a* politics and *a* law") but of establishing a juridico-political fraternity that serves the other in the "less bad" way.

51. Genesis Rabbah 9:13, cited in *Beyond the Verse*, 183, translation modified. See also *Beyond the Verse*, 66.

52. Critchley, "Five Problems," 97, 95, respectively.

53. *Beyond the Verse*, xvii.

54. Gilles Deleuze and Félix Guattari, *What Is Philosophy?* 109.

55. *Beyond the Verse*, 187.

56. *Beyond the Verse*, 179.

57. On this see Caygill, "Levinas's Silence." One could supply historical and biographical reasons for Levinas's ambivalence (the trauma of the Holocaust as a reflex for nationalism, the difference in conceiving of Zionism before 1967 and after, and so on). But these are no longer relevant to a contemporary investigation into Levinas's political theology, that is, into the implications of his secularized philosophy of Judaism ("ethics") for contemporary political analysis.

58. *Beyond the Verse*, 184.

59. Caygill, *Levinas and the Political*, 174.

60. Levinas, "Ethics and Politics," in *Levinas Reader*, 297.

61. *Difficult Freedom*, 217.

62. *Beyond the Verse*, xvii.

63. Such claims are insensitive to the details of the parable itself. For example, the beaten man on the side of the road is not dead but "half-dead" (Luke 10:30), and therefore would not render the priest impure. Moreover, the priest and the Levite are "going down from Jerusalem" (10:31), and thus away from the very temple they are said to venerate more than the half-dead man on the road. On this, see Michel Gourgues, "The Priest, the Levite, and the Samaritan Revisited," and Amy-Jill Levine, *The Misunderstood Jew*, 144–49.

64. On the origins of the conflict between Judeans and Samaritans, see II Kings 17; Josephus, *Antiquities* 9.277–91; and Emil Schürer, *The History of the Jewish People in the Age of Jesus Christ, Volume II*, 19–20. On the mutual antipathy

between Judeans and Samaritans, see Luke 9:52–53, John 4:9, and Josephus, *Antiquities* 18.2.6–7, 20.6.1–3, and *War* 2.232–37. For early rabbinic views that regard Samaritans as Israelites by law, see BT Kiddushim 75b, JT Ketuboth 3.1, 27a, and minor tractate *Kutim* 1.1. These and other rabbinic views are adduced by Reinhard Neudecker, "'And you shall love your neighbour as yourself—I am the Lord,' Lev. 19:18 in Jewish Interpretation," although his discussion does not mention the parable of the Good Samaritan. For evidence that Jews in the time of Jesus and even of Luke did not regard the Samaritans as Gentiles, see Lawrence Schiffman, "The Samaritans in Tannaitic Halakhah." Some of the material I present here is given more detailed treatment in Michael Fagenblat, "'Love your neighbor' in Jewish and Christian Ethics."

65. Victor Paul Furnish, *The Love Command in the New Testament*, 41. Another common observation that supports the view that the story of the Good Samaritan does not redefine the category of the neighbor refers to the decisive shift at the end of the story in which Jesus says to the lawyer, "'Which of these three seem to you to have become a neighbor (*plesion gegonenai*) to the man who fell among the robbers?' [The lawyer] said, 'The one who showed (*poeisas*) him mercy.' Jesus said to him, 'Go and do likewise'" (Luke 10:36–37). Here the Samaritan is not even the neighbor to be loved but a person who can teach the lawyer how a proper neighbor loves. This does not contradict my main interpretation. Those who emphasize the ill fit between the lawyer's question and Jesus' answer often suggest that Jesus' point is to show the lawyer that he was asking the wrong question: "Jesus then corrects the question by urging the questioner to consider his *own* responsibility; his concern should not be for who *the neighbor* is but for who *he himself* is in relation to the neighbor" (Furnish, 40). The story of the Good Samaritan *is* a critique of a narrowly construed notion of political fraternity, of the reduction of political fraternity to political ontology, but it does not attempt to dismantle the very idea of political fraternity. The Samaritan therefore plays two roles: he provides a model for how to love and he is emblematic of the repulsive dimension of the love command that obliges one to the despised neighbor.

66. Furnish, *The Love Command in the New Testament*, 41. Pope Benedict offers a better reading in his first encyclical, *Deus Caritas Est*, which calls for a love that "extends beyond the frontiers of the Church. The parable of the Good Samaritan remains as a standard which imposes universal love towards the needy whom we encounter 'by chance' (cf. Luke 10:31), whoever they may be." *Deus Caritas Est*, para. 25b. The Pope recognizes that the Church indeed has frontiers even as the commandment to love extends beyond them.

67. *God, Death, and Time*, 223.

68. Žižek, "A Plea for Ethical Violence," 140.

69. This has been well emphasized by Kenneth Reinhard in "The Ethics of the Neighbor: Universalism, Particularism, Exceptionalism."

70. As Josephus already remarked, the function of Jewish law includes "mutual communion" among Jews as well as "a general love of mankind" (*Apion* 2.15).

71. Žižek, "A Plea for Ethical Violence," 162.

72. *God, Death, and Time*, 174, 177, respectively.

73. Žižek, "A Plea for Ethical Violence," 162–63.

74. Santner, *On Creaturely Life*, 133. Since my position shares an evident proximity to Santner's, I should note that I do not accept Badiou's analysis, as Santner seems to (e.g., 127–29), according to which Law is essentially bound up with sin and death. The law is always both dead and undead and the task of the creature is to responsively undeaden the law in collectivities that are always already bound by it.

Bibliography

For the Hebrew Bible, I have relied on the *JPS Hebrew-English TANAKH* (Philadelphia: Jewish Publication Society of America, 1999); for the New Testament, *The Holy Bible: New Revised Standard Version with Apocrypha*, ed. Bruce M. Metzger (New York: Oxford University Press, 1991).

Ajzenstat, Oona. *Driven Back to the Text: The Premodern Sources of Levinas' Postmodernism.* Pittsburgh: Duquesne University Press, 2001.

———. "Levinas Versus Levinas: Hebrew, Greek, and Linguistic Justice." *Philosophy and Rhetoric* 38:2 (2005): 145–58.

Albertini, Franscesca. "Emmanuel Levinas' Theological-Political Interpretation of Moses Maimonides." In *Moses Maimonides (1138–1204): His Religious, Scientific, and Philosophical "Wirkungsgeschichte" in Different Cultural Contexts*, eds. Görge K. Hasselhoff and Otfried Fraisse, 573–85. Würzburg: Ergon Verlag, 2004.

Alexander, Philip S. "Pre-emptive Exegesis: Genesis Rabbah's Reading of the Story of Creation." *Journal of Jewish Studies* 43:2 (1992): 230–45.

Alston, William. "Christian Experience and Christian Belief." In *Faith and Rationality: Reason and Belief in God*, eds. Alvin Plantinga and Nicholas Wolterstorff, 103–34. Notre Dame, IN: University of Notre Dame Press, 1984.

Alter, Robert. *The Five Books of Moses: A Translation with Commentary.* New York: W. W. Norton, 2004.

Altmann, Alexander. *Moses Mendelssohn: A Biographical Study.* London: Routledge and Kegan Paul, 1973.

Amir, Yehoyada. "From Negation to Rehabilitation—Myth in Modern Jewish Thought." In *Myths in Judaism: History, Thought, Literature*, eds. Ithamar Gruenwald and Moshe Idel, 237–74. Jerusalem: Zalman Shazar Centre for Jewish History, 2004.

Anidjar, Gil. "*Our Place in al-Andalus*": *Kabbalah, Philosophy, Literature in Arab Jewish Letters.* Stanford, CA: Stanford University Press, 2002.

Arendt, Hannah. *The Human Condition.* 2nd ed. Chicago: University of Chicago Press, 1958.

Asad, Talal. *Genealogies of Religion: Discipline and Reasons of Power in Christianity and Islam.* Baltimore: Johns Hopkins University Press, 1993.

Atterton, Peter, Matthew Calarco, and Maurice Friedman, eds. *Levinas and Buber: Dialogue and Difference.* Pittsburgh: Duquesne University Press, 2004.

Augustine. *On Christian Doctrine.* Trans. Durant Waite Robertson. N.p.: Liberal Arts Press, 1958.

Bacry, Henri. *Emmanuel Levinas, philosophie et judaïsme.* Paris: COLLECTIF Press Editions, 2002.

Badiou, Alain. *Ethics: An Essay on the Understanding of Evil.* Trans. Peter Hallward. London: Verso, 2002.

———. *Polemics.* Trans. Steve Corcoran. London: Verso, 2006.

———. *Saint Paul: The Foundations of Universalism.* Trans. Ray Brassier. Stanford, CA: Stanford University Press, 2003.

Barth, Karl. *Church Dogmatics: Vol. III. The Doctrine of Creation. Part One.* Trans. J. W. Edwards, O. Sussey, and H. Knight. Edinburgh: T and T Clark, 1958.

Basser, Herbert W. *Studies in Exegesis: Christian Critiques of Jewish Law and Rabbinic Responses, 70–300 C.E.* Boston: Brill, 2000.

Batnitzky, Leora F. "Encountering the Modern Subject in Levinas." *Yale French Studies* 104 (2003): 6–21.

———. *Leo Strauss and Emmanuel Levinas: Philosophy and the Politics of Revelation.* New York: Cambridge University Press, 2006.

———. "On Reaffirming a Distinction Between Athens and Jerusalem." *Hebraic Political Studies* 2:2 (2007): 211–31.

Becker, Adam H., and Annette Yoshiko Reed, eds. *The Ways That Never Parted: Jews and Christians in Late Antiquity and the Early Middle Ages.* Tubingen: Mohr Siebeck, 2003.

Benedict XVI, Pope. *Deus Caritas Est.* At http://www.vatican.va/holy_father/benedict_xvi/encyclicals/documents/hf_ben-xvi_enc_20051225_deus-caritas-est_en.html.

Benor, Ehud Z. "Meaning and Reference in Maimonides' Negative Theology." *Harvard Theological Review* 88:3 (1995): 339–60.

Benz, Ernst W. "*Imago Dei*: Man as the Image of God." Trans. Alan F. Keele. *FARMS Review* 17:1 (2005). At http://farms.byu.edu/publications/review/?vol=17&num=1.

Bernasconi, Robert. "Heidegger's Destruction of Phronesis." *Southern Journal of Philosophy* 28 Supp. (1989): 127–47.

———. "One-Way Traffic: The Ontology of Decolonization and Its Ethics." In *Ontology and Alterity in Merleau-Ponty*, eds. G. Johnson and M. Smith, 67–80. Evanston, IL: Northwestern University Press, 1990.

———. "Rereading *Totality and Infinity*." In *The Question of the Other*, eds.

Arleen B. Dallery and Charles E. Scott, 23–34. Albany: State University of New York Press, 1989.

———. "Who Is My Neighbour? Who Is the Other? Questioning 'The Generosity of Western Thought.'" In *Ethics and Responsibility in the Phenomenological Tradition*, 1–31. Pittsburgh: Simon Silverman Phenomenology Center, Duquesne University, 1992.

Bernasconi, Robert, and David Wood, eds. *The Provocation of Levinas: Rethinking the Other*. London: Routledge, 1988.

Bernstein, Richard. *Radical Evil: A Philosophical Interrogation*. Cambridge: Polity, 2002.

Bird, Michael F. "The New Perspective on Paul: A Bibliographical Essay." At http://www.thepaulpage.com/Bibliography.html.

Blackburn, Simon. *Truth: A Guide for the Perplexed*. London: Allen Lane, 2005.

Blanchot, Maurice. *The Infinite Conversation*. Trans. Susan Hanson. Minneapolis: University of Minnesota Press, 1993.

———. *The Writing of the Disaster*. Trans. Ann Smock. Lincoln: University of Nebraska Press, 1986.

Blau, Yitzhak. "Flexibility with a Firm Foundation: On Maintaining Jewish Dogma." *Torah u-Madda Journal* 12 (2004): 179–91.

Blond, Phillip. "Emmanuel Levinas: God and Phenomenology." In *Post-Secular Philosophy: Between Philosophy and Theology*, ed. Phllip Blond, 103–20. London: Routledge, 1998.

Bolton, David, and Emmanuel Nathan. "New Understandings of Paul and His Jewish Heritage." At http://escholarship.bc.edu/cgi/viewcontent.cgi?article=1155&context=scjr.

Boyarin, Daniel. *Border Lines: The Partition of Judaeo-Christianity*. Philadelphia: University of Pennsylvania Press, 2004.

———. "By Way of Apology: Dawson, Edwards, Origen." *Studia Philonica Annual: Studies in Hellenistic Judaism* XIV (2004): 188–217.

———. *Intertextuality and the Reading of Midrash*. Bloomington: Indiana University Press, 1990.

———. "Midrash and the 'Magic Language.'" In *Derrida and Religion: Other Testaments*, eds. Yvonne Sherwood and Kevin Hart, 131–40. New York: Routledge, 2005.

———. *A Radical Jew: Paul and the Politics of Identity*. Berkeley: University of California Press, 1994.

Brandom, Robert B. *Articulating Reasons: An Introduction to Inferentialism*. Cambridge, MA: Harvard University Press, 2000.

Bright, John. *Jeremiah: Introduction, Translation, and Notes*. Garden City, NY: Doubleday, 1965.

Bruns, Gerald L. *Hermeneutics Ancient and Modern*. New Haven, CT: Yale University Press, 1992.

Buber, Martin. *On the Bible: Eighteen Studies*. Syracuse, NY: Syracuse University Press, 2000.

———. *Two Types of Faith*. New York: HarperCollins, 1983.

Bujis, Joseph A. "The Negative Theology of Maimonides and Aquinas." *Review of Metaphysics* 41 (June 1988): 723–38.

Buren, John van. *The Young Heidegger: Rumor of the Hidden King*. Bloomington: Indiana University Press, 1994.

Burrell, David. *Knowing the Unknowable God: Ibn-Sina, Maimonides, Aquinas*. Notre Dame, IN: University of Notre Dame Press, 1992.

Butler, Judith. "Ethical Ambivalence." In *The Turn to Ethics*, eds. Marjorie Garber, Beatrice Hanssen, and Rebecca L. Walkowitz, 15–28. New York: Routledge, 2000.

Caputo, John D. *Heidegger and Aquinas: An Essay on Overcoming Metaphysics*. New York: Fordham University Press, 1982.

———. *On Religion*. London: Routledge, 2001.

———. "People of God, People of Being: The Theological Presuppositions of Heidegger's Path of Thought." In *Appropriating Heidegger*, eds. James E. Falconer and Mark A. Wrathall, 85–100. Cambridge, UK: Cambridge University Press, 2000.

———. *The Weakness of God: A Theology of the Event*. Bloomington: Indiana University Press, 2006.

Caputo, John D., and Michael J. Scanlon, eds. *God, the Gift, and Postmodernism*. Indianapolis: Indiana University Press, 1999.

Caputo, John D., and Linda Martin Alcoff, eds. *St. Paul Among the Philosophers*. Indianapolis: Indiana University Press, 2009.

Cavell, Stanley. *Must We Mean What We Say?: A Book of Essays*. New York: Cambridge University Press, 1976.

———. *Philosophy the Day After Tomorrow*. Cambridge, MA: The Belknap Press of Harvard University Press, 2005.

Caygill, Howard. *Levinas and the Political*. London: Routlege, 2002.

———. "Levinas' Silence." In *Levinas, Law, Politics*, ed. Marinos Diamantides, 83–92. London: Routledge, 2007.

Celan, Paul. "The Meridian." Trans. Jerry Glen. *Chicago Review* 29:3 (1978): 29–40.

Chalier, Catherine. *La trace de l'infini: Emmanuel Levinas et la source hébraïque*. Paris: Cerf, 2002.

———. *Lévinas: L'utopie de l'humain*. Paris: Albin Michel, 1993.

———. "The Philosophy of Emmanuel Levinas and the Hebraic Tradition." In *Ethics as First Philosophy: The Significance of Emmanuel Levinas for Philosophy,*

Religion and Literature, ed. Adriaan T. Peperzak, 3–12. New York: Routledge, 1995.

———. *What Ought I to Do?: Morality in Kant and Levinas.* Trans. Jane Marie Todd. Ithaca, NY: Cornell University Press, 2002.

Chanter, Tina, ed. *Feminist Interpretations of Emmanuel Levinas.* University Park, PA: Penn State University Press, 2001.

Ciocan, Cristian, and George Hansel. *Levinas Concordance.* Dordrecht: Springer, 2005.

Clifford, Richard J. "The Hebrew Scriptures and the Theology of Creation." *Theological Studies* 46 (1985): 507–23.

Clifford, W. K. *The Ethics of Belief and Other Essays.* Amherst, NY: Prometheus Books, 1999.

Coady, C. A. J. *Testimony: A Philosophical Study.* Oxford, UK: Oxford University Press, 1992.

Cohen, Jonathan. "Educating for Spiritual Maturity: Hartman's Interpretation of Judaism as a 'Religion for Adults.'" In *Judaism and Modernity: The Religious Philosophy of David Hartman,* ed. Jonathan W. Malino, 111–32. Jerusalem: Shalom Hartman Institute, 2001.

Cohen, Richard A. *Elevations: The Height of the Good in Rosenzweig and Levinas.* Chicago: University of Chicago Press, 1994.

———, ed. *Face to Face with Levinas.* Albany: State University of New York Press, 1986.

Critchley, Simon. "Five Problems in Levinas's View of Politics." In *Levinas, Law, Politics,* ed. Marinos Diamantides, 93–106. London: Routledge, 2007.

Critchley, Simon, and Robert Bernasconi, eds. *The Cambridge Companion to Levinas.* Cambridge, UK: Cambridge University Press, 2002.

Dales, Richard C. "Maimonides and Boethius of Dacia on the Eternity of the World." *New Scholasticism* 56 (1982): 306–19.

———. *Medieval Discussions of the Eternity of the World.* Leiden: E. J. Brill, 1990.

———. "The Origin of the Doctrine of the Double Truth." *Viator* 15 (1984): 169–79.

Davidson, Donald. "Externalisms." In *Interpreting Davidson,* eds. Peter Kotatko, Peter Pagin, and Gabriel Segal, 1–16. Stanford, CA: CSLI Publications, 2001.

———. *Inquiries into Truth and Interpretation.* Oxford, UK: Clarendon Press, 1984.

———. *Subjective, Intersubjective, Objective: Philosophical Essays, Volume 3.* Oxford, UK: Oxford University Press, 2001.

Davidson, Herbert A. *Alfarabi, Avicenna, and Averroes, on Intellect: Their Cosmologies, Theories of the Active Intellect, and Theories of Human Intellect.* New York: Oxford University Press, 1992.

————. "Maimonides on Metaphysical Knowledge." *Maimonidean Studies* 3 (1992/93): 49–103.

————. "Maimonides' Secret Position on Creation." *Studies in Medieval Jewish History and Literature*, ed. I. Twersky, 16–40. Cambridge, MA: Harvard University Press, 1979.

————. "The Middle Way in Maimonides' Ethics." *Proceedings of the American Academy for Jewish Research* 54 (1987): 31–72.

Davies, Oliver. "Beyond the Language of Being: A Comparative Study of Meister Eckhart and Emmanuel Levinas." *Eckhart Review* 9 (Spring, 2000): 32–40.

Davies, Paul. "A Fine Risk: Reading Blanchot Reading Levinas." In *Re-Reading Levinas*, eds. Robert Bernasconi and Simon Critchley, 201–26. Bloomington: Indiana University Press, 1991.

————. "A Linear Narrative? Blanchot with Heidegger in the Work of Levinas." In *Philosophers' Poets*, ed. David Wood, 37–69. London: Routledge, 1990.

————. "On Resorting to an Ethical Language." In *Ethics as First Philosophy: The Significance of Emmanuel Levinas for Philosophy, Literature and Religion*, ed. Adriaan T. Peperzak, 95–104. New York: Routledge, 1995.

de Boer, Theodore. *The Rationality of Transcendence: Studies in the Philosophy of Emmanuel Levinas.* Amsterdam: J. C. Geiben, 1997.

de Leon, Moses. *Sefer Shekel ha-Kodesh.* Ed. Charles Mopsik. Los Angeles: Cherub Press, 1996.

Deleuze, Gilles, and Félix Guattari. *What Is Philosophy?* Trans. Hugh Tomlinson and Graham Burchell. London: Verso, 1994.

Derrida, Jacques. *Acts of Religion.* Ed. Gil Anidjar. New York: Routledge, 2002.

————. *Adieu to Emmanuel Levinas.* Trans. Pascale-Anne Brault and Michael Naas. Stanford, CA: Stanford University Press, 1999.

————. "At This Very Moment in This Work Here I Am." Trans. Ruben Berezdivin. In *Re-Reading Levinas*, eds. Robert Bernasconi and Simon Critchley, 11–50. Bloomington: Indiana University Press, 1991.

————. *Edmund Husserl's Origin of Geometry, an Introduction.* Lincoln: University of Nebraska Press, 1990.

————. *The Gift of Death.* Trans. David Wills. Chicago: The University of Chicago Press, 1995.

————. *On the Name.* Ed. Thomas Dutoit. Trans. David Wood, John P. Leavey Jr., and Ian McLeod. Stanford, CA: Stanford University Press, 1995.

————. *Speech and Phenomena and Other Essays on Husserl's Theory of Signs.* Evanston, IL: Northwestern University Press, 1973.

————. *Writing and Difference.* Trans. Alan Bass. Chicago: University of Chicago Press, 1978.

De Vries, Hent. *Minimal Theologies: Critiques of Secular Reason in Adorno and Levinas*. Trans. Geoffrey Hale. Baltimore: Johns Hopkins University Press, 2005.

Dews, Peter. "Disenchantment and the Persistence of Evil: Habermas, Jonas, Badiou." In *Modernity and the Problem of Evil*, ed. Alan D. Schrift, 51–65. Bloomington: Indiana University Press, 2005.

Diamond, James Arthur. *Maimonides and the Hermeneutics of Concealment*. New York: State University of New York Press, 2002.

Dostal, Robert J. "The Problem of '*Indifferenz*' in *Sein und Zeit*." *Philosophy and Phenomenological Research* 43:1 (1982): 43–58.

Dreyfus, Hubert L. *Being-in-the-World: A Commentary on Heidegger's "Being and Time," Division 1*. Cambridge, MA: MIT Press, 1991.

———. *Heidegger, Authenticity, and Modernity: Essays in Honor of Hubert L. Dreyfus, Volume 1*. Eds. Mark Wrathall and Jeff Malpas. Cambridge, MA: MIT Press, 2000.

Dunn, James D. G. *The New Perspective on Paul*. Rev. ed. Grand Rapids, MI: William B. Eerdmans, 2005.

Eco, Umberto, and Cardinal Martini. *Belief or Unbelief?: A Confrontation*. New York: Arcade, 2000.

Edwards, Mark J. *Origen Against Plato*. London: Ashgate, 2002.

Fagenblat, Michael. "Back to the Other Levinas: Reflections Prompted by Alain P. Toumayan's *Encountering the Other*." *Colloquy* 10 (2005): 298–313.

———. "Ethics and Halakhah in Levinas." *Shofar: An Interdisciplinary Journal of Jewish Studies* (2008): 97–119.

———. "*Il y a* du quotidian: Levinas and Heidegger on the Self." *Philosophy and Social Criticism* 28:5 (2002): 578–604.

———. "Lacking All Interest: Levinas, Leibowitz and the Pure Practice of Religion." *Harvard Theological Review* 97:1 (2004): 1–32.

———. "'Love your neighbor' in Jewish and Christian Ethics." In *Jewish Annotated New Testament*, eds. Marc Brettler and Amy-Jill Levine. New York: Oxford University Press, forthcoming.

Fishbane, Michael. *Biblical Myth and Rabbinic Mythmaking*. Oxford, UK: Oxford University Press, 2005.

———. *Biblical Text and Texture: A Literary Reading of Selected Texts*. Oxford, UK: Oneworld, 1998.

———. *The Kiss of God: Spiritual and Mystical Death in Judaism*. Seattle: University of Washington Press, 1994.

Frank, Daniel H. "Humility as a Virtue: A Maimonidean Critique of Aristotle's Ethics." In *Maimonides and His Time*, ed. E. Ormsby, 89–99. Washington, DC: Catholic University of America Press, 1989.

Frankenberry, Nancy K., ed. *Radical Interpretation in Religion.* Cambridge, UK: Cambridge University Press, 2002.

Friedman, R. Z. "Maimonides and Kant on Metaphysics and Piety." *Review of Metaphysics* 45 (1992): 773–801.

Frisch, Andrea. "The Ethics of Testimony: A Genealogical Perspective." *Discourse* 25:1–2 (2003): 35–54.

Furnish, Victor Paul. *The Love Command in the New Testament.* Nashville: Abingdon Press, 1971.

Furrow, Dwight. *Against Theory: Continental and Analytic Challenges in Moral Philosophy.* New York: Routledge, 1995.

Gadamer, Hans-Georg. *Truth and Method.* 2nd rev. ed. Trans. revised by Joel Weinsheimer and Donald G. Marshall. New York: Crossroad, 1989.

Gager, John G. *Reinventing Paul.* New York: Oxford University Press, 2000.

Gaston, Lloyd. *Paul and the Torah.* Vancouver: University of British Columbia Press, 1987.

Gersonides. *The Wars of the Lord.* 3 vols. Trans. Seymour Feldman. Philadelphia: Jewish Publication Society of America, 1984–1999.

Gibbs, Robert. *Correlations in Rosenzweig and Levinas.* Princeton, NJ: Princeton University Press, 1992.

———. "Height and Nearness: Jewish Dimensions of Radical Ethics." In *Ethics as First Philosophy: The Significance of Emmanuel Levinas for Philosophy, Religion and Literature,* ed. Adriaan T. Peperzak, 13–24. New York: Routledge, 1995.

———. *Why Ethics? Signs of Responsibilities.* Princeton, NJ: Princeton University Press, 2000.

Gibbs, Robert, and Elliot R. Wolfson, eds. *Suffering Religion.* London: Routledge, 2002.

Godlove, Terry F., Jr. "Saving Belief: On the New Materialism in Religious Studies." In *Radical Interpretation in Religion,* ed. Nancy K. Frankenberry, 10–24. Cambridge, UK: Cambridge University Press, 2002.

Gordon, Peter Eli. *Rosenzweig and Heidegger: Between Judaism and German Philosophy.* Berkeley: University of California Press, 2003.

Goshen-Gottstein, Alon. "The Body as Image of God in Rabbinic Literature." *Harvard Theological Review* 87:2 (1994): 171–95.

———. "Judaisms and Incarnational Theologies: Mapping Out the Parameters of Dialogue." *Journal of Ecumenical Studies* 39:3–4 (2002): 219–47.

Gourges, Michel. "The Priest, the Levite, and the Samaritan Revisited: A Critical Note on Luke 10:31–35." *Journal of Biblical Literature* 117:4 (1998): 709–13.

Green, Arthur. "Shekhinah, the Virgin Mary, and the Song of Songs: Reflections on a Kabbalistic Symbol in Its Historical Context." *AJS Review* 26:1 (2002): 43–44.

Green, Richard Firth. *A Crisis of Truth: Literature and Law in Ricardian England.* Philadelphia: University of Pennsylvania Press, 1999.

Greenberg, Moshe. *Studies in the Bible and Jewish Thought.* Philadephia: Jewish Publication Society, 1995.

Haar, Michel. "The Enigma of Everydayness." In *Reading Heidegger: Commemorations,* ed. John Sallis, 20–28. Bloomington: Indiana University Press, 1993.

———. "The Obsession of the Other: Ethics as Traumatization." *Philosophy and Social Criticism* 23:6 (1997): 95–107.

Habermas, Jürgen. "Work and Weltanschauung: The Heidegger Controversy from a German Perspective." Trans. John McCumber. *Critical Inquiry* 15:2 (1989): 431–56.

Hahn, Lewis Edwin, ed. *The Philosophy of Donald Davidson.* Chicago: Open Court, 1999.

Halbertal, Moshe. *Between Torah and Wisdom: Rabbi Menachem ha-Meiri and the Maimonidean Halakhists in Provence* (in Hebrew). Jerusalem: Magnes Press, 2000.

———. *Concealment and Revelation: Esotericism in Jewish Thought and Its Philosophical Implications.* Trans. Jackie Feldman. Princeton, NJ: Princeton University Press, 2007.

———. *Interpretative Revolutions in the Making: Values as Interpretative Considerations in Midrashei Halakhah* (in Hebrew). Jerusalem: Magnes Press, 1999.

———. "Maimonides' Book of Commandments: The Architecture of the Halakhah and the Theory of Its Interpretation" (in Hebrew). *Tarbiz* 59 (2000): 457–80.

———. "On Believers and Belief" (in Hebrew). In *On Faith: Studies in the Concept of Faith and Its History in the Jewish Tradition,* eds. Moshe Halbertal, David Kurzweil, and Avi Sagi, 29–36. Jerusalem: Keter, 2005.

Halbertal, Moshe, and Avishai Margalit. *Idolatry.* Trans. Naomi Goldblum. Cambridge, MA: Harvard University Press, 1992.

Handelman, Susan. *Fragments of Redemption: Jewish Thought and Literary Theory in Benjamin, Scholem, and Levinas.* Bloomington: Indiana University Press, 1991.

Hart, Kevin. "Jacques Derrida: The God Effect." In *Post-Secular Philosophy Between Philosophy and Theology,* ed. Phillip Blond, 137–48. London: Routledge, 1998.

———. *Trespass of the Sign: Deconstruction, Theology and Philosophy.* Cambridge, UK: Cambridge University Press, 1989.

Hartman, David. *A Living Covenant: The Innovative Spirit in Traditional Judaism.* Woodstock, VT: Jewish Lights, 1998.

———. *Maimonides: Torah and Philosophical Quest.* Philadelphia: Jewish Publication Society of America, 1976.

Harvey, Warren Zev. "Rabbinic Attitudes Toward Philosophy." In *"Open Thou*

Mine Eyes . . ." Essays on Aggadah and Judaica Presented to Rabbi William G. Braude on His Eightieth Birthday and Dedicated to His Memory, ed. H. Blumberg, 83–101. Jersey City, NJ: KTAV, 1992.

Hatley, James. "Levinas in the Jewish Context." *Philosophy and Rhetoric* 38 (2005): 173–89.

Hegel, G. W. F. *History of Philosophy*. Trans. E. S. Haldane and Frances H. Simson. London: Routledge and Kegan Paul, 1955.

Heidegger, Martin. *The Basic Problems of Phenomenology*. Rev. ed. Translation, introduction, and lexicon by Albert Hofstadter. Bloomington: Indiana University Press, 1988.

———. *Being and Time*. Trans. John Macquarrie and Edward Robinson. London: SCM Press, 1962.

———. *Identity and Difference*. Trans. Joan Stambaugh. New York: Harper, 1969.

———. *Pathmarks*. Ed. William McNeill. Cambridge, UK: Cambridge University Press, 1998.

———. *Plato's Sophist*. Trans. Richard Rojcewicz and André Schuwer. Bloomington: Indiana University Press, 1997.

———. *Sein und Zeit*. Frankfurt am Main: Vittoria Klostermann, 1976.

Hendley, Steve. *From Communicative Action to the Face of the Other: Levinas and Habermas on Language, Obligation and Community*. Lanham, MD: Lexington Books, 2000.

Hennessy, Scott. "Creation, Chaos, and the Shoah: A Theological Reading of the *Il y a*." In *Levinas and Biblical Studies*, eds. Tamara Cohn Eskenazi, Gary A. Phillips, and David Jobling, 49–64. Atlanta: Society of Biblical Literature, 2003.

Herzog, Annabel. "Benny Levy Versus Emmanuel Levinas on 'Being Jewish.'" *Modern Judaism* 26:1 (2006): 15–30.

Heschel, Abraham Joshua. *Prophetic Inspiration After the Prophets: Maimonides and Other Medieval Authorities*. Jersey City, NJ: KTAV, 1996.

Hirshman, Marc. "Love Thy Companion as Thyself: Musings on Its Interpretation in Tannaitic Literature and the Sermon on the Mount." In *Judaism and Modernity: The Religious Philosophy of David Hartman*, ed. Jonathan W. Malino, 213–22. Jerusalem: Shalom Hartman Institute, 2001.

Horner, Robyn. "On Lévinas' Gifts to Christian Theology." In *The Exorbitant: Emmanuel Levinas Between Jews and Christians*, eds. Kevin Hart and Michael Signer. New York: Fordham University Press, forthcoming.

Hoy, David. "Post-Cartesian Interpretation: Hans-Georg Gadamer and Donald Davidson." In *The Philosophy of Hans-Georg Gadamer*, ed. Lewis Edwin Hahn, 111–28. Chicago: Open Court, 1997.

Hunter, Ian. *Rival Enlightenments: Civil and Metaphysical Philosophy in Early Modern Germany.* Cambridge, UK: Cambridge University Press, 2001.

Husserl, Edmund. *Cartesian Meditations: An Introduction to Phenomenology.* Trans. Dorian Cairns. The Hague: Martinus Nijhoff, 1960.

Ibn Gabirol, Solomon. *Crown of Kingship ("Keter Malkhuth").* Ed. Yisrael Levin. Tel Aviv: Tel Aviv University, 1995.

Idel, Moshe. *Absorbing Perfections: Kabbalah and Interpretation.* New Haven, CT: Yale University Press, 2002.

———. *Kabbalah: New Perspectives.* New Haven, CT: Yale University Press, 1990.

James, William. "The Will to Believe." In *The Writings of William James: A Comprehensive Edition*, ed. John J. McDermott, 717–34. Chicago: University of Chicago Press, 1967.

Janicaud, Dominique, et al. *Phenomenology and the "Theological Turn": The French Debate.* New York: Fordham University Press, 2000.

Jonas, Hans. *The Gnostic Religion: The Message of the Alien God and the Beginnings of Christianity.* 2nd rev. ed. Boston: Beacon Press, 1963.

Kant, Immanuel. *Critique of Practical Reason.* Trans. Lewis White Beck. New York: Macmillan, 1993.

———. *Religion Within the Limits of Reason Alone.* Trans. Theodore M. Greene and Hoyt H. Hudson. New York: Harper Torchbook, 1960.

Kavka, Martin. *Jewish Messianism and the History of Philosophy.* Cambridge, UK: Cambridge University Press, 2004.

Kearney, Richard, and Joseph O'Leary, eds. *Heidegger et la question de Dieu.* Paris: Grasset, 1980.

Keller, Catherine. *Face of the Deep: A Theology of Becoming.* London: Routledge, 2003.

Kellner, Menachem. *Dogma in Medieval Jewish Thought: From Maimonides to Abravanel.* Oxford, UK: Oxford University Press, 1986.

———. *Maimonides' Confrontation with Mysticism.* Oxford, UK: Littman Library of Jewish Civilization, 2007.

———. *Maimonides on Judaism and the Jewish People.* Albany: State University of New York Press, 1991.

———. "The Virtue of Faith." In *Neoplatonism and Jewish Thought*, ed. Lenn E. Goodman, 195–205. Albany: State University of New York Press, 1992.

Kisiel, Theodore. *The Genesis of Heidegger's "Being and Time."* Berkeley: University of California Press, 1993.

Kister, Menachem. "*Tohu wa-Bohu*, Primordial Elements and *Creatio ex Nihilo.*" *Jewish Studies Quarterly* 14 (2007). At http://74.125.155.132/scholar?q=cache:H xtJRy6oQbgJ:scholar.google.com/+Kister,+Menachem,+%E2%80%9CTohu+ wa-Bohu&hl=en.

Knohl, Israel. *The Divine Symphony: The Bible's Many Voices.* Philadelphia: Jewish Publication Society, 2003.

——. *The Sanctuary of Silence: The Priestly Torah and The Holiness School.* Minneapolis: Fortress Press, 1995.

Kook, Abraham Isaac. *Abraham Isaac Kook: The Lights of Penitence, the Moral Principles, Lights of Holiness, Essays, Letters, and Poems.* Trans. and intro. Ben Zion Bokser. New York: Paulist Press, 1978.

——. *Orot* (in Hebrew). Jerusalem: Mosad Harav Kook, 1963.

Kosky, Jeffrey L. "Contemporary Encounters with Apophatic Theology: The Case of Emmanuel Levinas." *Journal for Cultural and Religious Theory* 1.3 (August 2000) (www.jcrt.org).

——. *Levinas and the Philosophy of Religion.* Bloomington: Indiana University Press, 2001.

Kraemer, David. "Formation of the Rabbinic Canon: Authority and Boundaries." *Journal of Biblical Literature* 110 (1991): 613–30.

Kreisel, Howard. "Imitatio Dei in Maimonides' *Guide of the Perplexed.*" *AJS Review* 19:2 (1994): 169–211.

——. *Prophecy: The History of an Idea in Medieval Jewish Philosophy.* Springer: Amsterdam, 2003.

Kripke, Saul. *Naming and Necessity.* Cambridge, MA: Harvard University Press, 1980.

Kugel, James L. *In Potiphar's House: The Interpretive Life of Biblical Texts.* Cambridge, MA: Harvard University Press, 1994.

Lacoue-Labarthe, Philippe. *Typography: Mimesis, Philosophy, Politics.* Stanford, CA: Stanford University Press, 1998.

Lear, Jonathan. *Happiness, Death, and the Remainder of Life.* Cambridge, MA: Harvard University Press, 2000.

Leibowitz, Yeshayahu. *The Faith of Maimonides.* Tel Aviv: MOD Books, 1987.

Lescourret, Marie-Anne. *Emmanuel Levinas.* Paris: Flammarion, 1994.

Levenson, Jon D. *Creation and the Persistence of Evil: The Jewish Drama of Divine Omnipotence.* Princeton, NJ: Princeton University Press, 1994.

——. *Sinai and Zion: An Entry into the Jewish Bible.* New York: HarperOne, 1987.

——. "The Universal Horizon of Biblical Particularism." In *Ethnicity and the Bible,* ed. Mark G. Brett, 143–70. Leiden: E. J. Brill, 1996.

Levinas, Emmanuel. *Alterity and Transcendence.* Trans. Michael B. Smith. New York: Columbia University Press, 1999.

——. *Autrement que savoir.* Paris: Éditions Osiris, 1988.

——. *Autrement qu'être ou au-delà de l'essence.* The Hague: Martinus Nijhoff, 1974. Trans. Alphonso Lingis as *Otherwise than Being or Beyond Essence.* The Hague: Martinus Nijhoff, 1981.

————. *Basic Philosophical Writings.* Eds. Adriaan Theodoor Peperzak, Simon Critchley, and Robert Bernasconi. Bloomington: Indiana University Press, 1996.

————. "Being Jewish." Trans. Mary Beth Mader. *Continental Philosophy Review* 40 (2007): 205–10.

————. *Beyond the Verse.* Trans. Gary D. Mole. London: Continuum International Publishing Group, 1994.

————. *Collected Philosophical Papers.* Trans. Alphonso Lingis. Pittsburgh: Duquesne University Press, 1998.

————. "The Contemporary Criticism of the Idea of Value and the Prospects for Humanism." In *Value and Values in Evolution,* ed. Edward A. Maziarz, 179–87. New York: Gordon and Breach, 1979.

————. "The Contemporary Relevance of Maimonides (1935)." Trans. Michael Fagenblat. *Journal of Jewish Thought and Philosophy* 16:1 (2008): 91–94.

————. *De l'existence à l'existent,* 2nd ed. Paris: Vrin, 1993. Trans. Alphonso Lingis as *Existence and Existents.* Boston: Kluwer Academic Publishing, 1978.

————. *Difficult Freedom: Essays on Judaism.* Trans. Seán Hand. Baltimore: Johns Hopkins University Press, 1990.

————. *En découvrant l'existence avec Husserl et Heidegger.* Paris: Vrin, 1994.

————. *Entre Nous: On Thinking-of-the-Other.* Trans. Michael B. Smith and Barbara Harshav. New York: Columbia University Press, 1998.

————. *Ethics and Infinity.* Trans. Richard A. Cohen. Pittsburgh: Duquesne University Press, 1985.

————. "Ethics and Politics." In *The Levinas Reader,* ed. Seán Hand, 289–97. Oxford, UK: Blackwell, 1992.

————. *Existence and Existents.* Trans. Alphonso Lingis. Boston: Kluwer Academic Publishing, 1978.

————. *God, Death, and Time.* Trans. Bettina Bergo. Stanford, CA: Stanford University Press, 2000.

————. "Il y a." *Deucalion* 1 (1946): 141–54.

————. *In the Time of the Nations.* Trans. Michael B. Smith. London: Continuum International Publishing Group, 1994.

————. *Nine Talmudic Readings.* Trans. Annette Aronowicz. Bloomington: Indiana University Press, 1994.

————. *Of God Who Comes to the Mind.* Trans. Bettina Bergo. Stanford, CA: Stanford University Press, 1998.

————. *On Escape.* Trans. Bettina Bergo. Stanford, CA: Stanford University Press, 2003.

————. *Otherwise than Being or Beyond Essence.* Trans. Alphonso Lingis. The Hague: Martinus Nijhoff, 1981.

———. *Outside the Subject.* Trans. Michael B. Smith. Stanford, CA: Stanford University Press, 1994.

———. "The Paradox of Morality: An Interview with Emmanuel Levinas." In *The Provocation of Levinas*, eds. Robert Bernasconi and David Wood, 168–80. London: Routledge, 1988.

———. "Philosophy and Awakening." Trans. Mary Quaintance. In *Who Comes After the Subject?* eds. Eduardo Cadava, Peter Connor, and Jean-Luc Nancy, 206–16. London: Routledge, 1991.

———. "'Preface' to Moïse Maimonide." In *Le livre des commandments*, traduit, commenté et annoté par Anne-Marié Geller, 9–11. Paris: L'âge d'homme, 1987.

———. *Proper Names.* Trans. Michael B. Smith. Stanford, CA: Stanford University Press, 1996.

———. "Secularization and Hunger." Trans. Bettina Bergo. *Graduate Faculty Philosophy Journal* 20:2–21:1 (1998): 3–12.

———. *The Theory of Intuition in Husserl's Phenomenology* [original 1930]. Trans. André Orianne. Evanston: Northwestern University Press, 1973.

———. *Time and the Other.* Trans. Richard A. Cohen. Pittsburgh: Duquesne University Press, 1990.

———. *Totalité et infini: Essai sur l'exteriorité.* The Hague: Martinus Nijhoff, 1961. Trans. Alphonso Lingis as *Totality and Infinity.* Pittsburgh: Duquesne University Press, 1969.

———. *Totality and Infinity.* Trans. Alphonso Lingis. Pittsburgh: Duquesne University Press, 1969.

———. "The Trace of the Other" (1963). Trans. Alphonso Lingis. In *Deconstruction in Context*, ed. Mark C. Taylor, 345–89. Chicago: University of Chicago Press, 1986.

———. *Unforeseen History.* Trans. Nidra Poller. Urbana: University of Illinois Press, 2004.

Levine, Amy-Jill. *The Misunderstood Jew: The Church and the Scandal of the Jewish Jesus.* New York: HarperOne, 2007.

Lobel, Diana. "'Silence Is Praise to You': Maimonides on Negative Theology, Looseness of Expression, and Religious Experience." *American Catholic Philosophical Quarterly* 76:1 (2002): 25–49.

———. *A Sufi-Jewish Dialogue: Philosophy and Mysticism in Bahya Ibn Pakuda's Duties of the Heart.* Philadelphia: University of Pennsylvania Press, 2007.

Lopez, Donald S., Jr. "Belief." In *Critical Terms for Religious Studies*, ed. Mark C. Taylor, 21–35. Chicago: University of Chicago Press, 1998.

Lorberbaum, Menachem. *Politics and the Limits of Law: Secularizing the Political in Medieval Jewish Thought.* Stanford, CA: Stanford University Press, 2001.

Lorberbaum, Yair. *Image of God: Halakhah and Aggadah* (in Hebrew). Tel Aviv: Schocken Books, 2004.

————. "Maimonides on Imago Dei: Philosophy and Law—the Crime of Murder, the Criminal Procedure and Capital Punishment" (in Hebrew). *Tarbiz* 68:4 (1999): 533–56.

————. "On Contradictions, Rationality, Dialectics, and Esotericism in Maimonides's *Guide of the Perplexed.*" *Review of Metaphysics* 55:4 (2002): 711–50.

Lyotard, Jean-François. "Levinas' Logic." In *Face to Face with Levinas*, ed. Richard A. Cohen, 117–58. Albany: State University of New York Press, 1986.

Maimonides, Moses. *Commentary to the Mishnah* (in Hebrew). 3 vols. Trans. Yosef Qafih. Jerusalem: Mosad Harav Kook, 1967.

————. *The Eight Chapters of Maimonides on Ethics (Shemonah Perakim): A Psychological and Ethical Treatise.* Ed. and trans. Joseph I. Gofrinkle. New York: Columbia University Press, 1966.

————. *Guide of the Perplexed.* Trans. Shlomo Pines. Chicago: University of Chicago Press, 1963.

————. *Mishneh Torah* (in Hebrew). 15 vols. Ed. Shabtei Frankel. Jerusalem: Shabtei Frankel Publishers, 2000.

Malcolm, Norman. *Thought and Knowledge: Essays by Norman Malcolm.* Ithaca, NY: Cornell University Press, 1972.

Malka, Salomon. *Emmanuel Levinas: His Life and Legacy.* Trans. Michael Kigel and Sonja M. Embree. Pittsburgh: Duquesne University Press, 2006.

Malpas, Jeff. *Donald Davidson and the Mirror of Meaning.* Cambridge, MA: Cambridge University Press, 1992.

Marion, Jean-Luc. *Being Given: Toward a Phenomenology of Givenness.* Trans. Jeffrey L. Kosky. Stanford, CA: Stanford University Press, 2002.

————. *God Without Being.* Chicago: University of Chicago Press, 1991.

————. *In Excess: Studies of Saturated Phenomena.* Trans. Robyn Horner and Vincent Berraud. New York: Fordham University Press, 2002.

————. "L'interloqué." In *Who Comes After the Subject?* eds. Eduardo Cadava, Peter Connor, and Jean-Luc Nancy, 236–45. London: Routledge, 1991.

————. "Metaphysics and Phenomenology: A Relief for Theology." Trans. Thomas A. Carlson. *Critical Inquiry* 20:4 (1994): 572–91.

————. "A Note Concerning the Ontological Indifference." Trans. Jeffrey L. Kosky. *Graduate Faculty Philosophy Journal* 20:2–21:1 (1998): 25–40.

————. "Thomas Aquinas and Onto-theo-logy." In *Mystics: Presence and Aporia*, eds. Michael Kessler and Christian Sheppard, 38–74. Chicago: University of Chicago Press, 2003.

May, Gerhard. *Creatio ex Nihilo: The Doctrine of "Creation Out of Nothing" in Early Christian Thought.* Trans. A. S. Worrall. Edinburgh: T and T Clark, 1994.

Mendelssohn, Moses. *Jerusalem, or on Religious Power and Judaism.* Trans. Allan Arkush. Introduction and Commentary by Alexander Altmann. Waltham, MA: Brandeis University Press, 1983.

Meskin, Jacob. "The Role of Lurianic Kabbalah in the Early Philosophy of Emmanuel Levinas." *Levinas Studies* 2 (2007): 49–78.

Miller, Patricia Cox. "Poetic Words, Abysmal Words: Reflections on Origen's Hermeneutics." In *Origen of Alexandria: His World and His Legacy*, eds. Charles Kannengiesser and William L. Petersen, 165–78. Notre Dame, IN: University of Notre Dame Press, 1988.

Mopsik, Charles. "La pensée d'Emmanuel Levinas et la Cabale." In *Emmanuel Levinas: Le Cahier de l'Herne*, eds. Catherine Chalier and Miquel Abensour, 428–41. Paris: Éditions de l'Herne, 1991.

Morgan, Michael L. *Discovering Levinas.* New York: Cambridge University Press, 2007.

Mortley, Raoul. *French Philosophers in Conversation: Levinas, Schneider, Serres, Irigaray, Le Doeuff, Derrida.* London: Routledge, 1991.

Moyn, Samuel. "Emmanuel Levinas's Talmudic Readings: Between Tradition and Invention." *Prooftexts* 23:3 (2003): 338–64.

———. "Judaism Against Paganism: Emmanuel Levinas's Response to Heidegger and Nazism in the 1930s." *History and Memory* 10:1 (1998): 25–58.

———. *Origins of the Other: Emmanuel Levinas Between Revelation and Ethics.* Ithaca, NY: Cornell University Press, 2005.

Nancy, Jean-Luc. *Being Singular Plural.* Trans. Robert D. Richardson and Anne E. O'Byrne. Stanford, CA: Stanford University Press, 2000.

———. "Sharing Voices." In *Transforming the Hermeneutic Context: From Nietzsche to Nancy*, eds. Gayle L. Ormiston and Alan D. Schrift, 211–59. Albany: State University of New York Press, 1990.

Neudecker, Reinhard. "'And You Shall Love Your Neighbour as Yourself—I Am the Lord' (Lev. 19:18) in Jewish Interpretation." *Biblica* 73 (1992): 496–517.

Niehoff, Maren. "*Creatio ex Nihilo* Theology in *Genesis Rabbah.*" *Harvard Theological Review* 99:1 (2006): 37–64.

Novak, David, *The Image of the Non-Jew in Judaism.* Lewiston, NY: Edwin Mellen Press, 1983.

Nulty, Timothy J. "Davidsonian Triangulation and Heideggerian Comportment." *International Journal of Philosophical Studies* 14:3 (2006): 443–53.

Ophir, Adi. "Evil, Evils, and the Question of Ethics." In *Modernity and the Problem of Evil*, ed. Alan D. Schrift, 167–87. Bloomington: Indiana University Press, 2005.

———. *The Order of Evils: Toward an Ontology of Morals.* Trans. Rela Mazali and Havi Carel. New York: Zone Books, 2005.

Otto, Rudolf. *The Idea of the Holy: An Inquiry into the Non-Rational Factor in the Idea of the Divine and Its Relation to the Rational.* Trans. J. W. Harvey. Oxford, UK: Oxford University Press, 1958.

Petrosino, Silvano. "L'idée de creation dans l'oeuvre de Lévinas." In *La différence comme non-indifférence: Éthique et altérité chez Emmanuel Levinas,* ed. Arno Münster, 97–107. Paris: Éditions Kimé, 1995.

Phillips, James. *Heidegger's Volk: Between National Socialism and Poetry.* Stanford, CA: Stanford University Press, 2005.

Pines, Shlomo. *Studies in the History of Jewish Thought.* Eds. Warren Zev Harvey and Moshe Idel. Jerusalem: Magnes Press, 1997.

Purcell, Michael. *Levinas and Theology.* Cambridge, UK: Cambridge University Press, 2006.

Putnam, Hilary. *The Collapse of the Fact/Value Dichotomy and Other Essays.* Cambridge, MA: Harvard University Press, 2002.

———. *Ethics Without Ontology.* Cambridge, MA: Harvard University Press, 2004.

———. "Introduction." In Franz Rosenzweig, *Understanding the Sick and the Healthy: A View of World, Man, and God,* trans. Nahum Glatzer, 1–20. Cambridge, MA: Harvard University Press, 1999.

———. "Levinas and Judaism." In *The Cambridge Companion to Levinas,* eds. Simon Critchley and Robert Bernasconi, 33–62. Cambridge, UK: Cambridge University Press, 2002.

———. "On Negative Theology." *Faith and Philosophy* 14:4 (1997): 407–22.

———. "Richard Rorty on Reality and Justification." In *Rorty and His Critics,* ed. Robert B. Brandom, 81–87. Malden, MA: Blackwell, 2000.

Raffoul, François, and David Pettigrew, eds. *Heidegger and Practical Philosophy.* Albany: State University of New York Press, 2002.

Ramberg, Bjørn T. *Donald Davidson's Philosophy of Language: An Introduction.* London: Basil Blackwell, 1989.

———. "Illuminating Language: Interpretation and Understanding in Gadamer and Davidson." In *A House Divided: Comparing Analytic and Continental Philosophy,* ed. C. G. Prado, 213–34. Amherst, NY: Humanity Books, 2003.

Ravitzky, Aviezer. "Samuel Ibn Tibbon and the Esoteric Character of the *Guide of the Perplexed.*" *Association of Jewish Studies Review* 6 (1981): 87–123.

———. "The Secrets of the *Guide to the Perplexed*: Between the Thirteenth and Twentieth Centuries." In *Studies in Maimonides,* ed. I. Twersky, 159–207. Cambridge, MA: Harvard University Center for Jewish Studies, 1990.

———. "To the Utmost of Human Capacity: Maimonides on the Days of the Messiah." In *Perspectives on Maimonides,* ed. Joel Kraemer, 221–56. London: Littman Library of Jewish Civilization, 1991.

Reinhard, Kenneth. "The Ethics of the Neighbor: Universalism, Particularism, Exceptionalism." *Journal of Textual Reasoning* 4:1 (2005). At http://etext.virginia.edu/journals/tr/volume4/index.html.

Ricoeur, Paul. "Experience and Language in Religious Discourse." In *Phenomenology and the "Theological Turn": The French Debate*, eds. Dominique Janicaud et al., 127–46. New York: Fordham University Press, 2000.

———. *Oneself as Another*. Trans. Kathleen Blamey. Chicago: University of Chicago Press, 1992.

———. *The Symbolism of Evil*. Trans. Emerson Buchanan. Boston: Beacon Press, 1967.

Robbins, Jill, ed. *Is It Righteous to Be? Interviews with Emmanuel Levinas*. Stanford, CA: Stanford University Press, 2001.

Rorty, Richard. "To the Sunlit Uplands." *London Review of Books* 24:21 (October 31, 2002).

Rose, Gillian. *The Broken Middle: Out of Our Ancient Society*. Oxford, UK: Blackwell, 1992.

———. *Judaism and Modernity: Philosophical Essays*. Oxford, UK: Blackwell, 1993.

Rosen, Stanley. *The Elusiveness of the Ordinary: Studies in the Possibility of Philosophy*. New Haven, CT: Yale University Press, 2002.

Rosenberg, Shalom. "The Concept of 'Emunah in Post-Maimonidean Philosophy." In *Studies in Medieval Jewish History and Literature. Volume II*, eds. Isadore Twersky and Jay M. Harris. Cambridge, MA: Harvard University Press, 1985.

Rosenzweig, Franz. *Philosophical and Theological Writings*. Translated, edited, notes and commentaries by Paul W. Franks and Michael Morgan. Indianapolis: Hackett, 2000.

Sadler, Ted. *Heidegger and Aristotle: The Question of Being*. London: Athlone Press, 1996.

Sagi, Avi, and Daniel Statman. *Religion and Morality*. Amsterdam: Rodopi Bv Editions, 1995.

Samuelson, Norbert M. *Judaism and the Doctrine of Creation*. Cambridge, UK: Cambridge University Press, 1994.

———. "Maimonides' Doctrine of Creation." *Harvard Theological Review* 84:3 (1991): 249–71.

Santner, Eric L. *On Creaturely Life: Rilke, Benjamin, Sebald*. Chicago: University of Chicago Press, 2006.

———. *On the Psychotheology of Everyday Life: Reflections on Freud and Rosenzweig*. Chicago: University of Chicago Press, 2001.

Saul, Nigel. "From Trothe to Truth." *Times Literary Supplement* (July 2, 1999), 27.

Schiffman, Lawrence H. "The Samaritans in Tannaitic Halakhah." *Jewish Quarterly Review* 75:4 (1985), 323–50.

Schmitt, Carl. *Political Theology: Four Chapters on the Concept of Sovereignty.* Trans. George Schwab. Chicago: University of Chicago Press, 2005.

Scholem, Gershom. *Major Trends in Jewish Mysticism.* London: Thames and Hudson, 1995.

———. "Sitra Ahra: Good and Evil in the Kabbalah." In *On the Mystical Shape of the Godhead: Basic Concepts in the Kabbalah*, trans. Joachim Neugroschel; translation edited and revised by Jonathan Chipman, 56–87. New York: Schocken Books, 1991.

Schrift, Alan D. "Introduction." In *Modernity and the Problem of Evil*, ed. Alan D. Schrift, 1–11. Bloomington: Indiana University Press, 2005.

Schürer, Emil. *The History of the Jewish People in the Age of Jesus Christ. Volume II*, rev. and ed. G. Vermes, F. Millar, and M. Black. Edinburgh: T & T Clark, 1979.

Schwartz, Michael. *Maimonides' Guide for the Perplexed* (Hebrew translation and commentary). 2 vols. Tel Aviv: Tel Aviv University Press, 2002.

Schwartz, Yossef. *"To Thee Is Silence Praise": Meister Eckhart's Reading in Maimonides' Guide of the Perplexed.* Tel Aviv: Am Oved, 2002.

Schwarzschild, Steven. "An Agenda for Jewish Philosophy in the 1980s." In *Studies in Jewish Philosophy: Collected Essays of the Academy for Jewish Philosophy, 1980–85*, ed. Norbert Samuelson, 101–25. Lanham, MD: University Press of America, 1987.

———. "Do Noahides Have to Believe in Revelation?" In *The Pursuit of the Ideal: Jewish Writings of Steven Schwarzschild*, ed. Menachem Kellner, 29–60. Albany: State University of New York Press, 1990.

Schweid, Eliezer. "'Prophetic Mysticism' in the Twentieth Century." *Modern Judaism* 14:2 (1994): 139–74.

Scult, Allen. *Being Jewish/Reading Heidegger: An Ontological Encounter.* New York: Fordham University Press, 2004.

Seeskin, Kenneth. *Jewish Philosophy in a Secular Age.* Albany: State University of New York Press, 1990.

———. "Judaism and the Linguistic Interpretation of Faith." In *Studies in Jewish Philosophy: Collected Essays of the Academy for Jewish Philosophy, 1980–1985*, ed. Norbert Samuelson, 215–34. Lanham, MD: University Press of America, 1987.

———. *Maimonides on the Origin of the World.* Cambridge, UK: Cambridge University Press, 2005.

———. *Searching for a Distant God: The Legacy of Maimonides.* New York: Oxford University Press, 2000.

Segal, Alan F. "Torah and *Nomos* in Recent Scholarly Discussion." In *The Other Judaisms in Late Antiquity*, 131–47. Atlanta: Scholars Press, 1987.

————. "Universalism in Judaism and Christianity." In *Paul in His Hellenistic Context*, ed. Troels Engberg-Pedersen, 1–29. Minneapolis: Fortress Press, 1995.

Shapiro, Marc B. *The Limits of Orthodox Theology: Maimonides' Thirteen Principles Reappraised.* Portland, OR: Littman Library of Jewish Civilization, 2004.

Shklar, Judith. *The Faces of Injustice.* New Haven, CT: Yale University Press, 1990.

Simon, Ernst. "The Neighbor (*Re'a*) Whom We Shall Love." In *Modern Jewish Ethics: Theory and Practice*, ed. Marvin Fox, 29–56. Columbus: Ohio State University Press, 1975.

Smith, Steven B. *Spinoza, Liberalism, and the Question of Jewish Identity.* New Haven, CT: Yale University Press, 1998.

Smith, Steven G. *Argument to the Other: Reason Beyond Reason in the Thought of Karl Barth and Emmanuel Levinas.* Chico, CA: Scholars Press, 1983.

Smith, Wilfred Cantwell. *Believing: An Historical Perspective.* Oxford, UK: Oneworld, 1998.

————. *Faith and Belief: The Difference Between Them* [1979]. Oxford, UK: Oneworld, 1998.

Solmsen, Friedrich. *Aristotle's System of the Physical World: A Comparison with His Predecessors.* Ithaca, NY: Cornell University Press, 1960.

Speiser, E. A. *Genesis: Introduction, Translation, and Notes.* Garden City, NY: Doubleday, 1964.

Spinoza, Benedict de. *Ethics.* Trans. R. H. M. Elwes. New York: Dover, 1955.

————. *A Theologico-Political Treatise and a Political Treatise.* Trans. R. H. M. Elwes. New York: Dover, 1951.

Stern, Joseph. "Maimonides' Demonstrations: Principles and Practice." *Medieval Theology and Philosophy* 10 (2001): 47–84.

————. "Maimonides' Epistemology." In *The Cambridge Companion to Maimonides*, ed. Kenneth Seeskin, 105–33. New York: Cambridge University Press, 2005.

Stowers, Stanley K. *A Rereading of Romans: Justice, Jews, and Gentiles.* New Haven, CT: Yale University Press, 1997.

Strauss, Leo. *Persecution and the Arts of Writing.* Chicago: University of Chicago Press, 1988.

Taminiaux, Jacques. *Heidegger and the Project of Fundamental Ontology.* Trans. and ed. Michael Gendre. Albany: State University of New York Press, 1991.

Taubes, Jacob. *The Political Theology of Paul.* Trans. Dana Hollander. Stanford, CA: Stanford University Press, 2004.

Taylor, Charles. *A Catholic Modernity?: Charles Taylor's Marianist Lecture.* New York: Oxford University Press, 1999.

Thomas, William. "Biblical Interpretation." In *The Cambridge Companion to Augustine*, eds. Eleonore Stump and Norman Kretzmann, 59–70. Cambridge, UK: Cambridge University Press, 2001.

Toumayan, Alain P. *Encountering the Other: The Artwork and the Problem of Difference in Blanchot and Levinas.* Pittsburgh: Duquesne University Press, 2004.

Trigano, Shmuel. "Levinas and the Project of Jewish Philosophy." Trans. Annette Aronowicz. *Jewish Studies Quarterly* 8:3 (2001): 279–307.

Tsumura, David Toshio. "The Earth in Genesis 1." In *"I Studied Inscriptions from Before the Flood": Ancient Near Eastern, Literary, and Linguistic Approaches to Genesis 1–11*, eds. Richard S. Hess and David Toshio Tsumura, 310–28. Winona Lake, IN: Eisenbrauns, 1994.

Twersky, Isadore. *Introduction to the Code of Maimonides (Mishneh Torah).* New Haven, CT: Yale University Press, 1982.

Urbach, E. E. "Whoever Saves One Soul . . ." (in Hebrew). In *The World of the Sages*, 268. Jerusalem: Magnes, 1988.

Vattimo, Gianni. *After Christianity.* Trans. Luca D'Isanto. New York: Columbia University Press, 2002.

———. *Belief.* Trans. Luca D'Isanto and David Webb. Oxford, UK: Polity, 1999.

———. *Beyond Interpretation: The Meaning of Hermeneutics for Philosophy.* Stanford, CA: Stanford University Press, 1997.

Vogel, Lawrence. *The Fragile "We": Ethical Implications of Heidegger's Being and Time.* Evanston, IL: Northwestern University Press, 1994.

Volpi, Franco. "*Being and Time*: A 'Translation' of the *Nichomachean Ethics*?" In *Reading Heidegger from the Start: Essays in His Earliest Thought*, eds. Theodore Kisiel and John van Buren, 195–211. Albany: State University of New York Press, 1994.

———. "Dasein as *Praxis*: The Heideggerian Assimilation and the Radicalization of the Practical Philosophy of Aristotle." In *Critical Heidegger*, ed. Christopher Macann, 27–66. London: Routledge, 1996.

Ward, Graham. *Barth, Derrida, and the Language of Theology.* Cambridge, UK: Cambridge University Press, 1995.

Weinsheimer, Joel. "Charity Militant: Toward a Post-Critical Hermeneutics." In *The Force of Tradition: Response and Resistance in Literature, Religion, and Cultural Studies*, ed. Donald G. Marshall, 39–54. Lanham, MD: Rowman and Littlefield, 2005.

Werblowsky, R. J. Zvi. "Faith, Hope and Trust: A Study of the Concept of Bittahon." In *Papers of the Institute of Jewish Studies, London*, ed. J. G. Weiss, 95–139. Jerusalem: Magnes, 1964.

Wheeler, Samuel C. *Deconstruction as Analytic Philosophy.* Stanford, CA: Stanford University Press, 2000.

Williams, Bernard. *Ethics and the Limits of Philosophy.* London: Fontana Press, 1985.

———. *Truth and Truthfulness: An Essay in Genealogy.* Princeton, NJ: Princeton University Press, 2002.

Winch, Peter. *Trying to Make Sense.* Oxford, UK: Basil Blackwell, 1987.

Winston, David. "The Book of Wisdom's Theory of Cosmogony." *History of Religions* 11:2 (1971): 185–202.

Wittgenstein, Ludwig. *Culture and Value: A Selection from the Posthumous Remains.* Oxford, UK: Blackwell, 1998.

———. *On Certainty.* Ed. G. E. M. Anscombe and G. H. von Wright, trans. Denis Paul and G. E. M. Anscombe. Oxford, UK: Blackwell, 1969.

———. *Philosophical Occasions, 1912–1951.* Indianapolis: Hackett, 1993.

Wolfson, Elliot R. "The Body in the Text: A Kabbalistic Theory of Embodiment." *Jewish Quarterly Review* 95:3 (2005): 479–500.

———. *Language, Eros, Being: Kabbalistic Hermeneutics and Poetic Imagination.* New York: Fordham University Press, 2004.

———. "Light Through Darkness: The Ideal of Human Perfection in the Zohar." *Harvard Theological Review* 81:1 (1988): 73–95.

———. "Secrecy, Modesty, and the Feminine: Kabbalistic Traces in the Thought of Levinas." *Journal of Jewish Thought and Philosophy* 14:1–2 (2006): 193–224.

———. *Through a Speculum That Shines: Vision and Imagination in Medieval Jewish Mysticism.* Princeton, NJ: Princeton University Press, 1994.

———. *Venturing Beyond: Law and Morality in Kabbalistic Mysticism.* New York: Oxford University Press, 2006.

Wolosky, Shira. *Language Mysticism: The Negative Way of Language in Eliot, Beckett, and Celan.* Stanford, CA: Stanford University Press, 1995.

Wright, Tamra. *Twilight of Jewish Philosophy.* Amsterdam: Harward Academic Publishers, 1999.

Wyschogrod, Edith. *Crossover Queries: Dwelling with Negatives, Embodying Philosophy's Others.* New York: Fordham University Press, 2006.

———. *Emmanuel Levinas: The Problem of Ethical Metaphysics.* 2nd ed. New York: Fordham University Press, 2000.

Wyschogrod, Michael. *The Body of Faith: God and the People of Israel.* Northvale, NJ: Jason Aaronson, 1996.

———. "A Jewish Perspective on Incarnation." *Modern Theology* 12:2 (1996): 195–209.

Yovel, Yirmiyahu. *Dark Riddle: Hegel, Nietzsche, and the Jews.* University Park: Penn State University Press, 1998.

Zarader, Marlène. *The Unthought Debt: Heidegger and the Hebraic Heritage.* Trans. Bettina Bergo. Stanford, CA: Stanford University Press, 2006.

Žižek, Slavoj. *On Belief.* London: Routledge, 2001.

———. "A Plea for Ethical Violence." In *The Neighbor: Three Inquiries in Political Theology,* eds. Slavoj Žižek, Eric L. Santner, and Kenneth Reinhard. Chicago: University of Chicago Press, 2005.

Index

ethical witness, 178–79, 180
ethics: of belief, 145; Christological
  interpretation, 176; and the claim of
  the Name, 129–33; cohistoricizing of,
  182–83; of covenantal faith, 150–56,
  162; and covenantal faithfulness, xxv,
  150–56; of *creatio ex nihilo*, 84–86;
  and creation, 29; criticisms of the
  "religious" elements of Levinas's
  ethics, 2–9, 18, 203*n*18; deformation
  of, 97–101; differences between
  Levinas's early and later works, 97–
  101; ethics of, xxi; of faith, 145, 145–47,
  146, 152, 154, 162, 163, 167, 168*69; as
  first philosophy, xxi, 196; and image
  of God, 88–91, 122; as individuated
  responsiveness, xx–xxi; Levinas's
  account, 18–20; metaphysical
  account, xxv; and political fraternity,
  187; post-metaphysical account,
  xxv; and responsibility, xx–xxi; and
  secularization, xi–xii; as secularized
  account of the Jewish covenant of
  faith, xxv; secularized theological
  concepts of, 196; of selfhood, 106–7
Ethics and the Limits of Philosophy
  (Williams), 200*n*15
eudemonia, 225*n*63
everyday life: particularity in, 79–84;
  responsibility in, 74–79
evil: and good, 150–56; Levinas's
  account of, 47, 212*n*25; mythic
  evil and political theology, 54–58;
  transcendence of, 47–54
existence, distinct from being, 212*n*22
externalism, 240*n*73

face, the: ethical significance of, xx–xxi,
  102; transcendence of, 7
faith: and action, 146–47; and belief,
  144–46, 160–61, 239*n*63; crises of,
  170; and righteousness, 235*n*22
family, the, 93
fecundity, 92–94, 224*n*54
Feuerbach, Ludwig, 45

Fishbane, Michael, 46, 54, 89
Fons Vitae (Ibn Gabirol), xxiii
Foucault, Michel, 75
Fox, Marvin, 5
Frank, Daniel, 119
fraternity: ambivalence of, 31, 179–88,
  209*n*92. *See also* ethical fraternity;
  political fraternity
freedom, defense of, 69
French philosophy, *laïcité*, xiv
French Republic, xiv, 183, 185, 187,
  225*n*60
French republicanism, 13, 184, 193
Freud, Sigmund, 215*n*72
Frisch, Andrea, 235*n*24
From Existence to the Existent (Levinas),
  xv, 34, 49, 70, 210*n*4

Gamaliel II, Rabban, 59, 216*n*86
Genesis I, myth of, 42–43, 53–55
Gentiles, 190, 249*n*64
Gersonides, 60
Gibbs, Robert, 8–9, 11–12, 205*n*38,
  224*n*54
glory, to the Name, 133–39, 232–33*n*51
God: kiss of, 105, 226*n*8; philosophical
  death of, 46. *See also* image of God;
  name of God
good, and evil, 150–56
Good Samaritan parable, 188–92,
  249*nn*65–66
goodness of the world, 47–54
Gordon, Peter Eli, 237*n*49
Goshen-Gottstein, Alon, 91, 176
Green, Richard Firth, 147
Greenberg, Moshe, 224*n*45
Guide of the Perplexed (Maimonides):
  audience of, xxii, 9*10, 242–43*nn*5–
  6; belief, 148; core truth of Judaism,
  10; creation as freedom, 70–73, 77,
  220*n*10, 220*nn*14–15; critique of
  Aristotle, 75, 76; kavod (glory), 133–
  36, 232–33*n*51; negative theology, 112–
  17, 120–121; revelation, 13; traces of
  transcendence, 110

Jewish philosophy, 9–11, 46, 68, 225*n*63
Jewish theology, recovery of, 143–44
Jewish thought, xxii
Jonas, Hans, 48
Judaic terms, in Levinas's philosophical
corpus, 27–29
Judaism: allegoresis of, 173; as ethics, 174–
75, 177–78, 186, 187; and heresy, 170,
242*n*87; as Law devoid of reason, 3–6;
Levinas's "invention" of, 7–8, 9, 32;
liturgy, xvi, 199*n*10; nonphilosophical
character of, 4; in opposition to
philosophy, 5–7; and philosophy,
9–14; as practice of religious
obligation, 141–43; secularized view,
178; Spinoza's interpretation, 3–4; as
"sublime Other of modernity," 202*n*5.
See also philosophy of Judaism
Judeans, relations with Samaritans, 189–
90, 249*n*64
Judeo-Christian heritage and tradition,
xii, 2, 16, 59, 69, 94, 98, 108, 178, 184,
187–88, 193, 196, 207*n*57, 225*n*60,
244*n*14

Kabbalah, 60–61, 201–2*n*4, 217*n*92,
218*n*105, 227*n*14, 227*n*17, 241*n*83
Kant, Immanuel, xi, 4, 46, 56, 68, 72,
202*n*9, 215*n*70, 225*n*63
Kantian morality, xvii–xx, 68–69, 219*n*1
Karo, Joseph, 129
Kavka, Martin, 226*n*63
kavod (glory), 133–37, 232*n*50, 232–33*n*51
Keller, Catherine, 61–63, 64, 218*n*98,
232–33*n*51
Kellner, Menachem, 25, 208*n*76, 217*n*91,
231*n*46, 232–33*n*51, 242*n*87
kenosis, 176
Keter Malkhut (poem), 109
Kierkegaard, Søren, 7, 165
kiss of God, 105, 226*n*8
Knohl, Israel, 37
Kook, Abraham Isaac, 142
Kosky, Jeffrey, 6–7, 26, 171, 203–4*n*25,
233*n*1

Kripke, Saul, 123, 125, 230*n*33
Kugel, James L., 201*n*19
Kuhn, Thomas, 75

laïcité, xiv
Lakish, Resh, 64
Leibowitz, Yeshayahu, 5, 142, 228*n*15,
234*n*10
lemor (Saying), 28–29, 209*n*86
Levenson, Jon D., 35–36, 152, 211*n*9,
234*n*19
Levinas, Emmanuel: appointments
as philosopher, xvi, 200*n*11;
commitment to Jewish education,
xv–xvi; "confessional" writings and
philosophical works, xiv, 69–70;
contribution to contemporary
phenomenology and moral
philosophy, xix–xxii, 200*n*15;
distinction between "confessional"
and philosophical writing, xiv, 1–2;
early career, xv–xvi; early works, 34–
35, 219*n*5; engagement with Judaism,
24–25; hermeneutical reading of his
work, 14–20; incarceration as POW,
xv, 33, 211*n*12; "infiltration" from
Judaism to his philosophy, xiv, 2,
201–2*n*4; influence of Heidegger,
xii–xiii; influence of the Holocaust,
xiv, xv–xvi, 38–39, 69, 199*n*4, 212*n*25;
influence of Kantian morality,
xvii–xx, 68–69, 219*n*1; influence of
Maimonides, xv, xvi, xxiv, 69, 70–73,
86–88, 96, 219*n*7; life and writings,
xiii–xiv; midrashic structure of
philosophical project, xxii, 27–32,
201*n*19; origins of his thought, 7–9;
philosophical approach to Judaism,
xiii; philosophical project, xvii–xxii;
Protestant and European sources
of his philosophy, xxiii–xxiv, 7–9,
171, 242*n*1; on relationship between
Israel, its law, and the Gentiles, 22–
27, 209*n*81; sources of his Judaism,
xvi, 199*n*10, 207*n*57, 224*n*52;

Cultural Memory | *in the Present*

Stefanos Geroulanos, *An Atheism that Is Not Humanist Emerges in French Thought*

Andrew Herscher, *Violence Taking Place: The Architecture of the Kosovo Conflict*

Hans-Jörg Rheinberger, *On Historicizing Epistemology: An Essay*

Jacob Taubes, *From Cult to Culture*, edited by Charlotte Fonrobert and Amir Engel

Peter Hitchcock, *The Long Space: Transnationalism and Postcolonial Form*

Lambert Wiesing, *Artificial Presence: Philosophical Studies in Image Theory*

Jacob Taubes, *Occidental Eschatology*

Freddie Rokem, *Philosophers and Thespians: Thinking Performance*

Roberto Esposito, *Communitas: The Origin and Destiny of Community*

Vilashini Cooppan, *Worlds Within: National Narratives and Global Connections in Postcolonial Writing*

Josef Früchtl, *The Impertinent Self: A Heroic History of Modernity*

Frank Ankersmit, Ewa Domanska, and Hans Kellner, eds., *Re-Figuring Hayden White*

Michael Rothberg, *Multidirectional Memory: Remembering the Holocaust in the Age of Decolonization*

Jean-François Lyotard, *Enthusiasm: The Kantian Critique of History*

Ernst van Alphen, Mieke Bal, and Carel Smith, eds., *The Rhetoric of Sincerity*

Stéphane Mosès, *The Angel of History: Rosenzweig, Benjamin, Scholem*

Alexandre Lefebvre, *The Image of the Law: Deleuze, Bergson, Spinoza*

Samira Haj, *Reconfiguring Islamic Tradition: Reform, Rationality, and Modernity*

Diane Perpich, *The Ethics of Emmanuel Levinas*

Marcel Detienne, *Comparing the Incomparable*

François Delaporte, *Anatomy of the Passions*

René Girard, *Mimesis and Theory: Essays on Literature and Criticism, 1959–2005*

Richard Baxstrom, *Houses in Motion: The Experience of Place and the Problem of Belief in Urban Malaysia*

Jennifer L. Culbert, *Dead Certainty: The Death Penalty and the Problem of Judgment*

Samantha Frost, *Lessons from a Materialist Thinker: Hobbesian Reflections on Ethics and Politics*

Regina Mara Schwartz, *Sacramental Poetics at the Dawn of Secularism: When God Left the World*

Gil Anidjar, *Semites: Race, Religion, Literature*

Ranjana Khanna, *Algeria Cuts: Women and Representation, 1830 to the Present*

Esther Peeren, *Intersubjectivities and Popular Culture: Bakhtin and Beyond*

Eyal Peretz, *Becoming Visionary: Brian De Palma's Cinematic Education of the Senses*

Diana Sorensen, *A Turbulent Decade Remembered: Scenes from the Latin American Sixties*

Hubert Damisch, *A Childhood Memory by Piero della Francesca*

José van Dijck, *Mediated Memories in the Digital Age*

Dana Hollander, *Exemplarity and Chosenness: Rosenzweig and Derrida on the Nation of Philosophy*

Asja Szafraniec, *Beckett, Derrida, and the Event of Literature*

Sara Guyer, *Romanticism After Auschwitz*

Alison Ross, *The Aesthetic Paths of Philosophy: Presentation in Kant, Heidegger, Lacoue-Labarthe, and Nancy*

Gerhard Richter, *Thought-Images: Frankfurt School Writers' Reflections from Damaged Life*

Bella Brodzki, *Can These Bones Live? Translation, Survival, and Cultural Memory*

Rodolphe Gasché, *The Honor of Thinking: Critique, Theory, Philosophy*

Brigitte Peucker, *The Material Image: Art and the Real in Film*

Natalie Melas, *All the Difference in the World: Postcoloniality and the Ends of Comparison*

Jonathan Culler, *The Literary in Theory*

Michael G. Levine, *The Belated Witness: Literature, Testimony, and the Question of Holocaust Survival*

Jennifer A. Jordan, *Structures of Memory: Understanding German Change in Berlin and Beyond*

Christoph Menke, *Reflections of Equality*

Marlène Zarader, *The Unthought Debt: Heidegger and the Hebraic Heritage*

Jan Assmann, *Religion and Cultural Memory: Ten Studies*

David Scott and Charles Hirschkind, *Powers of the Secular Modern: Talal Asad and His Interlocutors*

Gyanendra Pandey, *Routine Violence: Nations, Fragments, Histories*

James Siegel, *Naming the Witch*

J. M. Bernstein, *Against Voluptuous Bodies: Late Modernism and the Meaning of Painting*

Theodore W. Jennings, Jr., *Reading Derrida / Thinking Paul: On Justice*

Richard Rorty and Eduardo Mendieta, *Take Care of Freedom and Truth Will Take Care of Itself: Interviews with Richard Rorty*

Jacques Derrida, *Paper Machine*

Renaud Barbaras, *Desire and Distance: Introduction to a Phenomenology of Perception*

Jill Bennett, *Empathic Vision: Affect, Trauma, and Contemporary Art*

Ban Wang, *Illuminations from the Past: Trauma, Memory, and History in Modern China*

James Phillips, *Heidegger's Volk: Between National Socialism and Poetry*

Frank Ankersmit, *Sublime Historical Experience*

István Rév, *Retroactive Justice: Prehistory of Post-Communism*

Paola Marrati, *Genesis and Trace: Derrida Reading Husserl and Heidegger*

Krzysztof Ziarek, *The Force of Art*

Marie-José Mondzain, *Image, Icon, Economy: The Byzantine Origins of the Contemporary Imaginary*

Cecilia Sjöholm, *The Antigone Complex: Ethics and the Invention of Feminine Desire*

Jacques Derrida and Elisabeth Roudinesco, *For What Tomorrow . . . : A Dialogue*

Elisabeth Weber, *Questioning Judaism: Interviews by Elisabeth Weber*

Jacques Derrida and Catherine Malabou, *Counterpath: Traveling with Jacques Derrida*

Martin Seel, *Aesthetics of Appearing*

Nanette Salomon, *Shifting Priorities: Gender and Genre in Seventeenth-Century Dutch Painting*

Jacob Taubes, *The Political Theology of Paul*

Jean-Luc Marion, *The Crossing of the Visible*

Eric Michaud, *The Cult of Art in Nazi Germany*

Anne Freadman, *The Machinery of Talk: Charles Peirce and the Sign Hypothesis*

Stanley Cavell, *Emerson's Transcendental Etudes*

Stuart McLean, *The Event and Its Terrors: Ireland, Famine, Modernity*

Beate Rössler, ed., *Privacies: Philosophical Evaluations*

Bernard Faure, *Double Exposure: Cutting Across Buddhist and Western Discourses*

Alessia Ricciardi, *The Ends of Mourning: Psychoanalysis, Literature, Film*

Alain Badiou, *Saint Paul: The Foundation of Universalism*

Gil Anidjar, *The Jew, the Arab: A History of the Enemy*

Jonathan Culler and Kevin Lamb, eds., *Just Being Difficult? Academic Writing in the Public Arena*

Jean-Luc Nancy, *A Finite Thinking*, edited by Simon Sparks

Theodor W. Adorno, *Can One Live after Auschwitz? A Philosophical Reader*, edited by Rolf Tiedemann

Patricia Pisters, *The Matrix of Visual Culture: Working with Deleuze in Film Theory*

Andreas Huyssen, *Present Pasts: Urban Palimpsests and the Politics of Memory*

Talal Asad, *Formations of the Secular: Christianity, Islam, Modernity*